D0031368

THE LOGICAL FOUNDATIONS OF COGNITION
Edited by John Macnamara and Gonzalo E. Reyes

Vancouver Studies in Cognitive Science is a series of volumes in cognitive science. The volumes will appear annually and cover topics relevant to the nature of the higher cognitive faculties as they appear in cognitive systems, either human or machine. These will include such topics as natural language processing, modularity, the language faculty, perception, logical reasoning, scientific reasoning, and social interaction. The topics and authors are to be drawn from philosophy, linguistics, artificial intelligence, and psychology. Each volume will contain original articles by scholars from two or more of these disciplines. The core of the volumes will be articles and comments on these articles to be delivered at a conference held in Vancouver. The volumes will be supplemented by articles especially solicited for each volume which will undergo peer review. The volumes should be of interest to those in philosophy working in philosophy of mind and philosophy of language; to those in linguistics in psycholinguistics, syntax, language acquisition and semantics; to those in psychology in psycholinguistics, cognition, perception, and learning; and to those in computer science in artificial intelligence, computer vision, robotics, natural language processing, and scientific reasoning.

VANCOUVER STUDIES IN COGNITIVE SCIENCE
Forthcoming volumes

VOLUME 5   *Problems in Perception*
            Editor, Kathleen Akins, Philosophy
            University of Illinois - Champaign-Urbana

VOLUME 6   *The Biological Basis of Language*
            Editor, Myrna Gopnik, Linguistics
            McGill University

SERIES EDITORS

General Editor
  Steven Davis, Philosophy, Simon Fraser University
Associate General Editors
  Kathleen Akins, Philosophy, Simon Fraser University
  Nancy Hedley, Linguistics, Simon Fraser University
  Fred Popowich, Computing Science, Simon Fraser University
  Richard Wright, Psychology, Simon Fraser University

EDITORIAL ADVISORY BOARD

Susan Carey, Psychology, Massachusetts Institute of Technology
Elan Dresher, Linguistics, University of Toronto
Janet Fodor, Linguistics, Graduate Center,
  City University of New York
F. Jeffry Pelletier, Philosophy, Computing Science,
  University of Alberta
John Perry, Philosophy, Stanford University
Zenon Pylyshyn, Psychology, Rutgers University
Len Schubert, Computing Science, University of Rochester
Brian Smith, System Sciences Lab, Xerox Palo Alto Research Center,
  Center for the Study of Language and Information,
  Stanford University

BOARD OF READERS

William Demopoulos, Philosophy, University of Western Ontario
Allison Gopnik, Psychology, University of California at Berkeley
Myrna Gopnik, Linguistics, McGill University
David Kirsh, Cognitive Science,
  University of California at San Diego
François Lepage, Philosophy, Université de Montréal
Robert Levine, Linguistics, Ohio State University
John Macnamara, Psychology, McGill University
Georges Rey, Philosophy, University of Maryland
Richard Rosenberg, Computing Science,
  University of British Columbia
Edward P. Stabler, Jr., Linguistics,
  University of California at Los Angeles
Susan Stucky, Center for the Study of Language and Information,
  Stanford University
Paul Thagard, Philosophy Department, University of Waterloo

NATIONAL UNIVERSITY
LIBRARY   SAN DIEGO

the

logical

foundations

of

cognition

edited by John Macnamara
and Gonzalo E. Reyes

New York   Oxford
OXFORD UNIVERSITY PRESS
1994

Oxford University Press

Oxford New York Toronto
Delhi Bombay Calcutta Madras Karachi
Petaling Jaya Singapore Hong Kong Tokyo
Nairobi Dar es Salaam Cape Town
Melbourne Auckland

and associated companies in
Berlin Ibadan

Copyright 1994 by Oxford University Press, Inc.

Published by Oxford University Press, Inc.,
200 Madison Avenue, New York, NY 10016

Oxford is a registered trademark of Oxford University Press

All rights reserved. No part of this publication may be reproduced,
stored in a retrieval system, or transmitted, in any form or by any
means, electronic, mechanical, photocopying, recording or otherwise, without the prior permission of the publisher.

Library of Congress Cataloging-in-Publication Data
The Logical Foundations of Cognition/
edited by John Macnamara and Gonzalo E. Reyes
p. cm.   ISBN 0-19-509215-5 (cloth)
ISBN 0-19-509216-3 (paper)
1. Artificial Intelligence. 2. Language and languages.
3. Cognition
I. Macnamara, John, 1929-
II. Reyes, Gonzalo E., 1937-

2 4 6 8 9 7 5 3 1

Printed in the United States of America
on acid-free paper

Acknowledgments

About half of the papers in this collection began as contributions to a conference organized in Vancouver by the editors in February 1991 under the aegis of Vancouver Studies in Cognitive Science. We are deeply grateful to Steven Davis, general director of the conference series and general editor of the book series, for the invitation to hold an interdisciplinary conference on Logic and Cognition. He helped with all the financial aspects and with the practical details of running the conference. He has been an unfailing and patient source of advice and encouragement in editing the collection, making what might have been a tedious chore into a pleasant experience.

The main source of funds for the conference and published series came from the Social Sciences and Humanities Research Council of Canada, which we acknowledge with gratitude. We are also grateful to Simon Fraser University for financial support.

Other articles in this volume were solicited to supplement the conference papers. The collection as a whole is, we feel, more tightly knit than almost any conference proceedings. We are grateful to all contributors for sticking to the tasks assigned to them.

For an extraordinarily meticulous and scholarly editing of the text we thank Lindsey Thomas Martin and Eleanor O'Donnell. François Magnan undertook the editing of the two most technical papers, one by Magnan and Reyes and the other by La Palme Reyes, Macnamara, and Reyes. It was a headache-making task, and we are most grateful to him. We thank William Lawvere for suggesting improvements to the introduction.

Contents

Acknowledgments

Contributors

I. Theoretical Orientation

1. Introduction, 3
   John Macnamara and Gonzalo E. Reyes

2. Logic and Cognition, 11
   John Macnamara

3. Logic and Psychology: Comment on "Logic and Cognition," 35
   Hilary Putnam

4. Tools for the Advancement of Objective Logic: Closed Categories
   and Toposes, 43
   F. William Lawvere

II. Logic

5. Category Theory as a Conceptual Tool in the
   Study of Cognition, 57
   François Magnan and Gonzalo E. Reyes

6. Reference, Kinds and Predicates, 91
   Marie La Palme Reyes, John Macnamara and Gonzalo E. Reyes

III. Psychology

7. Foundational Issues in the Learning of Proper Names, Count
   Nouns and Mass Nouns, 144
   John Macnamara and Gonzalo E. Reyes

8. Prolegomena to a Theory of Kinds, 177
   Alberto Peruzzi

9. How Children Learn Common Nouns and Proper Names, 212
   D. Geoffrey Hall

10. Mental Logic and How to Discover It, 241
    Martin D. S. Braine

IV. Linguistics

11. The Semantics of Syntactic Categories, 264
   Emmon Bach

12. Some Issues Involving Internal and External Semantics, 282
   Francis Jeffry Pelletier

V. Intentionality

13. Husserl's Notion of Intentionality, 296
   Dagfinn Føllesdal

14. Referential Structure of Fictional Texts, 309
   Marie La Palme Reyes.

15. How Not to Draw the *de re/de dicto* Distinction, 325
   Martin Hahn

16. Cognitive Content and Semantics: Comment on "How Not to Draw the *de re/de dicto* Distinction," 354
   Philip P. Hanson

Contributors

Emmon Bach, Department of Linguistics,
University of Massachusetts, Amherst.
Martin D. S. Braine, Department of Psychology,
New York University.
Dagfinn Føllesdal, Department of Philosophy, University of Oslo.
Martin Hahn, Department of Philosophy, Simon Fraser University.
D. Geoffrey Hall, MRC Cognitive Development Unit, London.
Philip P. Hanson, Department of Philosophy,
Simon Fraser University
Marie La Palme Reyes, Department of Psychology,
McGill University.
F. William Lawvere, Department of Mathematics,
State University of New York, Buffalo.
John Macnamara, Department of Psychology, McGill University.
François Magnan, Département de mathématiques et de statisque,
Université de Montréal.
Francis Jeffry Pelletier, Department of Computer Science,
Department of Philosophy, University of Alberta.
Alberto Peruzzi, Department of Philosophy,
Università degli Studi di Firenze.
Hilary Putnam, Department of Philosophy, Harvard University.
Gonzalo E. Reyes, Département de mathématiques et de statistique,
Université de Montréal.

the
logical
foundations
of
cognition

1
Introduction

John Macnamara and Gonzalo E. Reyes

Further, we find the distinguishing characteristic of all cognitive phenomena
to be... reference to something as an object.

– Franz Brentano

We address this introduction to the casual reader who wishes to have a
brief sketch of the view of cognition that gave rise to this collection and
to the project that we believe is here launched. The introduction situates
the project historically, sketches how it relates to other projects, notably
standard experimental psychology, cognitive science and the philosophy of mind (including Husserl's approach). In doing so we contrive to
introduce the various papers in the collection, and present our particular view of how they contribute to the project. We also attempt to deal,
all too briefly, with certain near reflex objections to the view that there
can be a precise mathematical theory of cognition.

Cognition is just a learned word for acts of coming to know and states
of knowing, as well as for states of wanting and for decisions insofar as
they are guided by knowledge. We extend the term to include the theory of such acts and states. It is in this extended use that we permit ourselves the title of this volume: *The Logical Foundations of Cognition*.
Clearly we mean the logical foundations of the theory of cognition.

The study of cognition's logical foundations demands of contemporary readers a shift of attention and approach. Lance Rips (forthcoming)
remarks that traditionally, psychologists interested in cognitive processes have adopted either the psychometric approach or the experimental one. The psychometric approach is to devise tests of mental
traits or abilities - comprehension, sensitivity to others, intelligence and
so on - and to study correlations among test scores. The experimental
approach is more guided by theory. The main line is to devise experiments that test theories about mental operations. Today, experiment is
sometimes accompanied by computer modelling. Still computer modelling is sufficiently vigorous and autonomous to deserve a name of its
own: the modelling strategy.

While excluding none of the three approaches just mentioned, the present collection adopts a different one, which can properly be called the cognitive approach. This means that reference is the basic primitive. The collection is interdisciplinary but each essay is a contribution to the theory of reference. Of course we do not imagine that our project is the first to take reference seriously. We are inclined to believe, however, that nowhere in the contemporary scene does it have the central and foundational role that it has here. We see this volume as a first step towards the development of a unified theory of cognition in which reference is the basic primitive. From the perspective of the history of psychology, the ambition is far from being new. It is in fact a return to the interests and standpoint of the majority of psychologists through the ages. A few words to bring this out!

Following Aristotle's suggestion in *de Anima* (Book 3, chapter 3), the older test for whether a psychological phenomenon was cognitive was to see if the predicables 'true' and 'false' were applicable to it. For example, a man may feel sad but it makes no sense to ask if his sadness is true or false. In contrast, if he believes he was ill used, it makes perfect sense to ask if his belief is true or false. The test places sadness outside cognition and belief inside. This is not to deny that there may be cognitive components in states that might fairly be called states of sadness.

The intuition behind the Aristotelean view is that cognitive states and events claim that a certain state of affairs holds in the world. The claim may be true or false. To make any such claim, however, the mind must make contact with the world, the type of contact in which reference is central. That is, cognitive states have strings of interpreted symbols at their core. They may comprise much more than interpreted symbols but never less. Little wonder, then, that Franz Brentano, a neglected founder of modern psychology and himself a great Aristotelean scholar, should specify "reference to something as an object" as the distinguishing mark of the cognitive.

Partly to explore the theory of reference, Aristotle founded logic, which included his theory of the semantics of various classes of natural-language expressions. Today, with the aid of the mathematical theory of categories and especially its logical component, categorical logic, we are in a much stronger position to pursue Aristotle's original program. In fact we see the relation between categorical logic and cognition as parallel to that between calculus and dynamics. The motivation for taking this parallel seriously is the subject of John Macnamara's paper and Hilary Putnam's response to it. The more general theoretical relation between logic (objective and subjective) and cognition, as well as the appropriateness of category theory in the context, is explored in the paper by F. William Lawvere.

A common reaction is to say that the whole project is misguided on the grounds that the mind is not purely logical. The usual grounds for the negative reaction are that the mind is influenced by emotions and by defence mechanisms, which militate against dispassionate logic. The reaction seems fully justified insofar as it touches on what people say and on why they reach the conclusions they do. But this has little to do with the project. The project is to study the reference of natural-language expressions, such as the proper name 'Richard Nixon', the count noun 'dog', the mass noun 'water', the predicable 'sick'. It matters not at all whether speakers love or hate Richard Nixon, whether they use the name calmly or in anger; it picks out the same person regardless of the user's emotional state or political agenda. And so with the other types of expressions. This is parallel to the linguistic project of explaining why, say, English words in certain combinations are grammatical and in certain others ungrammatical. Linguistics does not propose to explain why anyone says anything; and neither need cognitive psychology.

Another source of hesitation is that logic deals with the way expressions ought to be interpreted and the way inferences ought to be drawn; in other words, that logic deals with idealizations of interpretation and deduction. Psychology, in contrast, is thought of as studying the facts of interpretation and the facts of how people draw conclusions, which are, often enough, erroneous from the logical point of view. When people hear a proposal to take the relation between logic and psychology as parallel to that between calculus and dynamics, they point out that calculus applies to dynamics under suitable idealization and simplification. For example, Galileo's mathematization of movement abstracted from friction and air resistance. Newton's first law of motion claims to describe motion in force-free space, which exists nowhere in reality. This approximation inspired the idealization and simplification that led to both calculus and the growth of physics. In this context, how are we to think of cognition?

Our answer has two parts. The first is to pass from natural languages with their many-faceted ambiguities to the language of thought, taking the latter to be unambiguous and semantically perspicuous. Two considerations encourage us in this move. One is that we are capable of grasping the distinct interpretations of sentences that have ambiguous expressions; and we can grasp the distinct logical structures that can correctly be associated with natural-language sentences. It follows not only that our minds are capable of grasping the various possibilities for interpretation, but that we have in our minds the expressive powers to represent them all perspicuously. It is natural to posit a language of thought in which to house these expressive powers – that is, a language of the mind into which natural-language sentences are compiled. The second consideration that supports the move to the language of thought is that there is at least one area of cognition where an enriched natural language is both unambiguous and semantically perspicuous, namely, the language of mathematics. This means that the language of mathematics actually instantiates the idealization we propose; although any particular use of it may depart to some extent from the ideal. (These remarks owe much to Michael Makkai.)

The second part of our answer to the query about idealization in cognition is bolder and more speculative. We see it as being similar in spirit to the postulation of those fundamental simplicities of dynamics, the Newtonian laws of motion. We postulate that the most basic properties of cognitive psychology, the underlying simplicities of cognition, show up as the universal properties of category theory. What this means is explained in the paper by François Magnan and Gonzalo E. Reyes, which is written as an introduction to category theory for mathematically unsophisticated readers. Several confirmatory examples are given in the paper by Marie La Palme Reyes, John Macnamara and Gonzalo E. Reyes, the paper by Macnamara and that by Macnamara and Reyes.

A preliminary word about why categorical logic and categorical models rather than classical logic and set-theoretic models. Classical logic, with its set-theoretic models, grew from the study of arithmetical sentences. Now arithmetic deals with objects that are eternal and unchanging, whereas the objects of most discourse are ephemeral and changeable. Moreover, set theory generally recognizes only a single primitive count noun, 'set'. In some versions, set theory recognizes a further count noun, namely 'Ur-element', whose interpretation is just anything that lacks members. Although the equality of two sets is definable in the theory as the relation of having the same members, this does not work for Ur-elements, precisely because they lack set-theoretic structure. It is simply assumed that urelements come equipped with a notion of equality and the matter is left at that. Even geometry as axiomatized by Hilbert (1902) has three primitive count nouns: 'point', 'line' and 'plane'. It is out of the question that all the kinds of everyday discourse – shoes, ships and sealing wax, cabbages and kings – should be reduced to a single kind. We regard the attempts of classical logicians to treat all these kinds as predicates of a universal kind THING as misguided and misleading. There are many reasons to reject the notion, the main one being that we have no access to such a kind - a kind that would pretend to embrace bicycles as well as mistakes in grammar. For we have no idea how to individuate objects under a totally unconstrained notion of thing (see the papers by Macnamara; Putnam; La Palme Reyes, Macnamara and Reyes). It follows that we need an alternative to classical logic. We call the alternative 'the logic of kinds' – a many-sorted logic.

The trouble with set theory runs deeper still. Although sets may have a rich ε-structure (given by members of members of...), especially in non-well-founded versions (see Aczel, 1988), there is a sense in which Sets are the most impoverished category. Functions among sets are not required to preserve this ε-structure and thus, from the standpoint of maps, objects in Sets look like unstructured collections of elements (which can be thought of as dots) on which functions may operate in an unconstrained way. The categorical point of view, in which objects and maps are both basic, requires that maps should preserve the structure of objects. In the category of Graphs, for instance, maps between graphs are constrained by the graph structure: they send vertices to vertices and arrows to arrows in such a manner as to preserve the incidence relations between vertices and arrows. By now we have a host of categories with set-like properties generalizing the catigory of Sets. These may profitably be substituted for sets in building models of cognitive processes. In fact, the mind is essentially involved with constructions that seem so natural and universal that they must be severely constrained. It follows that to capture these constructions precisely, we need a theory that makes provision for building in various constraints at the basic level. Category theory gives systematic ways to build and study examples with objects so structured as to force desired constraints.

Cognitive psychology, in the sense described, has only slight overlap with the discipline that nowadays bears the name 'cognitive science'. The overlap is in those areas that take reference seriously, such as word learning in children and the theory of concepts in adults. We hope the volume makes substantial contributions and clarifications in these areas. With the computer-modelling component of cognitive science, we take seriously the responsibility to go beyond standard experimental strategies in offering a unified theory of a significant portion of cognition. Computers, however, do not interpret their symbols into a reality external to the computer. Insofar as computer scientists attempt to model cognitive states, they require the stance that Jerry Fodor (1981) called methodological solipsism. The impact of this stance has been described somewhat aptly by the quip that methodological solipsism means psychology from the skin in. The world drops from sight, so to speak, and with it disappears reference to the world. This is by no means to deny a role for computers in modelling other areas of psychology, such as perception; nor, of course, does it deny the mind's computational abilities.

A question we are sometimes asked is how cognitive psychology in the Brentano tradition relates to the work of Edmund Husserl, Brentano's student. On the face of things, Husserl developed a theory of objects and of the cognition of objects, a theory that has points of contact with the modelling approach of cognitive science (see Dreyfus and Hall 1982, Introduction). Partly to handle this query, we asked Dagfinn Føllesdal to write the paper on Husserl. This paper serves two important functions. Føllesdal explains that Husserl abandoned Brentano's criterion for the mental (reference to something as an object) because Brentano had failed to give an adequate theory of fictional objects. While Husserl himself does not seem to have succeeded where Brentano failed, we feel that his concerns were fully justified. In her paper, Marie La Palme Reyes proposes a new solution to the problem of reference to fictional objects, a solution which we believe enables us to hold on to Bretano's characterization of the mental. Føllesdal goes on to explain Husserl's own theory of the mental construction of the objects of intentional states, his theory of noema. While there are undoubtedly insights of great value in Husserl's noema, we feel that the project as a whole must fail for want of an adequate theory of kinds to individuate and handle the identity of the objects of cognition. The inadequacy in Husserl's approach shows up in the handling of existence. His *epoché* or bracketing of existence attempts to sidestep the question of existence. To illuminate Husserl's thinking, Føllesdal draws attention to the duck/rabbit ambiguous figure which emphasized that how we construe a perceptual presentation may depend on nothing in the immediate perceptual array. This is even more obvious in "non-ambiguous" perception: how we construe the perceptual presentation afforded by, say, a boy – as a boy, a son, a person, an animal, etc. – may depend on nothing in the immediate perceptual array. For all that, BOY, SON, PERSON, ANIMAL are distinct though related kinds; and the existence of boys, sons, persons and animals seems quite unproblematic. This poses a challenge that, in our view, Husserl did not handle satisfactorily, that of accounting for the relations among such obviously related kinds as well as the relations among the varying ranges of existence of their members. For example, the range of existence for a boy and that for the related person is normally different. It follows that a boy is not identical with the related person. To handle such relations as that between the boy and the person is one of the basic tasks of the logic of kinds.

Another task in the realm of intentionality is to characterize the content of beliefs and to account for how beliefs are individuated; when to count two beliefs as the same belief and when to count them as different. Since beliefs are at the core of intentional (referential) states, this is obviously a key task to which philosophers have already devoted a great deal of attention. Martin Hahn and Philip Hanson devote their papers to this problem.

Theories of the semantics of natural-language expressions constrain psychological theories of the prerequisites for learning to interpret such expressions and theories of how they are learned. Macnamara and Reyes explore the psychological implications of the theory of kinds. Their paper together with the related paper by La Palme Reyes, Macnamara and Reyes are studied from the theoretical standpoint by Alberto Peruzzi and from the standpoint of experimental work with children by Geoff Hall. The collection as a whole emphasizes the extent of the logical resources that are involved in the simplest forms of everyday thought. Now, it is one thing to specify logical resources in a general way; it is another to specify the form in which they are realized in the mind. The latter is the problem that Martin Braine studies in his paper.

Another way to tackle Martin Braine's problem of discovering the mind's mental properties is to seek for linguistic universals. It is tempting to base one's claims about logical resources on intuitions about the semantic properties of the grammatical categories in the small number of languages with which one happens to be familiar. If, however, one claims a fundamental role in cognition for a certain logical structure, it is reasonable to ask if the logical structure shows up in all natural languages. The papers by Emmon Bach and Jeff Pelletier are devoted to this topic – linguistic universals related to the logical role of syntactic categories.

The work here presented is but a part of what has already been done and a mere fraction of what remains to be done.

It is not uncommon to hear the view that linguistic intuition is reliable enough to ground solid theories of syntax, morphology and phonology, but that semantic intuitions are guttering and unreliable. While not wishing to take anything from linguistic intuition, we wish to claim that the core intuitions relating to reference – the reference of proper names, count nouns, mass nouns and predicables – are as solid as anything in mathematics. We believe that this becomes apparent when reference is approached with sufficiently flexible mathematical tools. Our fond hope is that this collection of papers will help to spread this conviction. It was, we hasten to add, the conviction of Franz Brentano, and to a lesser extent, of that other founding father of modern psychology, Wilhelm Wundt (see Macnamara forthcoming). The generations that followed either sabotaged or lost sight of their psychological program. It is essential to set things to rights. The stakes are high, for apart from the proper understanding of logic, what is in play is the rightful position of cognition in the study of psychology.

References

Epigraph: Franz Bretano, *Psychologie vom empirischen Standpunkt*, my translation

Aczel, P. (1988). *Non-well-founded Sets*. Stanford, CA: CSLI Lecture Notes, No. 14

Dreyfus, H.L., and H. Hall (eds.) (1982). *Husserl, Intentionality and Cognitive Science*. Bradford/MIT Press

Fodor, J.A. (1981). *Representations: Philosophical Essays on the Foundations of Cognitive Science*. Cambridge, MA: Bradford/MIT Press

Hilbert, D. (1902). *The Foundations of Geometry*, trans. E.J. Townsend. Chicago: Open Court

Lawvere, F.W., and S.H. Schanuel (1991). *Conceptual Mathematics: A First Introduction to Categories*. Buffalo Workshop Press, P.O. Box 171, Buffalo, NY 14226, USA

Macnamara, J. (1992). The takeover of psychology by biology. In M. Pütz (ed.), *Thirty Years of Linguistic Evolution: Studies in Honour of René Dirven on the Occasion of His Sixtieth Birthday*, pp. 545-70. Philadelphia: John Benjamins

Rips, L. (forthcoming). *Logic and Cognition*. Cambridge, MA: Bradford/MIT Press

2
Logic and Cognition

John Macnamara

1. Introduction

The received position in logic and cognition is that the two subjects have little or nothing to do with one another. This position, adopted at the turn of the last century, is the result of two events. One was the divorce between philosophy and psychology. In the settlement after the divorce, logic, specifying standards of correct inference, went to philosophy, whereas to psychology went what were viewed as the facts of mental life. We can express the division of labour not too fancifully as:

$$\frac{\text{Standards of perfection}}{\text{Philosophy}} = \frac{\text{Facts}}{\text{Psychology}}$$

The second event was the close of the psychologism debate. That was the debate about the proper relation between logic and psychology. One side maintained that the foundations of logic rest on a psychological basis; that the truth of logical claims and the soundness of logical inference rules are guaranteed by the facts of psychology. This position in its full strength seems to orginate with Jakob Fries (1783-1844) and Friedrich Beneke (1798-1854) and was shared by many nineteenth-century logicians including John Stuart Mill. The debate was settled to most people's satisfaction by the appearance of two books: Gottlob Frege (1884), *The foundations of arithmetic;* and Edmund Husserl (1900), *Logical Investigations.* These books argued that:

(i)   Logic does not derive its basic principles from psychology.
(ii) Logic does not describe psychological states and events.

Elliott Sober (1978) captures something of the atmosphere of the times: "While the psychologists were leaving, philosophers were slamming the door behind them." This shows up in a third position, which Susan Haack (1978) attributes to Frege:

(iii) "Logic has nothing to do with mental processes." (P. 238)

While Frege certainly argued that logic had nothing to learn from psychology, it is not at all clear, as Notturno (1984) points out, that he denied that psychology could learn from logic.

For all that, (iii) describes well how psychologists regard logic. A search through some of the better known handbooks of psychology and cognitive science reveals either a total neglect of logic or the attitude that, at best, logic is a quarry from which to extract hypotheses for experimental investigation of human thought processes. An exception is the work of Jean Piaget, though he frequently attributed to children illogical schemata and inference rules, thus rendering the emergence of logically sound ones totally mysterious. One of the few psychologists to write about the psychologism debate is George Humphrey. In his influential book, *Thinking* (1951) Humphrey claims that Husserl's polemic against psychologism had "freed psychology from the shackles of logic" (p. 78). George Miller (1951) in the same year put the relation between the two disciplines as follows: "The fact is that logic is a formal system, just as arithmetic is a formal system, and to expect untrained subjects to think logically is much the same as to expect preschool children to know the multiplication table" (p. 806). A far cry from Leibniz's 'natural logic'!

As we will see, not all psychologists agree with Miller. At the same time, no psychology department, so far as I know, insists that its students study logic. The only formal tool insisted on for psychology students is statistics, which curiously does not enter the theory of psychology. The only formal tool insisted on for philosophy students is logic, where logic frequently plays an essential role in the theory. It is tempting, then, to set up the following equation:

$$\frac{\text{Logic}}{\text{Philosophy}} = \frac{\text{Statistics}}{\text{Psychology}}$$

Philosophers seem to think that logic is a useful tool with which to explore and express certain standards of perfection that apply to human reasoning. Since psychologists, by and large, have eschewed such standards, they see little need for an education in logic.

My strategy, after (1) this introductory section and (2) a note on the historical background to the division of labour between philosophy (with logic) and cognition, is (3) to argue briefly (because I have presented the case more fully in Macnamara 1986) that logic is highly relevant to cognitive psychology; (4) to argue at greater length, contrary to universal present-day belief, that logic has much to learn from psychology. (5) I claim, nonetheless, that logic is not grounded in psychology and that logic does not describe mental states and events. (6) The psychology I envisage is more comprehensive than that of most present-day psychologists, so I will make some remarks about what I take psychology to be. (7) I conclude with a statement intended to place in perspective the diverse elements in this paper.

My thesis is that logic and psychology mutually constrain each other in something like the way in which mathematics and physics constrain each other. Calculus, for example, was invented to express and handle concepts that are required in the study of physical forces and the movement of physical bodies. For all that, calculus is an analysis of mathematical continua, not of physical bodies or their movement in physical space. Calculus, then, has a life of its own apart from mechanics. At the same, time calculus is essential to the theory of mechanics in two ways: it is the principal language in which to express the theory (witness Hamilton's equations and Schrödinger's equation); it is the main conceptual tool that constrains the construction and testing of theory. Similarly, I hope to show, logic is an essential constituent of the theory of cognition: it supplies the appropriate mathematical language in which to express cognitive properties and processes and the appropriate mathematical instrument with which to explore them further. The properties and processes in question involve the ability to interpret symbols and to grasp the implications of relations among sentences. For all that, logic has a mathematical life of its own. Logic is no more cognition than calculus is mechanics – although logic is set up to express and handle the interpretation of symbols and the implications among sentences. In short, logic and cognition constrain each other as do calculus and mechanics.

In this connection, one can also point to the theory of linguistics and the psychological capacity to produce and recognize grammatical sentences. The theory of grammar and the theory of psycholinguistics mutually constrain one another. The example is less apt, however, inasmuch as normally one does not include semantics under grammar.

2. Historical Note on the Division of Labour between Philosophy and Psychology

I suspect that psychology turned its back on standards of perfection and on ideals when Thomas Hobbes adopted Galileo's kinematics as the model for psychology (see Macnamara 1990). Certainly physics (kinematics included) idealizes – to point centres of mass, to force-free spaces, to ideal gases. But the ideals are in the theory, not in the physical world described by the theory. A psychology that apes physics will also assume that the ideals are in theories about the mind rather than in mental reality. An example of a psychological ideal is the notion of an individual's true IQ, as the mean score obtained by the individual in an infinite series of intelligence tests without learning. In such a psychology, however, the ideals are not in the mind but in the theory; they are conveniences rather than aids to the development of theory.

How different is the approach to the human mind of St. Augustine or St. Thomas Aquinas? The older approach is still to be found in Descartes and Leibniz. The third set of objections to Descartes's *Meditations*, written by Hobbes (and Descartes's reply to them) already presage the disappearance of ideals from the subject matter or psychology. Let one example stand for all. In the fifth of the *Meditations*, Descartes had spoken of imagining a triangle which "although there may nowhere in the world be such a figure outside my thought, has nevertheless a determinate nature" (Vol. 1, p. 180). Obviously Descartes is speaking about a figure on an idealized plane bounded by three idealized lines (which, having no thickness, are necessarily invisible). To Hobbes the notion is incomprehensible: "If the triangle exists nowhere at all, I do not understand how it can have any nature;... The triangle in the mind comes from the triangle we have seen" (third set of objections to the *Meditations*; objection 14). Here is my point. If one denies any objective reality to ideals, one can, as Hobbes does, forget about any idealizing capacity in the mind. It seems as if this is what happened in the psychology that, in the wake of Hobbes, modelled itself on physics.

But ideals are too important to be abandoned altogether. A division of labour, well entrenched by Kant's time, assigns them to philosophy while assigning to psychology the facts of mental life – as though the ideals had no reality in mental life. In the following passage from Kant's *Logic*, we see the division of labour in full flower:

> Some logicians presuppose psychological principles in logic. But to bring such principles into logic is as absurd as taking morality from life. If we took the principles from psychology, i.e. from observations about our understanding, we would merely see *how* thinking occurs and *how it is* under manifold hindrances and conditions; this would therefore lead to the cognition of merely *contingent* laws. In logic, however, the question is not one of contingent but of *necessary* rules, not how we think but how we ought to think. The rules of logic, therefore, must be taken not from the *contingent* but from the necessary use of the understanding, which one finds, without any psychology, in oneself. (*Logic*, p. 16)

So the logician looks after the standards of perfect reasoning; the psychologist looks after the actual processes.The first important voice to be raised against this view of things is that of Noam Chomsky, albeit mainly in the domain of syntax. Is there not, however, a certain torsion in the distinction Kant wishes to maintain? If we have standards of perfection for our actual mental processes, and if psychology occupies itself with actual mental processes, why should psychology be barred from attempting to incorporate such standards in its scope and attempting to account for them? Is there any understanding the mind in its logical aspects, without access to the mind's logical standards? Is there any explaining people's satisfaction and dissatisfaction with particular arguments and their willingness to backtrack when logical error is pointed out to them? Indeed, is there any understanding their ability to recognize logical error in their own reasoning processes? Chomsky has resisted the settlement that linguists should concern themselves with linguistic competence (standards of linguistic perfection) and that psychologists should concern themselves with linguistic performance. In this, I believe, he is fully justified. By parity of reasoning, we should resist the corresponding division of labour in the area of logic. But I am getting ahead of myself.

To return to the main business at hand, the division of labour seems to survive to the present day. In "Epistemology Naturalized," Quine (1969) proposes psychology as our best shot at epistemology. But psychology will reveal only "how science is in fact" (p. 78). It will not give a logical justification for the conclusions of science. It is not the epistemological point that concerns me but the conception of psychology as a discipline that deals with facts to the exclusion, if I understand Quine, of standards of perfection.

A word about a possible source of confusion. It is frequently said that logic is a normative science, whereas psychology is not. Notice that Kant, in the passage cited above, says that logic is not about "how we think but how we ought to think." One also speaks about the *laws* of logic. This is all right provided we realize that the laws in question have only to do with the desire to achieve truth. As Husserl (1900/1970, pp. 88 ff.) pointed out, logical laws presuppose logical truth. The law of contradiction, for example, is to be respected in thinking not because it is a law but because it is true. Being normative, then, is not opposed to being true, to being a fact.

3. Logic Relevant to Cognitive Psychology

At the same time, there are some philosophers and psychologists who are uneasy with the orthodox position on how logic and cognition are related. Witness in particular Cohen (1981) and the numerous comments that accompany that paper. In the same spirit is Henle (1962), Pylyshyn (1972), Braine (1978; and this volume), Sober (1978), Rips (1983) and Macnamara (1986).

At its bleakest logic, elucidates certain uses of the connectives 'not', 'and' and 'or', certain uses of the words 'all' and 'some', as well as certain uses of logic's key words: 'true' and 'false'. It is obvious that any psychologist interested in explaining how children come to understand those uses of those expressions, or how they enter into the mental lives of adults, will want to learn what logicians have been able to discover about their interpretation. Indeed Quine (1970), Davidson (1980, essay 14) and Smedslund (1990) all say that there is no interpreting anyone who has a deviant logic of such expressions. Among the people we must interpret are logicians. It follows, on the view of the authors we are discussing, that we must interpret them as exploring certain ordinary-language uses of the expressions in question. Moreover, since the logicians explore the logical properties of these expressions more deeply than the rest of us, psychologists must turn to the logicians for a fuller understanding of these expressions, if they are to give an account of how those expressions (in those uses) are learned or how they are later deployed.

A less bleak logic will encompass proper names, count nouns, mass nouns, indexicals, predicables (mainly adjectival and verb phrases), the modal operators 'necessary' and 'possible' and a host of others. By a logic of such expressions, I mean an account of how they contribute to the truth-conditions of sentences in which they occur. That is the most accessible element in their interpretation. In *A Border Dispute,* I made an effort to spell all this out and to point in some detail to the psychological implications of the relevant logic. At the same time, I was careful to maintain the distinction between logic and psychology, and to avoid a psychologistic position. It seemed to me that logic stood little danger of being swallowed up in psychology if, for its purposes, psychology borrowed logical insights.

In *A Border Dispute,* however, I argued that classical logic is ill-equipped to handle the logic of ordinary discourse precisely because classical logic derives mainly from an analysis of arithmetical sentences. Arithmetic is an unusual domain of discourse because (a) the objects in the domain are eternal and unchanging; all their properties are necessary ones. And (b) only a single basic count noun is required in arithmetical sentences: 'number' or 'set' depending on the level of one's work. Any other count noun can be defined as a subset of numbers or sets – e.g., 'prime number', 'finite set'.

Most of ordinary discourse, in contrast,(a) deals with ephemeral and changing objects. And (b) it is quite improbable that the kinds of such discourse – dogs, ideas, molecules, etc. – can be reduced to a single kind or defined as subsets of a single kind. More of this below. It follows that classical logic needs to be substantially enriched if it is to be extended to parts of ordinary discourse that elude classical logic.

My general thesis is practically a tautology. It is that one guide to how to construct a logic richer than classical logic is the manner in which we interpret the expressions of ordinary language and the manner in which we grasp implications among ordinary-language sentences. These, however, are matters of psychological fact. It follows that psychological facts can guide the construction of logic. The logic so constructed is a mathematical object with a mathematical life of its own. It is not psychology. But in its construction, it is constrained by certain cognitive states and events. Although the thesis seems patently obvious, it has not been considered as seriously as it deserves in either the philosophical or psychological literature. The reason, I suspect, is fear of psychologism – a heresy so terrible that at the mention of the word, as Brentano (1874) says, "many a pious philosopher... crosses himself as though the devil himself were in it" (p. 306). The fear is quite ungrounded, as we will see when we have conceptualized more fully the relation between the two disciplines.

4. Psychological Contributions to Logic

Several papers recently argue the relevance of psychology to various philosophical enterprises. Ned Block (1981) claims that psychological studies of intelligence have a contribution to make to philosophical understanding of what it is to be intelligent. Adrian Cussins (1987) claims that psychological studies of concept formation are relevant to philosophical understanding of what it is to have a concept. I want to concentrate on logic.

My strategy is to present a series of psychological claims related to the interpretation of expressions and show how these claims were employed to constrain 'the logic of kinds'. By that I mean the category-theoretic semantics for a range of natural-language expressions developed by Gonzalo Reyes working in close collaboration with Marie Reyes and myself. I have chosen the psychological claims so that they permit a thumbnail sketch of the logic of kinds. It is not my purpose to defend that logic here. That would be to miss the point. My excuse for selecting certain psychological claims is my belief that the logic of kinds is interesting in itself. The logic owes much to the work of Peter Geach (1957, 1961, 1962, 1972), Aldo Bressan (1972), David Wiggins (1980) and Anil Gupta (1980). Further details of the logic are to be found in G.E. Reyes (1991), and M. Reyes (1988). The motivation for the logic, as well as an introduction to its mathematical formulation, is to be found in La Palme Reyes, Macnamara and Reyes (this volume).

Each psychological claim is to the effect that we can understand P or that we cannot understand Q. The claim that we can understand P is followed by the claim that there is a logic underlying the fact that we can. This is little more than the claim that there must be a theory of how we interpret P. The psychological claim points to a class of logics that takes cognizance of that fact. A psychological claim that we cannot understand Q is followed by the claim that logic should not assume that we can or require us to do so. Some psychological claims can be expressed equally well as linguistic claims. There is a most intimate relation between claims about the structure of language and claims about linguistic behaviour. Linguistic behaviour is to be explained by the mind's incorporation of linguistic properties. At the same time, natural languages have the properties they do only because those properties can be recognized by infants and manipulated by them without the type of metalinguistic assistance that second-language learners typically receive. In other words, there is a close fit between the mind's linguistic properties and the properties of natural languages.

I do not claim that we have infallible access to psychological facts. The claims I make are not particularly controversial, and some are downright obvious. I recognize, however, that seemingly obvious claims can be misleading, as Frege found to his dismay. I am fully prepared to accept the judgment of psychology (experimental or theoretical) or of logic on my putative psychological facts. For example, if my claims are shown to be inconsistent, I will abandon some of them, because inconsistent sentences jointly express nothing comprehensible. I will not take pains to defend my psychological proposals fully, since my purpose is mainly to illustrate how psychology constrains logic rather than to establish once and for all a particular set of psychological constraints.

Nor do I suggest that a particular psychological claim guides us to a unique logic. I am not even sure that all the relevant psychological facts guide us to a unique logic. Naturally, however, the constraints increase as the number of facts increases. Finally, I fully acknowledge that there may be routes other than the ones I propose to the particular logic we arrived at.

Psychological Claim 1: If we are faithful to our linguistic intuition, we attach certain quantifiers ('a', 'many', 'few', 'one', 'two', etc.) to count nouns only. On the universality of this claim, see Emmon Bach (this volume).

For example, we say 'a dog', 'another proof', but not *'two walkeds', *'many quickly', *'few hot'.

Psychological Claim 2: We cannot conceptually grasp an individual without the support of a count noun.

An indexical, such as 'this', will not do on its own. 'This', applied to an individual person, for example, may draw attention to the person or to the person's clothes, or appearance, or even manners. On its own, an indexical cannot unambiguously pick out any of those things. Neither can a predicable (adjectival or verb phrase) on its own. You cannot count whatever is blue in a room, because you do not know what to count as one blue – a whole blue shirt, or the sleeves separately on the grounds that they were sewn on, or the separate threads, or the fibres of the threads. It follows that a collection of predicables will not serve the purpose either. Neither will a proper name on its own. For one thing, most individuals do not have a proper name, so proper names could not be the general means of specifying an individual. When an individual is the bearer of a proper name, a count noun is needed to specify what the bearer is. Suppose you know who Steve is. You might be inclined to think that the name denotes the stuff in Steve's body, a certain mass of molecules. But that cannot be. Suppose Steve's body weighs 175 pounds; it is clear that such a mass of molecules was never born, although Steve was. By Leibniz's law, it follows that Steve is not identical with the molecules of which his body is formed, and hence that 'Steve' does not denote the stuff in Steve's body. What does it denote? The answer is a certain person. What individuates the bearer of the name and traces its identity correctly is the count noun 'person'. The bearer of a proper name always needs to be specified by a count noun.

These facts jointly point to a logic that recognizes count nouns as a logical category distinct from predicables. This is the major thesis of Gupta (1980). They also point to a logic in which any reference to an individual is typed by a count noun. (Individuation and identity in connection with mass nouns – such as 'water' and 'money' – requires a separate treatment that I do not propose to go into here.) This means that indexicals and proper names must be typed by a count noun. Referring definite descriptions wear their count noun visibly.

Psychological Claim 3: We cannot conceptually grasp an individual in a universal kind supposedly denoted by the count noun 'thing' or 'object'.

The reasons are similar to those that reveal the inadequacy of a predicable for the purpose of specifying an individual. If asked to count the things in a room, I do not know whether to count persons separately from their organs, and their cells separately from their organs, since all might be characterized as things. (Later we will see that there is a clear notion of a thing, or entity, in a subcategory of kinds, but it has nothing to do with a universal category of things). It follows that I cannot conceptually grasp an individual under the description 'thing'.

This fact supports the view that logic should not expect us to grasp an individual under the description 'thing'. Nor, what is almost the same, should it suppose that we have a notion of a bare particular – that is, of an individual that is untyped by a bona fide count noun such as 'bicycle', 'dog', or 'idea'. Now, on the Fregean approach, classical logic asks us to do just that. For that approach regiments 'Some man is tall' as:

(4.1) $\exists x$ (Man (x) and Tall (x))

The untyped variable is supposed to be interpreted into a universal kind THING. If one takes a more Peircean view, one may assume that the variable ranges over some more restricted domain of discourse. On that reading, one must accuse logicians of being sloppy, because they have not so specified the domain of discourse as to make adequate provision for the individuation of the individual that has the properties of being a man and being tall. Both readings place the count noun 'man' in subject position on equal logical footing with the predicable 'tall'. We can correct both defects at once if we replace (4.1) with:

(4.2) $\exists(x{:}Man)$ Tall (x)

which reads: 'some individual in the kind MAN is tall'. This is an example of restricted quantification, advocated by many logicians. There are other reasons, also supported by psychological observation, for such quantification. Bach (1989, chap. 4) points out that such expressions as 'most dogs' are uninterpretable in the way we naturally interpret them if quantification is unrestricted. The reason is that while it is true that most dogs have four legs, it is not true that most things are dogs and have four legs.

Notice the mutual determination of individual and kinds in the logic I am sketching. A kind is specified by its members; but the members are specified by the kind. This type of dialectical relation is familiar to psychologists from the writings of the Gestalt school. Gestalt psychologists observed that perceptual figures or wholes are determined by their perceptual parts, while the perceptual role of the perceptual part is determined by the perceptual whole of which it is a part. Another familiar example is supplied by language. A sentence is determined grammatically and semantically by its constituents, and the grammatical function and semantic role of a constituent is determined by the sentence to which it belongs. I merely point out that logic should respect the dialectical relation between individuals and the kinds to which they belong. All this signals a special status in logic for count nouns, which refer to kinds.

Psychological Claim 4: We employ the word 'dog' to refer to the dogs of times past and to future dogs as well as to present-day dogs.

In fact, we have no other means of referring to the whole kind DOG. This suggests the logical principle that the reference of the count noun 'dog', (i.e., the kind DOG) is independent of the time and circumstances of use, and so for all count nouns. We call this property of count nouns 'modal constancy', using the expression in a sense different from Gupta (1980). We mean by 'modal constancy' that the reference of a count noun cannot in general be identified with the members that happen to exist at the moment the word is used. Instead, it refers to a single, immense object, a kind that embraces all the members that ever were, are or will be. This suggests that a kind is an abstract object, and the simplest way to conceptualize it is as a set or more generally as an object in a category. In fact, in the logic of kinds, a kind is presented as a set together with an existence relation on the set assigning to each member the situations, both factual and counterfactual, of which the member is a constituent.

Psychological Claim 5: We cannot conceptually control the notion of a possible member of a kind.

Kinds are confined to members that are constituents of some factual situation. Quine (1961, p. 4) has asked the relevant question ("How many possible fat men can fit in a doorway?"). He seems perfectly justified in his scepticism about the possibility of a sensible answer, and, by implication,in his scepticism of the comprehensibility of the notion of a possible fat man.

In the logic of kinds, there are no possible fat men, only actual ones. We were supported in our stance by the grammar of ordinary language – which in turn gives rise to a highly relevant psychological claim. To illustrate, consider a couple, Derby and Joan, who have no daughter. We say that it might have been possible for them to have had a daughter; not that they might have had a possible daughter. No one would know how to treat a possible daughter. At the same time, Derby and Joan's daughter is not a constituent of any factual situation, only of counterfactual ones. To distinguish between her and actual daughters, Marie Reyes posited a higher-level predicate – 'to be considered as a daughter' – which can apply to sets of properties of persons. This suggestion has not been fully investigated yet, but if correct, it would make provision in the logic of kinds for individuals that are constituents of both factual and counterfactual situations. Only the latter are bona fide members of the kind; the former, confined to counterfactual situations, are members of a higher-order object. In this way, the logic of kinds caters for whatever was valuable in attempts to talk about possible individuals.

Psychological Claim 6: We cannot directly express identity across different kinds.

To illustrate, we may wish to claim that a boy is identical with the man he later became. But we cannot say that a certain boy is *the same boy* as a certain man, or that the boy is *the same man* as a certain man. As Hilary Putnam put it, in commenting on this paper, one cannot say 'I am the boy I once was.' He pointed out, however, that if there were talk of a certain boy 50 years ago, one might well say 'I am that boy'. But this does not mean that one is expressing identity across the kinds BOY and MAN. To begin with the 'I' in question is typed not by 'man' but by 'person', since it embraces the whole of a person's existence. The sentence 'I am that boy' expresses a relation between a certain boy and a certain person. The relation is signalled by the overworked copula. What precisely that relation is will become apparent when we see how to construct the notion of an entity in a system of kinds. There we will see that Putnam's is an important intuition.

A general theory that handles identity requires some sensitive regimentation of natural-language expressions. Sensitivity to the whole range of relevant intuition reveals that '=' is a typed predicable requiring that the referring expressions placed on its left and right to form a single sentence should both be typed by the same count noun. This is almost the same as Wiggins's (1980, chap. 1) thesis D. I come back to another related logical provision after the next claim.

Psychological Claim 7: We count passengers and persons differently (the example is from Gupta, 1980), and we can understand such ways of counting.

If you travel three times with Air Canada in 1991, you will be counted as three passengers, although you are only one person. Similar distinctions are made in counting patients and persons in hospitals, diners and persons in a restaurant, majors and persons in a university (there being persons who take joint majors), and so on.

If we cannot express either identity or lack of identity over different kinds, such as PASSENGER and PERSON, how do we avoid a bloated ontology in which there are persons besides passengers crowded into airplanes? The first thing to notice is that the kind PASSENGER is not included (set-theoretically) in the kind PERSON. Set-theoretic inclusion of A in B is one-one in this sense: for each member of A there is just one member of B, that is identical with it, and no member of B is identical with more than one member of A. It follows that the number of B's cannot be less than the number of A's. But the number of persons might well be less than the number of passengers. Set theoretic inclusion cannot handle this.

The logic of kinds handles it by positing an underlying map u between certain pairs of kinds - u: PASSENGER $\rightarrow$ PERSON. The map assigns to each passenger a person u(p). The theory posits similar maps - u': BOY $\rightarrow$ PERSON and u": MAN $\rightarrow$ PERSON. We now express the relation between the boy and the man he later became as an identity of underlying persons. If b is the boy and m the man, we say u'(b) = u"(m). While respecting the typing of '=' the move is a first step towards avoiding the bloated ontology that threatened. I will present a second step when discussing the notion of an entity in a subcategory of kinds.

Psychological Claim 8: We can understand fairy-tale metamorphoses in which, contrary perhaps to the laws of nature, a prince is transformed into a frog and back into a prince.

This was the point of departure for Marie La Palme Reyes (1988) to construct a logic that handles such understanding. She posited the existence in a counterfactual fairy-tale, world of counterparts of the kinds in the actual world with underlying morphisms between them. In La Palme Reyes (this volume) she keeps the language of fairy tales the same as ordinary English, and changes the interpretation. The intuition, a psychological one, is that the language of fiction and of non-fiction is the same; the difference is in the interpretation. She explains the understanding of the Frog-Prince and such stories by positing underlying maps between the fairy-tale kinds FROG' and PRINCE' on the one hand, and the fairy-tale ANIMAL' - u: FROG' → ANIMAL' and u': PRINCE' → ANIMAL' on the other. The identity of the frog-prince can then be understood as the identity of the underlying animal. The fact that we have to do, for example, with fairy-tale frogs and not real ones is signalled by the fact that the frogs in the story can talk. The storyteller invites us to posit new kinds appropriate for the story.

Psychological claim 9: We can understand systems whose logic is not classical.

Evert Beth and Saul Kripke have proposed distinct models for intuitionist logic. More impressive, however, is the fact that the internal logic of the open spaces in topology is intuitionistic. I find this more impressive because the topology of open spaces is entirely uncontrived – rather, it is discovered.

More generally, I believe that our ordinary semantic intuitions are local. They normally relate to small parts of the universe over short time intervals and have nothing very much to do with the rest of time and space. Coupling this with the discovery of intuitionist models in mathematics, I conclude that the logic of kinds should be classical (two-valued) only in special cases. It should make provision for intuitionism. In fact, the logic of kinds developed by Gonzalo Reyes is category-theoretic, which is naturally intuitionist, but also sufficiently general to embrace classical logic as a special case.

4a. Logical Constraints on Psychology

Lest I give the impression that the debt is all on one side, I would like to give one or two examples from our experience in which mathematical developments led to psychological illumination.

Case 1: Natural language is confusing in that a single expression can appear both as the subject of a sentence and as part of the predicate. Take 'passenger' and 'person' in

(4a.1)   This passenger is the woman I admire.

(4a.2)   This woman is a passenger.

We may wonder whether the expressions 'this passenger' and 'the woman I admire' in (4a.1) denote the same individual. Wiggins (1980, chap. 1) constructed a simple argument to the effect that individuation and identity tracing must be of a piece. More particularly, he showed that, granted Liebniz's law, if a and b are equal *qua* F and if a is a G, then a and b must be equal *qua* G. Now 'passenger' and 'woman' trace identity differently. It follows that 'this passenger' and 'the woman I admire' are not co-referential expressions; that the sentence cannot be construed as claiming that a certain passenger is a member of the kind WOMAN I ADMIRE. Wiggins's argument, which is completely mathematical, leads to illumination of how we interpret ordinary-language expressions. It led us to the conclusion that 'to be the woman I admire' in (4a.1) is in fact a predicable and not a referring expression at all. On the other hand 'this woman' in (4a.2) is a referring expression, being the subject of the sentence. And so 'woman' behaves differently from a semantic point of view in the two sentences.

These points are subtle and often concealed from direct intuition. The mathematics helps to disclose what is going on in the interpretation of ordinary-language expressions, that is, in the psychology. For additional arguments of a linguistic nature to the same effect, see Williams (1983).

Case 2: In the early days of working on the logic of kinds, we were puzzled about how to represent the 'is a' of ordinary language, as in 'A dog is an animal'. We saw that set-theoretic inclusion would not do. Gonzalo Reyes proposed that we employ the morphisms of which categorical logic is the study. The stimulus, so to speak, was psychological; the response was to employ a well-established mathematical tool. The move, however, helped to clear up several other difficulties in an unforeseen manner.

One was the semantic behaviour of predicables. In the logic of kinds, all predicables are typed by a count noun. It follows that there may be logical problems when a predicable is transferred from one count noun to another, as happens regularly in the syllogism. For examle, it was noticed in antiquity that even though every thief is a person, it does not follow that a good thief is a good person. Such cases are numerous. Although every person is an animal, a white person is not a white animal, white animals being exemplified by white rabbits, white rats and the like. Quite a different shade. Although every baby is a person, a big baby is not a big person. And so it goes on. Sometimes things are the other way around. Every basketball player is a person and a tall basketball player is a tall person; but if a tall person is a basketball player, it does not follow that he is a tall basketball player. Some predicables seem to pass from one count noun to another without faltering semantically. For example, a male baby is a male person, a 30-year-old thief is a thirty-year-old person; an injured basketball player is an injured person and an injured person who happens to be a basketball player is an injured basketball player.

Such observations have led to the development of a logic of predicables appropriate for the logic of kinds, and for this purpose the underlying maps proved indispensible. The basic idea in this development is that of the functoriality of predicables, or more vividly of their keeping phase as they 'move over' underlying maps in a system of kinds. 'Functorial' in this connection means, roughly, yielding the same truth-value. For more on this, see Reyes, La Palme Reyes and Macnamara (in preparation).

A second problem in which the underlying maps were invaluable is related to the notion of an entity in a subcategory of kinds. (This is where I fulfil my promise to say something about the interpretation of the words 'thing' and 'object'.) Our solution to the 'is a' problem had the merit of keeping distinct what ought to be kept distinct – passengers and persons, patients and persons, and so on. Bill Lawvere suggested in conversation that the categorical notion of the co-limit of a functor could be used to construct the kind ENTITY relative to a system of the category of kinds. The co-limit in question is obtained in two steps. First, take the disjoint union of all kinds in the subcategory and then divide the disjoint union by an equivalence relation, namely the equivalence relation generated by pairs of members of kinds that are in the underlying relation. To see what this means, consider a party at which there are men and women, wives and husbands, students and professors, Canadians and Irish people. The disjoint union assembles the lot keeping wives distinct from women, from professors and so on. The operation of dividing by the equivalence relation comes down to considering a particular woman, a particular wife and a particular professor, for example, as the same entity in the given system. Thus, although the host appreciates that each woman, each wife, each professor, each Canadian and each person at the party needs to be fed, he prepares only as many meals as there are entities at the party. In this case, natural language allows 'person' to cover the notion of entity in the system. Where, however, the higher-order word is a mass noun (say, 'food', one needs to construct the co-limit in a different way, identifying, for example, a portion of beef with a portion of meat to obtain the notion of a portion of STUFF in the system delimited by 'food'. The mathematics lead to a perfectly natural construal of the word 'thing', a construal which has exercised the minds of several philosophers, Gibbard (1975) and Gupta (1980), for example, without previous resolution.

I am not saying that 'thing' has no other uses. Obviously it sometimes functions as a variable over kinds, as in 'I saw something blue in the bushes'. In the notation already introduced, we might regiment that sentence as ∃(k:K)[Blue(k)], where K is a variable ranging over kinds and k is a variable ranging over individuals in K. There is, however, this other use of 'thing' or 'entity' that is revealed by the mathematical operations of taking the co-limit of a system of kinds and dividing it by an appropriate equivalence relation.

We are now in a position to take the second step to avoid a bloated ontology. For certain purposes we collapse across certain individuals in a system of kinds and, for example, treat a certain passenger and a certain person as identical. This also explains Putnam's intuition. The reason one can say 'I am that boy' is that one has constructed the kind ENTITY in the appropriate system, thus being entitled to treat a certain boy and a certain person as identical – not across the kinds BOY and PERSON but as members of the single kind ENTITY in the relevant system. Notice that one can also say 'That boy is (was) me' – which is to be expected, identity being a symmetrical relation.

The co-limit of which I speak is the co-limit of the functor that interprets a linguistic category N into the category K of kinds. At the linguistic level, one has morphisms among count nouns of the type 'dogs are animals', 'passengers are persons'. The functor that interprets such morphisms assigns to each a morphism of kinds, e.g., u:DOG → ANIMAL, u': PASSENGER → PERSON.

5. Type of Psychology Envisaged

It is evident in the foregoing that the psychology I envisage is not exclusively experimental. It makes substantial use of intuition. We describe a proposition as being intuitive when it presents itself to us as true without benefit of conscious reasoning or proof. The word 'intuition' comes from the Latin *intueri*, meaning 'to look at' or 'to gaze at'. As used by psychologists and philosophers, the word is a transparent metaphor. Just as we do not normally prove the existence of everyday objects that we can see with our eyes, so we say we do not normally prove the truth of certain propositions that we cannot verify directly by means of our senses. For example, I claimed that we so use the word 'dog' as to embrace dogs past and dogs to come, as well as present ones. I now claim that this psychological claim is intuitively obvious. By intuition I know that I so employ the word. I can, of course, check other people's intuitions by asking them, and I can also study accepted practice. But even then the evidence has to be generously interpreted. The relation between a person's use of 'dog' and dogs that have ceased to exist or that have not yet come into existence cannot be one that is directly verifiable by the senses. Admittedly, it is difficult to see how our senses verify that a person's use even of a dog's proper name denotes that dog when the dog is in full view of the speaker. Nevertheless, in whatever way our senses serve us in that case, they cannot serve us in the other, where the dogs do not even exist at the time of speaking.

A lifetime as an experimental psychologist makes me edgy in this connection. Psychologists rightly insist on empirical evidence for psychological claims: they are leery of intuitions. They suspect that in appealing to intuition you are appealing to introspection under another name. So a few reassuring words are necessary.

To begin, intuitions are part of ordinary experience and therefore they are empirical in the ordinary sense of the word. They are not experimental, but that is another matter. When you see a cow, the cow enters the experience but so, too, does the fact that you are *seeing* the cow, not touching or imagining her, and the fact that it is *you* and not some other person that is seeing her. Sometimes intuitions are obscure, and it may help to check yours against those of others, and even to count heads, as psychologists frequently do. At other times it may be important to check the intuition that you are *seeing* a cow, not imagining her, by attempting to touch the cow. Other intuitions are so clear that such checking seems superfluous. Mathematics pays great heed to intuition, and yet mathematics is the most sure-footed of the sciences, never having had to retract any widely held theory, in the way that even physics has. Some psychological intuitions (such as that one cannot count whatever is white in a room) seem to me as sound as any in mathematics. Of course, psychological intuition is not mathematical intuition. The content of one is psychology; that of the other is mathematics. Nevertheless there are important similarities. What I most object to in the division of labour between psychology and philosophy is that such obvious facts seem to be placed outside the purview of psychology. The only explanation that occurs to me is that psychologists are aping physicists – not as physicists really are, I fear, but as psychologists imagine them to be.

Franz Brentano saw all this, and although his main source for psychological truth was intuition or 'inner perception', he called his major book *Psychology from an Empirical Standpoint*. Another who sees it is Noam Chomsky, who all along has appealed to linguistic intuition as *empirical* evidence for linguistic theories.

Brentano was well aware of the pitfalls of introspection, which he was at pains to distinguish from intuition. Since psychologists have wisely turned their back on introspection, after some bad experiences, it is worthwhile quoting Brentano on the distinction between it and intuition or "inner perception" as he calls it in the passage I cite:

In observation, we direct our full attention to a phenomenon in order to apprehend it accurately. But with objects of inner perception this is absolutely impossible. This is especially clear with regard to certain mental phenomena such as anger. If someone is in a state in which he wants to observe his own anger raging within him, the anger must already be somewhat diminished, and so his original object of observation would have disappeared.... It is only while our attention is turned toward a different object that we are able to perceive, incidentally [*nebenbei*], the mental processes that are directed toward the object. (Brentano 1874, pp. 29-30)

The trouble is that introspection was thought by some to reveal directly the mind's representations and processes. Owing, however, to intentionality, such representations and processes are never directly available to the mind, only their objects are, the things that the representations and processes are about. That is why Brentano stresses that psychological intuition is incidental. When looking at the cow and attending to her, I am incidentally aware of my seeing. But if with introspective intent I attempt to study my seeing, I cease to attend to the cow and my perception of her is altered.

Most important, Brentano's appeal to intuition for psychological purposes is quite at odds with the Kantian division of labour that I have expressed in the equation:

$$\frac{\text{Standards of perfection}}{\text{Philosophy}} = \frac{\text{Facts}}{\text{Psychology}}$$

What he would most have objected to is the assumption that standards of perfection are irrelevant to the understanding of the human mind, as though access to such standards were not a psychological fact. For it is a psychological fact that the mind has access to standards of perfection that it can never fully realize in the extra-mental world: in measurement, in ease and grace of movement, in painting, sculpture and the musical arts, in dress, in interhuman relations, in ethics and of course in reasoning. It is equally a fact that we cannot have direct access to these standards by means of our external senses. In fact our main access to them is in intuition. So any psychology that eschews psychological intuition must be blind to perhaps the most important facts about the mind. And any psychology that ignores the mind's access to standards of perfection is not worthy of the name.

None of this is to deny that psychological surveys of intuition and psychological experiments have a place in the study of the mind in its logical aspects, or that such experiments have a contribution to make to

the development of a logic that is responsive to human thought processes. But it is not the purpose of this paper to highlight the experimental
approach.

6. Final Statement

There has been much controversy in recent years about the role of sentences in intentional states. Fodor (1975 and 1981) makes sentences and
propositional attitudes to sentences the essence of intentional states.
This is in fact the natural stance for workers in artificial intelligence, as
Pylyshyn (1984) points out. On the other hand, there are philosophers
who go so far as to deny the reality of intentional states altogether, notably Patricia Churchland (1986) and Paul Churchland (1984), and so
they have no important role for sentences in our mental lives. Others
such as Dennett (1987), Stich (1983) and Putnam (1988) take a somewhat
sceptical view about their role. Putnam in particular is impressed by
what he refers to as the holism of the mental. By this he means that it is
in general impossible to specify one belief without appealing to several
others, or at least presupposing them. I am sympathetic to his arguments, although like Fodor (1987), I hope that the holism of the mental
is local in the way that the meaning of the primitives in Hilbert's *Foundations of Geometry* is local.

Be all that as it may, I believe that we have to keep some place for sentences at the core of intentional states. Perhaps we need to keep much
more than sentences, but not less. The argument goes as follows. With
the *major et senior pars* of theoreticians, I claim that intentional states are
semantically evaluable. They specify, to within some degree, truth-conditions in some domain of objects. But we have seen that to grasp an object or objects conceptually, one has need of an appropriate count noun.
A sentence is required to fix the grammatical category and reference of
a particular linguistic form. It follows that to make the right type of conceptual contact with an individual, there is need of a count noun in a
sentence. It follows, further, that there is an essential role for sentences
in intentional states.

Logic is the mathematical language with which to express and explore the interpretation of constituents of sentences and the implica-
tional relations among sentences. It follows that logic is the appropriate
mathematical language with which to characterize essential elements in
intentional states, namely the interpretaion of linguistic symbols and
the ability to grasp implications among sentences. Not computation,
mind you. Computers, in Dennett's (1984, p. 28) apt phrase, are syntactic engines, not semantic ones. They are apt for modelling proof theory,

less apt for modelling model theory. In human cognition the most basic work to be done is in relation to the interpretation of symbols. It would seem that in this connection the computer is not a helpful tool.

Neither does the methodological solipsism help, which was advocated by Fodor (1981), and which is essential for artificial intelligence. Fodor takes the explanation of action in terms of beliefs and desires to be the core of cognitive psychology; and since beliefs and desires are logically opaque, he hopes that cognitive psychology can afford to ignore reference. This is a misconception. The main aim of cognitive psychology, as the name itself indicates, is to account for knowledge. Knowledge is a relation between the mind and the extra-mental world. Reference is the main ingredient in that relation. Reference is in fact logically prior to belief and belief-informed desire. It follows that Fodor's methodological solipsism is of little help. And with methodological solipsism must go the computer as an instrument for modelling cognitive states in their precisely cognitive respect.

Just as physics and mathematics mutually constrain each other (Galileo's insight), just as psycholinguistics and linguistics constrain each other (Chomsky's insight), so cognition and logic mutually constrain each other. We can express the relation as:

$$\text{Cognition} \Longleftrightarrow \text{Logic}$$

Perhaps it is only fair to attribute this insight to the father of logic, Aristotle.

Just as physics and mathematics do not collapse to a single subject, so cognition and logic do not collapse to a single subject. The basic mistake of the psychologistic logicians was to imagine that they do.

The logic of kinds of which I gave a thumbnail sketch is, in some obvious sense of the word, discovered by examining our interpretative practices. It is not a logic that one imposes in a brutal manner on the theory of cognition. It needs to be accommodated and expanded as one goes along and examines cognitive states and events. And while the logic of kinds takes on a mathematical life of its own, it retains a structural harmony with the basic facts of cognition. In one sense, then, the logic of kinds is objective; it is discovered by studying something objective, namely the category of kinds. The logic of kinds is also objective in another sense. It is the logic that appropriately mathematizes our conceptual grasp of objects.

I conclude by expressing a growing conviction that the mathematical tool best adapted to work in cognition is categorical logic. The logic of kinds is expressed in the terms of categorical logic. This is not an accident. Categorical logic is naturally intuitionist, though it can also be classical when the occasion arises. Natural logic is many-sorted, and categorical logic, because it treats morphisms as basic, seems specially adapted to deal with many-sorted systems. Natural logic involves the simultaneous handling of constancy and change, because change is conceivable only against a background of constancy. In the logic of kinds, the modally constant count nouns supply the background of constancy; predicables and modal connectives express change. Categorical logic, with its sensitivity to functoriality, is specially suited to handle such constancy and variability. For the same reason, categorical logic is the appropriate mathematical tool for handling that functor between linguistic structures and the structure of the non-linguistic that we call "interpretation". Categorical logic has worked out a generalized theory of the structures of truth-objects – against which classical logic's {0,1} appears as a special case. Its respect for functoriality makes categorical language the appropriate mathematical tool for mapping interpretations into truth-values. But I do not wish to encroach on the terrain of the other contributers to this volume, who will argue better than I can that categorical logic is the appropriate mathematical tool for the study of cognition.

I end by sharing with you a vision. It is that in cognition we are in the year 1690. Our calculus (categorical logic) has been invented – by Bill Lawvere, whom we are honoured to have in the audience. But it has only begun to be applied. My vision is of a deep and satisfying theory of the human mind developing and replacing tendencies in 'cognitive studies' that strike me for the most part as unworthy of their subject.

Acknowledgments

This paper, which was supported by a National Science and Engineering Research Council grant to the author, benefited from conversations with David Davies, Eric Lewis, Michael Makkai, and Storrs McCall. I am indebted to David Davies for a careful reading of an earlier version and many useful comments. It has also benefited greatly from the critique of Hilary Putnam, who was good enough to take on the task of commentator at the Vancouver Conference. It also reflects the comments and queries of many people who took part in the conference. Its debt to Bill Lawvere became too acute at times to avoid particular mention in the text. Only categorical logicians can appreciate its overall indebtedness to him. Since it might be shameful to disclose how much the paper owes to my dear friends Gonzalo and Marie Reyes, I merely thank them as though their contribution were nothing special.

References

Bach, E. (1989). *Informal Lectures on Formal Semantics*. New York: State University of New York Press

Block, N. (1981). Psychologism and behaviourism. *Philosophical Review*, 90: 5-43

Braine, M.D.S. (1978). On the relation between the natural logic of reasoning and standard logic. *Psychological Review* 85: 1-21

Brentano, F. ([1874] 1973). *Psychology from an Empirical Standpoint*. Translated by A.C. Rancurello, D.B. Terrel and L.L. McAlister. London: Routledge & Kegan Paul

Bressan, A. (1972). *A General Interpreted Modal Calculus*. New Haven, CT: Yale University Press

Churchland, P.M. (1984). *Matter and Consciousness*. Cambridge, MA: Bradford/MIT Press

Churchland, P.S. (1986). *Neurophilosophy*. Cambridge, MA: Bradford/MIT Press

Cohen, L.J. (1981). Can human irrationality be experimentally demonstrated? *Behavioral and Brain Sciences*. 4: 317-70

Cussins, A. (1987). Varieties of psychologism. *Synthese* 70: 123-54

Davidson, D. (1980). *Essays on Actions and Events*. Oxford: Clarendon

Dennett, D. (1984). *Elbow Room*. Cambridge, MA: Bradford/MIT Press

— (1987). *The Intentional Stance*. Cambridge, MA: Bradford/MIT Press

Descartes, R. (1641). *Meditations on First Philosophy*. In E.S. Haldane and G.R.T. Ross (eds.) *The Philosophical Works of Descartes* (2 vols.) Rpt. 1968. Cambridge University Press

Fodor, J.A. (1975). *The Language of Thought*. New York: Crowell

— (1981). *Representations*. Cambridge, MA: Bradford/MIT Press

— (1987). *Psychosemantics*. Cambridge, MA: Bradford/MIT Press

Frege, G. ([1884] 1959). *The Foundations of Arithmetic*. Translated by J.L. Austin. Oxford: Basil Blackwell

Geach, P.T. (1957). *Mental Acts*. London: Routledge & Kegan Paul

— (1961). *Aquinas*. In G.E.M. Anscombe and P.T. Geach *Three Philosophers*. Ithaca, NY: Cornell University Press, pp. 69-125

— (1962). *Reference and Generality*. Cornell University Press

— (1972). *Logic Matters*. University of California Press

Gibbard, A. (1975). Contingent identity. *Journal of Philosophical Logic*, 4

Gupta, A.K. (1980). *The Logic of Common Nouns*. New Haven, CT: Yale University Press

Haack, S. (1978). *Philosophy of Logics*. Cambridge: Cambridge University Press

Henle, M. (1962). The relation between logic and thinking. *Psychological Review*, 69: 366-78

Humphrey, G. (1951). *Thinking*. New York: Wiley

Husserl, E. ([1900] 1970). *Logical investigations*. 2nd ed., 1913. Translated by J.N. Findlay. London: Routledge & Kegan Paul

Kant, I. ([1800] 1974). *Logic*. Translated by R.S. Hartman & W. Schwarz. New York: Bobbs-Merrill.

Macnamara, J. (1986). *A Border Dispute: The Place of Logic in Psychology.* Bradford/ MIT Press

— (1990). Ideals and psychology. *Canadian Psychology*, 31: 14-25

Miller, G.A. (1951). Speech and language. In S.S. Stevens (ed.), *Handbook of Experimental Psychology*, New York: Wiley, pp. 789-810

Notturno, M.A. (1984). *Objectivity, Rationality and the Third Realm. Justification and the Grounds of Psychologism*. The Hague: Nijhoff

Putnam, H. (1988). *Representation and Reality.* Cambridge, MA: Bradford/MIT Press

Pylyshyn, Z. (1972). Competence and psychological reality. *American Psychologist*, 27: 546-52

— (1984). *Computation and Cognition*. Cambridge, MA: Bradford/MIT Press

Quine, W.V. (1961). *From a Logical Point of View.* Harvard University Press

— (1969). *Ontological Relativity and Other Essays*. New York: Columbia University Press

— (1970) *Philosophy of Logic*. Englewood Cliffs, NJ: Prentice-Hall

Reyes, G.E. (1991). A topos-theoretic approach to reference and modality. *Notre Dame Journal of Formal Logic*, 32: 259-391

Reyes, G.E., La Palme Reyes, M. and Macnamara, J. (in preparation). Functoriality and grammatical role in syllogisms.

Reyes, M. [La Palme] (1988). A Semantics for Literary Texts. PhD thesis in Interdisciplinary Studies, Concordia University, Montreal

Rips, L.J. (1983). Reasoning as a central intellective ability. In R.J. Sternberg (ed.), *Advances in the Study of Human Intelligence*. Hillsdale: Erlbaum

Smedslund, J. (1990). A critique of Tversky and Kahneman's distinction between fallacy and misunderstanding. *Scandanavian Journal of Psychology*, 31: 110-20

Sober, E. (1978). Psychologism. *Journal for the Theory of Social Behavior*, 8: 165-92

Stich, S.P. (1983). *From Folk Psychology to Cognitive Science*. Bradford/MIT Press

Wiggins, D. (1980). *Sameness and Substance*. Oxford: Basil Blackwell

Williams, E. (1983). Semantic vs. syntactic categories. *Linguistics and Philosophy*, 6: 423-46

3

Logic and Psychology

Hilary Putnam

John Macnamara has provided us with a nuanced and impressive defence of the mutual relevance of logic and psychology, one which concedes the correctness of Kant's warning against psychologizing the notion of logical validity, while cautioning us against leaping to the conclusion that logic and psychology have nothing to learn from each other. I agree heartily with what he has to say to us on these general topics, and I also agree with a number of his more specific claims. However, for the time being I find that I must remain a "fence-sitter" with respect to some of the lessons that Macnamara wants logic to learn from psychology. Macnamara has done us a great service by proposing these lessons, but in one or two cases the details are difficult and controversial and (it seems to me) there are other conclusions to be drawn from some of the data Macnamara marshalls. Still, it is no small achievement to have put such a discussion on the agenda.

But before we turn to questions of detail, let us look at the general themes of Macnamara's fascinating lecture. The psychological facts which interest Macnamara are facts about human conceptual equipment. This is obscured by the way some of them are stated. Thus Psychological Claim 1 looks like a fact about the conceptual roles of certain quantifiers in English, rather than a psychological fact at all. (I take it that 'psychological facts' are supposed to be empirical, and it is not an *empirical* fact that 'few water' does not make sense, although it is an empirical fact that English speakers use a quantifier *[few]* with this particular conceptual role.) However, Macnamara takes care to immediately add "On the universality of this claim, see Emmon Bach (this volume)." Thus it is clear that the fact to which he refers is that the presence of quantifiers with these particular conceptual roles is a linguistic universal; and I agree with Macnamara and with Chomsky that such universals indicate something about human mentality. (I would go further and argue that even if something is only *almost universal*, in the sense that, say, *with rare exceptions, all human languages have property P*, that too indicates something important about human mentality.)

Macnamara argues at length that the structure of (linguistically universal) human concepts can be a fertile source for the construction of new logical formalisms, and I agree. The quantifiers 'few' and 'most' have, of course, already received some formal study, but, as Macnamara rightly points out, the possibilities go much further: his special project is to advance the study of the logic of *kinds,* and the mathematical tools he favours come from category theory (and from the applications of category theory made by his co-workers Gonzalo Reyes and Marie Reyes).

One of Macnamara's *bêtes noires* is the idea that 'logic' must be identified with classical logic (and classical logic in turn with the study of the validity and satisfiability of formulas involving the standard list of a half dozen or so 'logical constants'). Here Macnamara might have added that the standard list of 'logical constants' is more to be explained on historical than on logico-mathematical grounds. For Aristotle's medieval successors A, E, I, and O were logical constants (meaning 'All... are...', 'Some... are...', 'No... are...', and 'Some... are not...', and subject to the implicit restriction that the class of ... must not be empty); these have disappeared as primitives, to be defined in terms of the quantifiers (themselves suggested to Peirce, who introduced the now-standard notation, by the Σ and Π of analysis), while the concept of a set (which did not exist, in anything like the present understanding of it, until the nineteenth century), or, what comes to the same thing, the ε of set membership, has been promoted to the list! And (according to the late G.E.L. Owen) the principle that *every assertion is simply true or false* was deeply problematic for Plato and Aristotle, not just because of cases like the sea fight which has not yet taken place (is it *now* true or false that the Greeks will win?), but because so many assertions seem to need a further qualifier to make sense. Sometimes the problematic status of the principle of bivalence is swept under the rug in logic classes by saying something like, "In an ideal language," or "We shall assume that every predicate has been given perfectly precise truth conditions," as though we has any idea what such an 'ideal language' could be. ("You still owe me a definition of 'precise'," Wittgenstein remarks in the *Investigations*). In particular, I applaud Macnamara's trenchant observation that "classical logic is ill-equipped to handle the logic of ordinary discourse precisely because classical logic derives mainly from an analysis of arithmetical sentences." Macnamara is right in urging us not to delimit the scope of 'logic' once and for all, and right in urging us to pay attention to modal logic, to intuitionist logic, to relevant logic, and – as already remarked, this is his special concern – to the logic of kinds. (Incidentally, I myself have urged that more attention be paid to certain problems connected with bivalence, in particular problems connected with Skolemization and problems connected with the nature of vagueness; and have suggested a liberalized intuitionist logic as one solution, in Putnam (1983, Chapters 1 and 15).

Macnamara's Psychological Claims 2 and 3

It is now time to examine the particular psychological claims Macnamara makes, and the lessons he draws from them. In the light of what I have already said, it will be clear that I have no problems with Psychological Claims 1 and 9. I also have no problems with 4, 5 and 8, and I do not have anything of particular interest to add to them. My problems with 6 and 7 will be the subject of the next section. In the present section I want to comment on 2 and 3.

Let me quote from Macnamara's paper: "Psychological Claim 2: We cannot conceptually grasp an individual without the support of a count noun." Once again we have a psychological claim worded as a claim about conceptual impossibility. To tease out the empirical content of the claim, we have to look at Macnamara's discussion. For example, Macnamara writes, "You cannot count whatever is blue in a room because you do not know what to count as one blue – a whole blue shirt, or the sleeves separately on the grounds that they were sewn on, or the separate threads, or the fibres of the threads." I am struck by (what seems to me) the psychological unreality of this remark. I am quite sure that if one instructed a child above the age of five (or an adult uncorrupted by philosophy!) "Count all the blue things in this room, and give me the number," the subject would count the shirt and *not* the threads, and *not* the separate sleeves, and *not* the fibres, etc.! On the other hand, if there is a blue sofa with cushions which lift off in the room, the subject might well ask, "Do you want me to count each cushion separately or only the whole sofa?"

What I think this shows is that 'blue thing' (though not, I agree 'blue' by itself) can function as a supporting count noun, although it has a certain degree of ambiguity. But note: 'thing', in 'blue thing', does not mean 'entity' or 'object' in the logician's sense. Sleeves and threads are things we can quantify over. The empirical fact is that, in ordinary language, the word 'thing' does not mean 'anything you can quantify over'. 'Thing' has, of course, many uses even in ordinary language (e.g., 'The thing I was trying to remember'). But in 'blue thing' it means something like a physical object which is separate from others, which satisfies Aristotle's criterion for wholeness (you can move it about, and the parts stay in the same arrangement), which we experience as a single Gestalt. I think it is true that we frequently use 'thing' as a count noun in ordinary language in such a sense, and we rarely (apart from the relatively artificial contexts of philosophy and logic) use it to cover everything we quantify over. And this *is* a fact of psychological significance.

Macnamara should agree, I think, because he himself, later in his paper shows how to construct just such context-sensitive notions of 'thing' in his own system of categorial logic. Let me note, in passing, that the logician's notion of an 'object' is not really one notion but *an indefinitely extendable family of notions* (On this, see Putnam (1990, Chapter 6).

Macnamara's next example also deserves a comment. Macnamara says, "Suppose you know who Steve is. You might be inclined to think that the name denotes the stuff in Steve's body, a certain mass of molecules. But that cannot be. Suppose Steve's body weights 175 pounds; it is clear that such a mass of molecules was never born, although Steve was.... What individuates the bearer of the name and traces its identity correctly is the count noun 'person'. The bearer of a proper name always needs to be specified by a count noun."

Macnamara's point seems right to me, but the example is not convincing because a materialist (e.g., David Lewis) would say that Steve is identical with the mereological sum of all the *time-slices* of molecules which have been part of his (four-dimensional, space-time) body since conception, rather than with the mereological sum of the molecules which are part of his body *now*. The four-dimensional object Lewis is talking about does have different weights at different times, and Lewis would deny that it "was never born." It is because Macnamara takes "the stuff in Steve's body" to be a *three-dimensional* object while identifying Steve with a *four-dimensional* object that his quick proof of nonidentity works.

What can we say about this? (I discuss these issues in Putnam 1990, pp. 26-28, by the way.) One move, due to Saul Kripke, is to argue that Steve and the mereological sum of all the time-slices of molecules which are or have been part of Steve's body cannot be identical because they have different *modal* properties. (The mereological sum could not *have consisted of different time-slices of molecules*, but different molecules, and *a fortiori* different time-slices of molecules, could have been part of Steve's body.) Indeed, by this argument, the mereological sum is not only not identical with Steve; it is not even identical with Steve's *body*. Lewis's reply is to say that when we say that "different molecules, and *a fortiori* different time-slices of molecules, could have been part of Steve's body," all we mean is that a *counterpart* of Steve could have consisted of different molecules. Quine would disagree with both Kripke and Lewis; Quine would say that Steve is identical with a space-time region, not with time-slices of molecules (and block Kripke's 'modal' argument by *rejecting modality*). As I wrote in a previous publication [Putnam (1990), *loc. cit.*], using the example of a chair rather than of a person:

> Are chairs really *identical* with their matter, or does a chair somehow coexist in the same space-time region with its matter while remaining numerically distinct from it? And is their matter really identical with the [electromagnetic, gravitational, etc.] fields? And are the fields really identical with the space-time region? To me it seems clear that at least the first, and probably all three of these questions are nonsensical. We can formalize our language in the way Kripke would, and we can formalize our language in the way Lewis would, and (thank God!) we can leave it unformalized and not pretend the ordinary language 'is' obeys the same rules as the sign '=' in systems of [standard] formal logic. Not even God could tell us if the chair is 'identical' with its matter, and not because there is something He doesn't know. (Putnam 1990, pp. 26-28)

In sum, I agree with Macnamara that in ordinary language Steve is not treated as either identical or non-identical with 'the stuff in Steve's body', whether we take that stuff to be molecules, time-slices of molecules, a space-time region, or whatever. Metaphysicians have created *alternative languages* in which Steve is identified with something in a different category, like a space-time region, but the question "Which of these metaphysical theories is really true?" is senseless. None of them is "really true"; and if we want a formalization of our natural language that observes the way we actually think and speak (and shall doubtless go on thinking and speaking), then we should go with Macnamara and not assume that cross-category identities are well formed in cases like this. (Whether *every* count noun generates a category, as Macnamara urges, is a question I discuss in the next section; certainly 'person', 'space-time region', 'number' do function as different categories, in the sense that we do not – unless we are philosophers – pretend to understand identity statements that cross them.)

Finally, I agree with Macnamara that understanding a proper name like 'Steve' requires associating it with the appropriate category (knowing that the 'Steve' in question is a person, or a cat, or an automobile, or whatever).

Psychological Claim 3 ("We cannot conceptually grasp an individual in a universal kind supposedly denoted by the count noun 'thing' or 'object'") has, in effect, just been discussed as well.

Macnamara's Psychological Claims 6 and 7

Claim 6 ("We cannot directly express identity across different kinds") is one of the claims with respect to which I am not convinced. Certainly there are *some* kinds across which we cannot 'express identity' in natural language, as I have just agreed. But Macnamara means every count noun to count as a kind for this purpose, and this seems immensely counter-intuitive. Thus, Macnamara writes, "Sensitivity to the whole range of relevant intuitions reveals that '=' is a typed predicable requiring that the referring expressions placed on its left and right to form a single sentence, should both be typed by the same count noun."

The example Macnamara employs to illustrate this claim is that "we cannot say that a certain boy is *the same boy* as a certain man, or that the boy is *the same man* as a certain man." As as datum this is undeniable, but this is a case in which I shall draw a different conclusion from the data.

First of all, it is important to remember that predicates like 'boy' and 'man' have a time-argument in natural language. When an imprecise specification of the time-argument suffices, the time-argument is expressed by *tense*: thus, *John is a boy* or *John was a boy* or *John will be a boy* A logician might write 'Boy(John, t_{now})' or 'Boy(John, t_{past})' or 'Boy (John, t_{future})". Of course, when we want to, we can make the time argument explicit: thus, *John was a boy in 1970* .But this fact is enough to explain why we cannot say "the boy you were talking about is the same boy as Steve", where Steve is a grown man; for, by the standard elimination of definite descriptions, this would imply

$$(Ex)(Boy(x, t_{now}) \ \& \ x=Steve \ \& \ (Ey)(Boy(y, \text{time you referred to}) \ \& \\ \text{you talked about } y \ \& \ y=x))$$

and this implies the false 'Boy(Steve, t_{now})'. I agree however, that 'The boy is the same man as Steve' is deviant, but I would account for this by noting that sentences which begin 'The boy is ...' normally mean that some x such that Boy(x, t_{now}) is...; 'The boy that was is the same man as Steve' is not deviant, and Macnamara's theory predicts that it should be. Note that I used classical logic in the above symbolization, with no restriction on the use of '=' across kinds. Similarly, instead of regarding MEN, BOYS and PERSONS as completely distinct kinds, as Macnamara does, and invoking a morphism u: MEN – PERSONS and a morphism u': BOYS – PERSONS, and interpreting the statement that a certain boy is now a man as meaning 'u (the BOY referred to) = u' (the MAN referred to)', which is Macnamara's solution, I would simply interpret such a statement as saying that $(Ex)[x = \iota y(Boy(y, t_{past})$ & y was referred to as a boy in some contextually definite conversation) & $x = \iota y(Man(y, t_{now})$ & y was referred to as a man is some contextually definite conversation)). If we are trying to reconstruct natural language, I agree with Macnamara that there are good reasons, which have already been discussed, for taking the quantifier '(Ex)' to range over a category like PERSONS and not over a fictitious totality of all entities, but I see no need to deny that a person can literally *be* a boy (at one time) and a man (at a different time). A corollary is that the behavior of transitory properties like 'is a boy' and 'is a man' is not compelling evidence for Macnamara's thesis that count nouns must be recognized as 'kinds' across which identity makes no sense.

I take it that Claim 7 ("We count passengers and persons differently, … and we can understand such ways of counting") is intended as further evidence for Claim 6. My way of accounting for the data in this case would be somewhat different from the strategy I followed in the BOYS/ MEN case. Although 'passenger' is also a transitory property of persons, something additional is involved in this example. Macnamara writes, "If you travel three times with Air Canada in 1991, you will be counted as three passengers, although you are only one person." But, it seems to me, this is only partly true. In some contexts (annual bookkeeping, say), what Macnamara says is quite true. But in other contexts (changing a ticket, for example) we might get 'The passenger came on flight 109 and she continued on flight 311', and in this case the passenger is counted as *one* passenger, although she flies twice. The fact is that there is an ancient (and still usual) meaning of 'passenger' in which passengers are persons, and a bookkeeping artifactual use in which passengers are no more real persons than the dollars in an electronic transaction are real dollars (a logician might say that the bookkeeper's 'passengers' are abstract entities). In the sense in which passengers are bookkeepers' fictions (or abstract entities), they are of course not persons, but in such a sentence as 'The passenger who stepped off the plane was the first woman astronaut', I see no reason to deny that 'woman' and 'passenger' are predicates of *one and the same person*. I would symbolize this sentence as:

$$\iota x(Passenger(x, t_{past1}) \text{ & x stepped off the plane}) = \iota x(Woman(x) \text{ & } Astronaut(x, t_{past2})),$$

where 't_{past1}' and 't_{past2}' are to be interpreted as constants for contextually definite past times. Here the sign '=' may be restricted to PERSONS, but no restriction to smaller kinds (Passenger, Woman, Astronaut) is required. (It follows that I do not accept Macnamara's interpretation of sentences [4a.1] and [4a.2] a little later in the paper.)

In my view, our disagreements highlight a possible danger in the use of new ideas in logic as paradigms for the interpretation of sentences in natural language: one can become wedded to a symbolism, and then the symbolism may be forced upon inappropriate phenomena, rather than functioning as a guide to new insights. But Macnamara himself warns against this very danger, when he says that his logic of kinds "is not a logic that one imposes in a brutal manner on the theory of cognition. It needs to be accommodated and expanded as one goes along and examines cognitive states and events." I look forward to the continuation of the work that Macnamara and his co-workers have undertaken, and to the continuation of the discussion that it has provoked.

References

Putnam, H. (1983). *Realism and Reason: Philosophical Papers, Volume 3.* Cambridge: Cambridge University Press

— (1990). *Realism with a Human Face.* Cambridge, MA: Harvard University Press

4

Tools for the Advancement of Objective Logic: Closed Categories and Toposes

F. William Lawvere

The thesis is that the explicit adequate development of the science of knowing will require the use of the mathematical theory of categories. Even within mathematical experience, only that theory has approximated a *particular* model of the general, sufficient as a foundation for a *general* account of all particulars. Arising 50 years ago from the needs of geometry, category theory has developed such notions as adjoint functor, topos, fibration, closed category, 2-category, etc., in order to provide:

(1) A guide to the complex, but very non-arbitrary constructions of the concepts and their interactions which grow out of the study of space and quantity.

It was only the relentless adherence to the needs of that basic subject that made category theory so well-determined yet powerful. When some schools of category theory have gone astray, it has usually been due either to neglecting too long that specific goal of studying space and quantity better, or to ossifying some partial determination of what space and quantity are. If we replace "space and quantity" in (1) above by "any serious object of study," then (1) becomes my working definition of *objective logic*. Of course, when taken in a philosophically proper sense, space and quantity do pervade any serious field of study. Category theory has also objectified as a special case:

(2) The subjective logic of inference between statements. Here statements are of interest only for their potential to describe the objects which concretize the concepts; here by describing, we mean both commenting on the objects constructed and indicating desiderata for their construction.

Specifically, we need, for example, a mathematical model of the following philosophical position. Within thinking:

(a) Subjective logic is a part of objective logic, which also reflects and partly guides construction in the latter.
(b) Thinking itself is a part of being, which reflects being and guides our action on it.
(c) One of the many aspects of being is (b) itself, which is therefore reflected to manifest itself as (a).
(d) Considered as a process within being, (a) is a central feature of thinking which a *science* of thinking must address.

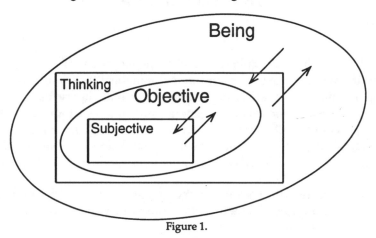

Figure 1.

I believe that there is a second central feature of thinking: individuals think, but so do clans, "schools of thought," professions, social classes, nations, etc.; thinking takes place in brains, but also in schools, newspapers, meeting houses, etc. – i.e., in material institutions which people have created for the purpose of mutually transforming individual thinking and collective thinking into each other.

An explicit philosophy, dealing with both the mutual transformation of subjective logic and objective logic, as well as the mutual transformation of individual thinking and collective thinking, could be very helpful (for example, when reforming the schools) and adequate mathematical models will be an essential basis of clarity.

1. Categorical Refinement of a Hegelian Principle

A very generally occurring specific kind of process is the following. A category $\mathcal{B}$ of *particulars* is presented to thought and measured against an abstract distillation $\mathcal{V}$ of previous concrete thoughts. There results an *abstract general* $\mathcal{A}$ partly expressing the essence of $\mathcal{B}$ but permitting calculation and speculation within itself. The acquisition of $\mathcal{A}$ permits the construction of the *concrete general* C, a category pictured as containing both all the possible objects of essence $\mathcal{A}$ as well as all the $\mathcal{A}$-respecting transformations and comparisons between these possible objects. At least as important as the calculation in $\mathcal{A}$ is our power to investigate by pure thought the objects in C (recording perhaps some of the results in $\mathcal{A}$) and thus to create plans. In particular, there is a functor $\mathcal{B} \longrightarrow C$ reflecting (partly) each of the original particulars as one among the $\mathcal{A}$-possibles.

Mathematical experience has shown that the above description can be made even more precise and productive. In order that the measuring can compare $\mathcal{B}$ and $\mathcal{V}$, $\mathcal{V}$ must also be a category. While a theory $\mathcal{A}$ *may* have (within the abstract general) a useful subjective presentation $\mathcal{A}' \longrightarrow \mathcal{A}$ by means of "primitives" and "axioms," its objective result, the concrete general C, depends only on $\mathcal{A}$ itself as the category presented. The kind $\mathcal{D}$ of category that $\mathcal{A}$ is desired to be, must be a kind in which $\mathcal{V}$ participates too. Then an explicit model of the process can be given as follows:

$$\mathcal{A} \subseteq \operatorname{Hom}(\mathcal{B}, \mathcal{V})$$

a category of functors from $\mathcal{B}$ to $\mathcal{V}$ and all natural transformations between them. This is the idea of "natural structure"[1] (distilled in my 1963 doctoral thesis from examples in algebraic topology; there 'structure' is taken in the sense of an abstract general). This $\mathcal{A}$ typically specifies not only the theorems true for all objects in $\mathcal{B}$, but also the kind of formulas appropriate to $\mathcal{B}$ among which the theorems are found; externally specified primitives are not presupposed. Then:

$$C = \mathcal{D}\operatorname{Hom}(\mathcal{A}, \mathcal{V})$$

the category of $\mathcal{D}$-preserving structures of kind $\mathcal{A}$ valued in $\mathcal{V}$. Here 'structure' is taken in its concrete general aspect. Thus, relative to $\mathcal{D}$ and $\mathcal{V}$, the comparison functor $\mathcal{B} \longrightarrow C = \mathcal{B}^{**}$ is seen as an instance of the standard Fourier map to the double dual, familiar from the work of Stone, Pontrjagin and others in the 1930s that made explicit the relation:

$$D^{*}\text{-spaces} \Longleftrightarrow (\text{D-algebras of variable quantities})^{\mathrm{op}}$$

as an adjoint pair of functors with constant quantity V taken as dualizing object/space. There are many kinds of spaces, for we can take D = Boolean (with V = 2) or continuous or smooth or combinatorial, etc.; that is, D functions as an abstract general. These all arose from looking at particular spaces and their relationships. Similarly, the doctrine $\mathcal{D}$ can be not only the notion of finite cartesian products (as in universal algebra), but also of Barr regular (as in positive logic, etc.), and the concrete generals C which arise belong to $\mathcal{D}^*$-Cat where $\mathcal{D}^*$ is a dual doctrine, as the work of Makkai and others has richly demonstrated. Change of doctrines $\mathcal{D}' \longrightarrow \mathcal{D}$, with its functorially induced changes in the rest, is as much an everyday tool as is interpretation $\mathcal{A}' \longrightarrow \mathcal{A}$ of theories or morphisms M $\longrightarrow$ M' of $\mathcal{A}$-structures in C, since all these have long been recognized to take place in categories, with all which that implies. For example, an interpretation $\mathcal{A}' \longrightarrow \mathcal{A}$ of abstract generals functorially induces a functor $C \longrightarrow C'$ in the opposite direction which compares the corresponding concrete generals. For example, if my previous experience $\mathcal{B}$ with cats has led to a theory $\mathcal{A}$ which includes that they have long tails, dropping that axiom leads to an $\mathcal{A}'$ and a resulting C' which would provide for the possibility of the broadening of my experience when I meet a Manx.

While subjective logic in the narrow sense might take $\mathcal{V}$ just as truth-values, a better example is the category of abstract sets and arbitrary mappings (but for Lie theory, e.g., it might be appropriate to take something much richer, such as the category of smooth spaces, as the distillation of knowledge presumed to be acquired). The category $\mathcal{V}$ of sets obeys various rich doctrines as alluded to above, but it is already quite fruitful just to let $\mathcal{D}$ recognize merely that $\mathcal{V}$ is a category. The possible $\mathcal{D}^*$s are then abstract theories of sets whose particular concretes include not only the constant $\mathcal{V}$ but also the categories of variable and cohesive "sets" which may arise, for example, as categories $\mathcal{B}$ of particulars to be measured. Measurement of a given $\mathcal{B}$ might reveal, for example, a pair of functors:

$$\mathcal{B} \overset{A}{\underset{P}{\rightrightarrows}} \mathcal{V}$$

assigning sets to each particular, and measurement might even reveal a triple of transformations:

$$A \overset{r}{\underset{t}{\overset{s}{\rightrightarrows}}} P$$

which are natural (i.e., homogeneous with respect to all particular comparisons B $\longrightarrow$ B' in $\mathcal{B}$) and satisfy, for example, sr = 1_P = tr. An initial version of $\mathcal{A}$ would be just the *finite* category:

defined by the same equations. Then $C = \mathcal{D} \operatorname{Hom}(\mathcal{A}, \mathcal{V})$ is the infinitely rich category of concrete reflexive graphs whose scientific interest and technological utility will probably never be exhausted; the functor $\mathcal{B} \longrightarrow C$ reveals that each of our given particulars B "is" at least a reflexive graph whose points P(B) are provided by $\mathcal{B}$ also with a set A(B) of arrow connections and with maps s(B), t(B), r(B) specifying which points are the source and target of given arrows and which arrow is the null loop at each point.

2. Deepening, Metrics, Unity and Identity of Adjoint Opposites

In the above example I have used the pregnant observation of Macnamara and the Reyes that the logical interpretation of the word 'is' should be just a *map* in an appropriate category, *not* necessarily an inclusion map: to do otherwise is a cheap source of paradoxes. A related observation concerns the interpretation of 'and': it is well known that in a category $\mathcal{A}$, categorical product is the right adjoint of the diagonal functor $\mathcal{A} \xrightarrow{\Delta} \mathcal{A} \times \mathcal{A} \xrightarrow{\times} \mathcal{A}$ (where $\mathcal{A} \times \mathcal{A}$ is the product in $\mathcal{D}$-Cat), and that if $\mathcal{A}$ consists only of inclusions (i.e., $\mathcal{A}$ is a poset as in propositional logic) then product reduces to conjunction. It is even exploited in proof theory that for any category $\mathcal{A}$, the poset reflection $\mathcal{A} \xrightarrow{\exists} \mathcal{A}_0$ maps products to conjunctions. However, as pointed out by Schanuel, the most direct interpretation of everyday 'and' is very often product in a non-poset, such as 'the position of the bird is determined by its altitude *and* the point on the earth beneath it'.

As posets often need to be deepened to categories to accurately reflect the content of thought, so should inverses, in the sense of group theory, often be replaced by adjoints. Adjoints retain the virtue of being uniquely determined reversal attempts, and very often exist when inverses do not.

Great mathematical philosophers, such as Grassmann 150 years ago, recognized the distinction between synthetic operations such as addition and the corresponding analytic operations such as subtraction, but the nature of the correspondence cannot be characterized in terms of inverses, even for the posetal case of non-negative real numbers, where the truncated difference is indeed the adjoint:

$$x + a \geq y$$

$$x \geq y \, \Delta \, a$$

This is the invertible rule which guides our calculation with bank accounts, etc., $y \, \Delta \, a$ being always non-negative. In that example we could recover the group property by passing to a larger system, but at the loss of the useful criterion $a \geq b$ iff $b \, \Delta \, a = 0$. However, if $+$ denotes an *idempotent* operation such as subjective disjunction of statements or objective union of closed regions in space, then there is no group enveloper, but the analytic adjoint 'yes..., but not...' operation may exist. This adjointness is all that is needed (together with the usual lattice axioms, which are also just adjointnesses) to derive the properties of the topologically crucial boundary operation:

$$\text{boundary (A)} \;\underset{\text{def}}{=}\; A \text{ and (yes but not A)}$$

Sometimes a given functor has both left and right adjoints. For example, the inclusion of truth values $V_0 \longrightarrow V_\infty$ into distance values, wherein true is 0 ("right on") and false is ∞ ("making it true is prohibitively expensive"), has both left and right adjoint retractions, one (feasibility) whereby every finite distance is true and the other (frugality) whereby every non-zero distance is too much to be truly necessary and hence false. Now, both V_0, V_∞ are closed categories and hence serve, in a way related to but different from the ways discussed in section 1, as abstract generals: the corresponding concrete generals are the categories of posets and of metric spaces (not necessarily symmetric, with distance-decreasing maps) respectively. The trio of little adjoints covariantly induces bigger ones: a poset is a special metric space in which all distances are either 0 or ∞ but the points of a metric space are ordered in two extreme ways, frugality saying $x \longrightarrow y$ iff it costs nothing, but feasibility permitting $x \overset{\bullet}{\longrightarrow} y$ iff the cost is finite. (There are many precise determinations of the category V_∞ of distances; for example, some have ∞ = one trillion, so finite just means "under budget.") This feasibility relation induces an equivalence relation on points (and on maps) of metric spaces, two points x, y being in the same component iff the distances in both directions are finite; this decomposition, in spite of its purely logical character, turns out to be intimately related to the geometrical notion of *rotations*, for these are essentially the only automorphisms of metric spaces which retain any activeness after this components functor has neglected all those which move all points by at most a bounded distance.

As another example of how the theory of closed categories can explicitly guide the study of metric spaces, note that the family of intervals [0,d] in V_∞ provides a special family of metric spaces. Any small family of objects in a complete category raises two questions: are the functions (or properties), i.e., the maps in the category whose codomains are in the family, coadequate to determine every object in the category? And are the paths (or probes), i.e., the maps in the category whose domains are in the family, adequate to determine every object? Isbell in 1960 showed the importance of these questions. A fundamental adjoint construction by Kan (1958) has given rise to a measure of the failure of adequacy by the so-called adequacy comonad $\Gamma X \xrightarrow{\ e\ } X$, where Γ is an endofunctor of the big category giving for every object X the best approximation to it which can be reconstructed from the results of probing it with paths parameterized by objects in the given small family, and where e is the natural transformation directly comparing the approximation with the X being investigated (so adequacy holds if e is an isomorphism). In our example, where the big category is the concrete general of all metric spaces determined by the closed category V_∞ of distances and where the small family is the family of intervals [0,d], for d finite from V_∞ itself, the path-approximation ΓX to X turns out to be the *geodesic remetrization* of X; for example, if X is the surface of the earth metrized by its obvious embedding in the earth itself, then $\Gamma X \xrightarrow{\ e\ } X$ is the distance decreasing map from the same surface metrized by minimum-distance paths which stay on the surface.

Conversely, many notions suggested by the study of metric spaces, such as radius, engulfing, etc., have precise analogues for concrete generals enriched in any (even non-posetal) closed categories V.

Sometimes (opposite to the case discussed above) a functor p which has both adjoints is itself a common retraction for both of its adjoints. Any such functor is a precise realization of the allegedly nebulous notion *unity-and-identity-of-opposites*. For the two adjoints are then two inclusions of subcategories, united in the domain of p, opposite in the precise sense given by the adjointness itself, yet both identical in themselves with the codomain of p; moreover, for each object X in the domain of p there is a well-defined "interval" $L_p (pX) \longrightarrow X \longrightarrow R_p (pX)$ with endpoints in the two opposite subcategories, within which X must lie, but determined only by the partial knowledge pX about X. As a very simple example, consider the case where p is any surjective, order-preserving map of finite, totally ordered sets. A more general image is that the domain of p is structured as a "cylinder" with two identical ends which are the two subcategories and with threads running through it from each object on the left end to the corresponding object on the right end; all the objects with a given p-value are on one thread, and certain of the comparison maps between them point along the thread. Functoriality gives ways of passing between threads. However, in many examples even the approximating interval around X is not a poset; also special care must be taken not to assume that the two opposite subcategories are disjoint, for the two ends of the cylinder often touch in certain points.

From examples previously discussed, we can assemble an example of UIAO (unity and identity of adjoint opposites). Reinterpret the distance category V_∞ as a category of times and consider the functor category $\mathcal{V}V_\infty^{op}$: its objects are systems of sets X_t (for t in V_∞) of possible states equipped with a definite law of becoming $X_t \longrightarrow X_s$ for $s \geq t$ which satisfies the evident transitivity conditions, and its maps $X \longrightarrow Y$ are systems $X_t \longrightarrow Y_t$ of $\mathcal{V}$-maps which compatibly compare the two respective laws of becoming. There are two opposite subcategories of very special systems: in one the change of states $X_0 \longrightarrow$ can be arbitrary, but $X_t \longrightarrow X_s$ for $s \geq t > 0$ is always an identity map so that "everything happens right at the beginning"; in the other $\longrightarrow X_\infty$ can be arbitrary but $X_t \longrightarrow X_s$ for $\infty > s \geq t$ is always an identity so that "everything happens right at the end." Suppose, for an arbitrary X, that we know only $Y = p(X) = [X_0 \longrightarrow X_\infty]$, a pair of sets structured by a single map, but that we are as yet ignorant of the details of what happened in between. Then we can start further investigation from two approximations LY $\longrightarrow X \longrightarrow$ RY where LY, RY are in the two opposite subcategories and the arrows are maps in $\mathcal{V}V_\infty^{op}$. The two subcategories are in themselves isomorphic to $\mathcal{V}V_0^{op}$: (which has as objects single maps $Y_{true} \longrightarrow Y_{false}$ of sets) and the functor p which adjointly unites them is induced by our previous inclusion $V_0 \longrightarrow V_\infty$. Here the categories V_0, V_∞ are playing a different role as abstract generals, more akin to the one discussed in section 1: they specify kinds of models of becoming.

Also a concrete general $\mathcal{U}$ of being, whose abstract general specifies a kind of cohesiveness or unity of being, may participate in UIAO's. To take an example, Cantor's abstraction process $\mathcal{B} \longrightarrow \mathcal{V}$, assigning to particular cohesive spaces their abstract sets of points, extend (along $\mathcal{B} \longrightarrow \mathcal{B}^{**}$ $\overset{=}{\underset{def}{}}$ $\mathcal{U}$) to a functor p whose left and right adjoint inclusions are the subcategory $\mathcal{V} \longrightarrow \mathcal{U}$ of discrete spaces and $\mathcal{V} \longrightarrow \mathcal{U}$ of codiscrete spaces respectively. The contradictory properties of an abstract set, namely that its points are completely distinguished yet indistinguishable by any clear property, are resolved into two opposite spaces with the same points: the discrete one in which no connected motion exists to blur them and the codiscrete one in which every point is instantly blurred into every other one; though there is the canonical LS $\longrightarrow$ RS map of discrete to codiscrete which induces an isomorphism on S upon applying p, typically the only maps ("clear properties") from a codiscrete to a discrete space are constant. The relevant abstract generals say that a map in $\mathcal{U}$ should preserve cohesion, but a discrete space D has zero cohesion to preserve, so maps $D \longrightarrow X$ are arbitrary on points; dually, a codiscrete space C has in a vacuous way infinite cohesion, so again maps $X \longrightarrow C$ are arbitrary on points; these remarks explain the two adjointnesses. The notion of connected movement in a space X (discrete or not) can be usefully modelled by maps $T \longrightarrow X$ in $\mathcal{U}$ where T is a connected space; meaning that $\pi(T)$ is one point where π is the further left adjoint $\mathcal{U} \longrightarrow \mathcal{V}$ to the discrete inclusion and called 'the set of connected components of ___'.

Objective logic must recognize the quality of dimensionality in spaces and construct quantity-types for measuring it. I have outlined elsewhere (Lawvere 1991b) a program for doing this in terms of intermediate UIAO's $\mathcal{U} \longrightarrow \mathcal{U}_n \longrightarrow \mathcal{V}$ related by a left-to-right "crossover" determination of Hegel's jump idea. I showed its correctness in some important examples, and in particular defined dimension one as the lowest UIAO between $\mathcal{U}$ and $\mathcal{V}$ for which $\pi(L_n X) = \pi X$ for all spaces X in $\mathcal{U}$, that is, all connecting which can be done can be achieved with one-dimensional paths. However, here I will approach dimension more directly in connection with a combinatorial example.

3. Realization of Plans

One should not despise the codiscrete spaces $\mathcal{V} \longrightarrow \mathcal{U}$, for their very contrast with the discrete ones permits them to be seen as connected "blobs" of various dimensions which can be glued into quite arbitrary combinatorial plans. What such a plan envisages is a real space (or building, etc.) to be constructed, using previously-acquired components: a two-point blob is imagined as a continuous one-dimensional segment with two endpoints, a three-point blob as a continuous two-dimensional triangle with three edges, a four-point blob as a three-dimensional tetrahedron, etc. The simplest example of a non-codiscrete space obtained by gluing together blobs is a *one* - dimensional triangle consisting only of the edges. Certain considerations would require that even the one-dimensional segment be recognized to have an infinite-dimensional microstructure, but whatever may be the precise nature of these real components to be used in carrying out the plans, their specification can be considered to be a standard additionally given functor $\mathcal{V} \longrightarrow \mathcal{U}$. Both the gluing of codiscrete pieces to see plans and also the gluing of standard pieces to carry them out, are realized as colimits in the category $\mathcal{U}$. The standard-space functor $\mathcal{V} \longrightarrow \mathcal{U}$ induces an adjoint pair:

$$\mathcal{U} \xLeftarrow{\quad\quad} \mathcal{V}^{\mathcal{V}^{op}}$$

where each space is considered as the structured ensemble of possible probings of it by standard spaces, and the left adjoint return "realizes" any conceivable $\mathcal{V}^{op} \xrightarrow{\;P\;} \mathcal{V}$ by using it as a scheme to glue together standard pieces. But wait.

As the relation between the subjective and objective can be reflected into the subjective, for example, as the relation between presentations by axioms and invariant theories within the abstract general, so can it be reflected into the objective, as in our present description, using concrete generals of spaces and of combinatorial plans, etc. But there is a difference. Speculation costs little, and it seems that calculation can go on indefinitely; thus perhaps countable infinity is not such a bad idealized model of those aspects of subjectivity. By contrast, a plan which can be carried out must be finite.

Thus we introduce a reduction $\mathcal{V}^{\mathcal{V}^{op}} \longrightarrow \mathcal{U}'$ of our dreamy scale of plans, in order that the composite $\mathcal{U}' \xrightarrow{\text{left adj.}} \mathcal{V}^{\mathcal{V}^{op}} \longrightarrow \mathcal{U}$ comes closer to modelling constructions which can really be done. For example, all homotopy types of spaces arise from the standard choice $\mathcal{U}' = \mathcal{V}^{\mathcal{K}_0^{op}}$, where $\mathcal{K}_0 \longrightarrow \mathcal{V}$ (inducing the reduction) is just the inclusion of the category of finite sets. In general, such a composite $\mathcal{U}' \longrightarrow \mathcal{U}$ reflects, within objective logic, the subjective-objective opposition itself; it is the concrete result of a comparison between two abstract theories of space, a combinatorial one and a continuous one.

4. Detailed Models of Becoming

Sometimes the objects in being to be constructed are actually in the realm of thinking (in the broad material sense we are giving to thinking). For example, a book may be constructed from an outline. There are also shorthand notes for delivering a speech (wherein the symbols in the combinatorial plan are to be realized by syllables of sound) and librettos for operas with musical symbols, etc. If we regard the desired product to be an audio tape of the speech or a video tape of the opera, then the geometric sort of realization discussed in section 3 applies. However, in those cases the plan is primarily a plan for a *performance*, a kind of becoming that we must also effectuate when we actually *carry out* the construction of a house or of a machine. The study of the categories and functors appropriate to this problem sometimes goes under the name of "control theory," but these categories have also specific features in common with those arising in continuum mechanics in connection with the tempering of metals, etc. They involve taking into the already acquired $\mathcal{V}$ (hence into the abstract generals $\mathcal{A}$ which arise) a model of time which is not merely a poset or group, but is a category which also contains the possible controlling processes as maps. The corresponding concrete generals are categories whose objects consist of systems of states evolving in a (partly) controlled manner.

Apart from generalities about evolution of states (controlled or not), there are two further important features which make possible specific mathematical treatment. First, states are states *of* a body (often the relation is contravariant) and bodies have parts. The part-whole relation is not merely a poset, but rather each part is included in the whole in two senses, since each part is both itself *and* its relationship; we can call these two kinds of arrows the passive and active inclusions. In its purest form such a body is the category B:

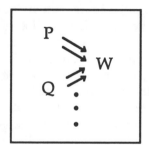

equipped with a faithful labelling functor to:

whose sections correspond to the parts. A system of states for B is a functor $B^{op} \xrightarrow{\ X\ } \mathcal{V}$ (where $\mathcal{V}$ might be taken as sets or spaces). The passive maps in B then induce projections $X(W) \longrightarrow X(P)$ for each part P, each state of the whole involving in particular a state of P; these taken together induce a map $X(W) \longrightarrow \Pi_{p \neq w} X(P)$ into the product of the state spaces of all the parts. One usually assumes that this passively induced map is an isomorphism or at least an inclusion: the state of the whole is nothing but collectively the states of all its parts. But there are still the maps $X(W) \longrightarrow X(P)$ obtained by applying X to the *active* maps in B;

these help to express how the collective state will *influence* the state of each part P. An appropriate model of *time* in this context is as *another* functor $B^{op} \xrightarrow{\quad T \quad} \mathcal{V}$ in the same category as X. The passively induced maps $T(W) \longrightarrow T(P)$ are *individually* assumed to be isomorphisms if we want to express that in a motion or development of B as a whole, the times of each part are synchronized. But there are still the *actively*-induced maps $T(W) \longrightarrow T(P)$ which I will take as expressing the *delay* with which the individual states of P can respond to the influence of the collective states. Then a motion or development of B which follows the specific laws inherent in X and T is just any map $T \longrightarrow X$ which is homogeneous (or natural) with respect to *each* of the maps in B. In systems amenable to differential equations, the delays are taken as infinitesimal translations, but they may also be the finite delays inherent in physical connecting "wires."

The second important feature (making calculation feasible) of the evolution of bodies with parts is the following. In the thinking of the body politic, democracy begins with the people U whom individual P knows. Similarly, in a fluid body, the immediate influence on the motion of a particle P comes from the particles very close to it, considered, in partial-differential equations, to constitute an infinitesimal neighborhood U of P. Thus, we can deepen our "purest" model B by introducing an intermediate layer of objects U with sub-whole inclusions $U \longrightarrow W$, across which some of the passive and active inclusions of the various P's factor. The new category $\hat{B} \supset B$ obtained depends on the precise interlocking of these sub-wholes (essentially a binary relation between P's and U's). If the state functor X previously discussed is the restriction of an X defined on $\hat{B}$, then the *active* influences factor as:

$$X(W) \longrightarrow X(U) \longrightarrow X(P)$$

making explicit the way in which the immediate influence of the state of the whole on P's state depends only on the state of his neighbours (of course including his own state $X(U) \longrightarrow X(P)$, due to the factored *passive* inclusion $P \longrightarrow U$). The product condition placed previously on X becomes over $\hat{B}$ the inverse limit condition $X(W) = \lim X(U)$, the well-defined part (of the product over all objects of $\hat{B}$) consisting of logically possible collective states.

If $\mathcal{V}$ is a topos, so are the categories $\mathcal{V}^{B^{op}}$, $\mathcal{V}^{\hat{B}^{op}}$ in which our state and time objects reside and map into each other; there are many objects in these categories which satisfy neither of the two extreme isomorphism conditions. But some of these objects serve, as in other parts of topos theory, to internalize (to the concrete general determined by the abstract body structure B) the logical and other algebraic calculations we may need to do on functions of state and time. There may also be means, available to objective logic, for making precise the idea that the sub-wholes U of W are qualitatively smaller, as is true at least in the case of the partial-differential equations of continuum motion. Namely, certain very special objects D in $\mathcal{V}$ admit use as "fractional exponents," via a functor $(\ )^{1/D}$ right adjoint to the usual function-space functor $(\ )^D$. In the same way, the idea that the time delays in T are "immediate" may be made precise.

Conclusion

Despite some simplifications in the above, needed for rapid description, I hope that I have made clear that there is a great deal of useful precision lying behind my illustrations, and a great deal to be developed on the same basis. Thus I believe to have demonstrated the plausibility of my thesis that category theory will be a necessary tool in the construction of an adequately explicit science of knowing.

Note

1 A simple example of natural structure: Galois observed that the roots of a particular polynomial equation can be permuted, leading to a certain *group* G as abstract general. The corresponding concrete general is the category of all possible permutation representations of G. (It can be shown that each of these possibles actually arises from a suitable system of polynomial equations.) This example is related to another one. Over a particular domain in the plane, there are varialbe quantities; it was observed that these quantities can be added and multiplied, leading to the abstract general D which is the *algebraic theory of commutative rings*. The corresponding concrete general is the category of all possible commutative rings. (Algebraic geometry shows that every one of these possibles, C, is actually the system of all variable quantities over a suitable domain space, whose dimension and quality depends on the ring C.

References

Cantor, G. (1895) Beiträge zur Begründung der transfiniten Mengenlehre, *Math. Annalen* 46: 481-512

Isbell, John (1960). Adequate subcategories. *Illinois Journal of Mathematics* 4(4): 541-52

Kan (1958). Adjoint functors. *Transactions of the American Mathematical Society* 87: 294-329

Lawvere, F. W. (1963). Functorial semantics of algebraic theories. *Proceedings of the National Academy of Science, USA* 50(5): 869-72

— (1969). Adjointness in foundations. *Dialectica*, 23: 281-96

— (1973). Metric Spaces, generalized logic and closed categories *Rendiconti del Seminario Matematico e Fisico di Milano*, 43: 135-66

— (1986). Taking categories seriously. *Revista Colombiana de Matematicas* 20: 147-78

— (1991a). Intrinsic Co-Heyting boundaries and the Leibniz rule in certain toposes. *Category Theory Proceedings Como 1990. Springer Lecture Notes in Mathematics* 1488: 279-81

— (1991b). Some thoughts on the future of category theory. *Category Theory Proceedings Como 1990. Springer Lecture Notes in Mathematics* 1488: 1-13

Lawvere, F.W., and S.H. Schanuel (1991). *Conceptual Mathematics: A First Introduction to Categories*. Buffalo Workshop Press, P.O. Box 171, Buffalo, NY 14226, USA

MacLane, S. and I. Moerdijk (1992). *Sheaves in Geometry and Logic: A First Introduction to Topos Theory*. New York: Springer-Verlag

Macnamara and Reyes (this volume). Foundational issues in the learning of proper names, count nouns and mass nouns

Makkai, M. (1987). Stone duality for first order logic. *Advances in Mathematics* 65(2): 97-171

Moerdijk, I., and G. Reyes (1991). *Models for Smooth Infinitesimal Analysis*. New York: Springer-Verlag

Pontrjagin, L. (1939). *Topological Groups*. Princeton, NJ: Princeton University Press

Schanuel, S.H. (1991). Negative sets have Euler characteristic and dimension.

Stone, M.H. (1937) Applications of the theory of Boolean rings to general topology

5

Category Theory as a Conceptual Tool in the Study of Cognition

François Magnan and Gonzalo E. Reyes

1. Introduction

The aim of this paper is to introduce category theory as a conceptual tool in the study of cognition. We believe that category theory has several advantages over set theory as a guide in analyzing and conceptualizing basic intentional abilities of the human mind such as the abilities to refer, to count and to learn.

These advantages result from the following considerations that we hope to clarify and justify as we go along:

1. Category theory is a generalization of set theory in the sense that the latter appears as a limiting case which may be accommodated within the former. As a consequence, category theory is able to provide means to avoid over-determinations resulting from peculiarities of set theory.
2. Category theory provides means to circumscribe and study what is universal in mathematics and other scientific disciplines. By identifying logic with the study of what is universal category theory supplies the means to describe such a logic, the objective logic of the discipline in question.

We illustrate consideration (1) with an example. We all know from high school that some quantities are scalars (temperature, pressure), whereas others are vectors (velocity, force).The latter have not only magnitude but direction. As physics developed, the need for a generalized notion of vector was felt and the question arose how one should define such a notion. The answer turned out to be both deep and simple: a generalized vector is an element of a vector space, i.e., of an algebraic structure satisfying some simple laws. Thus, we do not over-determine a generalized vector by defining it as a kind of "super-arrow" with more directions and further angles (including possibly solid ones) and satisfying complicated conditions which generalize those of high school vectors. Using an Aristotelian term, we could say that the essence of a vector is its belonging to a vector space.

A similar development has taken place in logic. Modern logic, in the form that originated from Frege, Peano and Russell arose from the study of arithmetic and set theory. As it developed, the need was felt to generalize the notion of set. This need was felt particularly when people tried seriously to apply logic to natural languages. The objects referred to in such languages are ephemeral and changing, unlike numbers and sets, which are timeless and constant. Category theory gives us the means to define a generalized (or variable/cohesive) set as an object of a category satisfying some properties (a topos), without the temptation to go into over-determinations such as: "it is a family of sets varying continuously over a Hausdorff topological space and such that..." Of course, for some toposes such a description of a generalized set is possible. Notice that this is analogous to our vector-space example: generalized vectors may be described in terms of angles, etc. for vector spaces of dimensions up to three.

As an example of this way of thinking, the reader may consult Reyes (1991a), Reyes and Zolfaghari (1991b) for an approach to modal logic that avoids such over-determinations as possible worlds, possible situations, alternative relations and so on. Once again, the resulting modal operators may be described in terms of some of these notions in particular cases.

With respect to consideration (2), some historical notes may help the reader to place the theory of categories in the correct perspective.

Category theory was created in the earlier 1940s by S. Eilenberg and S. MacLane to guide some complicated computations involving passage to the limit in algebraic topology. During the 1950s it was the study of concrete problems in algebraic topology, complex analysis, functional analysis and algebraic geometry that led people like Kan and Grothendieck to further advances such as the discovery of adjoint functors, abelian categories and homological algebra. Since then, and especially during the last 20 years, category theory has increasingly found its vocation as a foundational discipline capable of clarifying (and sometimes even expanding) our understanding of mathematical knowledge and its applications. This change is mainly due to the discovery of F. W. Lawvere that some categories may be viewed as universes of variable/cohesive sets, capable of modelling theories that lack models in the more rigid universe of constant sets. Already, category theory has been applied to a variety of subjects ranging from physics to linguistics.

It was a fundamental discovery that most of the basic notions and constructions in all of these fields may be characterized by so-called universal properties, properties which may be formulated in terms of a very few primitives: object, morphism, domain (of a morphism), codomain (of a morphism) and composition. These primitives generalize those of set, function, domain and codomain, respectively, of set theory. We shall see several examples of universal properties in this paper. Universality may also be described in terms of adjoint functors (as we shall see in section 3), which Lawvere sees as expressing the objective dialectical relations at the heart of a given field. Considering logic as the study of what is universal, then, we arrive at what Lawvere calls the objective logic of the field, a logic to be discovered rather than postulated at the outset. In this way, classical logic appears as a particular presentation of the objective logic of the category of constant sets. On the other hand, the logic of the universe of graphs is richer and subtler and it exhibits phenomena not to be found in the classical logic (see Reyes and Zolfaghari [1991b]). To see how the search for a logic can be carried out, see section 2, where we argue that counting implies that the logic of finite sets is classical.

Besides these considerations of a rather general nature, there is one which is specific to cognition: the human mind has the ability to carry out a large number of constructions (probably following "blueprints" of some kind) that seem so natural and so universal that they must be severely constrained. (See section 2 for some examples). It follows that we need an adequate theory to describe constructions that are naturally constrained. But as we saw, category theory is precisely such a theory. We may even suggest that universals of the mind may be expressed by means of universal properties in the theory of categories and much of the work done up to now in this area seems to bear out this suggestion.

The paper is divided into two parts. In the first (section 2) we introduce informally some of the main categorical themes by means of an analysis of the process of counting. By discussing the process of counting in some detail, we give evidence that this universal ability of the human mind may be conveniently conceptualized in terms of this theory of universals which is category theory. (For more on category theory as a theory of universals, see Ellerman [1988]).

In the second part (section 3) we give rigorous definitions of categories, functors, natural transformations and adjoint functors and illustrate these notions, whenever possible, with examples from logic and linguistics rather than from mathematics.

2. Counting

Counting is certainly one of the mind's fundamental abilities. We do not want to develop a theory of the mental processes involved in counting but to express a few basic facts that underly this ability. The first thing required for counting is that the objects to be counted be clearly delimited in such a way that they become definite and distinguishable. For instance, it seems doubtful that we can count all animals. On the other hand, we can count the dogs in a particular room. This "collection into a whole of definite and separate objects" is precisely what Cantor calls a set (*Menge*) and thus we may say that counting applies to sets rather than mereological wholes such as heaps. As Frege pointed out, the same mereological whole consisting of marching soldiers may be counted as one army, ten regiments or 30,000 men. The result of counting the elements of a set is a natural number, the number of elements in the set, provided that the set is finite. We shall write $\#A$ for the number of elements of the (finite) set A. Before going into the process of counting itself, let us remark that counting is simplified by using arithmetical operations such as addition, multiplication and exponentiation between natural numbers. Thus, to count the apples contained in a bag we may put them first into two smaller bags, count the apples in each bag and add the numbers thus obtained. On the other hand, if the objects to be counted are nicely ordered in an array such as a chess board, we may count the columns and the rows separately and then multiply the resulting numbers. The arithmetical operations on natural numbers are the reflection of more basic operations between (finite) sets. The first example exhibits the set-theoretical operation of taking the union of two disjoint sets as the operation underlying addition. In the second example, it is rather the (cartesian) product of the two sets that underlies multiplication. Furthermore, ordinary laws that relate these arithmetical operations turn out also to be reflections of laws that relate the underlying set-theoretical operations.

Before we go into details, let us recall the definitions of the set-theoretical operations mentioned above. Given any sets A and B, we define their *cartesian product* to be the set $A \times B = \{(a, b) : a \in A, b \in B\}$. In other words, the cartesian product of A and B is the set consisting of ordered pairs of elements, the first from A and the second from B. Similarly, given any sets A and B (which may partly overlap or even be equal) we define their *disjoint union* $A + B$ to be the ordinary union of the (disjoint) sets $A \times \{0\}$ and $B \times \{1\}$. This means that an element of the disjoint union is either of the form $(a, 0)$ or of the form $(b, 1)$. Notice that the disjoint union of $\{0, 1\}$ and $\{0, 1, 2\}$ has 5 elements, whereas their ordinary union has only 3. The last operation we consider is exponentiation: given A and B as before, we define B^A to be the set of functions from A to B. In other words, an element of B^A is a function whose domain is A and whose codomain is B.

We may now formulate the relation between ordinary arithmetical operations and their underlying set-theoretical operations as follows (where A and B are finite sets):

Proposition 2.1.
1. $\#(A + B) = \#A + \#B$
2. $\#(A \times B) = \#A \times \#B$
3. $\#(B^A) = (\#B)^{(\#A)}$

Similarly, we could formulate corresponding relations between arithmetical and set-theoretical operations at the level of laws. As an example, lets us notice that the distributive law $n \times (p + q) = n \times p + n \times q$ follows from the following proposition (where A, B and C are finite sets):

Proposition 2.2. There is a one-to-one correspondance between $A \times (B + C)$ and $A \times B + A \times C$.

The set-theoretical operations underlying the arithmetical ones are so natural that they are taken for granted when counting, which creates the impression that they are not involved in this process. We believe that these operations constitute universal "blueprints" of the mind and we may ask what distinguishes them from others. Set theory does not give us too much help with this problem. Indeed, from a purely set-theoretical point of view, nothing seems to distinguish these operations from countless others that may be defined starting from two sets. To make things worse, the definition of disjoint union is rather artificial. The main point is to transform the original sets so as to make them disjoint and this could be achieved in a variety of ways. How can one decide which, if any, is the right operation?

It is at this point that category theory comes to our rescue with a new idea: instead of seeing a cartesian product as a set, let us view it as a structure consisting of a set *together* with the relations between this set and the original ones. This structure satisfies a universal property which essentially characterizes it. We need, of course, to specify the relations between the cartesian product of two sets (as defined above) and the original sets. These relations are given by functions. Since the notion of function is so fundamental, we pause to describe it in some detail.

2.1. Sets and Functions

A *function* consists of three things: a starting set called *domain* or *source*, an ending set called *codomain* or *target* and a rule that assigns to each member of the domain, one and only one member of the codomain. As an example, consider the rule that assigns to each busdriver in Montreal the bus line to which he or she is attached. Defining the set of bus drivers of Montreal as domain and the set of bus lines as codomain, we have defined a function. We can show all these constituents in a diagram like the following:

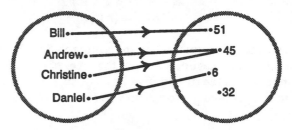

It is easy to see that there is always a very trivial function 1_A between any set A and itself, namely, the one that assigns to each element a of A the same member a. This function is called the *identity function* on A.

Functions are closed under several operations. One of the most basic is *composition*. This concept comes very naturally when we start dealing with functions. In our previous example, we could have introduced another function that would have the set of bus lines as domain, the set of possible bus routes as codomain and that would assign to each bus line the route it regularly follows. We can then represent this situation with the following diagram in which R1 stands for route 1, etc.:

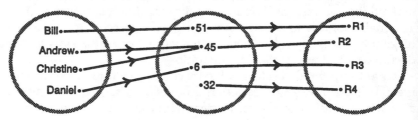

If we follow the arrows from bus drivers to bus lines and then to routes we can now assign a route to each driver. This gives us a function having the set of bus drivers as domain and the set of routes as codomain:

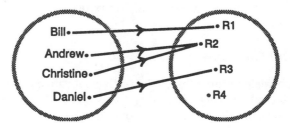

This new function is called *composition* of the original functions. It is clear that we can compose any two functions such that the codomain of one is the same set as the domain of the other. The notation we will use for the composition of $A \xrightarrow{f} B$ and $B \xrightarrow{g} C$ will be $A \xrightarrow{g \circ f} C$. It can be seen fairly easily that composition is associative, that is, if we have three functions $A \xrightarrow{f} B$, $B \xrightarrow{g} C$ and $C \xrightarrow{h} D$, then the compositions $h \circ (g \circ f)$ (h composed with $g \circ f$) and $(h \circ g) \circ f$ ($h \circ g$ composed with f) are the same function. The composition with identity functions does nothing, that is, if we have a function $A \xrightarrow{f} B$, then $f \circ 1_A = f = 1_B \circ f$.

We are now ready to describe the categorical cartesian product of two sets. Suppose that we have three bags of apples denoted by 1, 2, 3, each containing two apples, one green, G and another red, R. Diagrammatically:

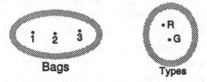

Bags   Types

We can now make a list of all the elements of the (ordinary) cartesian product as follows: $(1, G)$, $(2, G)$, $(3, G)$, $(1, R)$, $(2, R)$, $(3, R)$. This set is clearly in one-to-one correspondence with the set of all the apples and may be identified with it. For instance, $(2, G)$ corresponds to the green apple in the second bag. The relations between the ordinary cartesian product and the original sets may be described by two functions. The first has the ordinary or set-theoretical cartesian product as domain, the set $\{1, 2, 3\}$ of bags as codomain and assigns to each apple the bag that contains it. The other has also the cartesian product as domain but has the set $\{G, R\}$ as codomain and assigns to each apple its type (green or red).

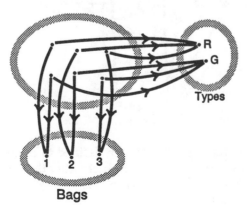

Bags

As we said before, the basic idea is now to characterize the structure consisting of the (ordinary) cartesian product *together* with these two special functions (rather than of the cartesian product alone) among sets plus a couple of functions having the same codomains as our two special functions. Let us call such a structure a *fork*. Thus a fork consists of a set X (the "handle") together with a couple of functions having X as domain: the $\{1, 2, 3\}$-"prong" whose codomain is the set of bags and the $\{G, R\}$-"prong" whose codomain is the set of types. We now consider the fork having the cartesian product as handle, the function which assigns to each apple the bag where it came from as $\{1, 2, 3\}$-prong and the function which assigns to each apple its type as the $\{G, R\}$-prong. Such a fork has the following universal property: given any other fork, say fork', there is a unique function f from the handle of fork' into the product set (handle of our original fork) that respects the prongs in the following sense. If a member x of the handle of fork' is assigned to bag 2 (by the $\{1, 2, 3\}$-prong of fork') and assigned to type R (by the $\{G, R\}$-prong of fork') then $f(x)$ must be $(2, R)$. The fact that f respects the prongs can be expressed more generally in terms of composition of functions as follows: if we compose a prong of our original fork with f we get the corresponding prong in fork'. A fork having this universal property will be called a *terminal* fork. The following diagram illustrates the situation:

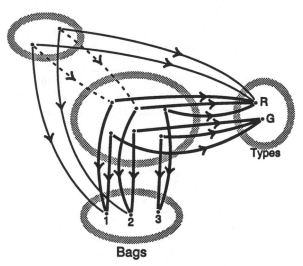

Bags

The *categorical cartesian product* is then defined to be any terminal fork. It would be more correct to say *a* product rather that *the* product in this definition, but two terminal forks are "essentially" the same in a sense to be made precise later on.

We can describe in a similar way the sum (or disjoint union) of two sets. Let A and B be two finite sets. We saw before how to form the disjoint union $A + B$ of those sets. The sum of A and B will be defined as the diagram:

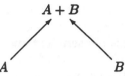

instead of just the set $A + B$. A diagram of the form:

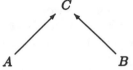

will be called a *cofork* for A and B. The sum is clearly a cofork and its specificity is guaranteed by a universal property. The sum is an initial cofork. This means that if we take any other cofork (like the one displayed above) there will be a unique function $A + B \longrightarrow C$ that respects the prongs of the cofork (in a sense analogous to the one we have given in the definition of product).

We will see later how the definitions of product and disjoint union (or coproduct) may be formalized in the general context of category theory.

2.2. Counting as a Process

Although we have set the stage for counting, counting itself involves other structures that reflect the mind's ability to iterate. To conceptualize this notion, we notice that we iterate or repeat processes and a process is usually conceptualized as a function. To iterate the function is to compose it with itself. This does not always make sense but only at times when, for instance, the domain coincides with the codomain. This leads to the notion of an evolutive set or discrete dynamical system. An *evolutive set* is a function whose domain coincides with its codomain. Thus, an evolutive set is a set with an endofunction.

There are cases where processes are not readily presented as functions. How can we consider the turning of the earth around the sun as an endofunction? What would its domain be? This example and several others seem to require a more abstract conceptualization: a set (whose elements are thought of as processes) together with a binary operation (thought of as composition) satisfying some conditions. These considerations suggest the use of the more abstract notion of *monoid* to conceptualize iteration. However, it is a basic result of Cayley that any abstract monoid may be represented as an evolutive set.

With these structures in place, let us see what is involved when we count a crowd of people in a room. We first choose one person and give her the number 1, proceed to choose a second person and give her the number 2 and so on until everybody has been chosen once and given a number. These successive choices amount to associating the structure of an evolutive set with the set of persons (the endofunction assigns to each person the one that is chosen next and with the last that person herself). The evolutive set is endowed with a starting point (the first person chosen) together with a function from the set of people into the set of natural numbers 1, 2, 3, ... The number assigned to the last person chosen is precisely the number of people sought. We can picture such a structure by drawing a dot for each member of the set we want to count and an arrow from each dot to the dot counted next. In this way we get things like:

Once again we see a blueprint of the mind in action whose prototype is the evolutive set I of natural numbers 1, 2, 3, ... with successor as the endofunction and 1 as the starting point. What characterizes this system as distinct from other evolutive sets? The answer (due to Lawvere) is given by the following universal property: it is the initial evolutive set with starting element. More precisely, we have the following:

Proposition 2.3. Given any evolutive set A with endofunction f and starting element a, there is exactly one function from I into A which preserves the structure in the following sense: it assigns 1 to a and whenever n is assigned to x, then $n + 1$ is assigned to $f(x)$, the successor of x.

In particular, there is a unique structure preserving function from I into the evolutive system of the people in the room induced by the successive choices. Notice that if there are, say, 15 people, the last person will be assigned to all numbers from 15 on. This gives an equivalent way of counting: the first natural number to which the last person is assigned is the number of people sought.

Counting a set A appears, then, as associating the generic structure of an evolutive set having a starting element with A and mapping the blueprint I into A in the only way that preserves the structure.

Notice that the number of elements of a set is defined in terms of the set in question *enriched* with a structure of evolutive set with starting element. Since there may be several ways to introduce such a structure on a set (just start with a different person and make different choices for second, third, etc.) it is not clear (from this definition) that the number in question is independent of the choice of such a structure. We have, however, the following fundamental result:

Proposition 2.4. Two evolutive sets with starting elements whose underlying sets are in bijective correspondance have the same number of elements.

These considerations of the actual process of counting have an interesting corollary about the "logic of the stage", that is, about the logic of those "collections into a whole of definite and separate objects": it is Boolean. Indeed, let S be such a collection that may be counted by a natural number and let T be a subcollection, namely those already counted. To keep on going, we need to be able to decide, given an arbitrary element of S whether it has been counted already (i.e., whether it belongs to T) or not. In other words, the subcollections of S constitute a Boolean algebra. We have not started with a ready-made logic that we impose on these collections. Rather, we discover their logic by assuming that the operation of counting is applicable to them. This is one example of a main theme in this paper: objective versus subjective logic.

Before we leave this subject, we would like to point out that we have only scratched the surface of a large topic. Fascinating mathematical problems have appeared when dealing with the psychology of counting from a perspective similar to ours (cf. Bénabou [1991]). On the other hand, the psychology of counting (of which this section gives a glimpse) is a largely unexplored area which certainly deserves to be studied.

3. Basic Notions in Category Theory

Notice that in the previous section we did not define products (and disjoint unions) as sets of ordered pairs of elements (as is usually done in set theory), but in terms of universal properties described using only the basic notions of set, function, domain (of a function), codomain (of a function), identity (function) and composition (of functions). Category theory starts with the realization that most constructions in mathematics may be defined by universal properties, provided that we generalize these basic set-theoretical notions. Thus, the basic notions of category theory are: object, morphism, domain (of a morphism), codomain (of a morphism), identity (morphism) and composition (of morphisms).

3.1. Towards a Definition of a Category

Before going into the formal definition, we give an example of a category that is very far from the finite sets that we have (implicitely) described. Its objects will be people (rather than sets) and its morphisms, family relations (rather than functions). Let us take a "universe" consisting of four persons (the objects of the category): Franz, Hermann, Julie and Amschel. Morphisms will be family relations. More precisely, a morphism from (a person) A to (a person) B will be the description of B relative to A within the family. The domain of a morphism from A to B is A and its codomain is B. In the following diagram, morphisms are represented by arrows:

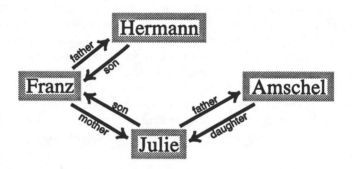

For instance, the arrow going from *Franz* to *Hermann* can be read as: "The father of Franz is Hermann." Now that we have objects and morphisms we naturally want to know how to compose the morphisms and what are the identity morphisms.

The identity morphims on a object A is a distinguished arrow starting from A and ending at A. In our example, the identity arrow on *Franz* will be interpreted as: "Franz is Franz." The notion of composition is also very straightfoward in this case. If we compose the two following arrows:

we get

Thus we identify 'The father of the mother of Franz is Amschel' with 'The grandfather of Franz is Amschel'. Of course, if we wanted to apply this to a concrete family, things could become more complicated because we would have to take into account the fact that everybody has two grandfathers and that a father may have more that one son, etc. Clearly, we could solve these difficulties but to do so would make the language heavier and would in no way help the reader to grasp the basic notions of category theory or prepare him to understand the general notion of a category.

If we draw our diagram again and add the identity arrows and all the arrows needed to compose any pair of arrows we get the following (by making the required identifications):

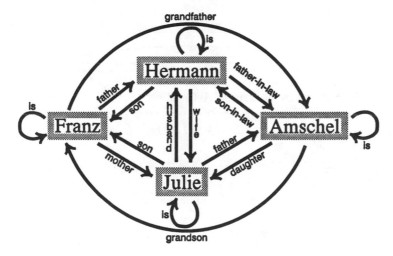

We can ask whether the properties of composition of functions remain true in this new context of family relations (rather than functions). In particular, is composition associative in our example? The reader can convince himself of the associativity of the composition by checking that 'The father of the wife of the man who is the father of Franz' and 'The father of the woman that is the wife of the father of Franz' are equivalent descriptions for 'The grandfather of Franz' (follow the diagram!). The other property of composition is that the composition of a morphism f with any identity morphism (of the source or the target of f) gives f itself. This is also true in our example, since 'The father of the person that is Franz is Hermann' is the same as 'The father of Franz is Hermann'.

After these examples we are ready to give the definition of a category:

Definition 3.1 A category $\mathfrak{C}$ is a collection of objects $Ob(\mathfrak{C})$ and a collection of morphisms $Ar(\mathfrak{C})$ (also called arrows or maps) such that for each morphism of $Ar(\mathfrak{C})$ we can associate a domain object in $Ob(\mathfrak{C})$ (from which the morphism starts) and a codomain object in $Ob(\mathfrak{C})$ (at which the morphism ends) in a way that the following properties hold:

1. For each object $A \in Ob(\mathfrak{C})$ we have a special morphism $1_A \in Ar(\mathfrak{C})$ that has A both for domain and codomain and that is called identity on A.

2. If we have two morphisms $f, g \in Ar(\mathfrak{C})$ such that the codomain of f is the same object as the domain of g then there exists a morphism $g \circ f$ in $Ar(\mathfrak{C})$ starting from the domain of f and ending at the codomain of g. This morphism is called the composition of f and g.

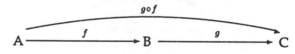

3. If $A \xrightarrow{f} B$ in a morphism in $Ar(\mathfrak{C})$ then

$$f \circ 1_A = f = 1_B \circ f$$

4. If $A \xrightarrow{f} B$, $B \xrightarrow{g} C$ and $C \xrightarrow{h} D$ are three morphisms in $Ar(\mathfrak{C})$ then

$$(h \circ g) \circ f = h \circ (g \circ f)$$

3.2. Examples of Categories

We now look at some simple examples of categories. The reader is invited to verify that all the properties needed are satisfied in those examples.

Example 1. Finite sets with functions clearly form a category, as we have seen in the first section.

Example 2. The family consisting of Hermann, Franz, Julie and Amschel together with their (family) relations also form a category.

Example 3. To each formal system we can associate a category whose objects are the well-formed formulas of the formal system. We also choose to put one and only one map going from formula A to formula B if we can prove B under the assumption of A i.e., $A \to B \iff A \vdash B$. Clearly, from each formula A we can trivially prove A ($A \vdash A$) so that for every object A we have an identity morphism, namely, the only morphism from A to A. Composition also comes very naturally. If we can prove B from A and C from B, then (by modus ponens) we can prove C from A ($A \vdash B$, $B \vdash C \Rightarrow A \vdash C$).

Example 4. We now define what is called "the nominal category of a subject" (introduced by M. LaPalme, J. Macnamara and G. E. Reyes in this volume). Objects are taken to be the count nouns of a subject. Take, for instance, zoology as the subject. The objects will then be the count nouns 'dog', 'mammal', 'whale', etc. We recognize a morphism from A to B if the sentence 'an A is a B' is correct in the subject of interest (correct, in the sense that you will find it in dictionaries). For example, there is a map from 'whale' to 'mammal' because it is the case that 'a whale is a mammal' is a correct sentence. There is no map from 'dog' to 'cat' because a dog is not a cat. The domain of a map is a count noun in subject position. The codomain is a count noun in predicate position. Identity maps are given by valid sentences of the form 'a whale is a whale'. Finally, composition is given by modus ponens: 'a whale is a mammal', 'a mammal is an animal' therefore 'a whale is an animal'.

Example 5. The category of evolutive sets (or discrete dynamical systems) whose objects are of the type (A, f) where A is a set and $A \xrightarrow{f} A$ is a function. We can give a very suggestive graphic representation of objects of this kind. First, we draw a dot for each member of the set A. Next, for each member $x \in A$, we draw an arrow that starts at the dot representing x that points at the dot representing $f(x)$ (the image of x by f). We get diagrams like these:

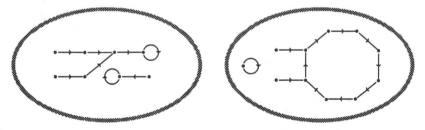

The justification of the name "dynamical system" appears through this representation. If we select a dot in the diagram – as initial state of the system – , then each time we apply f we move (in a completely determinate manner) to the next state of the system and so on. We usually call f the "evolution" of the dynamical system.

Clearly, they are a generalisation of sets because we can consider a plain set A as the dynamical system $(A, 1_A)$ (where 1_A is the identity function on A) where no movement exists. Dynamical systems are sets with a further structure on them. In fact, we can consider dynamical systems as "sets that internally develop" (as Lawvere as pointed out). One of our main points can be formulated here. Category theory gives us much richer structures than plain set theory. This gives us one reason to believe that category theory is a better source than set theory for models of cognitive processes.

Remember that morphisms in a category are very important constituents. So, we must give a precise definition of morphisms between two evolutive sets (A, f) and (B, g) to put a category structure on this universe. Perhaps we could define such a morphism as a simple function $\Phi : A \longrightarrow B$. Clearly, all the conditions imposed in the definition of a category would be satisfied by this choice. But, it would not be a very clever choice because morphisms of this form do not take into account the evolutions f and g of the discrete dynamical systems. With these morphisms we would get a category that is essentially the same as the category of sets. The evolution functions f and g should, then, play a role in the definition of morphisms.

We give them a role by defining a morphism $(A, f) \overset{\Phi}{\longrightarrow} (B, g)$ as a function $\Phi : A \longrightarrow B$ with further restrictions. We want Φ to preserve the evolutions in the following sense: If Φ sends $a \in A$ to $b = \Phi(a) \in B$, then the evolution of a (namely $f(a)$) must be sent by Φ to the evolution of b (namely $g(b)$). Using a mathematical notation, this fact is expressed by $\Phi(f(a)) = g(\Phi(a))$ for all $a \in A$. These morphisms are structure-preserving. They are clearly what we were looking for.

Example 6. Our last example will be the category of (multiple oriented irreflexive) graphs. Graphs are objects composed of dots and arrows. Each arrow has a source dot and a target dot. When the source and the target are the same for a particular arrow we call it a loop. The following picture shows an example of a graph:

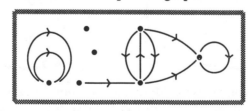

Mathematically we describe a graph G as a set of dots G_0, a set of arrows

G_1 and two functions $s, t : G_1 \longrightarrow G_0$ that assign to each arrow its source and its target respectively. We use the notation (G_0, G_1, s, t) to refer to such a structure.

To get a category, we also need to define a notion of morphism between graphs. We will say that a dot and an arrow are incident if the dot is the source or the target of the arrow (we also say in this case that they are in a relation of incidence). If $G = (G_0, G_1, s_G, t_G)$ and $H = (H_0, H_1, s_H, t_H)$ are two graphs, we define a morphism of graphs $\Phi : G \longrightarrow H$ as a pair of functions (Φ_0, Φ_1) (where $\Phi_0 : G_0 \longrightarrow H_0$ and $\Phi_1 : G_1 \longrightarrow H_1$) that respect the incidence relations, i.e., $\Phi_0(s(f)) = s(\Phi_1(f))$ and $\Phi_0(t(f)) = t(\Phi_1(f))$ for all arrows $f \in G_1$. These mathematical relations only mean that the source of an arrow f in G must be sent by Φ_0 to the source of the arrow to which Φ_1 sends f in H (the same restrictions apply for the targets). These retrictions on Φ rule out morphisms that would separate an arrow from its incident dots by sending the dots to a place different from where the arrow is sent. Graphs can also be viewed as a generalisation of sets if we consider graphs with no arrows.

3.3. Generalized Elements in a Category

The last five examples given above are far removed in nature from simple sets. In fact, neither a formula nor a count noun is a set; evolutive sets and graphs are not just plain sets but sets with further structures on them. A fortiori, morphisms in these categories are not plain functions. Nevertheless, there is a sense in which objects of a category may be represented as sets of generalized elements and morphisms, as functions between such sets. To see this, let $1 = \{0\}$ be the singleton whose only element is 0. We claim that there is a one-to-one correspondence between elements of A and functions from 1 into A: with $a \in A$ we associate the function $a : 1 \longrightarrow A$ which sends the unique element of its domain, 0, into a. Conversely, with $f : 1 \longrightarrow A$ we associate the element $f(0) \in A$. These associations establish the required one-to-one correspondence. We may thus identify elements of A with functions $1 \longrightarrow A$ and this allows us to view elements as particular functions, namely, those whose domains are singletons. Let us define a *generalized element* of an object A of a category to be a morphism $X \longrightarrow A$, where X is again an object of the category. If we want to make explicit the dependency on X, we shall talk of an X-*element* of A or an element of A parametrized by X. A morphism $f : A \longrightarrow B$ may be represented as an actual function from the generalized elements of A into the generalized elements of B as follows: given a generalized X-element of A, $a : X \longrightarrow A$, the composition $f \circ a$ is a generalized X-element of B.

We now give an example of generalized elements in the category of graphs. Let X be the graph consisting of only one dot a and one loop l. We consider all the morphisms from X to an arbitrary graph G. This collection is the collection of X-elements of G. What does an element of this collection look like? To construct a morphism $X \xrightarrow{\Phi} G$, we first need to give an image to a, that is, to select a dot $\Phi_0(a)$ in G. We also need to give an image to the loop l and so we select an arrow $\Phi_1(l)$ in G. According to the rules for the morphisms in graphs, the source of $\Phi_1(l)$ and its target must both be $\Phi_0(a)$ (because a and l have this incidence relation in X by the very definition of loops). We have found that an X-element of G is simply a loop of G so that X is a special graph that has the ability to extract the loops from any graph. The reader is encouraged to see how this representation works in our four other examples of categories.

Using these generalized elements, we will now discuss the generalization of the notions of a monic, epic and bijective function from the theory of sets to the context of category theory.

3.4. Monomorphism, Epimorphism and Isomorphism

Let $f : A \longrightarrow B$ be an ordinary function between sets. Recall that this function is monic (or one-to-one) if, whenever a and a' are two elements of A which are sent by f into the same element of B, i.e., $f(a) = f(a')$, then $a = a'$. In other words, different elements of the domain have different values in the codomain. As an example consider a classroom during a lecture in which nobody is standing. The function which assigns to each person the chair he is sitting in is monic precisely when no two people sit in the same chair.

The natural generalization of this notion to the context of category theory is by defining a morphism $f : A \longrightarrow B$ to be monic or a monomorphism if the actual function from generalized elements of A into generalized elements of B which represents f is monic. We thus arrive at the following:

Definition 3.2. A morphism $A \xrightarrow{i} B$ is a monomorphism if for any object T and morphisms $T \xrightarrow{s_1} A$, $T \xrightarrow{s_2} A$ the fact that:

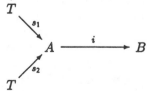

commutes (meaning that $i \circ s_1 = i \circ s_2$) must imply that $s_1 = s_2$. In this case we write $A \xhookrightarrow{i} B$ instead of just $A \xrightarrow{i} B$.

We say that a diagram commutes if, for any pair of objects in the diagram, all paths between them give rise to the same morphism if we compose the morphisms in each path. For example, to say that the following diagram commutes:

$$
\begin{array}{ccc}
A & \xrightarrow{\ f\ } & B \\
{\scriptstyle h}\downarrow & & \downarrow{\scriptstyle g} \\
C & \xrightarrow{\ i\ } & D
\end{array}
$$

means that $i \circ h = g \circ f$ because there are two paths going from A to D (first f followed by g and also h followed by i).

Recall that a function $f : A \longrightarrow B$ between sets is epic or surjective if every element in the codomain comes from an element of the domain; if, in other words, for each $b \in B$ there is an $a \in A$ such that $f(a) = b$. If we go on to define a morphism $f : A \longrightarrow B$ in a category to be epic or to be an epimorphism by requiring that the representing function (between generalized elements) should be epic or surjective, we obtain a very strong notion. Indeed, assuming that for every generalized element $b : X \longrightarrow B$, there is a generalized element $a : X \longrightarrow A$ such that $f \circ a = b$. In particular, this must be true for $1_B : B \longrightarrow B$ and hence we obtain a generalized element $s : B \longrightarrow A$ such that $f \circ s = 1_B$. In other words, f must have a right inverse (s), generally referred to as a section (of f). Conversely, if f has a section, one may conclude that the representing function of f is surjective. This notion is important in several categorical contexts and is called a *split epi*. For some purposes, however, it is too strong and we would like to define a weaker notion of epimorphism.

To do so, let us return to our definition of products and coproducts. The reader may have observed that these are very symmetric. In fact, one may reverse all morphisms in the definition of either to obtain the definition of the other. We say that they are duals. This gives a hint to the solution of our problem: define epimorphism to be the dual of monomorphism. Thus we arrive at the following:

Definition 3.3. A morphism $X \xrightarrow{\ s\ } A$ is called epimorphism if, for any object T and each pair of morphisms $A \xrightarrow{\ s_1\ } T$, $A \xrightarrow{\ s_2\ } T$, we have that $s_1 = s_2$ from the fact that following diagram commutes:

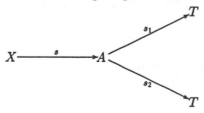

Finally, let us see how to generalize the notion of bijection to the categorical context. Following the straightforward approach of representing a morphism $f : A \longrightarrow B$ as a function between generalized elements, it is natural to define f to be an isomorphism if its representing function is bijective, i.e., monic and epic. A moment's reflection allows us to reformulate this definition as follows:

Definition 3.4. A morphism $A \xrightarrow{f} B$ is called isomorphism if there is a morphism $B \xrightarrow{g} A$ such that $g \circ f = 1_A$ and $f \circ g = 1_B$.

3.5. Universal Constructions in Categories

We are now in a position to define products and coproducts as well as some other operations defined by universal properties in an arbitrary category.

3.5.1. Initial and Terminal Objects

In section 3.3 we tried to capture the notion of an element of a set purely in terms of the basic notions of set, function, domain, codomain, identity and composition. We would have succeeded but for the fact that we had to introduce a special set 1 having exactly one element (that we called "0"), i.e., a singleton. The question naturally arises whether we can define singletons in terms of our basic notions. The answer is yes: a singleton S is characterized by the universal property that there is exactly one function from any set X into S (indeed, the function which assigns the only element of S to each element of the set X). This allows us to define the corresponding categorical notion:

Definition 3.5. A terminal object of a category $\mathfrak{C}$ is an object $1 \in Ob(\mathfrak{C})$ such that, for every object $X \in Ob(\mathfrak{C})$, there is one and only one morphism:

$$X \xrightarrow{\ !\ } 1$$

By the process of reversing all the arrows we may define the dual notion:

Definition 3.6. An initial object of a category $\mathfrak{C}$ is an object $0 \in Ob(\mathfrak{C})$ such that, for every object $X \in Ob(\mathfrak{C})$, there is one and only one morphism:

$$0 \xrightarrow{\ !\ } X$$

An important fact is that any two terminal objects (as well as any two initial objects) in a category are uniquely isomorphic. In other words, if T and T' are two terminal objects, then there is a unique isomorphism between the two. Because of this, it is customary to collapse all terminal objects into a representative and talk about *the* terminal object.

Looking back at our examples, we find that in the category of finite sets the initial object is the empty set ∅. This may seem rather twisted at first because a function from the empty set to another set seems to mean nothing. However, the function that does nothing satisfies our definition of function and it is clearly unique because we cannot construct two different functions ∅ ⟶ A (To do so we would have to give a different image to an element of ∅ in each function. But by definition ∅ does not have elements). The notions of terminal and initial objects do not exist in the nominal category nor in the category of family relations. In the category of well-formed formulas of a formal system, initial objects are contradictions (statements that are always false like $P \wedge \neg P$) for the simple reason that from them we can prove anything and that morphisms between two objects in this category are always unique when they exist. Still, in this category the terminal objects are clearly tautologies (statements that are always true, like $P \vee \neg P$) for the reason that we can prove a tautology from any statement. In the category of evolutive sets the terminal objects are of the form $(\{*\}, Id)$ where $\{*\}$ is a singleton and Id is the identity function on this singleton. The initial object (unique in this case) is the empty evolutive set having as evolution the only possible endofunction $\emptyset \overset{!}{\longrightarrow} \emptyset$. We invite the reader to find initial and terminal objects in the category of graphs.

3.5.2. Products and Coproducts

We have seen in section 2.1 how to define the notion of product in terms of sets and functions alone. We may now give the definition of a (categorical) product of two objects in a category:

Definition 3.7. Let $\mathfrak{C}$ be a category. A product of two objects $A, B \in Ob(\mathfrak{C})$ is an object $P \in Ob(\mathfrak{C})$ together with two morphisms $P \overset{p_A}{\longrightarrow} A$ and $P \overset{p_B}{\longrightarrow} B$ such that, for any object $X \in Ob(\mathfrak{C})$ equipped with a pair of morphisms $X \overset{f}{\longrightarrow} A$, $X \overset{g}{\longrightarrow} B$, there is one and only one morphism $X \overset{h}{\longrightarrow} P$ (usually we use the notation $\langle f, g \rangle$ for h) such that the following diagram commutes:

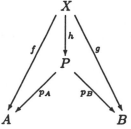

We can also see the product as a terminal fork. To do this, we first need to define the category of forks on two objects A and B. The objects of this category are forks on A and B. If we have two forks:

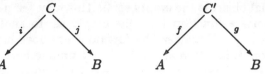

then a morphism from the C fork to the C' fork is defined as a morphism $C \xrightarrow{h} C'$ (this last morphism is actually in the category $\mathfrak{C}$) such that the following diagram commutes:

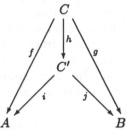

It is clear that a terminal object in this category of forks is a product of A and B.

We use a Gentzen notation to express universal mapping properties. For the product, we get:

$$\frac{C \to A \times B}{C \to A \; , \; C \to B}$$

This means that with each morphism from an object C to the product object $A \times B$ we can associate a morphism from C to A and another from C to B and conversely. The reader is invited to go back to the example of bags of apples to verify his understanding of the above definition.

Another example of product is the following: a chess board is a square divided into 8 rows and 8 columns. Each player has a set of pieces that are placed on the board. A possible way to describe all the positions of the pieces on the board at any time in the game is to systematically draw the board with each of the pieces in its position.

Another way would be to assign to each column, a letter (from A to H) and to each row, a number (from 1 to 8). We could then say where a particular piece is placed by giving the letter of its column and the number of its row (like C3). The reason why we can do this is that the board is the product of the set of possible rows and the set of possible columns. The following diagram describes the integration of the notion of product in this example:

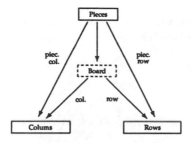

Our last example of product will be the product in the category of a formal system. What could satisfy the definition of product in this category? The product of two objects A and B must be an object P with two morphisms $P \to A$ and $P \to B$ such that, for every other object C and morphism $C \to A$, $C \to B$, there is one and only one morphism $C \to P$ such that a given diagram commutes (see the definition of product). In our particular category the product of formulas A and B must be a formula P from which we can prove both A and B and such that it is provable from any other formula C that could also prove both A and B. There is clearly one way of constructing the product: by letting $P = A \wedge B$ (the conjuction of the two formulas). We could have let $P = \neg(\neg A \vee \neg B)$ but this formula is clearly equivalent to the first. In fact, we can prove easily that all the products of two given objects in a category are isomorphic (this follows from the fact that any two terminal objects are isomorphic).

The dual notion of product is called "coproduct" and is defined as follows:

Definition 3.8. Let $\mathfrak{C}$ be a category. A co-product of two objects $A, B \in Ob(\mathfrak{C})$ is an object $S \in Ob(\mathfrak{C})$ with two morphisms $A \xrightarrow{sA} S$ and $B \xrightarrow{sB} S$ such that, for all objects $X \in Ob(\mathfrak{C})$ and all pairs of morphisms $A \xrightarrow{f} X$, $B \xrightarrow{g} X$, there exists one and only one morphism $S \xrightarrow{h} X$ such that the following diagram commutes:

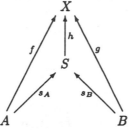

Again we can synthetise this definition in the following notation:

$$\frac{A + B \to C}{A \to C \ , \ B \to C}$$

What does the coproduct look like in our category of finite sets? A picture is enough to give the idea:

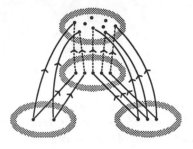

The coproduct in the category of finite sets is *sum*. We see in the above picture that $2 + 3 = 5$. We begin to see the advantages of expressing concepts in the categorial language. We have found a very intimate relation between product and sum. Naturally, the coproduct in the category of a formal system will be disjunction of formulas. We leave the verification of these facts to the reader.

3.5.3. Equalizers and Coequalizers

To introduce the notion of an equalizer we imagine a schoolteacher that in the middle of a term decides to assign new seats to his students. Suppose he wants to know which students remained in their old places. To make the change amounts to defining two functions o and n from the set S of students to the set C of chairs. These functions assign to each student his old and new chair respectively. The question is then to find the students who did not change places. From a set-theoretical point of view, the answer is obvious: it is the set $E = \{x \in S : o(x) = n(x)\}$. This set E is called the (set-theoretical) equalizer of o and n and we may try to characterize this set purely in terms of sets and functions. Just as in the case of products, the solution is to characterize the structure consisting of E *together* with the inclusion map e of E into S, rather than the set E alone. We can picture this structure as the diagram:

$$E \xrightarrow{\;\;e\;\;} S \overset{o}{\underset{n}{\rightrightarrows}} C$$

By going from sets to an arbitrary category and representing E as a set of generalized elements and e as a function between sets of generalized elements, we arrive naturally at the following definition:

Definition 3.9. A pair consisting of an object E and an arrow $E \xrightarrow{e} A$ in a category $\mathfrak{C}$ is called an equalizer of a pair of arrows $f, g : A \to B$ if

$f \circ e = g \circ e$ and, for every arrow $C \xrightarrow{h} A$ such that $f \circ h = g \circ h$, there is a unique arrow $C \xrightarrow{k} E$ such that the following diagram commutes:

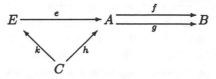

As in previous cases, two equalizers are uniquely isomorphic.

The dual notion of an equalizer is called a coequalizer. We do not give the precise definition since it is the symmetric counterpart of the above definition: just reverse all the arrows! A simple example of a coequalizer can be given in the category of graphs.

Suppose we have two graphs G_1 and G_2 such that G_1 consists of only one dot (no arrows) and G_2 consists of two dots with an arrow linking them. We define two morphisms $s, t : G_1 \longrightarrow G_2$. The morphism s sends the dot of G_1 to the source of the arrow in G_2 and the morphism t sends the dot of G_1 to the target of the arrow in G_2. A coequalizer for this pair of morphisms must be a graph X and a morphism $e : G_2 \longrightarrow X$ such that $e \circ s = e \circ t$ and that is universal among similar objects. It is easy to see that the two dots in G_2 must be sent to a unique dot in X to satisfy the required condition. Consequently, there must be a loop in X for a morphism like e to exist. We must also verify that X together with e has the universal property of coequalizer; that is, if we have another morphism $e' : G_2 \longrightarrow X'$ such that $e' \circ s = e' \circ t$, then there must exist a unique morphism $X \xrightarrow{x} X'$ such that $x \circ e = e'$. Since X' has the same property as X, it must also contain a loop. The arrow in G_2 must be sent to a loop l in X' by e' so that there is a unique way of sending the loop X to l.

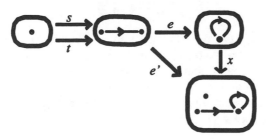

3.5.4. Exponential Objects

In the first section we pointed out that the set-theoretical operation of exponentiation B^A (for the set of all functions from A to B) generalizes the corresponding operation between natural numbers. This notation is very suggestive if we take into account our previous formula telling that $\#(B^A) = \#A^{\#B}$. How do we characterize this operation by means of a universal property?

Let us imagine a computer that is programmed to compute the values of functions from A to B when presented with elements of A. You could give the computer a function $A \xrightarrow{f} B$ (i.e., an element of B^A) and an element $a \in A$, and it would give as answer the element of $b \in B$ where f sends a. The program in the computer would be a function $B^A \times A \xrightarrow{ev} B$ that does the following: $ev(\langle f, a \rangle) = f(a)$ (given a pair consisting of an function f and an element $a \in A$, it computes $f(a)$). This function is called the *evaluation function*. This function is, in a way, the best possible choice among all other functions of the form $C \times A \xrightarrow{g} B$. This is expressed precisely in the following definition:

Definition 3.10. Let $\mathfrak{C}$ be a category in which there are products, and let $A, B \in Ob(\mathfrak{C})$. A morphism $B^A \times A \xrightarrow{ev} B$ is called an evaluation morphism if, for all morphisms $C \times A \xrightarrow{f} B$, there exists a unique morphism $\lceil f \rceil : C \longrightarrow B^A$ for which the following diagram commutes:

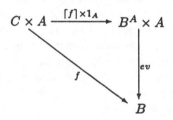

The universal property of the exponential object can be expressed by a very simple correspondence:

$$\frac{C \to B^A}{C \times A \to B}$$

An interesting example of exponential objects can be found in our category of a formal system. We are looking for an object B^A (a formula) that has the property that, if we can deduce it from C, then we can deduce B from $C \times A$ (that is $C \wedge A$); conversely, if we can deduce B from $C \wedge A$, then we should be able to deduce B^A from C alone. Symbolically we have:

$$\frac{C \vdash B^A}{C \wedge A \vdash B}$$

The obvious candidate for B^A is $A \Rightarrow B$. Of course, if $C \vdash A \Rightarrow B$, then $C \wedge A \vdash (A \Rightarrow B) \wedge A$ so that $C \wedge A \vdash B$ by modus ponens. Conversely, if $C \wedge A \vdash B$, then by Herbrand's deduction theorem we have that $C \vdash A \Rightarrow B$. Categories for which cartesian products as well as exponentials of two objects exist are called *cartesian closed categories*.

3.6. Functors

We have so far introduced as basic concepts the notions of object and morphisms. Morphisms, as we have seen, can be viewed as links between objects. In the present section, we investigate links between categories, the functors.

By way of introducing this notion, consider the canonical interpretation of the nominal category $\mathfrak{N}$ into the category of sets that assigns to the count noun 'dog', say, the set $\|DOG\|$ of all dogs. Recalling that morphisms in the nominal category were identifications of the type 'a dog is a mammal', it seems natural to interpret such a morphism as the function from the set $\|DOG\|$ of all dogs to the set $\|MAMMAL\|$ of all mammals that assigns to each dog his counterpart in the set of mammals. Identity morphisms of the type 'a dog is a dog' may be interpreted as the identity function 1_{DOG}. Finally, composition of morphisms of the nominal category may be interpreted naturally as composition of the corresponding functions. In other words, the canonical interpretation is just a function from objects and morphisms of $\mathfrak{N}$ into objects and morphisms of SET which preserve, in an obvious sense, the structure of the category. We thus arrive at the following:

Definition 3.11. Let $\mathfrak{C}$ and $\mathfrak{D}$ be two categories. A functor $F : \mathfrak{C} \to \mathfrak{D}$ is a mapping that assigns to each object $A \in Ob(\mathfrak{C})$, an object $F(A) \in Ob(\mathfrak{D})$ and to each morphism $A \xrightarrow{f} B$ in $\mathfrak{C}$, a morphism $F(f) : F(A) \longrightarrow F(B)$ in $\mathfrak{D}$ such that $F(1_X) = 1_{F(X)}$ and $F(g \circ f) = F(g) \circ F(f)$.

We can give another simple example of functors. To do so, let us define a very simple category $\mathfrak{L}$. It has only one object (which will be called "$*$"), the identity morphism 1 and an infinite class of morphisms $\alpha, \alpha^2, \alpha^3 \ldots$. In pictures:

Clearly, all these morphisms start and end at the only object available.

The composition of morphisms in this category is naturally defined by the following rule:

$$\alpha^m \circ \alpha^n \equiv \alpha^{m+n}$$

For example, $\alpha^3 \circ \alpha = \alpha^4$. The composition with the identity morphism is forced by the definition of a category, i.e., $1 \circ \alpha^m = \alpha^m$. This may seem very abstract since no meaning was actually given to the object or the morphisms. The flexibility of the definition of a category allows us to do that.

In itself, $\mathfrak{L}$ does not appear to be very interesting but it becomes so when we look at functors $F : \mathfrak{L} \to \mathfrak{Set}$ (where $\mathfrak{Set}$ is the category of set and functions). In fact, such a functor is simply a set $F(*)$ (image of the object of $\mathfrak{L}$ by F) and a class of functions $F(\alpha^m)$ (images of the morphisms in $\mathfrak{L}$). By the definition of functor we have that:

$$F(\alpha^m) = F(\alpha \circ \alpha^{m-1}) = F(\alpha) \circ F(\alpha^{m-1}) = \ldots = \underbrace{F(\alpha) \circ \ldots \circ F(\alpha)}_{m \text{ times}}$$

This last equation tells us that the image of α^m for any given m is strictly determined by composing $F(\alpha)$ with itself m times. We can conclude from this that a functor $F : \mathfrak{L} \to \mathfrak{Set}$ is simply a set A (corresponding to $F(*)$) and a function $A \xrightarrow{f} A$ (corresponding to $F(\alpha)$), i.e., an evolutive set or discrete dynamical system.

3.7. Natural Transformations

Natural transformations are, in spite of their names, usually not very "natural" for a beginner in category theory. In fact, it is a complicated notion which, however, is fundamental in category theory. So fundamental is it that Mac Lane has said that categories and functors were precisely invented to give a precise meaning to this particular notion. Natural transformations are links between functors, and so, links between links (see Mac Lane 1988).

As we did for functors, we introduce this notion through an example, namely, the category of evolutive sets or discrete dynamical systems. We leave justifications for the notion of natural transformation in the context of linguistics to M. La Palme, J. Macnamara and G. Reyes (this volume). The main observation is that evolutive systems may be represented as functors. Natural transformations are what correspond to morphisms between such systems.

Once we have represented evolutive sets as functors, the question is: how to represent morphisms of evolutive sets? Recall that a morphism $(A, f) \xrightarrow{\Phi} (B, g)$ in the category of evolutive sets is a function $A \xrightarrow{\Phi} B$ that preserves the evolution in the following sense: for each $a \in A$ we require that $\Phi(f(a)) = g(\Phi(a))$. In words, the evolution of a point $a \in A$ must be sent by Φ to the evolution of the point $\Phi(a)$ in B. This can also be expressed by the commutativity of the following diagram:

$$
\begin{array}{ccc}
F(*) & \xrightarrow{\ F(\alpha)\ } & F(*) \\
{\scriptstyle\Phi}\downarrow & & \downarrow{\scriptstyle\Phi} \\
G(*) & \xrightarrow{\ G(\alpha)\ } & G(*)
\end{array}
$$

If we remember that dynamical systems are functors of the type $F : \mathfrak{L} \to \mathfrak{Set}$, we see that the morphisms between dynamical systems are in fact morphisms between functors. Following this lead one arrives at the following:

Definition 3.12. Let $\mathfrak{C}$ and $\mathfrak{D}$ be two categories. Let $F, G : \mathfrak{C} \to \mathfrak{D}$ be two functors. A natural transformation $\tau : F \dot{\longrightarrow} G$ is a class of morphisms containing a morphism $F(X) \xrightarrow{\tau_X} G(X)$ in $Ar(\mathfrak{D})$ for each $X \in Ob(\mathfrak{C})$ and such that, for every morphism $X \xrightarrow{f} Y$ in $Ar(\mathfrak{C})$, the following diagram commutes:

$$
\begin{array}{ccc}
F(X) & \xrightarrow{\ F(f)\ } & F(Y) \\
{\scriptstyle\tau_X}\downarrow & & \downarrow{\scriptstyle\tau_Y} \\
G(X) & \xrightarrow{\ G(f)\ } & G(Y)
\end{array}
$$

Notice that natural transformations themselves between functors from a category $\mathfrak{C}$ to a category $\mathfrak{D}$ form a category. The reader is invited to define identity morphisms and composition. Now that functors have been integrated in the context of categories, we can apply to them the language developed in the previous sections. For example, two functors $F, G : \mathfrak{C} \to \mathfrak{D}$ are isomorphic if there are natural transformations $\tau : F \dot{\longrightarrow} G$ and $\eta : G \dot{\longrightarrow} F$ such that $\eta \circ \tau = 1_F$ and $\tau \circ \eta = 1_G$.

3.8. Adjoint Functors

In the present section we give some simple examples of adjoint functors. The first example is concerned with modal operators in logic, more particularly with a pictorial way to represent these operators. The second example will show how to view products and coproducts in a category as adjoints to a functor.

Our first example requires the definition of a special category whose objects are figures of the plane. This category will have one and only one morphism between a figure A and a figure B if and only if the figure A is contained in the figure B. This category is usually called $\mathcal{P}(\mathbf{R}^2)$. Now, suppose that there is a square grid covering the whole plane. We now define two functors $\Box, \Diamond : \mathcal{P}(\mathbf{R}^2) \to \mathcal{P}(\mathbf{R}^2)$ relative to this grid.

The □ functor assigns to a figure A all the squares in the grid that are "necessarily" contained in A; that is the squares that are completely covered by A. The ◇ functor assigns to a figure A all the squares in the grid that are "possibly" contained in A; that is the squares that are partly or totally covered by A. The next pictures show how the functors operate:

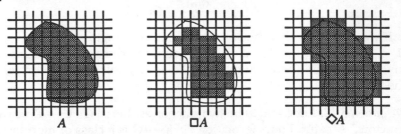

$$A \qquad \square A \qquad \diamond A$$

The reader may check that we have the following relation between these functors: if X and Y are figures, then X is contained in $\square Y$ if and only if $\diamond X$ is contained in Y or, with our usual notation:

$$\frac{X \to \square Y}{\diamond X \to Y}$$

We shall say that □ and ◇ are adjoint functors and, more precisely that ◇ is a left adjoint of □. In symbols: $\diamond \dashv \square$. The reader familiar with modal logic will recognize a particular determination of the operators of necessity and possibility.

Before stating our second example, we must define a particular category that can be built from any category $\mathfrak{C}$. We will denote this category by $\mathfrak{C} \times \mathfrak{C}$. Its objects are pairs of objects (A, B) where $A, B \in Ob(\mathfrak{C})$. A morphism $(A, B) \to (C, D)$ is simply a pair of morphisms (f, g) where $A \xrightarrow{f} C$ and $B \xrightarrow{g} D$.

There is clearly a functor $\Delta : \mathfrak{C} \to \mathfrak{C} \times \mathfrak{C}$ that assigns to each object $A \in Ob(\mathfrak{C})$ the object $(A, A) \in Ob(\mathfrak{C} \times \mathfrak{C})$ and, to each morphism $A \xrightarrow{f} B$ in $Ar(\mathfrak{C})$, the morphism $(f, f) \in Ar(\mathfrak{C} \times \mathfrak{C})$. This functor gives rise to two different adjunctions as follows: Assume that $\mathfrak{C}$ has products as well as coproducts. Then we can define two functors $Prod, Coprod : \mathfrak{C} \times \mathfrak{C} \to \mathfrak{C}$ as $Prod(A, B) \equiv A \times B$ (the categorical product) and $Coprod(A, B) \equiv A + B$ (the coproduct). The following properties hold for them:

$$\frac{\dfrac{\dfrac{X \to Prod(A, B)}{X \to A \ , \ X \to B}}{(X, X) \to (A, B)}}{\Delta(X) \to (A, B)} \qquad \frac{\dfrac{\dfrac{Coprod(A, B) \to Y}{A \to Y \ , \ B \to Y}}{(A, B) \to (Y, Y)}}{(A, B) \to \Delta(Y)}$$

The situation can be pictured as:

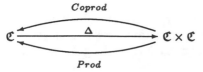

We say in this case that *Prod* is the right adjoint of Δ and that *Coprod* is the left adjoint of Δ (i.e., *Coprod* $\dashv \Delta \dashv$ *Prod*). We are now ready to give a precise meaning to the notion of adjunction:

Definition 3.13. Let $F : \mathfrak{C} \to \mathfrak{D}$ and $G : \mathfrak{D} \to \mathfrak{C}$ be two functors between categories $\mathfrak{C}$ and $\mathfrak{D}$. We say that F is left adjoint to G (or that G is right adjoint to F) if we have a bijective correspondence:

$$\frac{F(A) \overset{x}{\longrightarrow} B}{A \underset{\bar{x}}{\longrightarrow} G(B)}$$

for all $A \in Ob(\mathfrak{C})$ and all $B \in Ob(\mathfrak{D})$. Furthermore, this bijection must be natural in the following sense: For each morphism $A' \overset{f}{\longrightarrow} A$ and $B \overset{g}{\longrightarrow} B'$ we must have the following correspondences (where all the triangles commute):

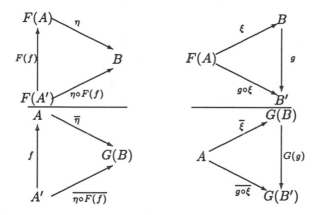

which mean in particular that $\overline{g \circ \xi} = G(g) \circ \bar{\xi}$ and $\bar{\eta} \circ f = \overline{\eta \circ F(f)}$. In this case we write $F \dashv G$.

3.9. Limits and Colimits

Our last subject will be limits and colimits. These notions will synthesize almost all universal properties we have defined so far in categories. As their name suggests, they are dual notions. For this reason, we will only give here the definition of limit and leave to the care of the reader the formal description of the notion of colimit.

We will use the formulation 'D is a diagram of $\mathfrak{C}$' to describe a family $\{D_i\}_{i \in I}$ of objects of $\mathfrak{C}$ with some morphisms $D_i \overset{x}{\longrightarrow} D_j$ (of $\mathfrak{C}$) linking these objects. The word 'diagram' still bears the same meaning we have used informally in the previous sections when we were talking about commutativity of diagrams. A diagram is, in some sense, just a part of a category.

Sometimes, in particular categories, we can build a kind of super-fork for a diagram. Let $\mathcal{C}$ be a category and D a diagram in $\mathcal{C}$. A super-fork for D must have an handle $X \in Ob(\mathcal{C})$ and a prong $X \xrightarrow{f_i} D_i$ for each object D_i in the diagram D. We also require a super-fork to be compatible with the diagram D. To do this, we require that the prongs of the super-fork obey the following: whenever two prongs form a triangle with an arrow in D, this triangle must be commutative. The next picture shows the context of a super-fork:

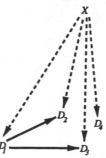

The category-theory representative of super-forks is usually called *cone*. We now give a precise definition for it:

Definition 3.14. Let D be a diagram in a category $\mathcal{C}$. A cone for D is an object X of $\mathcal{C}$ together with a family of arrows $\{X \xrightarrow{f_i} D_i\}_{i \in I}$ (where $\{D_i\}_{i \in I}$ is the family of objects of D) such that, for all arrows $D_i \xrightarrow{x} D_j$ of D, the following diagram commutes:

It is easy to see that super-forks are a generalisation of forks. If we take the diagram consisting of only two objects D_1 and D_2 (no arrows) in $\mathcal{C}$ then we realize that a super-fork for this diagram is simply a fork for D_1 and D_2 (an handle X and two prongs):

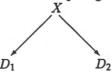

As we have noticed before, a product of two objects in a category is a terminal object in the category of forks on those two objects. If we pursue the generalisation, we are led to define a category of super-forks and define limits as terminal super-forks. The objects of this category are super-forks for the diagram D. If X and X' are two super-forks for D, then we define a morphism from X' to X to be a morphism $X' \xrightarrow{f} X$ in $\mathfrak{C}$ such that, for each object D_i in D, the triangle formed by the X'-prong on D_i, the X-prong on D_i and f commutes. We then simply define the notion of limit as a terminal object in this category of super-forks. Another clearly equivalent and perhaps simpler definition of the notion of limit is the following:

Definition 3.15. A limit for a diagram D (of a category $\mathfrak{C}$) is a cone X for D such that, for every other cone X' of D, there is one and only one morphism f such that:

commutes for all the D_i.

As we have seen a categorical product of A and B is clearly a limit for the diagram consisting of only the objects A and B. The colimit of the same diagram would naturally lead us to the coproduct (or sum). The limit of the empty diagram (no objects and therefore no arrows) is simply a terminal object for the category. We can see this by verifying the definitions. What is a cone for the empty diagram? Clearly, every object of the category is a cone for the empty diagram. So that a terminal cone is just a terminal object. We leave to the reader the verification that an equalizer is a limit for:

$$D_1 \rightrightarrows D_2$$

We use the epithet *complete* for categories in which limits of all diagrams exist. We call a category co-complete if colimits of all diagrams exist.

As a last remark we want to emphasize the fact that there is a special relation between limits and left adjoints. If a functor $F : \mathfrak{C} \longrightarrow \mathfrak{D}$ is the left adjoint of some functor and when $\mathfrak{C}$ and $\mathfrak{D}$ are complete categories, then F must preserve the limits. For example, in the case of product this implies that $F(A \times B) = F(A) \times F(B)$. Further, if $\mathfrak{C}$ and $\mathfrak{D}$ are co-complete categories then right adjoints preserve colimits.

Acknowledgments

We are indebted to John Macnamara for his many very helpful comments on the paper. Both authors were partially supported by individual grants from Canada's National Science and Engineering Research Council (NSERC).

References

Bénabou, J. (1991). Seminaire 1990-1991, *Cahiers de poétique comparée, Mezura* 25

Ellerman, D. P. (1988). Category theory and concrete universals. *Erkenntnis* 28: 409–429

Goldblatt, R. (1984). *Topoi: The Categorical Analysis of Logic*. 2th Ed. New York, NY: North Holland

La Palme, Marie, John Macnamara and Gonzalo E. Reyes (this volume). Reference, kinds and predicates

Lawvere, F. W. and S. H. Schanuel (1991). *Conceptual Mathematics: A First Introduction to Categories*. Buffalo, NY: Buffalo Workshop.

Mac Lane, S. (1988). *Categories for the Working Mathematician*. Graduate Texts in Mathematics 5, New York, NY: Springer-Verlag

Pawlak, Z. (1982). Rough sets. *International Journal of Information and Computer Science* 11: 145–172

Reyes, G. E. (1991a). A topos-theoretic approach to reference and modality. *Notre Dame Journal of Formal Logic* 32: 3, 359-391

Reyes, G. E. and Houmann Zolfaghari (1991b). Topos-theoretic approaches to modality. *Proceedings of the 1990 Como Meeting on Category Theory*, forthcoming in Springer-Verlag Lecture Notes in Mathematics

6

Reference, Kinds and Predicates

Marie La Palme Reyes, John Macnamara
and Gonzalo E. Reyes

The aim of this paper is to present a theory of reference for proper names (PNs), count nouns (CNs) and predicables (mainly adjectives, adjectival phrases, verbs, verb phrases).

The paper is divided into three sections and an Appendix. In the first, we describe briefly some theses on reference. These theses express the logical prerequisites for reference to take place. The second section, which is the core of the paper, describes a mathematical theory that is based on these theses. This theory, the theory of reference mentioned above, constitutes the foundation for the semantics of kinds and predicates.

The third section, which is devoted to some applications of the theory, is divided into three parts. In the first, we discuss and apply the notion of an underlying map which is directly linked to reference and kinds. In the second, we discuss some transformations that such parts of speech as CNs, MNs (mass nouns) and predicables may undergo and we provide semantical counterparts for these transformations. In the third, we mention some problems and possible developments of our theory. In the Appendix, we sketch a proof of a soundness theorem for the formal system introduced in the second section.

Our aim is to achieve an objective presentation of the logic of reference in a sense that we hope to make clear as we go along. Category theory gives us the tools needed for such an enterprise and consequently we will assume some knowledge of the basic notions of this theory in the mathematical section (for an introduction, see Magnan and Reyes this volume). We will see that concepts that are usually taken as primitive may be defined in categorical terms and that their relations may be studied "objectively" inside the theory, rather than postulated by ad-hoc axioms. Most important among these is the notion of entity and the corresponding relation of coincidence among members of different kinds. An analogy may clarify what we have in mind: the ancient Greeks considered the notion of space as an horizon. Space contained geometrical objects, but for them space itself was not a geometrical object. In consequence, it was impossible for them to study the connections between space and geometrical objects, such as the sphere, inside the space. For us, on the other hand, space itself is a geometrical object. It is on the same footing as the sphere, say, and modern geometry has developed means to study the rich connections among all of these geometrical objects. In a similar vein, in spite of the fundamental role that the notion of entity plays in logic, we feel that heretofore it has been seen as an horizon and, as a consequence, that the relation of entity to more usual kinds such as DOG, PERSON, has been either missed or misunderstood.

Earlier versions of the two first sections may be found in M. Reyes (1988) and in G. E. Reyes (1991).

1. Theses on Reference

The theses on reference in this section relate to the logic of natural language in respect of PNs, CNs, MNs and predicables. These expressions by no means exhaust the domain of reference. For instance, descriptions, demonstratives and pronouns are also referring expressions, but we will not study them in this paper. By the logic of a natural language, we understand partly an account of the contribution of parts of speech such as a PN like 'Freddie' or a CN like 'dog' to the truth conditions of the sentences in which they occur. We take this to be specifying the references of 'Freddie' and 'dog'. Expressions of these types combine to form sentences such as 'Freddie is a dog' whose interpretations are functions of the references of the separate expressions. This is one way of putting Frege's principle of compositionality for sentences. But, by the logic of a language we also mean the study of such relations as that between DOG and ANIMAL, the construction of a notion of entity that would permit us to treat a particular dog and a particular animal as a single entity, the study of predicables in relation to the nouns that typed them and the effect of such typing on inferences among sentences, etc.

To avoid misunderstanding, let us mention at the outset that we do not try to reduce the notion of reference to a physical, physiological or "natural" one. We just state some properties that this relation, reference, reveals on analysis. Whether reference may be reduced to any of the categories above is, for the purpose of the analysis, quite irrelevant. In this we follow at least the spirit of Kripke (1980) whose theory of names does not eliminate intentionality.

It is a remarkable property of natural languages that a PN, say, 'Picasso' picks out its referent uniquely every time it is uttered, regardless of whether its referent is present, of whether we know Picasso's whereabouts at that moment, of whether or not we are able to recognize Picasso and of whether or not we are referring to events that took place in the past or events that may take place in the future. What semantical structure should we postulate to ground such referential capabilities? The answer that we offer here has evolved from several sources. On the one hand some of the theses were inspired by earlier work of Macnamara (1982, 1986) based in part on work done by Gupta (1980), Geach (1972, 1980), Bressan (1972), Wiggins (1980). On the other hand, some aspects of the mathematical semantics developed here can be found in G. E. Reyes (1991), in G. E. Reyes and Zolfaghari (1991), in M. Reyes (1988) which, in turn, draw on categorical logic, a subject started by Lawvere in the 1960s and developed by him and several authors since then.

We view reference as the basic relation between language and reality, or, rather, between the words in some linguistic categories and reality. The emphasis on reference as the basic relation between language and reality puts us at odds with a strong idealist current in contemporary thought about the semantics of natural languages as exemplified, for instance, in Eco, Santambrogio and Violi (1988). It is not our intention to launch a full attack on this position, but rather to show that our realistic approach to reference leads to a logic that we believe has both depth and elegance; one that yields rich insights for linguistics and the theory of mind. For a critical review of the above book see Macnamara (1989).

1.1. PNs Refer Rigidly.

A PN, say 'Nixon', has the property of picking out its unique referent throughout all actual as well as counterfactual situations, past, present and future of which Nixon is a constituent. A biographer of Nixon would use the single PN 'Nixon' to refer to the boy who grew up in California, the young politician who won his first election and the president who was forced to resign from office, regardless of the different times and situations. The biographer may be unsure whether Nixon won his first election by fraudulent means and he may discuss both the possibility that he did employ such means and the possibility that he did not to arrive at the truth. In other words, he must consider counterfactual as well as factual situations (since clearly both possibilities cannot be realized) involving Nixon, the referent of 'Nixon', in order to describe the actual course of events. Similarly, to explain Nixon's actions, the biographer should entertain a series of possibilities about Nixon's motives and evaluate them critically. The point is that we are forced to consider counterfactual situations about the referent of the PN 'Nixon'. The rigidity of the reference of a PN has been forcefully argued by Kripke (1980).

The role of counterfactual situations in determining the actual is further exemplified in classical Mechanics. To determine the real trajectory of a body, we use the calculus of variations and compute the Lagrangian of all its possible trajectories, most of which are only logically, not physically, possible. We choose as the real trajectory the one for which the Lagrangian has a minimum (or stationary) value. The possible is essential to describe the real.

PNs should be contrasted in this respect with descriptions, such as 'the President of the United States', and pronouns, such as 'you', whose referents vary systematically with the occasion of use. Notice, however, that several people may have the same name, say 'Nixon', and hence, as Barwise and Perry (1983) have insisted, the person referred to by the PN 'Nixon' depends also on the occasion of use. Nevertheless, PNs are still rigid in the weaker sense that their referents do not vary systematically with the occasion of use.

1.2. Reference to an Individual by Means of a PN Involves a Kind.

This assertion, which characterizes the approach we are developing, rests on the observation that to specify the referent of the PN 'Nixon', individuate him and trace his identity throughout all actual and counterfactual situations we need a kind. Kinds are typically interpretations of CNs. (Interpretations of MNs will be considered later.) Take the kind PERSON (we will always use capital letters when referring to the interpretations of expressions of the language) which is the interpretation of the CN 'person'. Such a kind is a set with further structure, but for the present purposes assume that kinds are just sets. When we say that a certain object is individuated, we mean that it is in a kind, so individuation is in fact the membership relation of set. The expression "tracing identity" that is common in the philosophical literature we understand as the relation of equality of the set. In this we differ from philosophers who attach the notion of "tracing identity" to the notion of time: the identity of a person, for instance, being "assembled" or "traced" through successive slices of time. We treat the identity of a person as primitively given by the kind PERSON. We say that membership and equality, or individuation and identity tracing are of a piece and are given by the kind. We cannot have equality without having membership and vice versa. Incidentally mathematics never separates these two notions. A last remark is that we will use the notion of situations heuristically for the time being, but we promise to come back to it. Let us return to the example of 'Nixon' and the necessity for a kind to be involved in reference to the bearer of the name. The boy in California, the young politician and the president remained one and the same person, although he successively stopped being a boy, a young politician and a president. As Aristotle emphasized, change requires something to change. The boy changes and becomes an adult but to understand the link between the two there must be something that remains the same. There must be a constancy that underlies the change of the boy into the adult. We claim that such a constancy is supplied by a kind to which the individual experiencing the change belongs.

Fairy tales may seem to provide counter-examples, for they frequently tell of changes of species. It may be contrary to biological laws that a prince should be turned into a frog, but such changes are intelligible even to children. One way to explain this is to appeal to a kind such as ANIMAL. The prince and the frog are the same animal. Logic requires such a kind, though the story teller may not name it explicitly, see M. Reyes (this volume). Moreover, successful reference requires adequate provision for individuating the target of reference. This means that a PN must be typed by a CN; 'Nixon', for example, is typed by 'person'. On the other hand, speakers who use the name 'Nixon' need not refer to the kind PERSON. Otherwise there would be an infinite and disastrous regress; because they would also have to refer to the kind that individuates that kind, and so on for ever. In passing we remark that although there is no individuation apart from kinds, successful identification of an individual does not require reference to the relevant kind. For example, a dog may succeed in identifying his mistress without any use whatever of a CN. Perhaps the dog's task is simplified by his being oblivious to the fact that his mistress may be a woman, a professor, a mother as well as being a person (see also section 3.3).

One might imagine at first that the job of specifying the bearer of PN and tracing its identity might be performed by a demonstrative, like 'this', or a pronoun, like 'she'. Demonstratives are often used to teach PNs, as in "This is John". Can it be that demonstratives individuate the bearer of the PN or do they themselves need to be supported in their semantic role by a kind? As Wittgenstein has pointed out, demonstratives are woefully vague. Suppose you see an elephant at the zoo pacing up and down and someone says "Look at this", to what does 'this' refer? It could refer to the elephant, but it could also refer to his trunk, or the texture of his skin or to his way of walking. To make the reference precise a kind is needed and in this case even the utterance of the CN which is interpreted by that kind is needed. It follows that if after the introduction "This is John" the name 'John' does not inherit the indeterminism of the demonstrative, then some unspoken factor has specified the reference of the demonstrative. Similar remarks apply to pronouns. If, on their own, demonstratives and pronouns fail to specify the bearer of a PN, then neither do they trace the bearer's identity on their own.

1.3. Any Reference to an Individual Involves a Kind.

This assertion is a generalization of the preceding one. PNs are just one type of expression among several that refer to individuals: descriptions, demonstratives, indexicals, pronouns, etc. These differ from PNs by not referring rigidly. There is, however, a definite sense in which to refer is to refer rigidly. In this sense, even descriptions refer rigidly. Consider the description 'the President of the United States'. It is true that the person picked out by this description depends in a systematic way on occasions of use and it is this feature that we emphasize when we say that descriptions do not refer rigidly. But notice that once a person has been picked out, once the reference has been fixed, this expression refers as fixedly as a PN. Indeed we can understand sentences such as 'the President of United States was not born in California', though he was not a president at the time of his birth. Such expressions refer to one and the same person throughout all real and counterfactual situations in which this person appears. It follows that the kind involved in the reference is not PRESIDENT but rather PERSON tacitly understood.

We now consider some alternative approaches to the problem of individuating and tracing the identity of an individual. Aristotle seems to have searched for a solution to the problem by using his distinction between substance and accident, allowing accidents to change and tracing identity through substance. Substance, for Aristotle, is metaphysically complex, being composed of matter and form. For example, he assumed that a common ovine form (nature) explained why two sheep are sheep (sharing membership in the kind SHEEP). What made the two distinct, according to Aristotle, was distinctness of matter. But now consider the CN 'river'. What are we to take as its substance? The answer 'water' suggests itself. 'Water', however, is not a CN but a MN, and therefore it fails to specify what to count as 'a water'. If such a term is interpretable, it could only mean something like 'a body of water'. The proposal thus amended would amount to tracing the identity of rivers through the kind BODY OF WATER quite in agreement with the thesis 1.2. Unfortunately this does not work either, since the body of water in a river is continuously changing and hence the identity of a river is left unaccounted for. This observation owes much to our reading of Geach (1957, p. 71).

There is a modern, more sophisticated, version of Aristotle's suggestion: trace the identity of, say, Nixon through the matter of his body conceptualized now as the molecules (or atoms or elementary particles) that make up his body. Once again this amounts to a proposal to use a kind such as BUNCH OF MOLECULES to trace Nixon's identity. But this will not do the job: the bunch of molecules that constituted Nixon's

body at the time of his birth is quite different from the one that constituted his body at the time he celebrated his first year in the presidency.
It follows that Nixon may not be identified with a bunch of molecules
and that BUNCH OF MOLECULES does not trace his identity in the
proper manner.

Leibniz had an answer to the problem of identity which is genuinely
different from Aristotle's and also from ours. He attempts to individuate
and trace the identity of an individual by specifying its predicates.
He makes the tacit and apparently plausible hypothesis that CNs and
predicables have the same logical role; thus, he places membership in
the kind, say SHIRT, on the same logical footing as the interpretation
of 'to be white', for instance. Usual formalizations of first-order logic
have followed him in this respect. From our realist point of view, which
starts from the relation of reference, this position still amounts to tracing
identity of individuals through a kind, although a universal kind of bare
particulars such as 'entities' or 'things' or 'objects' or 'individuals'. We
view some of the arguments offered in this section as an indication
that we have no conceptual access to a domain of bare particulars.
On the other hand, Leibniz's position does not seem incoherent for
somebody who rejects reference altogether, a nominalist like Leibniz,
for instance, or an idealist like several modern philosophers (assuming
that nominalism or idealism, as the case may be, is itself coherent; a
non-trivial assumption!).

From a logical point of view, the demonstrative in 'This is John'
does not specify the reference of 'John' given all the ambiguity of the
demonstrative 'this'. Similarly, from a purely logical standpoint it is
logically impossible to count whites in a room where there is, among
other things, a white shirt. We cannot know what to count as one white
given the fact that the pockets, the sleeves and even threads or fibers may
be regarded as different whites. On the other hand, it is a psychological
fact that people can refer to a person by saying "This is John" and
can count whites in a room with some measure of success. It follows,
therefore, that in both cases an implicit notion of entity is at work. In the
first case, the implicit notion seems to be PERSON, whereas in the other
it may be REASONABLY SIZED OBJECT IN A ROOM. Furthermore,
this notion of entity is not postulated but constructed from the kinds
that are exemplified in a given situation. We will come back to this point
in section 2.3. We believe that this notion of entity is so readily available
that we have the impression that no kind is involved in referring, and
this it is that makes Leibniz's view so tempting.

We consider the notion of kind as basic. This notion cannot be reduced
to more basic notions. Of course this does not preclude the possibility of
having a well founded and rich theory of kinds. Set theory is similar in

this respect. The notion of set cannot be reduced to more basic notions. This fact, however, does not preclude the development of a very rich theory such as set theory (axiomatized by Zermelo-Frankel, say) which is also based on an undefinable and unanalyzed notion of set. In spite of this, set theory has brought new and higher standards of correctness to the whole of mathematics. Kinds are the constitutive domains which allow us to use quantifiers and the equality symbol correctly. We will not assume that we have an infallible criterion (psychological or otherwise) to decide whether two members of a given kind are identical, but we will postulate that there is a truth in the intuition that they are, regardless of our ability to establish it. All that we can assert is that a kind has members that are individuated and that it makes sense to say that two members are identical. This is quite clear for such kinds as BOY and BICYCLE.

This thesis applies also to individuals referred to by means of MNs. When we use 'water' we may refer to a particular member of the kind LIQUID, as in the expression 'Water is H_2O'. This kind, since it is the interpretation of a CN, is conceptualized as a discreet space or set without further structure whose members, besides water, include milk, wine, orange juice, etc. But we could also refer to a 'quantity of water' or a 'portion of water' as in the expression 'The water poured on the oleander during the summer'. In this case the kind involved in the reference is PORTION OF WATER or QUANTITY OF WATER which we conceptualize as the supremum of several smaller portions of water all contained in a $\bigvee$-lattice. (See section 2.5.6. We will discuss relations between kinds in section 3.1.)

1.4. Kinds are Modally Constant.

This means that the kind WOMAN, for example, is a constant set that does not change as young girls grow up to become women and as old women die. As a consequence, the statement 'All women are mortal' makes reference to all women independent of times and situation. Contrast this with the variable set PRESENT SENATORS. The membership of such a set changes from time to time. The powerful intuition that we can talk of dead women as well as future ones supports our claim that WOMAN is modally constant, picking out the set of all women who ever were, are or will be. And the expression 'All women' picks out all women, not just those who are present in the situation referred to. Following a different line of thought Putnam (1978) came to the same conclusion.

In claiming that all kinds are modally constant we differ from Gupta (1980, p.27) who claims that BACHELOR is not modally constant because a person who is a bachelor may cease to be a bachelor. PERSON in contrast, he would hold to be modally constant because the individual who is a person cannot cease to be a person. There are several things wrong with this claim. One of them is that it fails to take account of our ability to understand fairy tales in which persons cease to be persons and become frogs, for instance. It seems to us that the distinction between "substance sorts" and "non-substance sorts" does not survive the serious consideration of fairy tales.

We believe, however, that Gupta's idea of a substance sort derives from a valuable intuition that can be traced to Aristotle. There are several passages scattered through Aristotle's writings claiming that for each individual there is a unique kind. For each such individual he expects a unique answer to the question "What is it?", an answer giving the "essential nature" of the individual. (See, for instance, J. Barnes 1984 *Post. Ana.* 90a30 and 92a6; *Topics* 101b39; *Metaphysics* 1031b20.) Our view is that what is guiding Gupta, as Aristotle before him, is an intuition of a psychologically privileged unique kind related to each perceptual formation of a perceptual figure. The psychological basis for this claim is spelled out at length in Macnamara and G. E. Reyes (this volume). We draw attention to two features of the Aristotle-Gupta intuition. One is the uniqueness of the supposed substance sort that is determined by the relevant psychological principles. The second is to remark with Quine, that the notion of what is essential depends on the kind considered. Quine (1960, p. 199) pointed out that the properties essential to a mathematician *qua* mathematician include rationality, whereas those essential to the same mathematician *qua* cyclist do not. Although Quine is unhappy with any form of modal logic (probably because he allows bare particulars), the point just stated is a valid one, provided the kinds in question specify the same individual. There are no logically privileged kinds.

Another reason for postulating that all kinds are constant is that Gupta's theory rests on a distinction between essential and accidental properties, substance sorts being based on essential properties and other sorts being based on accidental ones. While not adverse to the distinction, we do not wish to rest the foundation of our semantics on so thorny an issue. We handle the distinction in our own way in the following thesis.

1.5. Predicates of Kinds and Not Kinds Themselves Are Subject to Change and Modalities.

First, a remark on usage: we use the word 'predicate' to mean property and 'predicable' for the linguistic expressions that express a predicate.

As we have seen in the preceding thesis, kinds remain constant from situation to situation; they are the standards of constancy against which we understand change and modalities. Part of the burden of change and modalities is carried by predicates and not by kinds themselves. In particular, necessity and possibility apply to predicates of a given kind. For example, 'to be a boy' (not to be confused with membership in the kind BOY) is a necessary predicate of the kind BOY. That is any boy is a boy, necessarily; no person is necessarily a boy, though he may at one time be a boy. A member of the kind PASSENGER is, *qua* passenger, necessarily a passenger.

We think that attempts to apply modalities to kinds themselves to form new "kinds" such as "POSSIBLE APPLE", "POSSIBLE CAR", "POSSIBLE BOY" and "POSSIBLE MAN" in the manner employed by Gupta (1980) to define "modal constancy" are not well founded. There are serious difficulties with the interpretation of such expressions as 'possible apple' and 'possible boy' as kinds. Does a portion of apple jelly count as a possible apple on the grounds that it came from a single apple? Or again, does a piece of junk metal count as a possible car. Quine (1953) asked the question: "How many possible men are there in that doorway?" These observations show that a putative kind POSSIBLE MAN would be rather uncontrollable and will not perform the functions of a genuine kind (e.g., individuation). On the other hand, we may ask of a given fruit whether it is possibly an apple. The intuition that "apples are necessarily apples" that Gupta tried to express by means of POSSIBLE APPLE, should be expressed rather as: "the interpretation of the predicable 'to be an apple' of the kind FRUIT is a necessary predicate of certain fruits." We cannot eliminate the kind FRUIT in this formulation, since the statement "the interpretation of the predicable 'to be an apple' of the kind INGREDIENT IN A RECIPE is a necessary predicate of certain ingredients in a recipe" should be false for cooking to be possible at all. Interestingly, possible objects seem to be ruled out by Aquinas (1964) in his commentary on Aristotle's *Metaphysics*.

Our way of considering possibility and necessity agrees with the grammar of these notions as M. Reyes (1988) pointed out. Suppose we find an archeological site with skeletons of some anthropoids. If we are asked whether some are humanoids, we could naturally reply that "three of these are possibly the skeletons of humanoids," but we would not say "there are three skeletons of possible humanoids." Similarly, we do not say that Mr. and Mrs. X have twelve possible children, but rather that it is possible for Mr. and Mrs. X to have twelve children. None of this is to deny that a kind POSSIBLE CHILD (PC) might be constructed on the basis of the kind CHILD. The non-real members of

PC would be confined to counterfactual situations. They would satisfy the concept of a child, whatever that turns out to be. Naturally, the theory of how PC is constructed would require considerable, as yet unknown, mathematical resources. If successful, however, we would manage to handle such cases as that proposed by Bach (1986) in which a man is correctly said to be writing a novel even if the novel is never finished.

Although kinds are modally constant, members of kinds may change and even come into existence and cease to exist though we can still refer to them. To account for the fact that members are constituents of some situations and not of others, we assume that kinds come equipped with a predicate of existence or constituency. This is the function that associates with a particular member of a kind, the set of actual and counterfactual situations of which he is a constituent.

We remark briefly that situations do not constitute a kind as, for instance, dogs do. They are, rather, a logical tool which can be "extracted" if one wishes from the structures that allow us to interpret our language. Because of this we are able to speak about counterfactual or possible situations as a *façon de parler* without running into difficulties with possible members of a kind. We do not postulate a kind SITUATIONS as we postulate a kind DOG. We will come back to this question in section 2.1.

Predicables such as 'is sick', 'is pale' and 'is a passenger', since they are related to situations, enable us to handle change. A person may be sick or may be a passenger in one situation and not in another. We must remember that there is a difference between being a member of a kind K and having the property of 'being a K'. Most treatments of modal logic interpret the modal connectives 'possible' and 'necessary' in relation to possible worlds. A possible world is taken to be a fully determinate universe. Take the claim that it would have been possible for you to sit on the armchair, when you actually sat on the sofa. To interpret the possibility in question most logicians appeal to a universe in which everything is just as it actually is except that you are sitting in the armchair rather than on the sofa. Some, like Kripke, claim that the state of a possible world is a matter of stipulation. Mates (1986, chap. 14) queries whether our stipulated world in which everything is unchanged except where you are sitting might not be inconsistent. He points out that our knowledge of the actual world is so limited that we simply do not know what changes we can stipulate without running foul of the laws of nature.

We hold that modal intuitions are local. They are confined to the situations that are relevant to the conversation in which the modal claim is made. What is more, we do not require that even in the local situation everything except where you sit is held constant from the factual situation to the counterfactual one. All we claim is that we can interpret locally the claim that you might have sat in the armchair; we know what the local situation would have to be like for the claim to be true.

Since modal claims are interpreted by means of situations rather than by means of possible worlds, it follows that the logic of kinds which we present is intuitionist, not classical. Classical logic claims that every proposition is either true or false. The distinguishing characteristic of intuitionist logic is that it allows that some propositions may be neither true nor false.

1.6. All Predicates Are Typed by Kinds.

This thesis will receive a more precise formulation in the next section but for the moment we will give some examples that, we hope, will convey what we mean. Sommers (1982, p. 297) has already drawn attention to the fact that certain predicables seem to have no applicability in certain domains. For instance, 'sick' may be applied to persons, dogs and even plants, but it seems to be meaningless when applied to electrons and natural numbers. This leads us to interpret a predicable as a family of predicates, a family indexed by the system of kinds that belong to its domain of application. We insist that the domain should be a system of kinds and not an unstructured class of kinds. This is one way in which our approach differs from that of Sommers. We will try to make our meaning more intuitively accessible.

Everyone knows that 'addled' can be applied only to eggs and brains. They may not appreciate how widespread the phenomenon of typing is in natural languages. The predicable 'dull' denotes quite different attributes as applied to days, knives, boys and courses. 'Run' applied to dogs and governments denotes very different actions. Plato drew attention to the fact that although every thief is a person, a good thief is not usually a good person. Similarly, although every baby is a person, a big baby is not a big person. Although every person is an animal, it does not follow that a white person is a white animal, since white animal is exemplified by white rabbits and white mice, whose covering is of a quite different shade from the skin of white people. At the same time not all predicables behave in this way. A male baby is a male person; every winged bird is a winged animal; every old passenger is an old person; and so on.

This concludes the first section. We do not pretend that these theses exhaust the properties of reference, we might have added some more or presented them in a more economical way since, for instance, the third thesis is a generalization of the second. Our purpose was different. We wanted to stress some of the logical prerequisites necessary for reference to happen at all. These logical prerequisites are usually overlooked or ignored or dismissed.

2. Mathematical Formulation of the Theory of Kinds

2.1. Situations

Let $\mathcal{P} = < P, \leq >$ be a non-empty pre-ordered set; namely, $\leq$ satisfies $U \leq U$ and if $W \leq V$ and $V \leq U$ then $W \leq U$. We think of P as a set of "factual and counterfactual" situations, and of $\leq$ as the relation of "having more information than", namely, $V \leq U$ whenever V has more information than U.

A set D is *downward closed* if whenever $U \in D$ and $V \leq U$ then $V \in D$. We define:

$$\Gamma(\Omega) = \{D \subseteq P : D \text{ is downward closed}\}$$

(Both Γ and Ω and hence $\Gamma(\Omega)$ have definite meanings in topos theory. Here, however, $\Gamma(\Omega)$ turns out to be the set of downward closed subsets of P.) Clearly $\Gamma(\Omega)$ is a distributive lattice with respect to the set-theoretical operations of union ($\cup$) and intersection ($\cap$) and has a smallest ($\emptyset$) as well as a largest (P) element. In fact, more is true of this lattice. But first let us give the following definitions. A *Heyting algebra* is a bounded distributive lattice L with an "implication" operation:

$$\Rightarrow: L \times L \longrightarrow L$$

satisfying the following condition:

$$x \leq y \Rightarrow z \text{ iff } x \wedge y \leq z$$

for all $x, y, z \in L$. A *co-Heyting algebra* is a bounded distributive lattice L with a "subtraction" operation $\backslash : L \times L \longrightarrow L$ satisfying the following condition:

$$x \backslash y \leq z \text{ iff } x \leq y \vee z$$

for all $x, y, z \in L$. A *bi-Heyting algebra* is a bounded lattice that is both a Heyting and a co-Heyting algebra.

Proposition 2.1.1. $\Gamma(\Omega)$ is a bi-Heyting algebra.

Proof. It is clear that $\Gamma(\Omega)$ is closed under arbitrary unions and intersections. We may define implication ($\Rightarrow$) and subtraction ($\backslash$) as follows:

$$D \Rightarrow D' = \cup\{D'' \in \Gamma(\Omega) : D \cap D'' \subseteq D'\}$$

$$D \backslash D' = \cap \{D'' \in \Gamma(\Omega) : D \subseteq D' \cup D''\}$$

Implication and subtraction have the following fundamental properties (adjointness):

$$D'' \subseteq D \Rightarrow D' \; iff \; D \cap D'' \subseteq D'$$

$$D \backslash D' \subseteq D'' \; iff \; D \subseteq D' \cup D''$$

To help us understand situations better, let us take a particular case. Let $P = \{U_0, ..., U_8\}$ such that:

Let $\{U_0, ..., U_4\}$ be D_1 and $\{U_5, ..., U_7\}$ be D_2 so:

$$\Gamma(\Omega) = \{P, \emptyset, D_1, D_2, \{U_0\}, \{U_2\}, \{U_4\}, \{U_5\}, \{U_7\}, \{U_8\}, \{U_0, U_2\}, ...\}$$

We say that a downward closed set is a *connected component* of P if there is a "chain" between any two situations in the set. So D_1, D_2 and $\{U_8\}$ are the connected components of P in this example. The connected components are like instantaneous snapshots. Going along the chain is like making different enlargements of the same snapshot. Factual and counterfactual situations belong to different connected components.

2.2. Kinds and Predicates

We define a *kind* as a couple (A, ϵ_A) where A is a set and $\epsilon_A : A \longrightarrow \Gamma(\Omega)$ is a map. We think of kinds as interpretations of count nouns (CNs) such as 'person', 'dog', 'animal'. The interpretation of 'dog', for instance, is the set DOG of all dogs that ever were, are or will be together with the map $\epsilon_{DOG} : DOG \longrightarrow \Gamma(\Omega)$, which associates with a particular dog, say Freddie, the set of situations of which Freddie is a constituent. Notice that if $U \in \epsilon_{DOG}(Freddie)$ and $V \leq U$, then the information that Freddie is a constituent is preserved from U to V, namely, $V \in \epsilon_{DOG}(Freddie)$, and so $\epsilon_{DOG}(Freddie) \in \Gamma(\Omega)$. Notice also that 'Freddie' is a proper name and is interpreted as a member of the kind DOG in keeping with thesis 1.2. (To simplify the notation we will often replace the couple (A, ϵ_A) by A.)

Kinds constitute a category $\mathcal{K}$ under the following definition of morphism: a *morphism* $f : (A, \epsilon_A) \longrightarrow (B, \epsilon_B)$ is a function $f : A \longrightarrow B$ such that $\epsilon_A(a) \subseteq \epsilon_B(f(a))$ for all $a \in A$. In fact, the category of kinds constitutes a category of fuzzy sets. Our interpretation, however, is not one of fuzzy membership but of degree of constituency or, more intuitively, of extent of existence. The properties of the category of kinds are: it has products (needed to handle n-place predicables), coproducts (needed to handle the notion of entity) and exponentials (also needed to handle predicables).

Proposition 2.2.1 The category $\mathcal{K}$ of kinds is a distributive, complete and co-complete category with exponentials

Proof. What this means is that $\mathcal{K}$ has arbitrary products (in particular, a terminal object 1), arbitrary coproducts (in particular, an initial object 0), equalizers, coequalizers and exponentials.

Products. The terminal object is $1 = (\{*\}, \epsilon_{\{*\}})$ where $\epsilon_{\{*\}}(*) = P \in \Gamma(\Omega)$. The product of (A, ϵ_A) and (B, ϵ_B), for instance, is the diagram:

$$(A \times B, \epsilon_{A \times B})$$
$$\pi_A \swarrow \qquad \searrow \pi_B$$
$$(A, \epsilon_A) \qquad\qquad (B, \epsilon_B)$$

where $\epsilon_{A \times B}(a, b) = \epsilon_A(a) \cap \epsilon_B(b)$. The general case is obtained in the same way. The fundamental property of products is that a morphism from any object (C, ϵ_C) of the category into the product of two objects (A, ϵ_A) and (B, ϵ_B), for instance, is the same as the couple of morphisms from (C, ϵ_C) into (A, ϵ_A) and (C, ϵ_C) into (B, ϵ_B), namely that:

$$\frac{(C, \epsilon_C) \longrightarrow (A \times B, \epsilon_{A \times B})}{(C, \epsilon_C) \longrightarrow (A, \epsilon_A), \ (C, \epsilon_C) \longrightarrow (B, \epsilon_B)}$$

Equalizers. The equalizer, for instance, of two morphisms:

$$(A, \epsilon_A) \ \underset{g}{\overset{f}{\rightrightarrows}} \ (B, \epsilon_B)$$

is the diagram:

$$(E, \epsilon_E) \overset{q}{\longrightarrow} (A, \epsilon_A) \ \underset{g}{\overset{f}{\rightrightarrows}} \ (B, \epsilon_B)$$

where:

$$E \overset{q}{\longrightarrow} A \ \underset{g}{\overset{f}{\rightrightarrows}} \ B$$

is an equalizer, namely, $E = \{a \in A : f(a) = g(a)\}$ and q is the inclusion map. We define $\epsilon_E(a) = \epsilon_A(q(a))$.

Coproducts. The initial object 0 is $0 = (\emptyset, \epsilon_\emptyset)$ where $\epsilon_\emptyset$ is the only function $\emptyset \xrightarrow{\epsilon_\emptyset} \Gamma(\Omega)$. The coproduct, for instance, of (A_0, ϵ_0) and (A_1, ϵ_1) is the diagram:

$$(A_0 + A_1, \epsilon_{A_0+A_1})$$

$$(A_0, \epsilon_{A_0}) \qquad (A_1, \epsilon_{A_1})$$

such that:

$$A_0 + A_1 = \{(a,0) : a \in A_0\} \cup \{(a,1) : a \in A_1\},$$

$\epsilon_{A_0+A_1}(a,0) = \epsilon_{A_0}(a)$ and $\epsilon_{A_0+A_1}(a,1) = \epsilon_{A_1}(a)$

The fundamental property of the coproduct is similar to that of the product:

$$\frac{(A+B, \epsilon_{A+B}) \longrightarrow (C, \epsilon_C)}{(A, \epsilon_A) \longrightarrow (C, \epsilon_C), (B, \epsilon_B) \longrightarrow (C, \epsilon_C)}$$

Coequalizers. The coequalizer of two morphisms:

$$(A, \epsilon_A) \; \underset{g}{\overset{f}{\rightrightarrows}} \; (B, \epsilon_B),$$

for instance, is the diagram:

$$(A, \epsilon_A) \; \underset{g}{\overset{f}{\rightrightarrows}} \; (B, \epsilon_B) \xrightarrow{[\ ]} (C, \epsilon_C)$$

where:

$$A \; \underset{g}{\overset{f}{\rightrightarrows}} \; B \xrightarrow{[\ ]} C$$

is a coequalizer, namely, $C = \{[b] : b \in B\}$ where $[b]$ is the equivalence class of b for the smallest equivalence relation containing the couples $\{(f(a), g(a)) : a \in A\}$ and $\epsilon_C([b]) = \bigvee_{x \in [b]} \epsilon_B(x)$.

Exponentials. The exponential of the kind (B, ϵ_B) to the kind (A, ϵ_A) is the diagram:

$$(B^A, \epsilon_{B^A}) \times (A, \epsilon_A) \xrightarrow{ev} (B, \epsilon_B)$$

where:

$$B^A \times A \xrightarrow{ev} B$$

is the exponential of the kind B to the kind A, namely:

$$B^A = \{A \xrightarrow{f} B\},$$

$$ev(f, a) = f(a) \in B$$

and:

$$\epsilon_{B^A}(f) = \bigcap_{a \in A} \{\epsilon_A(a) \Rightarrow \epsilon_B(f(a))\}$$

The exponential has the following fundamental property (adjointness):

$$\frac{(C, \epsilon_C) \longrightarrow (B^A, \epsilon_{B^A})}{(C, \epsilon_C) \times (A, \epsilon_A) \longrightarrow (B, \epsilon_B)}$$

We say that the first map is the exponential transpose of the second map.

This category is distributive in the sense that finite products distribute over finite coproducts (even arbitrary coproducts in this case): $A \times 0 \simeq 0$ and that:

$$A \times (B + C) \simeq A \times B + A \times C$$

Indeed, this category is even locally distributive and thus according to Lawvere (in press), the category of kinds constitutes a category of spaces.

To complete the proof one should check the universal properties of products, equalizers, coproducts, etc. □

Since colimits are especially important in the development of our theory we will construct them explicitly in the next section. By a general theorem of category theory, colimits exist since we have an initial object, coproducts and coequalizers.

Furthermore, $\mathcal{K}$ is not the category of $\Gamma(\Omega)$-valued sets (see Fourman and Scott 1979 for an exposition of this category). We do, however, have an obvious functor that sends an object (A, ϵ_A) of $\mathcal{K}$ into an object (A, δ_A) of $\Gamma(\Omega)$- valued sets. We define $\delta_A : A \times A \longrightarrow \Gamma(\Omega)$ as $\delta_A(a, a') = \{U \in \epsilon_A(a) : a = a'\}$ and notice that a morphism $f : (A, \epsilon_A) \longrightarrow (B, \epsilon_B)$ is sent into the map $F : A \times B \longrightarrow \Gamma(\Omega)$ given by:

$$F(a, b) = \{U \in \epsilon_A(a) : f(a) = b\}$$

where:

$$\delta_A(a, a') = \{U \in \epsilon_A(a) \cap \epsilon_A(a') : a = a'\} \in \Gamma(\Omega)$$

and:

$$F(a, b) = \{U \in \epsilon_A(a) : f(a) = b\} \in \Gamma(\Omega)$$

We define a *predicate* of a kind A to be a map $\phi : A \longrightarrow \Gamma(\Omega)$. We think of predicates of A as the interpretation of predicables (adjectives, VP, etc.) such as 'white', 'mortal', 'run' and 'find something' sorted by the CN whose interpretation is the kind A. For instance, the predicate RUN of the kind PERSON is the map:

$$RUN : PERSON \longrightarrow \Gamma(\Omega)$$

which associates with a person, say John, the set of situations in which John runs. Once again it is easy to see that RUN(JOHN) is a downward closed set, i.e., is a member of $\Gamma(\Omega)$.

We define an *ϵ-predicate* of a kind (A, ϵ_A) as a predicate ϕ of the kind (A, ϵ_A) such that $\phi(a) \subseteq \epsilon_A(a)$ for all $a \in A$. (We will come back to the notion of ϵ-predicate in section 2.4.) ϵ-predicates constitute a category $Pred_\epsilon(\mathcal{K})$ with the following definition of objects and morphisms: an *object* is a couple (A, ϕ) where A is in fact an abbreviation for the kind (A, ϵ_A) and:

$$\phi : A \longrightarrow \Gamma(\Omega)$$

is an ϵ-predicate of A, that is $\phi(a) \subseteq \epsilon_A(a)$ for all $a \in A$. A *morphism*:

$$f : (A, \phi) \longrightarrow (B, \psi)$$

is a map $f : A \longrightarrow B$ in $\mathcal{K}$ such that:

$$\phi(a) = \epsilon_A(a) \cap \psi(f(a))$$

We have an obvious forgetful functor:

$$\mathcal{F} : Pred_\epsilon(\mathcal{K}) \longrightarrow \mathcal{K}$$

sending the object (A, ϕ) into A and f into itself. (We remark that predicates also constitute a category, but we shall not use it here.)

2.3. Entities for a System of Kinds

In this section we define a notion of entity for a system of kinds. A system of kinds is a functor:

$$I : \mathcal{L} \longrightarrow \mathcal{K}$$

where $\mathcal{L}$ (thought of as a nominal category) is a small category and $\mathcal{K}$ is the category of kinds. We define the entity for the system to be the colimit of the functor I (thought of as interpretation).

We now give an explicit description of the colimit. Consider the set:

$$E_0 = \{(a, i) : a \in I(i)\}$$

We define an equivalence relation on E_0 as follows: $(a, i) \sim (b, j)$ iff there is a chain:

in $\mathcal{L}$ and elements $a_k \in I(i_k)$ where $(0 \leq k \leq n)$ such that $a = a_0$, $b = a_n$, and $I(i_k{\rightarrow}i_{k-1})(a_k) = a_{k-1}$, $I(i_k{\rightarrow}i_{k+1})(a_k) = a_{k+1}$.

This is the smallest equivalence relation containing $((a, i), (b, j))$ whenever $\exists \alpha : i {\longrightarrow} j$ such that $I(\alpha)(a) = b$.

Now let $E = E_0/\sim$, the set of equivalent classes:

$$\{[(a, i)] : a \in I(i)\}$$

We define the relation ϵ_E as follows:

$$\epsilon_E([(a, i)]) = \bigcup\{\epsilon_{I(j)}(b) : (a, i) \sim (b, j)\}$$

It is easy to check that (E, ϵ_E) is the colimit of I. Notice that we have a canonical map:

$$\eta_i : I(i) {\longrightarrow} E$$

given by $\eta_i(a) = [(a, i)]$.

We define a *coincidence relation*:

$$\delta_I : E_0 \times E_0 {\longrightarrow} \Gamma(\Omega)$$

$U \in \delta_I((a, i), (b, j))$ iff there is a chain as before in $\mathcal{L}$ and elements $a_k \in I(i_k)$ where $(0 \leq k \leq n)$ such that $a = a_0, b = a_n$, and $I(i_k{\rightarrow}i_{k-1})(a_k) = a_{k-1}$, $I(i_k{\rightarrow}i_{k+1})(a_k) = a_{k+1}$, and $U \in \epsilon_{I(i_k)}(a_k)$ for $(0 \leq k \leq n)$.

Example: If we take Joe to be a man and l to be a liar, we understand Joe and l to be coincident at U if $U \in \delta_I((Joe, man), (l, liar))$ that is, precisely when at U, Joe is a l. Other examples will be given later. The following result is easily checked.

Proposition 2.3.1. The coincidence relation δ_I has the following properties:

1. $\delta_I((a, i), (b, j)) = \delta_I((b, j), (a, i))$

2. $\delta_I((a, i), (b, j)) \cap \delta_I((b, j), (c, k)) \subseteq \delta_I((a, i), (c, k))$

3. $\delta_I((a, i), (b, j)) \subseteq \epsilon_{I(i)}(a) \cap \epsilon_{I(j)}(b)$.

2.4. Predicates of a System of Kinds

We define an ϵ-predicate (existence predicates) of a system $I : \mathcal{L} \longrightarrow \mathcal{K}$ of kinds to be a family $(\phi_i)_{i \in |\mathcal{L}|}$ such that each ϕ_i is an ϵ-predicate of the kind $I(i)$. (Here as well as in the sequel, we use $| \mathcal{C} |$ for the class of objects of the category $\mathcal{C}$.)

We say that an ϵ-predicate $(\phi_i)_i$ of I is *natural* (or *functorial*) iff there is a functor:

$$\Phi : \mathcal{L} \longrightarrow Pred_\epsilon(\mathcal{K})$$

such that the diagram:

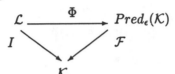

commutes, and for each $i \in | \mathcal{L} |$, $\Phi(i) = (I(i), \phi_i)$. $Pred_\epsilon(\mathcal{K})$ is the category of ϵ-predicates and $\mathcal{F}$ the forgetful functor. Equivalently, $(\phi_i)_i$ is natural if for every $\alpha : i \rightarrow j \in \mathcal{L}$, $\phi_i = \epsilon_{I(i)} \cap (\phi_j \circ I(\alpha))$, i.e., the diagram:

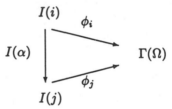

commutes "up to existence".

We say that an ϵ-predicate $(\phi_i)_i$ for I is *extensional* iff:

$$\phi_i(a) \cap \delta_I((a, i), (b, j)) \subseteq \phi_j(b)$$

for all $i, j \in | \mathcal{L} |$, $a \in I(i)$, $b \in I(j)$.

Proposition 2.4.1. An ϵ-predicate for a system I of kinds is natural iff it is extensional

Proof. $\Leftarrow$:) Let $\alpha : i \rightarrow j \in \mathcal{L}$. Given $a \in I(i)$, we have to check that:

$$\phi_i(a) = \epsilon_{I(i)}(a) \cap \phi_j(I(\alpha)(a))$$

Let $b = I(\alpha)(a)$. If $U \in \phi_i(a)$, then $U \in \epsilon_{I(i)}(a)$ since $((\phi_i)_i$ is a ϵ-predicate). Since $I(\alpha)$ is a morphism of $\mathcal{K}$, $U \in \epsilon_{I(j)}(b)$ and this shows that $U \in \delta_I((a, i), (b, j))$. By extensionality of $(\phi_i)_i$ we conclude that $U \in \phi_j(b)$. A similar argument shows that:

$$\epsilon_{I(i)}(a) \cap \phi_j(I(\alpha)(a)) \subseteq \phi_i(a)$$

$\Rightarrow$:) Let $(\phi_i)_i$ be a natural ϵ- predicate. We have to show that:

$$\phi_i(a) \cap \delta_I((a,i),(b,j)) \subseteq \phi_j(b)$$

Let $U \in \phi_i(a)$, $U \in \delta_I((a,i),(b,j))$. We proceed by induction on the length of the chain defining δ_I (see section 2.3). Let us do just the case n=1 to see what is involved: there is a diagram:

in $\mathcal{L}$ and an element $a_1 \in I(i_1)$ which is sent into $a \in I(i)$ by $I(i_1{\to}i)$ and into $b \in I(j)$ by $I(i_1{\to}j)$ such that:

$$U \in \epsilon_{I(i)}(a) \cap \epsilon_{I(i_1)}(a_1) \cap \epsilon_{I(j)}(b)$$

By naturality of $(\phi_i)_i$:

$$\phi_{i_1}(a_1) = \epsilon_{I(i_1)}(a_1) \cap \phi_i(a)$$

and this implies that $U \in \phi_{i_1}(a_1)$. Using naturality once again:

$$\phi_{i_1}(a_1) = \epsilon_{I(j)}(b) \cap \phi_j(b)$$

and this implies that $U \in \phi_j(b)$. $\square$

We define an ϵ-predicate $(\phi_i)_i$ of I to be *lax natural* if for every α : $i{\longrightarrow}j \in \mathcal{L}$:

$$\phi_i \leq \epsilon_{I(i)} \cap (\phi_j \circ I(\alpha))$$

and an ϵ-predicate is *anti-lax natural* if for every $\alpha : i{\longrightarrow}j$:

$$\phi_i \geq \epsilon_{I(i)} \cap (\phi_j \circ I(\alpha))$$

We remark that it is possible to see an ϵ-predicate as a natural transformation which justifies our terminology, but we will not go into this further. To illustrate these definitions we note: (1) The predicate TALL for the system of kinds consisting of PERSON, BASKETBALL PLAYER and the underlying function:

BASKETBALL PLAYER$\longrightarrow$PERSON

is lax natural: a tall basketball player is a tall person although a tall person who is a basketball player may not be a tall basketball player. (2) The predicate TALL for the system of kinds consisting of BABY, PERSON and the morphism of kind (in this case, underlying map) BABY$\longrightarrow$PERSON is anti-lax natural: a tall baby is not a tall person. (3)

The predicate MALE for the system of kinds of (2) is natural: a baby is male if and only if the person underlying the baby is male.

We finish this section with a result whose importance will be apparent in section 3.2. Let $I : \mathcal{L} \longrightarrow \mathcal{K}$ as before. We define the category $\mathcal{P}(\mathcal{L})$ as follows: Its objects are couples (i, Φ) where $i \in| \mathcal{L} |$ and $\Phi : \mathcal{L} \longrightarrow Pred_\epsilon(\mathcal{K})$ such that:

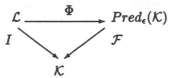

commutes and $\Phi(i) = (I(i), \epsilon_{I(i)})$ for all $i \in| \mathcal{L} |$.

Its morphisms $(i, \Phi) \longrightarrow (j, \Psi)$ are couples consisting of a morphism $i \longrightarrow j \in \mathcal{L}$ and a natural transformation $\Phi \xrightarrow{\alpha} \Psi$ such that $\alpha(i) = Id_{I(i)}$ $\forall i \in| \mathcal{L} |$.

Proposition 2.4.2. The forgetful functor $\mathcal{P}(\mathcal{L}) \xrightarrow{U} \mathcal{L}$ sending (i, Φ) into i has a left adjoint $P \dashv U$

Proof. The proof will appear elsewhere. We just mention that the action of P on objects is the following: $P(i) = (i, \Phi)$ where:

$$U \in \Phi(j)(b) \iff \exists a \in I(i) \ \ U \in \delta_I((a,i),(b,j))$$

for all $b \in I(j)$.

The interest of this proposition lies in its application to linguistics (as we shall explain in section 3.2): if $\mathcal{L}$ is a category of CNs (see section 2.5.2) and I is the canonical interpretation of CNs into the corresponding kinds, then every CN in the category, say 'dog', gives rise to an ϵ-predicate which all dogs possess, namely, TO BE A DOG. The proposition says that this predicate is "the smallest" among extensional ϵ-predicates having this property.

2.5. Language and Interpretation

2.5.1. Sorts, Terms and Formulas

We define *sorts* by recursion as follows:

1. CNs of the English vocabulary are *basic sorts*: 'man', 'person', etc.

2. $1, \Omega$ ("propositions") and O ("object" or "entity") are *sorts*.

3. If X, Y are *sorts*, so are $X \times Y$ and Y^X.

4. Nothing else is a *sort*.

We remark that we have not sought to limit the operations on sorts. We could enrich our operations to include, for instance, disjoint unions. In what follows $(t : X)$ is a sorted term whose sort is X.

We define *terms* by recursion as follows:

1. If $c \in Con$ where Con is a set of constants, then $(c : X)$ is a *term*, a *sorted constant term*. For instance, if $John \in Con$, then $(John : person)$ is a sorted constant. If $meet \in Con$, then $(meet : \Omega^{person \times person})$ is a sorted constant, if $run \in Con$, then $(run : \Omega^{person})$, $(run : \Omega^{dog})$ are sorted constants. In this way we specify the meaningful context for the constants we are using. For instance, $(run : \Omega^{person})$ and $(run : \Omega^{dog})$ may be terms but unless we are writing poetry we will probably exclude $(run : \Omega^{numbers})$ as a term. In section 2.5.5 we relax the sorting constraint and introduce the notion of generic predicables. We also have $(* : 1)$ as a sorted constant but we do not add, for instance, $(* : person)$.

2. If $x \in Var$ where Var is an infinite set of unsorted variables, then $(x : X)$ is a term, a *sorted variable term*.

3. If $(t : X)$ and $(s : X)$ are terms, then $(< (t : X), (s : Y) >: X \times Y)$ is a *term*.

4. If $(t : Y)$ is a term and $(x : X)$ is a sorted variable, then $(\lambda(x : X)(t : Y) : Y^X)$ is a *term*.

5. If $(t : Y^X)$ and $(s : X)$ are terms, then $((t : Y^X)^{\iota}(s : X) : Y)$ is a *term*. We use Lambek's notation "ι" to indicate the result of evaluating $(t : Y^X)$ at $(s : X)$.

6. $(\top : \Omega)$ and $(\bot : \Omega)$ are *terms* (sorted constants).

7. If $(t : X)$ and $(s : X)$ are terms, then $((t : X) = (s : X) : \Omega)$ is a *term*.

8. If $(t : X)$ and $(s : Y)$ are terms, then $((t : X) \asymp (s : Y) : \Omega)$ is a *term*.

9. If $(\phi : \Omega)$ and $(\psi : \Omega)$ are terms, then $((\phi : \Omega) \Delta (\psi : \Omega) : \Omega)$ are *terms* where $\Delta \in \{\wedge, \vee, \rightarrow, \backslash\}$.

10. If $(\phi : \Omega)$ is a term and $(x : X)$ is a sorted variable, then $(\forall(x : X) (\phi : \Omega) : \Omega)$ and $(\exists(x : X) (\phi : \Omega) : \Omega)$ are *terms*.

11. If $(\phi : \Omega)$ is a term, then so are $(\Box\phi : \Omega)$ and $(\Diamond\phi : \Omega)$, $(\Box^{*}\phi : \Omega)$ and $(\Diamond^{*}\phi : \Omega)$.

12. Nothing else is a *term*.

We remark that the formulation of terms proceeds by concatenation and that we do not allow cuts to take place, so that when we come to the interpretation we know exactly how every term entering the expression is sorted.

Formulas are defined to be terms of sort Ω. Whenever it is clear from context what our intentions are we will write a formula simply as 'ϕ' instead of '$(\phi : \Omega)$'. We use the following abbreviations:

If $(t : X)$ is a term, we let $E(t : X) \equiv (t : X) \asymp (t : X)$.

If ϕ is a formula, we let $\neg\phi \equiv \phi \to \perp$ and $\sim \phi \equiv \top \backslash \phi$.

We shall assume that we have defined the usual notions of substitution of a term for a variable, of a term or formula for a free variable, of a term being free for a variable in a term or in a formula, etc. Notice that we need to define these notions for sorted variables. We will now illustrate with some examples how terms are formed.

Notice that we can, for instance, write the formation of terms with $\exists$ as:

$$\frac{(\phi : \Omega), \ (x : X)}{(\exists(x : X)\,(\phi : \Omega) : \Omega)}$$

and read it as "if $(x : X)$ is a sorted variable and $(\phi : \Omega)$ is a formula, then $(\exists(x : X)\,(\phi : \Omega) : \Omega)$ is a formula." We will use that form to present the examples.

1. 'Somebody meets John' (we use the abbreviation 'p' for 'person'):

$$\frac{(meet : \Omega^{p \times p}), \ \dfrac{(x{:}p), \ (John{:}p)}{(<(x{:}p), \ (John{:}p)>{:}p \times p)}}{\dfrac{(x : p), \ ((meet : \Omega^{p \times p})^!(< (x : p), (John : p) >: p \times p) : \Omega)}{(\exists(x : p)((meet : \Omega^{p \times p})^!(< (x : p), \ (John : p) >: p \times p) : \Omega) : \Omega)}}$$

2. 'Those who meet John' (we suppose that 'those' is typed by 'person' ['p']). We obtain the following expression:

$$(\lambda(x : p)((meet : \Omega^{p \times p})^!(< (x : p), \ (John : p) >: p \times p) : \Omega) : \Omega^X)$$

2.5.2. The Nominal Category

So far we have studied sorts, terms and formulas but we have not taken into account the identifications that natural language uses all the time, such as 'a dog is an animal'. To study these identifications, we need the notion of an entity for a system of kinds that we introduced in section 2.3. We must structure the basic sorts so that they form a category that we call the nominal category $(\mathcal{N})$. We first form a nominal graph, which we exemplify by:

$$\boxed{\text{a man}} \xrightarrow{is} \boxed{\text{a person}} \boxed{\text{a man}} \xrightarrow{is} \boxed{\text{a primate}} \xrightarrow{is} \boxed{\text{a mammal}}$$

Notice that we interpret the copula connecting nouns as a morphism of the category.

We then complete these graphs in the following way:

1. Whenever we have a box, we add an arrow. For instance, to the box

$$\boxed{\text{a man}}$$

we add the arrow $\xrightarrow{is}$ as follows:

$$\boxed{\text{a man}} \xrightarrow{is} \boxed{\text{a man}}.$$

This represents the identity map.

2. Whenever we have two arrows, the co-domain of one being the domain of the other, we add an arrow that is the composition of the two arrows. For instance from

$$\boxed{\text{a man}} \xrightarrow{is} \boxed{\text{a primate}} \xrightarrow{is} \boxed{\text{a mammal}}$$

we obtain an arrow

$$\boxed{\text{a man}} \xrightarrow{is} \boxed{\text{a mammal}}$$

which is the composition map. This is in keeping with natural-language intuitions.

The nominal graph thus completed forms a category. This nominal category represents some of the identifications that are normal in natural languages (for instance, those that are standard in dictionaries). Notice that the nominal category can be seen as a deductive system where the identity map corresponds to the axiom 'a man is a man' and the composition map corresponds to the rule of inference:

$$\frac{\textit{a man is a primate, a primate is a mammal}}{\textit{a man is a mammal}}$$

2.5.3. Interpretation of the Nominal Category

An *interpretation of* $\mathcal{N}$ is a functor:

$$\|...\| : \mathcal{N} \longrightarrow \mathcal{K}.$$

For instance, if $\underline{A}$ is a CN (basic sort), then we interpret $\underline{A}$ as a kind $\|\underline{A}\|$ where $\|\underline{A}\| = (A, \epsilon_A)$. Thus $\|...\|$ is a family of kinds indexed by CNs and MNs. It respects the structure of $\mathcal{N}$ in the sense that we have a morphism:

$$u : \|\underline{A}\| \longrightarrow \|\underline{B}\| \ \in \mathcal{K}$$

whenever we have

$$\boxed{\text{a } \underline{A}} \xrightarrow{\ is\ } \boxed{\text{a } \underline{B}}$$

in $\mathcal{N}$. We say that such a u is an underlying morphism.

We now define an interpretation of the language relative to an interpretation of $\mathcal{N}$. We extend the interpretation of the basic sorts given by the functor $\|...\|$ to all sorts as follows:

1. The sort 1 is interpreted as $\|1\| = (\{*\}, \epsilon_{\{*\}})$ which is the terminal object in $\mathcal{K}$. The sort Ω is interpreted as $\|\Omega\| = (\Gamma(\Omega), \epsilon_T)$, that is, the set of downward closed situations. The sort O is interpreted as the co-limit in $\mathcal{K}$ of the interpretation functor restricted to the CNs of the nominal category.

2. If the sorts X, Y have been interpreted then:

$$\|X \times Y\| = \|X\| \times \|Y\| \text{ and } \|X^Y\| = \|X\|^{\|Y\|}$$

For each term $(t : X)$ and each sequence $(x_1, ..., x_n)$ of distinct variables such that the free sorted variables of $(t : X)$ are among the elements of $((x_1 : X_1), ..., (x_n : X_n))$, we define by recursion:

$$\|((x_1 : X_1), ..., (x_n : X_n)) : (t : X)\| : \|X_1\| \times ... \times \|X_n\| \longrightarrow \|X\|$$

abbreviating $(x_1 : X_1), ..., (x_n : X_n)$ to $\vec{X}$ whenever possible.

1. $(c : X)$ being a sorted constant, we let $\|(c : X)\| \in \|X\|$ or equivalently $\|(c : X)\| : 1 \longrightarrow \|X\|$. We let $\|(\vec{X}) : (c : X)\| : \|X_1\| \times ... \times \|X_n\| \longrightarrow \|X\|$ be interpreted as the constant map whose value is $\|(c : X)\|$.

2. $(x_i : X_i)$ being a sorted variable, we let:

$$\|(\vec{X}) : (x_i : X_i)\| : \|X_1\| \times ... \times \|X_n\| \xrightarrow{\ \pi_i\ } \|X_i\|$$

be π_i the ith projection.

3. $(t : X)$ and $(s : Y)$ being terms and the free sorted variables of $(t : X)$, and $(s : Y)$ being among the elements of $(\vec{X})$, then:

$$\|(\vec{X}) :< (t : X), (s : Y) >: X \times Y\|$$

$$=< \|(\vec{X}) : (t : X)\|, \|(\vec{X}) : (s : Y)\| >$$

4. $(x : X)$ being a sorted variable, $(t : Y)$ a term and the free variables of $(t : Y)$, among the elements of $(\vec{X})$, then:

$$\|(\vec{X}) : \lambda(x : X)(t : Y) : Y^X\| : \|X_1\| \times \ldots \times \|X_n\| \longrightarrow \|Y\|^{\|X\|}$$

is defined to be the exponential transpose of the map:

$$\|(\vec{X}, (x : X)) : (t : Y)\| : \|X_1\| \times \ldots \times \|X_n\| \times \|X\| \longrightarrow \|Y\|$$

5. $(t : Y^X)$ and $(s : X)$ being terms whose free variables are among the elements of $(\vec{X})$, then:

$$\|(\vec{X}) : (t : Y^X)'(s : X) : Y\|$$

$$= ev(< \|(\vec{X}) : (t : Y^X)\|, \|(\vec{X}) : (s : X)\| >)$$

where $ev : \|Y\|^{\|X\|} \times \|X\| \longrightarrow \|Y\|$ is the evaluation map.

We will now use a shorthand notation to simplify the statement of the next clauses. We will use the forcing notation and say that:

$$U \Vdash \phi[a_1, \ldots, a_n] \overset{def}{\Leftrightarrow} U \in \|(\vec{X}) : (\phi : \Omega)\|(a_1, \ldots, a_n)$$

when $a_1 \in \|X_1\|, \ldots, a_n \in \|X_n\|$. A formula ϕ is forced at a situation U under the assignment $(a_1, \ldots, a_n)$ if and only if the situation U belongs to the set of downward closed situations interpreting the formula ϕ under the assignment $(a_1, \ldots, a_n)$.

6. $U \Vdash \top[\vec{a}]$ always and $U \Vdash \perp[\vec{a}]$ never; writing $[\vec{a}]$ for $[a_1, \ldots, a_n]$.

7. $U \Vdash (t : X) = (s : X)[\vec{a}]$ iff $\|(\vec{X}) : (t : X)\|(\vec{a}) = \|(\vec{X}) : (s : X)\|(\vec{a})$.

8. $U \Vdash (t : X) \asymp (s : Y)[\vec{a}]$ iff $U \in \delta_{\|\ldots\|}(\|(\vec{X}) : (t : X)\|(\vec{a}), \|(\vec{X}) : (s : Y)\|(\vec{a}))$.

9. $U \Vdash \phi \wedge \psi[\vec{a}]$ iff $U \Vdash \phi[\vec{a}]$ and $U \Vdash \psi[\vec{a}]$.

10. $U \Vdash \phi \vee \psi[\vec{a}]$ iff $U \Vdash \phi[\vec{a}]$ or $U \Vdash \psi[\vec{a}]$.

11. $U \Vdash \phi \longrightarrow \psi[\vec{a}]$ iff $\forall V \leq U$ if $V \Vdash \phi[\vec{a}]$ then $V \Vdash \psi[\vec{a}]$.

12. $U \Vdash \neg \phi[\vec{a}]$ iff $U \Vdash \phi \longrightarrow \perp[\vec{a}]$ iff $\forall V \leq U$ $V \not\Vdash \phi[\vec{a}]$.

13. $U \Vdash (\phi \backslash \psi)[\vec{a}]$ iff $\exists V \geq U$ $V \Vdash \phi[\vec{a}]$ and $V \not\Vdash \psi[\vec{a}]$.

14. $U \Vdash \sim \phi[\vec{a}]$ iff $\exists V \geq U$ $V \not\Vdash \phi[\vec{a}]$.

15. $U \Vdash \exists (x : X) \phi[\vec{a}]$ iff there is $a \in \|X\|$ such that $U \Vdash \phi[\vec{a}, a]$.

16. $U \Vdash \forall (x : X) \phi[\vec{a}]$ iff $\forall V \leq U$ $V \Vdash \phi[\vec{a}, a]$ for all $a \in \|X\|$.

17. $U \Vdash \Diamond \phi[\vec{a}]$ iff $\exists V$ such that $V \Vdash \phi[\vec{a}]$.

18. $U \Vdash \Box \phi[\vec{a}]$ iff $\forall V$ $V \Vdash [\vec{a}]$.

19. $U \Vdash \Diamond^* \phi[\vec{a}]$ iff $\exists V \in \Pi(U)$ such that $V \Vdash \phi[\vec{a}]$, where $\Pi(U)$ is the connected component of $U \in P$, namely those elements V that can be reached from U by a zigzag $U \geq U_1 \leq \ldots \geq U_n \leq V$.

20. $U \Vdash \Box^* \phi[\vec{a}]$ iff $\forall V \in \Pi(U)$ $V \Vdash \phi[\vec{a}]$.

Proposition 2.5.1. If $U \Vdash \phi[\vec{a}]$ and $V \leq U$, then $V \Vdash \phi[\vec{a}]$. This expresses the functoriality of the forcing relation

Proof. The proof is done by induction on formulas and is straightforward. To illustrate, we do the proof for $\neg$, $\exists$ and $\Diamond^*$.

($\neg$) We have $U \Vdash \neg \phi[\vec{a}]$ and $V \leq U$; we show that $V \Vdash \neg \phi[\vec{a}]$. So, given a $W \leq V$, we show that $W \not\Vdash \phi[\vec{a}]$. But by the definition of forcing for $\neg$ we have $\forall W' \leq U$ $W' \not\Vdash \phi[\vec{a}]$. So in particular for $W \leq V$.

($\exists$) We have $U \Vdash \exists x \phi[\vec{a}]$ and $V \leq U$; we show that $V \Vdash \exists x \phi[\vec{a}]$. Hence we show that $\exists b \in \|X\|$ such that $V \Vdash \phi[\vec{a}, b]$. But by hypothesis $\exists a \in \|X\|$ such that $U \Vdash \phi[\vec{a}, a]$ and by the induction hypothesis $V \Vdash \phi[\vec{a}, a]$ and we take $b = a$.

($\Diamond^*$) $U \Vdash \Diamond^* \phi[\vec{a}]$ and $V \leq U$. Clearly $V \Vdash \Diamond^* \phi[\vec{a}]$ since $\Pi(U) = \Pi(V)$. We may think of $\Pi(U)$ as a set of situations which are accessible from U.

We can finally define the basic notion of *validity* of a sentence, a sentence being a formula without free variables. A sentence σ is *valid* (in $\Gamma(\Omega(1))$) if and only if $1 \Vdash \sigma[\,]$, where $[\,]$ is the empty sequence of assignments. More generally, we say that a formula is *valid* if and only if the sentence that is its universal closure, is valid.

2.5.4. *Formal System*

We will now describe a formal system for "modal higher order theory" based on Gentzen's sequents. These expressions, following Boileau and Joyal (1981), will be of the form $\Gamma \vdash_{\vec{X}} \phi$, where Γ is a finite set of formulas of the language of modal higher order theory already described, ϕ a single formula and $\vec{X}$ a finite set of sorted variables containing all the free sorted variables of Γ and ϕ. We shall assume that these expressions satisfy the following rules. This system follows, in part, Lambek and Scott (1986, p.134) which in turn is based on Gentzen's work (see Szabo 1969).

1. *Structural rules*

   1.1 $\quad p \vdash_{\vec{X}} p$

   1.2 $\quad \dfrac{\Gamma \vdash_{\vec{X}} p \quad \Gamma \cup \{p\} \vdash_{\vec{X}} q}{\Gamma \vdash_{\vec{X}} q}$

   1.3 $\quad \dfrac{\Gamma \vdash_{\vec{X}} q}{\Gamma \cup \{p\} \vdash_{\vec{X}} q}$

   1.4 $\quad \dfrac{\Gamma \vdash_{\vec{X}} q}{\Gamma \vdash_{\vec{X},(x:X)} q}$

   1.5 $\quad \dfrac{\Gamma \vdash_{\vec{X},(x:X)} \phi}{\Gamma[(t:X)/(x:X)] \vdash_{\vec{X}} \phi[(t:X)/(x:X)]}$

   where $\phi[(t:X)/(x:X)]$ means substituting t for x in ϕ, $(t:X)$ being free for $(x:X)$ in ϕ and Γ.

2. *Logical rules*

   2.1 $\quad p \vdash_{\vec{X}} \top$ and $\perp \vdash_{\vec{X}} p$

   2.2 $\quad r \vdash_{\vec{X}} p \wedge q$ iff $r \vdash_{\vec{X}} p$ and $r \vdash_{\vec{X}} q$
   $\quad p \vee q \vdash_{\vec{X}} r$ iff $p \vdash_{\vec{X}} r$ and $q \vdash_{\vec{X}} r$

   2.3 $\quad p \vdash_{\vec{X}} q \rightarrow r$ iff $p \wedge q \vdash_{\vec{X}} r$
   $\quad p \backslash q \vdash_{\vec{X}} r$ iff $p \vdash_{\vec{X}} q \vee r$

   2.4 $\quad p \vdash_{\vec{X}} \forall (x:X)\phi$ iff $p \vdash_{\vec{X},(x:X)} \phi$
   $\quad \exists (x:X)\phi \vdash_{\vec{X}} p$ iff $\phi \vdash_{\vec{X},(x:X)} p$

   provided that $(x:X)$ is not a sorted variable in $\vec{X}$.

3. *Identity rules*

   3.1 $\quad \vdash_{\vec{X}} (t:X) = (t:X)$

   3.2 $\quad (t:X) = (s:X), \phi[(t:X)/(x:X)] \vdash_{\vec{X}} \phi[(s:X)/(x:X)]$
   provided that $(t:X)$ and $(s:X)$ are free for $(x:X)$ in ϕ. (Leibniz's law).

4. *Rules on special symbols*

   4.1 $\quad \vdash_{(x:1)} (x:1) = (*:1)$

   4.2 $\quad < (t:X),(s:X) >=< (u:X),(v:X) > \vdash_{\vec{X}} (t:X) = (u:X)$
   $\quad < (t:X),(s:X) >=< (u:X),(v:X) > \vdash_{\vec{X}} (s:X) = (v:X)$

4.3
$$\frac{\Gamma, \quad (z:Z) = <(x:X),(y:Y)> \vdash_{\vec{X},(x:X),(y:Y),(z:Z)} \phi}{\Gamma \vdash_{\vec{X},(z:Z)} \phi}$$

provided that $(x:X)$ and $(y:Y)$ are not free in Γ or ϕ.

5. *Coincidence rules*

5.1 $\vdash_{\vec{X}} (x:X) \asymp (x:X)$

5.2 $(x:X) \asymp (y:Y) \vdash_{\vec{X}} (y:Y) \asymp (x:X)$

5.3 $(x:X) \asymp (y:Y), \quad (y:Y) \asymp (z:Z) \vdash_{\vec{X}} (x:X) \asymp (z:Z$

5.4 $(x_1:X_1) \asymp (y_1:Y_1),...,(x_n:X_n) \asymp (y_n:Y_n)$
$\vdash_{\vec{X}} < (x_1:X_1),...,(x_n:X_n) > \asymp < (y_1:Y_1),...,(y_n:Y_n) >$

In the rules 5.1-5.4, the sorted variables are sorted variables of basic sorts.

6. *Rules for the λ-calculus*

6.1 $\vdash_{\vec{X}} ((\lambda(x:X)(t:Y):Y^X)^!(x:X):Y) = (t:Y)$

provided that $(x:X)$ is not a variable in $\vec{X}$.

6.2 $\vdash_{\vec{X}} \lambda(x:X)\phi((t:X)) = \phi[(t:X)/(x:X)]$

provided that $(t:X)$ is free for $(x:X)$ in ϕ.

6.3
$$\frac{\Gamma \vdash_{\vec{X},(x:X)} (t:X) = (s:X)}{\Gamma \vdash_{\vec{X}} \lambda(x:X)(t:X) = \lambda(x:X)(s:X)}$$

7. *Rules for modal operators $\square$ and $\diamond$*

7.1 $\square\phi \vdash_{\vec{X}} \phi \qquad \phi \vdash_{\vec{X}} \diamond\phi$

7.2 $\square\phi \vdash_{\vec{X}} \square\square\phi \qquad \diamond\diamond\phi \vdash_{\vec{X}} \diamond\phi$

7.3 $\phi \vdash_{\vec{X}} \square\diamond\phi \qquad \diamond\square\phi \vdash_{\vec{X}} \phi$

7.4 $(x:X) = (y:Y) \vdash_{\vec{X}} \square((x:X) = (y:X))$

7.5
$$\frac{\phi \vdash_{\vec{X}} \psi}{\square\phi \vdash_{\vec{X}} \square\psi}$$

7.6
$$\frac{\phi \vdash_{\vec{X}} \psi}{\diamond\phi \vdash_{\vec{X}} \diamond\psi}$$

7.7 $\vdash_{\vec{X}} \diamond\phi \leftrightarrow \neg\square\neg\phi$
$\vdash_{\vec{X}} \square\phi \leftrightarrow \sim \diamond \sim \phi$

7.8 $\vdash_{\vec{X}} \square\phi \vee \neg\square\phi$
$\vdash_{\vec{X}} \diamond\phi \vee \neg\diamond\phi$

8. *Rules for modal operators* $\square^*$ *and* $\diamondsuit^*$. The rules 8.1 to 8.8 are the same as the corresponding one from 7.1 to 7.8.

8.9
$$\frac{\vdash_{\vec{x}} \phi \vee \neg\phi}{\phi \vdash_{\vec{x}} \square^*\phi}$$

The *-modal operators were introduced by Reyes and Zolfaghari (In press). They show that these operators are definable from '$\neg$' and '$\sim$' in σ-complete bi-Heyting algebras. There are connections between all these modal operators, namely:

$$\square \leq \square^* \leq Id \leq \diamondsuit^* \leq \diamondsuit$$

This can be proved in our system, i.e., $\square\phi \vdash_{\vec{x}} \square^*\phi$, etc. In a model based on a pre-ordered set P, $\square^*$ and $\square$ coincide as well as $\diamondsuit^*$ and $\diamondsuit$ precisely when P is connected. The *-modal operators are also interesting from a philosophical point of view specially in relation to the discussions on excluded middle and determinism since they characterize sentences which satisfy the excluded middle as being precisely the necessary ones.

This completes our system. We have not tried to describe it in the simplest or most economical manner. In fact, some of the rules are redundant but we have included them for the sake of symmetry. For instance, the rule 8.4 can be derived from the other axioms and rules of inference since one can show $x = y \vee \neg(x = y)$.

We can now formulate a soundness theorem for our system whose proof will be sketched in the Appendix. In order to formulate it, we need the following definition: $\Gamma \models_{\vec{x}} \phi$ if and only if $\forall U \in P \,\forall(a_1, \ldots, a_n) \in \|X_1\| \times \ldots \times \|X_n\| \,(U\Vdash\Gamma[a_1, \ldots, a_n] \Rightarrow U\Vdash\phi[a_1, \ldots, a_n])$ where $\vec{X}$ contains all the free sorted variables of Γ and ϕ and $U\Vdash\Gamma[a_1, \ldots, a_n]$ iff $U\Vdash\gamma[a_1, \ldots, a_n]$ for all $\gamma \in \Gamma$.

Theorem 2.5.2. (Soundness) If $\Gamma \vdash_{\vec{x}} \phi$, then $\Gamma \models_{\vec{x}} \phi$

2.5.5. *Interpretation of Generic Predicables*

In colloquial language expressions such as 'meet' and 'run' are unsorted, as we see if we look them up in a dictionary. 'Meet' appears by itself illustrated by some examples from its domain of application. We see the same phenomenon in mathematics where, for instance, '+' can be applied to natural, rational, real or complex numbers. This feature is what Reynolds (1980) calls "genericity" or "parametricity". The trouble with the language as we have introduced it is lack of provision for generic predicables. We have made provision only for such sorted terms as $meet((x : person), (x : dog))$. The interpretation is then overdetermined by the sorts. To arrive at the generic predicable we erase the sorts of the sorted free variables in *meet*. Thus we obtain $meet(x, y)$ which is a generic predicable. The question now is how to interpret such predicables. The answer is simple. We define:

$$\|(x, y) : meet(x, y)\| :| \mathcal{N}^2 | \longrightarrow | Pred_\epsilon(\mathcal{K}) |$$

as the function Φ in the following commutative diagram:

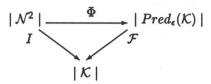

where $I(\underline{A}, \underline{B}) = \|\underline{A}\| \times \|\underline{B}\|$. For instance, '$p$' stands for person, and 'd' for dog.

$$\|(x, y) : meet(x, y)\|(p, d) = (\|p\| \times \|d\|, \|p\| \times \|d\| \longrightarrow \Gamma(\Omega))$$

where $\|p\| \times \|d\| \longrightarrow \Gamma(\Omega)$ is $\|((x : p), (y : d)) : meet((x : p), (y : d)) : \Omega\|$. The value of this function for a particular person and a particular dog is the set of all situations in which that particular person meets that particular dog.

In general, from $t((x_1 : \underline{A}_1), ..., (x_n : \underline{A}_n))$ we form the generic predicable $t(x_1, ...x_n)$ which is interpreted as:

$$\|(x_1, ..., x_n) : t(x_1, ..., x_n)\| :| \mathcal{N}^n | \longrightarrow | Pred_\epsilon(\mathcal{K}) |$$

and:

$$\|(x_1, ..., x_n) : t(x_1, ..., x_n)\|(\underline{A}_1, ..., \underline{A}_n)$$
$$= (\|\underline{A}_1\| \times ... \times \|\underline{A}_n\|, \|(x_1 : \underline{A}_1), ..., (x_n : \underline{A}_n) : t((x_1 : \underline{A}_1), ..., (x_n : \underline{A}_n))\|)$$

We say that the generic predicable t is natural if its interpretation extends to a functor (denoted by the same "Φ")

$$\Phi : \mathcal{N}^n \longrightarrow Pred_\epsilon(\mathcal{K}).$$

We can also define the notion of lax-natural and anti-lax-natural. For example, 'meet' is natural since, if a man and a puppy, say, are constituents of a given situation, then the man meets the puppy (at that situation) if and only if the underlying person meets the underlying dog.

2.5.6. Interpretation of Mass Nouns

In this section we will briefly touch upon the interpretation of mass nouns (MNs) by showing how they can be accommodated in the theory of kinds. First, we give some definitions. A $\bigvee$-*lattice* is a poset (a partially ordered set) in which every subset has a supremum. A morphism of $\bigvee$-lattices is a set-theoretical function between their underlying sets which preserves all suprema.

MNs will be interpreted as kinds of the form $(O(W), \epsilon_{O(W)})$ where $O(W)$ is the $\bigvee$-lattice. The use of 'O' in this notation comes from topology where it is customary to use $O(X)$ to denote the $\bigvee$-lattice of open sets of a topological space X. For instance, 'water' will be interpreted as the $\bigvee$-lattice of portions of water generated by actual portions of water. Examples would be the portion consisting of the water in the bath and the water in the sink and also the quantity of water poured on a given plant during a year. (This description is somewhat inaccurate since we believe that there is no absolute notion of portion of water, but only a notion of portion of water relative to a substance or stuff such as food or chemical substance. For further information see a forthcoming paper by the authors.)

Kinds corresponding to the interpretation of MNs constitute a category $\mathcal{M}$, the category of masses or quantities or, as we prefer to say, aggregates. A morphism of $\mathcal{M}$:

$$f : (O(W), \epsilon_{O(W)}) \longrightarrow (O(V), \epsilon_{O(V)})$$

is a function from $f : O(W) \longrightarrow O(V)$ such that $\epsilon_{O(W)} \leq \epsilon_{O(V)} \circ f$ and f is a morphism of $\bigvee$-lattice; that is, f is both a morphism of kinds and a morphism of $\bigvee$-lattice. We give two examples of morphisms. The first:

$$(O(\text{ICE}), \epsilon_{O(\text{ICE})}) \longrightarrow (O(\text{WATER}), \epsilon_{O(\text{WATER})})$$

is the underlying map of that which is expressed in colloquial language as "ice is water". And the second:

$$(O(\text{GOLD}), \epsilon_{O(\text{GOLD})}) \longrightarrow (O(\text{METAL}), \epsilon_{O(\text{METAL})})$$

interprets the colloquial "gold is metal".

The category $\mathcal{M}$ is complete, co-complete and linear (in the sense defined below). Thus it is a category of quantities in the sense of Lawvere (in press). Conveniently enough, colloquial language uses the expression 'quantity of water' in a sense that fits precisely Lawvere's notion.

A category C is said to be *linear* if the following conditions are satisfied:

1. C has finite products and coproducts (including terminal and initial objects: 1 and 0, respectively);

2. the unique morphism $0 \longrightarrow 1$ is an isomorphism;

3. the canonical morphism $A + B \longrightarrow A \times B$ obtained from the morphisms:

$$(1_A, 0_{AB}) : A \longrightarrow A \times B$$

and:

$$(0_{BA}, 1_B) : B \longrightarrow A \times B$$

is an isomorphism, where 0_{AB} is the composite of $A \longrightarrow 1$, $1 \sim 0$ and $0 \longrightarrow B$.

The fact that a category $\mathcal{C}$ is linear allows us to define a structure of semi-group on the set $\mathcal{C}(A, B)$ of morphisms from A to B. In the case that concerns us, this structure is a $\bigvee$-lattice.

MNs and CNs are usually convertible into each other. For instance, the CN 'wine', whose interpretation consists of Sauterne, Claret, Burgundy, etc. may be converted into the MN 'wine' whose interpretation is the set of portions or quantities of wine. In our context these transformations are derived ultimately from the adjoint functors $(G \dashv Q)$ between the categories $\mathcal{M}$ and $\mathcal{K}$.

$$\mathcal{M} \xrightarrow{Q} \mathcal{K} \xrightarrow{G} \mathcal{M}$$

where G corresponds to the colloquial expression 'group of' and appears as a universal way of converting a CN into a MN; Q corresponds to the colloquial expression 'quantity of' or 'portion of' and acts as a universal way of converting MNs into CNs. Notice however that the objects of $\mathcal{M}$ have already been constructed as kinds, hence Q is just the obvious forgetful functor. Furthermore this interpretation treats expressions like 'group of' and 'quantity of' not as CNs but as functors.

In analogy with the notion of entity for a system of kinds in $\mathcal{K}$, we can form the notion of stuff for a system of aggregates of $\mathcal{M}$. For example, a piece of cotton is a piece of material; these pieces can be identified as being a single piece of stuff. G provides a way to link these two fundamental notions of the category of kinds. Furthermore, notice that a predicate for a system of aggregates $I : \mathcal{L} \longrightarrow \mathcal{M}$ may be defined to be a predicate for the system of kinds $Q \circ I : \mathcal{L} \longrightarrow \mathcal{K}$.

Before leaving this topic, let us dispel some possible misunderstandings. We first notice that the word 'water' may be seen both as a PN denoting a member of the kind LIQUID and as a MN denoting the aggregate of its portions. This is definitely not the case with 'ship of Theseus'. This expression is a PN that denotes a member of the kind SHIP but it is not the aggregate of its parts, i.e., it is not a MN. Similarly, a particular drink of gin and tonic, say, is a member of the kind DRINK, but a drink is not the aggregate of its parts. A drink is, in fact, a highly intentional object. Thus, we may add some gin to somebody's drink without creating a new drink or destroying the old one.

Finally let us notice that, unlike many authors who have written about MNs, we have not assumed that aggregates have Boolean structure. The reason is that in our main examples, underlying maps such as:

$$(O(\text{ICE}), \epsilon_{O(\text{ICE})}) \longrightarrow (O(\text{WATER}), \epsilon_{O(\text{WATER})})$$

do not preserve the top element (since not all the water in the world is ice). It follows that if we assumed that portions of ice as well as portions of water had Boolean structure, the morphisms between them could not be Boolean homomorphisms, but morphisms of $\bigvee$-lattice. This shows that to interpret MNs into Boolean structures is to overdetermine them: it precludes the construction of STUFF for a system of aggregates. Indeed, the category of complete Boolean algebras with $\bigvee$-lattice morphisms lacks co-equalizers and even equalizers. To see the lack of co-equalizers, take the $\bigvee$-lattice endomorphism τ of the Boolean algebra of two elements $2 = \{0, 1\}$ defined by $\tau(0) = 0$ and $\tau(1) = 0$. It is easy to see that the diagram:

$$2 \overset{Id}{\underset{\tau}{\rightrightarrows}} 2$$

does not have a co-equalizer or, equivalently, since τ is idempotent, an equalizer. Co-equalizers are essential to construct STUFF for a system of aggregates, just as they are to construct ENTITY for a system of kinds.

3. Applications

3.1. Kinds and Their Underlying Maps

In this section we apply the theory of kinds to solve some well-known problems in the philosophical literature. Furthermore, we argue that there is a need for a notion of underlying map among kinds as distinct from set-theoretical inclusion. We also argue that there is a need for a notion of generalized or "local" underlying map between kinds.

We begin with a famous problem in the theory of identity, the paradox of the ship of Theseus. The paradox was proposed in antiquity and has been reformulated many times. The most tantalizing formulation is that of Hobbes in his book *Concerning Body* (1839, chap 11, sect 17). In that version the Athenians preserved the ship of Theseus for many years, replacing damaged parts until not a plank of the original was left. Others collected the discarded planks, reassembled them in the original order and made a ship of them. "This," says Hobbes, "without doubt had also been the same numerical ship with that which was at the beginning; and so there would have been two ships numerically the same, which is absurd." We must concede that the conclusion is absurd but argue that it does not follow from the premises. The paradox presupposes that a ship belongs indifferently to the kind SHIP or the kind SHIP PARTS; that is, that a ship is identical with its parts and that we can use either kind to trace its identity. Allowing that, any change in ship parts implies a change in ship. On the other hand, common sense suggests that one can change a plank in the ship of Theseus without its ceasing to be the same ship. It follows that a ship is not identical with the collection of its parts and that only the kind SHIP traces its identity in the proper manner.

Of course the question remains as to the relation between SHIP and SHIP PARTS. The relation is similar to that between PERSON and BUNCH OF MOLECULES, between CLAY, STATUE and PORTION OF CLAY, between DRINK OF GIN AND TONIC and QUANTITY OF GIN AND TONIC. We conceptualize such relations as a family of functions $(f_U)_{U \in P}$ between the corresponding kinds; for instance:

$$f_U : \text{PERSON}(U) \longrightarrow \text{BUNCH OF MOLECULES}(U), \quad \forall U \in P.$$

These functions are not independent of situations since they are subject to the following constraint: let $V \leq U$ be given, then:

$$
\begin{array}{ccc}
 & f_U & \\
\text{PERSON(U)} & \longrightarrow & \text{BUNCH OF MOLECULES(U)} \\
\downarrow & & \downarrow \\
 & f_V & \\
\text{PERSON(V)} & \longrightarrow & \text{BUNCH OF MOLECULES(V)}
\end{array}
$$

is a commutative diagram and:

$$\text{PERSON (U)} = \{p \in PERSON : U \in \epsilon_{\text{PERSON}}(p)\}$$

The commutativity of this diagram expresses no more than the fact that increasing information does not change the bunch of molecules that make up the person. In spite of the similarity, this is not an underlying relation such as DOG $\longrightarrow$ ANIMAL. The last associates to each dog the underlying animal in a way that is independent of any situation. On the other hand, the bunch of molecules that make up a person clearly depends on situations: the bunch of molecules that constitutes Nixon's body at present is not the same as the bunch that constituted his body at the time of his birth. One way to sum up the difference is to say that the relation between PERSON and BUNCH OF MOLECULES is "locally" underlying.

We go on to make some observations about genuine underlying relations, which played so crucial a role in our treatment of predicates and in the construction of ENTITY and STUFF. There is such a relation between the kind PASSENGER and the kind PERSON. This example is due to Gupta (1980) and is a modern version of the problem of counting heralds that comes from the Middle Ages. We cannot express the relation between these two kinds as a set-theoretical inclusion, since a single person may be counted by airline companies as many passengers. Furthermore, persons are no longer passengers when their journeys end, but they do not cease to be persons. So, as we saw in section 2.5.2, we conceptualize the expression 'a passenger is a person' by positing a map. On u we impose the condition that if a passenger p is a constituent of a situation, the person $u(p)$ is also a constituent of the same situation. We say that $u(p)$ is the person underlying p and that u is an underlying map.

These maps enable us to express the identity of a baby with the man he later becomes by saying that the person underlying the baby is the same person as that underlying the man. This sidesteps what would otherwise be an impossibility: to say of a baby that he is the same baby as a man.

Putnam's answer to this problem seems different (see for instance Putnam [this volume]). He denies that there is a question of identity across kinds and recognizes only one bona fide kind in these examples, namely, the kind PERSON. For him, our kinds BABY, MAN and PASSENGER are constructed as predicates of persons or, rather, as subkinds (in our sense) of PERSON× TIME of persons indexed by times (or, maybe, by time slices). Thus, in his view:

$$\imath x\ (Passenger(x, t_{past1}) = \imath x(Passenger(x, t_{past2}))$$

(where x ranges over the kind PERSON) would express the connection between passengers and persons that we conceptualized in terms of underlying maps: two passengers may underlie the same person. But other problems cannot be solved by invoking the notion of "instants of time" or "time slices", though they can be solved with the notion of underlying map. Let us consider the case of majors in a North American university. A single person can be both a major in philosophy and a major in mathematics during the same period of time. The departments of Philosophy and Mathematics will separately include the student in their lists of majors, and the university will count two majors although only one person and only one time slice are involved. Other such examples are patients and professors. A single person can simultaneously be the patient of a urologist and of a heart specialist; that is, be two patients. A person can be a professor in two separate universities during the same time. There are many such examples. Undoubtedly, sufficient ingenuity would permit another construction to handle such cases, but whatever the ingenuity, the outcome must be exactly what we have stipulated. Thus, in Putnam's handling of the relation between passengers and persons, our underlying map PASSENGER⟶ PERSON surfaces as the first projection from PERSON× TIME into PERSON. We believe our approach is preferable because it involves fewer philosophical commitments. We are not assuming that PERSON is logically privileged and that the other relevant kinds should be constructed from it. But we do not debar such construction.

As a last application, let us look at a fairy tale in which a prince is metamorphosed into a frog. How can we conceptualize the assertion that says "the prince is a frog." Equality will not do, since PRINCE and FROG are different kinds. But notice that there is an animal underlying the frog and the prince. The assertion says that the animal underlying the frog is the same as the one underlying the prince. This example and others are discussed in La Palme Reyes (1988 and this volume).

At the bottom of all these examples lies the problem of bare particulars or the problem of positing just one basic sort in the language and interpreting it as the universal kind. We have seen that the natural logic that we extract from the study of reference is a many sorted logic. Now we can ask the following question: Can a member of a kind K belong to a different kind L? Geach (1980) answers affirmatively. Furthermore, he says that equality is relative to a kind and that it is possible for x and y to be identical in K ($x =_K y$) and not identical in L ($x \neq_L y$). But Wiggins (1980) remarks that $x =_K y \longleftrightarrow x =_L y$ by Leibniz's law. We reformulate Wiggins's proof in the following way:

Theorem 3.1.1. $x =_L y \longrightarrow x =_K y$

Proof. By Leibniz's law, see section 2.5.4, we have $x =_L y$, $\phi(x) \vdash_{x,y} \phi(y)$. Let ϕ be the following property:

$$\phi(u) \equiv x =_K u$$

Then we have $\phi(x) \equiv x =_K x$. So from:

$$x =_L y, \quad x =_K x \vdash_{x,y} x =_K y$$

and $\vdash_{x,y} x =_K x$, we conclude $x =_L y \vdash_{x,y} x =_K y$. In other words, $\vdash_{x,y} x =_L y \longrightarrow x =_K y$.

Since we accept Leibniz's law, we interpret Wiggins's argument as showing that we cannot separate membership in a kind (individuating) and equality (tracing the identity). The argument supposed that it makes sense to say of an x that it belongs to two distinct kinds K and L. But we cannot do that if the kinds are PASSENGER and PERSON, because Wiggins's argument shows that:

$$x =_{\text{PERSON}} y \longleftrightarrow x =_{\text{PASSENGER}} y$$

which is false, since the identity of a person is traced differently from that of a passenger. Wiggins's assumptions do not preclude an x from belonging to two different kinds K and L as long as there is an injective underlying map between them, as between BOY and PERSON.

There are many reasons why we reject the doctrine of bare particulars or bare entities but this does not imply that we reject the notion of entity altogether. The kinds ENTITY and STUFF play a very important role in our theory. But they are kinds that are defined by categorical means on the basis of systems of more fundamental kinds or aggregates and are quite controllable. We already gave some arguments for the need of these kinds and will give more. Notice, however, that the doctrine of bare particulars does violence to grammar, which in all languages distinguishes common nouns from predicables. Furthermore the doctrine of bare particulars implies a universality of predicates, in the sense that predicates apply to individuals independent of any further properties they may have. But this is simply not the case. Take an entity which is a person that happens to be a baby, in fact, a big baby. Standard treatments regiment this information as:

$$(Person(e) \wedge Baby(e) \wedge Big(e))$$

where e stands for an entity. From this regimentation it follows that if e is a big baby, e is thereby a big person, which is contrary to common sense. The remedy is to disallow bare particulars and pay attention to the difference in logical role between common nouns and predicables. This is to recognize that predicables are logically typed by the common nouns they modify.

In further support of our position we recall that Frege got into trouble because he assumed that there are bare particulars, a position he may well have been led to by his study of Leibniz. Solutions to Russell's antinomy, which showed up the error of Frege's system, run parallel to our own position. Russell's own solution was the theory of types, in which the expressions at each level are typed by those on the level above. Zermelo's solution was to require that the specification of any set presupposes that the members of the newly specified set already belong to another set. In their own way both solutions debar uncontrolled access to bare particulars. We might add that Bernays's way of handling Russell's antinomy is to distinguish between sets and classes. This is a solution based on a distinction between sorts. (The interested reader can consult Paul J. Cohen (1966).) All of these solutions, then, are in harmony with our own fundamental position.

In concluding this section we recall two reasons for having underlying maps in our theory. With underlying maps we can account for some puzzling phenomena of natural languages. We have already mentioned one: even if babies are persons, big babies are not big persons. On the other hand, male babies are obviously male persons. To understand what is going on, it is not enough to postulate kinds BABY and PERSON; we also have to consider the underlying map u: BABY$\longrightarrow$ PERSON. The other reason for positing underlying maps is that they permit the construction of the controllable kinds ENTITY and STUFF which are so essential to the handling of natural-language identifications.

3.2. Grammatical Transformations and Their Semantical Counterparts

We have already drawn attention in section 2.5.6 to the fact that MNs and CNs are usually convertible into each other. A MN such as 'water' may be converted into the CN 'portions of water' or 'quantities of water' by prefixing the partitive expression 'portions of' or 'quantities of'. Conversely, the CN 'dog' may be converted into its plural form 'dogs' or more precisely and more universally, into 'group of dogs', which semantically is a MN, by prefixing the collective 'group of'. In that same section we formulated semantical counterparts of these grammatical transformations in terms of functors between the categories of kinds $\mathcal{K}$ and the category of aggregates $\mathcal{M}$. The fact that the interpretation of 'group of' is functorial is revealed by such observations as that a group of dogs is a group of animals, which reflects the underlying relation between the kinds DOG and ANIMAL. Furthermore, the adjointness relation between the functors G (which interprets 'groups of') and Q (which interprets 'quantities of'), namely $G \dashv Q$, shows that the syntactical operation of converting a CN into its plural form is the universal way of converting a CN into a MN.

In terms of these adjoint functors and a notion of substance or stuff we can define further transformations such as the conversion of PNs into MNs. For instance the PN 'water' whose interpretation is a member of the kind LIQUID may be converted into the MN 'water' whose interpretation is the $\bigvee$-lattice of portions of water. (Further details may be found in a forthcoming paper by the authors.)

In this section we give several examples of similar grammatical transformations and argue for their universality. Although several of these transformations have been pointed out in the linguistic literature, the main novelty of our approach is to provide semantical counterparts in terms of category theory.

The operation that transforms a CN into its plural form has been investigated by Jackendoff (1991) but he does not provide a semantical interpretation. The fact that plural CNs behave like MNs was pointed out earlier by Bennett (1979). In fact, plural CNs have no plurals; like MNs they do not take the articles 'a' and 'another'; like MNs they do take 'the' and 'a lot of'; the referent of 'dogs' in most usages may be combined (and sometimes divided) and still appropriately called 'dogs'. There are some differences: for example, plural CNs take plural verbs; plural CNs but not MNs take 'few'; MNs but not plural CNs take 'a little'.

The adjointness relation between the functors Q and G and the corresponding conclusion that taking plurals is the universal way of converting a CN into a MN suggests that these functors represent linguistic universals. This seems to be corroborated by the fact that languages like Japanese, which do not distinguish CNs from MNs at the syntactic level, do so at the semantic level and require expressions equivalent to 'quantity of' and 'group of' to licence the application of certain quantifiers to MNs and CNs. Thus in order to apply the quantifier *san* (three) to *mizu* (water) the partitive *bai no* (portion of) is required as in the phrase *san bai no mizu* (three portions of water). On the other hand Japanese employs the collective *no mure* in place of the English 'group of': *Inu no mure* ("group of dogs", literally "dog of group"), and *Dobutsu no mure* ("group of animals"). And, as functoriality of the interpretation of *no mure* requires, an *inu no mure* is a *dobutsu no mure*. (We owe these examples to Yuriko Oshima-Takane.)

We turn now to another transformation among grammatical categories, namely that between CNs and predicables. Each CN and each MN can be transformed into a predicable. For instance the CN 'dog' can be transformed into the predicable 'to be a dog' which may be typed by a variety of CNs such as 'mammal', 'animal', etc. The study of this transformation is highly relevant to syllogistic reasoning in which CNs are (tacitly) transformed into predicables to formulate syllogisms. (See La Palme Reyes, Macnamara and Reyes (forthcoming) for further details about this and other problems concerning syllogisms.) We just mention the syllogism in Barbara:

> All passengers are persons
> All persons are mortal
> ―――――――――――――――――
> All passengers are mortal

Here the so-called middle term, namely 'person', occurs first as part of the predicable 'to be a person' and then as a genuine CN. Certainly some connection must be established between the two in order to conclude the validity of the argument. Since the notion of validity is a semantical one, we need to give an account of the relations between the kind PERSON and the predicate TO BE A PERSON. This is precisely what we did in section 2.4. There we showed that given the system of kinds:

$$\|...\| : \mathcal{N} \longrightarrow \mathcal{K}$$

the predicate TO BE A PERSON was the initial object in the (partially) ordered category of all extensional predicates Φ of the system $\|...\|$ such that:

$$\Phi(person) = (\|person\|, \epsilon_{\|person\|})$$

Once again, this universal property suggests that the functor P of section 2.4 represents a linguistic universal.

Of course we can ask whether there is a natural way of transforming a predicable into a CN and, correspondingly, whether there is a functor between predicates (of a system of kinds) and the category of kinds. For extensional predicates we proceed as follows: an extensional predicate (of a system of kinds) gives rise to a predicate on the ENTITY of the system. But as M. La Palme Reyes (1988) showed there is a one-to-one correspondence between ϵ-predicates and subkinds of a given kind. We have succeeded in this way in associating a subkind of ENTITY with an extensional predicate.

The categorical imperative suggests that an understanding of a subject requires the organization of the subject matter in categories, i.e., in collections of objects together with the structure preserving transformations between them. As Lawvere has emphasized in his lectures, a category provides means to comply with two requirements which at first sight look contradictory:

1. Each particular object is completely fixed and definite.

2. Each object can immediately be transformed in determinate ways into other objects.

Applying this insight to linguistics suggests that an understanding of language requires a study not only of the usual grammatical "categories" but of their transformations. The work reported in this paper should be considered as a starting point of a general theory of transformations of grammatical categories in both its syntactical and semantical aspects. The rest of this section is intended to indicate some transformations which may be amenable to the methods developed in this paper.

Many languages such as Latin, Irish and English, have verbal nouns or gerunds. Gerunds behave very much like ordinary MNs. For example, we have 'I prefer standing to sitting', which is quite on a par with 'I prefer apple juice to cider'. So one says "much standing is fatiguing" not "*many standing is fatiguing"; or "I had to do a lot of standing" not "*I had to do a large number of standing".

This transformation from a verb into a gerund applies to every verb in the language including the auxiliaries 'doing', 'being' and 'having'. The only exceptions are the modals, 'could', 'will', 'ought', etc. Romance languages, unlike Latin, tend not to have gerunds but they all have infinitives which also behave like ordinary MNs: "I like to stand". Notice, furthermore, that gerunds and infinitives lend themselves to the same sort of measures as other MNs. For example, we can say "standing two hours in line" or "to stand two hours in line." There are also transformations from gerunds and infinitives into count nouns as in 'periods standing in line' or 'periods of standing in line'. All of this suggests that gerunds and infinitives, like MNs, should be interpreted as $\bigvee$-lattices. Thus, one can speak of all the standing done by the whole human race, or by the Irish people, or by John.

The formation of gerunds and infinitives from verbs has been studied intensively but from the syntactical point of view only. Indeed, Chomsky's study of verbal nominalizations (1970) led to the development of $\overline{X}$-grammar, Jackendoff (1977). But the semantical aspects of these transformations remain to be explored.

All verbs in English with the exception of the auxiliaries and modals have gerundives and participles, that is, they all give rise through transformations to adjectives. So the verb 'travel' has a gerundive 'travelling' as in 'travelling companion' or 'travelling bag'. Participles we can illustrate by 'a much travelled man'. The semantics of gerundives is more complicated than that of the gerunds. For example, travelling companions do not need to be travelling to satisfy that description. Likewise a reading group does not need to be reading to satisfy the description. These examples indicate that the semantical relations between verbs and their gerundives are complicated and probably not accountable for in our context. On the other hand, the semantical relations between verbs and participles seem to be more straightforward. A well read man is one who has read a lot; a travelled man is one who has travelled a lot, etc.

English is particularly flexible in allowing common nouns to be transformed into verbs. You can "hand your cup" or "cup your hand"; "police the house" or "house the police". Here, the semantical relations among such transforms seem to be more regular and predictable.

Clark and Clark (1979) have drawn attention to the set of ad hoc transformations that can be performed on proper names as, for instance, in 'Do not try to do a Richard Nixon on me' or 'Don't try to Nixon me' or

'That is a typical Nixon remark'. Here the semantics of such expressions are as complicated as those of metaphors and quite probably cannot be explained as logical relations of the kind described in this paper.

Other transformations include the agentive morpheme 'er' added to verbs to form a CN: e.g., 'drive-driver'; 'watch-watcher'; 'own-owner'; 'knock-knocker'; 'slip-slipper'. Here the verb is read as typed by a particular CN: for instance 'drive' is typed by 'person'. In this case, the derived nominal may be interpreted as the subkind of PERSON corresponding to the predicate TO DRIVE, in other words, the kind of persons who drive. This situation has already been discussed at the beginning of this section. Similarly, in English 'knock' as typed by 'person' leads to 'knocker' whose interpretation is the subkind of PERSON corresponding to the predicate TO KNOCK. But 'knocker' can also denote the kind that consists of the instruments supplied for knocking with. A similar ambiguous example is 'drawer'. In this case, the semantical relations seem rather complicated.

We conclude what might otherwise be a long list by noting that most adjectives can be transformed to yield abstract nouns: 'white-whiteness'; 'true-truth'; 'hot-heat'; 'near-nearness', etc. Sometimes the transformation is unmarked morphologically: 'The wall is red' becomes 'The red of the wall'. We can do no more at this point than draw attention to the phenomenon and note that the conceptualization of abstract nouns requires mathematical resources that go beyond what we have outlined for CNs and MNs. (See the next section for a suggestion about the right context to interpret abstract nouns.)

3.3. Comments, Questions and Possible Developments

In this final section we raise some questions and we comment on some aspects of our topic that did not find their place in the main text.

The main observation is that the presentation of our paper was chosen with a reader innocent of topos theory in mind. Indeed, we worked consistently with sets only, although we used a non-standard notion of set of truth-values $\Gamma(\Omega)$ (rather than $\{0,1\}$) and consequently a non-standard notion of predicate. This set of truth-values consists of downward closed subsets of a pre-ordered set $\mathcal{P}$ of "possible situations". This has misled some critics into thinking that these "possible situations" were assumed to constitute a kind like DOG, an assumption that would contradict thesis 1.5.

Our starting point is really a topos defined over $Sets$ which satisfies some conditions spelled out in Reyes and Zolfaghari (1991). Kinds are defined to be constant objects in this topos (together with an ϵ-relation). A very special case of a topos satisfying these conditions is $Sets^{\mathcal{P}^{op}}$, the topos of "Kripke trees". The main reason for choosing it is that it is probably the topos most familiar to logicians and philosophers (besides *Sets*). In particular, validity in this topos is defined by means of the ordinary Kripke forcing.

By using the results of Reyes (1989) the topos-theoretic approach and the approach through sets with non-standard truth values are equivalent as far as kinds are concerned. Using this equivalence, we have translated everything from the topos context (where things are natural) into our non-standard set-theoretical context. In particular, the forcing relation defined in the section 2.5.3 is just the translation of the ordinary forcing relation of the topos.

Sometimes, the price to pay is the adhoc appearance of some of our notions and constructions. An example is the notion of a generalized underlying relation, which in spite of its formidable appearance is nothing but the translation of the notion of a morphism among kinds in the topos. In other cases, the price is higher.

Kinds and their predicates do not exhaust the semantical universe. Abstract nouns, for instance, do not seem to refer to kinds directly. It seems plausible that the interpretations of abstract nouns live in the topos as non-constant objects and that it is here that we can relate DOG and DOGHOOD. We plan to return to this question in a future paper. Finally, by excluding toposes, we left out of consideration categories such as reflexive graphs that offer rich possibilities to visualize and easily compute bi-Heyting operations as well as modal operators (see Reyes and Zolfaghari [in press]).

We would like to point out that Lawvere has suggested to us that kinds themselves should be conceptualized as categories rather than sets with an existence predicate. This would impose a 2-category structure on $\mathcal{K}$, the category of kinds, a notion that would require technical developments that go far beyond the elementary level of our paper. This suggestion remains to be explored.

We have not discussed a question that may have occured to the reader: reference to an individual requires a kind that individuates it and traces its identity. What about reference to a kind? By the same argument, reference to the kind DOG implies the existence of a new kind to which DOG belongs. At this point, the spectre of an infinite regress arises: Does the possibility of referring to 'Freddie' imply, after all, the existence of a rather paradoxical kind of kinds? Does this kind belong to itself?

We do not have a definite answer to this question. Recently, some topos-theoretic models of theories allowing kinds that belong to themselves have been constructed (see Hyland and Pitts 1987), but it seems that in referring to a particular dog, say Freddie, a kind is involved for reference to take place, although this kind need not itself be referred to.

Finally, something very similar to our nominal category (with underlying maps that need not be monic) has been introduced quite independently from us by theoretical computer scientists (see Reynolds 1980). And, just as our motivation was to state the functoriality of predicates along underlying maps (say from dogs to animals) in order to validate syllogistic reasoning, so theirs was, at least in part, to state the functoriality of operations along change of types (of + from the natural numbers to the reals, for example) to achieve agreement of the results. It is gratifying to see that work on problems in such different domains seems to have converged on a single solution.

4. Appendix

In this Appendix we sketch a proof of the soundness theorem (2.5.2) whose statement we recall:

Theorem 4.1.1. (Soundness) If $\Gamma \vdash_{\vec{X}} \phi$, then $\Gamma \models_{\vec{X}} \phi$

Proof. We shall say that a sequence $\Gamma \vdash_{\vec{X}} \phi$ is valid if $\Gamma \models_{\vec{X}} \phi$ and that a rule of inference is valid if the validity of the premisses implies the validity of the conclusion. The proof of this theorem is long and proceeds by showing that all axioms and rules of inference are valid. For most axioms and rules of inference this is quite straightforward, the only tricky verifications being those connected with substitution of terms. To handle these, we need a substitution lemma as is customary in soundness proofs.

Lemma 4.1.2. (Substitution) If:

1. $(\vec{X})$ and $(y : Y)$ are distinct sorted variables,

2. $(s : Y)$ is free for $(y : Y)$ in $(t : X)$, i.e., the substitution is proper,

3. $FV((t : X)[(s : Y)/(y : Y)]) \subseteq (\vec{X})$, where $FV(-)$ means the free variables of the expression contained in $(-)$,

then:
$$FV((t : X)) \subseteq (\vec{X}), (y : Y) \, ,$$
$$FV((s : Y)) \subseteq (\vec{X})$$

and:
$$\|(\vec{X}) : (t : X)[(s : Y)/(y : Y)]\|(\vec{a})$$
$$= \|(\vec{X}, (y : Y)) : (t : X)\|(\vec{a}, \|(\vec{X}) : (s : Y)\|(a))$$

where:
$$(\vec{a}) = (a_1, ..., a_n) \in \|X_1\| \times ... \times \|X_n\|$$

and:
$$a \in \|Y\|$$

Proof. The proof proceeds by induction on terms. Let us illustrate this proof for the case of $((t : Z^X)^{\iota}(q : X) : Z)$ We must show that:

$$\|(\vec{X}) : ((t : Z^X)^{\iota}(q : X) : Z)[(s : Y)/(y : Y)]\|(\vec{a})$$

$$= \|(\vec{X}, (y : Y)) : ((t : Z^X)^{\iota}(q : X) : Z)\|(\vec{a}, \|(\vec{X}) : (s : Y)\|(\vec{a}))$$

By definition of substitution, we have:

$$\|(\vec{X}) : ((t : Z^X)^{\iota}(q : X) : Z)[(s : Y)/(y : Y)]\|$$

$$= \|(\vec{X}) : ((t : Z^X)[(s : Y)/(y : Y)]^{\iota}(q : X)[(s : Y/(y : Y)] : Z)\|$$

By definition of $((t : Z^X)^{\iota}(q : X) : Z)$ we have:

$$\|(\vec{X}) : ((t : Z^X)[(s : Y)/(y : Y)]^{\iota}(q : X)[(s : Y)/(y : Y)] : Z)\|=$$
$$\|(\vec{X}) : evo < m, n >\|$$

where m and n are respectively:

$$m = \|(\vec{X}) : (t : Z^X)[(s : Y)/(y : Y)]\|$$

$$n = \|(\vec{X}) : (q : X)[(s : Y)/(y : Y)]\|$$

To apply the induction hypothesis, we must verify (1), (2) and (3).

(1) is verified by hypothesis.

(2) is verified since the fact that $(s : Y)$ is free for $(y : Y)$ in $((t : Z^X)^{\iota}(q : X) : Z)$ implies that $(s : Y)$ is free for $(y : Y)$ in $(t : Z^X)$ and $(s : Y)$ is free for $(y : Y)$ in $(q : X)$.

(3)
$$FV((t : Z^X)[(s : Y)/(y : Y)]) \subset (\vec{X})$$

and:
$$FV((q : X)[(s : Y)/(y : Y)]) \subset (\vec{X})$$

since:
$$FV(((t : Z^X)^{\iota}(q : X) : Z))[(s : Y)/(y : Y)]) \subset (\vec{X})$$

by definition. Hence:

$$\|(\vec{X}) : (t : Z^X)[(s : Y)/(y : Y)]\|(\vec{a})$$

$$= \|(\vec{X}, (y : Y)) : (t : Z^X)\|(\vec{a}, \|(\vec{X}) : (s : Y)\|(\vec{a}))$$

and:

$$\|(\vec{X}) : (q : X)[(s : Y)/(y : Y)]\|(\vec{a})$$

$$= \|(\vec{X}, (y : Y)) : (q : X)\|(\vec{a}, \|(\vec{X}) : (s : Y)\|(\vec{a}))$$

and we thus obtain:

$$\|(\vec{X}) : ((t : Z^X)^{\iota}(q : X) : Z)[(s : Y)/(y : Y)]\|(\vec{a})$$

$$= \|(\vec{X}) : evo < m, n >\|$$

where:

$$m = \|(\vec{X}, (y : Y)) : (t : Z^X)\|(\vec{a}, \|(\vec{X}) : (s : Y)\|(\vec{a}))$$

and:

$$n = \|(\vec{X}, (y : Y)) : (q : X)\|(\vec{a}, \|(\vec{X}) : (s : Y)\|(\vec{a})).$$

Finally:

$$\|(\vec{X}) : ((t : Z^X)^{\iota}(q : X) : Z)[(s : Y)/(y : Y)]\|(\vec{a})$$

$$= \|(\vec{X}) : ((t : Z^X)^{\iota}(q : X) : Z)\|(\vec{a}, \|(\vec{X}) : (s : Y)\|(\vec{a})) \quad \square$$

For terms of sort Ω (formulas), the preceding lemma can be formulated as follows: $U \Vdash \phi[(s : Y)/(y : Y)][\vec{a}]$ if and only if $U \Vdash \phi[\vec{a}, \|(\vec{X}) : (s : Y)\|(\vec{a})]$. The proof proceeds by induction on the formulas.

We remark that if $(y : Y) \in (\vec{X})$, we can always change $(y : Y)$ to another variable that has not appeared before, $(t : X)[(s : Y)/(y : Y)] = ((t : X)[(z : Y)/(y : Y)][(s : Y)/(z : Y)])$, where $(z : Y) \notin FV((t : X))$ (see van Dalen 1983).

To illustrate the proof of the soundness theorem, we verify it for the following rules (see section 2.5.4): the structural rule 1.5, the logical rule 2.3 and the rules 7.7 and 7.8 for modal operators.

1.5. Assume $\Gamma \models_{\vec{X},(x:X)} \phi$ and show that:

$$\Gamma[(t : X)/(x : X)] \models_{\vec{X}} \phi[(t : X)/(x : X)]$$

Let U and $(\vec{a}) \in \|X_1\| \times ... \times \|X_n\|$ be given and, on the assumption that $U \Vdash \Gamma[(t : X)/(x : X)][(\vec{a})]$, show that $U \Vdash \phi[(t : X)/(x : X)][(\vec{a})]$. Since the hypotheses of the lemma of substitution are satisfied:

$$U \Vdash \Gamma[(t:X)/(x:X)][(\vec{a})] \text{ iff } U \Vdash \Gamma[\vec{a}, \|(\vec{X}):(t:X)\|(\vec{a})]$$

But by hypothesis:

$$\forall U, \forall \vec{a}, b \ U \Vdash \Gamma[\vec{a}, b] \implies U \Vdash \phi[\vec{a}, b]$$

We choose then $b = \|(\vec{X}):(t:X)\|(\vec{a})$ and conclude:

$$U \Vdash \phi[\vec{a}, \|(\vec{X}):(t:X)\|(\vec{a})]$$

2.3. We must show that:

$$p\backslash q \models_{\vec{X}} r \iff p \models_{\vec{X}} q \lor r$$

($\Rightarrow$) Let $U \Vdash p[\vec{a}]$ and $U \nVdash q[\vec{a}]$. From now on we will leave out the " $\vec{a}$ ". So, by the definition of $\models$ for \ we have $U \Vdash (p\backslash q)$ and hence $U \Vdash r$.
($\Leftarrow$) Let $U \Vdash (p\backslash q)$. Hence $\exists V \geq U$ such that $V \Vdash p$ and $V \nVdash q$. Hence we have that $V \Vdash r$, (the other possibility is ruled out since $V \nVdash q$). We then conclude $U \Vdash r$ by functoriality of the forcing relation.

7.7. We show that $\models_{\vec{X}} \Diamond \phi \leftrightarrow \neg\Box\neg\phi$, namely, given U, $U \Vdash \neg\Box\neg\phi$ if and only if $U \Vdash \Diamond \phi$. We leave out as before "$\vec{a}$ ". But by definition:

$$U \Vdash \neg\Box\neg\phi \text{ iff } \forall V \leq U \ V \nVdash \Box\neg\phi$$

$$\text{iff } \forall V \leq U \neg(\forall W \ W \Vdash \neg\phi)$$

$$\text{iff } \forall V \leq U \ \exists W \ W \nVdash \neg\phi$$

$$\text{iff } \forall V \leq U \ \exists W \neg(\forall W' \leq W \ W' \nVdash \phi)$$

$$\text{iff } \forall V \leq U \ \exists W \exists W' \leq W \ W' \Vdash \phi$$

$$\text{iff } \exists W \ W \Vdash \phi \text{ iff } U \Vdash \Diamond \phi$$

7.8. We show that given U, $U \Vdash \Box\phi \lor \neg\Box\phi$. By definition of forcing, we must then show:

$$U \Vdash \Box\phi \text{ or } U \Vdash \neg\Box\phi$$

equivalently:

$$\forall V \ V \Vdash \phi \text{ or } \forall W \leq U \ W \nVdash \Box\phi$$

equivalently:

$$\forall V \ V \Vdash \phi \text{ or } \forall W \leq U \neg(\forall V \ V \Vdash \phi)$$

equivalently:

$$\forall V V \Vdash \phi \text{ or } \forall W \leq U \exists V V \nVdash \phi$$

and finally:

$$\forall V V \Vdash \phi \text{ or } \exists V V \nVdash \phi$$

which is true.

Starting from the axioms and rules of inference that we have stated in section 2.5.4, we can deduce theorems in the usual way. For instance, let us prove the following theorem.

Theorem 4.1.3. (Constant domain) $\forall (x : X)(\sigma \vee \phi(x : X)) \longleftrightarrow \sigma \vee \forall (x : X)\phi(x : X)$ where $(x : X)$ is not a free variable of σ.

Proof. Assume (1) $p \vdash_{\vec{x}} \forall (x : X)(\sigma \vee \phi(x : X))$ and apply the logical rule 2.4 to obtain (2) $p \vdash_{\vec{x} \vee (x:X)} \sigma \vee \phi(x : X)$. Then by applying the logical rule 2.3 we obtain (3) $p \backslash \sigma \vdash_{\vec{x} \vee (x:X)} \phi(x : X)$. Then by applying 2.4 again, we obtain (4) $p \backslash \sigma \vdash_{\vec{x}} \forall (x : X)\phi(x : X)$ and finally by applying once more 2.3 we obtain (5) $p \vdash_{\vec{x}} \sigma \vee \forall (x : X)\phi(x : X)$.$\square$

We remark that in general, these arguments are not valid in a topos for which the set $P(A)$ of subobjects of a given object A constitutes a co-Heyting algebra, with a subtraction operation $\backslash_A : P(A) \times P(A) \longrightarrow P(A)$ satisfying the adjunction:

$$\frac{F \backslash G \subseteq H}{F \subseteq G \cup H}$$

where F, G are subobjects of A. The reason is that $\pi^*(F \backslash G) \neq \pi^* F \backslash \pi^* G$ for:

$$A \times B \xrightarrow{\pi} A.$$

But this is precisely what is involved in the step from (3) to (4) in the proof of the last theorem. However, since we interpret kinds as constant objects in the topos, this property is satisfied, (see Reyes and Zolfaghari [in press]).

Acknowledgments

We would first like to express our gratitude to Bill Lawvere for his encouragement and for several suggestions that have helped to improve our paper in substantial ways. In particular, he suggested the notion of entity for a system of kinds, a notion that is central to the whole development. We have also profited from the study of his paper (this volume).

We would also like to thank Houman Zolfaghari. Some of the work reported in this paper was done in collaboration with him and we are grateful for the continuing interest he has shown in our work.

John Macnamara and Gonzalo Reyes gratefully acknowledge the support of individual grants from the Canada's National Science and Engineering Research Council (NSERC). Marie La Palme Reyes gratefully acknowledges support of a post-doctoral fellowship from Canada's Social Sciences and Humanities Research Council (SSHRC).

References

Aquinas, St Thomas (1964). *In Duodecim Libros Metaphysicorum Aristotelis Expositio.* Bk 4, Lectio 2, Para 558. M-R. Cathala and R.M. Spiazzi (eds.). Turin: Marietti Press

Aristotle (1984). *The Complete Works of Aristotle.* Barnes, J. (ed.) Vol. 1. Bollingen series. Princeton, NJ: Princeton University Press

Bach, E. (1986). The algebra of events. *Linguistics and Philosophy* 9: 5-16

Barwise, J., and J. Perry (1983). *Situations and Attitudes.* Cambridge, MA: Bradford/MIT Press

Bennett, M. (1979). Mass nouns and mass terms in Montague grammar. In S. Davis and M. Mithun (eds.) *Linguistics, Philosophy and Montague Grammar.* Austin, TX: University of Texas Press

Boileau, A., and A. Joyal (1981). La logique des topos. *Journal of Symbolic Logic* 46: 6-16

Bressan, A. (1972). *A General Interpreted Modal Calculus.* New Haven, CT: Yale University Press

Chomsky, N. (1970). Remarks on Nominalization. R. Jacobs and P. Rosenbaum (eds.), *Readings in English Transformational Grammar.* Waltham, MS: Ginn, 184-227. In N. Chomsky (1972), 11-61

Chomsky, N. (1972). *Studies on Semantics in Generative Grammar.* The Hague: Mouton

Clark, E. V., and H. H. Clark (1979). When nouns surface as verbs. *Language* 55: 767-811

Cohen, P. J. (1966). *Set Theory and the Continuum Hypothesis.* New York: W. A. Benjamin.

van Dalen, D. (1983). *Logic and Structure.* 2nd Ed. Universitext. Berlin: Springer-Verlag

Eco, U., M. Santambrogio and P. Violi (eds.) (1988). *Meaning and Mental Representation.* Bloomington, IN: Indiana University Press

Fourman, M. P., and D. S. Scott (1979). Sheaves and logic. In M. P. Fourman, C. J. Mulvey and D. S. Scott (eds.), *Applications of Sheaves.* Lecture Notes in Mathematics 753. Berlin: Springer-Verlag

Geach, P. T. (1957). *Mental Acts*. London: Routledge and Kegal Paul

Geach, P. T. (1972). *Logic Matters*. Berkeley, CA: University of California Press

Geach, P. T. (1980). *Reference and Generality*. 3rd Ed. Ithaca, NY: Cornell University Press

Gupta, A. K. (1980). *The Logic of Common Nouns*. New Haven, CT: Yale University Press

Hobbes, T. (1839). *Concerning Body*. In W. Wolesworth (ed.) *The English Works of Thomas Hobbes* Vol. 1. London: J. Bohn

Hyland, J. M. E., and A. M. Pitts (1987). The theory of constructions: categorical semantics and topos-theoretic models. In John W. Gray and André Scedrov (eds.) *Categories in Computer Science and Logic*. American Mathematical Society, Providence, RI. Contemporary Mathematics 92: 137-199

Jackendoff, R. (1977). $\overline{X}$-*Syntax: A Study of Phrase Structure*. Linguistic Inquiry Monograph 2. Cambridge, MA: MIT Press

Jackendoff, R. (1991). Parts and boundaries. *Cognition* 41: 9-45

Kripke, S. A. (1980). *Naming and Necessity*. Oxford: Basil Blackwell

Lambek, J., and P. J. Scott (1986). *Introduction to Higher Order Categorical Logic*. Cambridge Studies in Advanced Mathematics 7. Cambridge: Cambridge University Press

La Palme Reyes, M., J. Macnamara and G. E. Reyes (Forthcoming) Functoriality and grammatical role in syllogisms.

La Palme Reyes, M. (This volume). Referential structure of fictional texts

Lawvere, F. W. (in press). Categories of space and of quantity. In Proceedings of the conference on Structures in Mathematical Theories, San Sebastian (September 1990)

Lawvere, F. W. (This volume). Tools for the Advancement of Objective Logic: Closed categories and toposes.

Macnamara, J. (1982). *Names for Things: A Study of Human Learning*. Cambridge, MA: Bradford/MIT Press

Macnamara, J. (1986). *A Border Dispute: The Place of Logic in Psychology*. Cambridge, MA: Bradford/MIT Press

Macnamara, J. (1989). Review of *Meaning and Mental Representations* by U. Eco, M. Santambrogio and P. Violi (eds.), (1988). *Journal of Language and Social Psychology* 8: 349-353

Macnamara, J., and G. E. Reyes (This volume). Foundational issues in the learning of proper names, count nouns and mass nouns

Magnan, F., and G. E. Reyes (This volume). Category theory as a conceptual tool in the study of cognition

Mates, B. (1986) *The Philosophy of Leibniz*. Oxford: Oxford University Press

Putnam, H. (1978). The meaning of "meaning". In K. Grunderson (ed.), *Language, Mind and Knowledge*. Minnesota Studies in the Philosophy of Science. Minnesota: University of Minnesota Press

Putnam, H. (This volume). Logic and psychology

Quine, W. V. (1953). *From a Logical Point of View*. Cambridge, MA: Harvard University Press

Quine, W. V. (1960). *Word and Object*. Cambridge, MA: MIT Press

Reyes, G. E. (1989). Non-standard truth values and modalities. In *Proceedings of 1989 Sienna Meeting on Modal and Tense Logics*

Reyes, G. E. (1991). A topos-theoretic approach to reference and modality. *Notre Dame Journal of Formal Logic* 32: 359-91

Reyes, G. E., and H. Zolfaghari (1991). Topos-theoretic approaches to modality. In A. Carboni, M. C. Pedicchio and G. Rosolini (eds.). *Category Theory*, Proceedings, Como 1990. LNM 1488. Berlin: Springer Verlag

Reyes, G. E., and H. Zolfaghari (In press). Bi-Heyting algebras, toposes and modalities

Reyes, M. (1988). *A Semantics for Literary Texts*. Ph.D thesis. Montréal: Concordia University

Reynolds, J. (1980). Using category theory to design implicit conversions and generic operators. In Neil D. Jones *Proceedings of the Aarhus Workshop Semantics-Directed Compiler Generation*. Lecture Notes in Computer Science 94. Berlin: Sringer Verlag

Sommers, F. (1982). *The Logic of Natural Language*. Oxford: Clarendon Press

Szabo, M. E. (1969). *The Collected Papers of Gerhard Gentzen*. Studies in Logic and the Foundations of Mathematics. Amsterdam: North-Holland Publishing Company

Wiggins, D. (1980). *Sameness and Substance*. Oxford: Basil Blackwell

7

Foundational Issues in the Learning of Proper Names, Count Nouns and Mass Nouns

John Macnamara and Gonzalo E. Reyes

Although the foundations laid down in La Palme Reyes, Macnamara and Reyes (this volume) are crucial to the psychology of word learning, they are not in themselves psychology but logic. This paper bridges the gap. It begins with a general statement about the problem of explaining how anyone learns proper names, count nouns and mass nouns. It goes on to lay down a psychological postulate from which, in conjunction with the theses laid down in La Palme Reyes, Macnamara and Reyes (this volume), we draw two conclusions of paramount importance for the theory of learning in general. We next proceed, in the light of our logical and psychological foundations, to specify what the learner must express at the point of learning a proper name, a count noun or a mass noun. For simplicity we confine ourselves to basic-level count nouns and mass nouns. We do not carry out a comprehensive review of the experimental literature. That task we leave to Geoff Hall in the article that follows this one.

1. General Statement of the Problem of Explaining Word Learning

Introduction

Explaining how children can learn proper names, count nouns and mass nouns are particular cases of explaining how anyone can learn anything, a problem that Bertrand Russell (1948) formulated strikingly: "How comes it that human beings, whose contacts with the world are brief and personal and limited, are nevertheless able to know as much as they do know?" We, too, might ask of a particular child learning a particular count noun: How is it that he or she can learn 'dog'? Notice that the sceptic's rejoinder that our knowledge is an illusion is irrelevant in relation to the language, since the sceptic has to rely on knowledge of language even to state his thesis.

There are many problems for the learner to solve, some well-known and some not. To make things concrete, imagine a boy of about 15 months who hears the word 'dog' correctly applied to Freddie, a puppy. By way of introducing our topic, we list a number of the main problems that the child has to solve to be able to use the word correctly. (1) Does 'dog' denote an attribute (e.g., colour), an action (e.g., sniffing), a kind (e.g., DOG), or an individual in a kind (e.g., Freddie)? (2) Granted 'dog' denotes a kind, is it a kind to which the whole dog belongs or just a part? Is it the dog's face or the visible exterior parts, or does it embrace the invisible interior parts? (3) Granted 'dog' denotes a kind to which the whole dog belongs, which kind is it? Reasonable candidates might be PHYSICAL OBJECT, LIVING BEING, ANIMAL, BLACK ANIMAL, MALE ANIMAL, DOG, POODLE, PET, DOMESTIC ANIMAL. Quine (1960, chap. 2) has pointed out that things may be much worse, because there are lots of "unreasonable" but applicable candidates, e.g., UNDE-TACHED DOG PARTS, SLICES OF DOG TIME. (4) To what grammatical category does the word 'dog' belong? Without an answer to this question, the child will not be able to use the word grammatically. While at first he may use the word on its own, before long he will be combining it with other words to make skeletal sentences.

Similar problems confront the child in the process of learning a proper name such as 'Freddie' or a mass noun such as 'water'. These are all problems that the child must grapple with independently in the sense that parents and friends cannot explain to him what 'dog' means and how the word is classified grammatically. To do so would presuppose a considerable knowledge of his mother tongue (which we assume to be English). But this is precisely what he is just beginning to acquire.

These or similar problems have been recognized since antiquity. In the *Meno*, Plato states his celebrated paradox of learning as follows: "But how will you look for something when you don't in the least know what it is? How on earth are you going to set up something you don't know as the object of your search? To put it another way, even if you come right up against it, how will you know that what you have found is the thing you didn't know?" Applied to the little boy, the paradox suggests that he can discover the meaning and grammatical categories of the words he hears only if he already knows them. If our analysis is correct, it is clear that the child, searching for the interpretation of the word 'dog' and for the grammatical category to which the word belongs, must be greatly constrained in the hypotheses that he entertains and in his interpretation of the scant evidence. Our task is to describe these constraints, and to go on from there to give psychological explanations of the workings of the child's mind.

We try to state our problem, à la Chomsky, by first representing, in a manageable way, the knowledge attained by the child during the process of learning. Then we try to answer the question of how he acquired this knowledge, basing ourselves on well-motivated psychological theses.

Our approach is a reworking of Macnamara (1986), where an account of how children may solve many of the above questions was proposed also in the form of a representation of the child's knowledge. As we will see, such representations take us right into fundamental questions of the appropriate logic (and semantics) of the grammatical categories that interest us.

Since representations of the learner's knowledge are at the core of our theory, we must clarify our notion of representation. A representation need not resemble what it represents in the way a map or a photograph do. For example, in dynamics the trajectory of a projectile is represented by a system of equations, which enable one to calculate height, velocity and direction at each point in the trajectory. There is no suggestion that the projectile itself is computing any of these values. Similarly, there is no suggestion in our representations that children express the knowledge in precisely the form we offer. Rather, we claim that they must represent the same information in some manner. In particular, we do not expect that children can tell other people the information they have learned. We do, however, expect them to reveal their knowledge indirectly, in their utterances and actions.

We adopt the strategy of representing a child's possible "states of knowledge" as nodes of a tree growing downwards from its root (like phrase-structure trees). At each node we specify a couple consisting of a fragment of a many-sorted language L and a fragment of its metalanguage ML (both explained below) that represent the knowledge of the system at that state. This specification is subject to the following constraint: whenever a node q is immediately below another node p, the fragments at p are subfragments of those at q. In other words, knowledge increases as we go down the tree. The knowledgeable reader will recognize something very similar to the Kripke representation of Brouwer's idealized mathematician (see, e.g., Dalen, 1983). At a given time during the process of learning, the cognitive system of the child is in a state of knowledge that is represented by a node in the tree together with its specified fragments. If we make the simplifying assumption that the child does not forget, his knowledge will increase and hence his cognitive system will determine a downward "trajectory" through the nodes, starting from the root of the tree. At the root there is a stock of primitive symbols and primitive rules of interpretation. Growth may take place in several ways: by extending the vocabulary with new count nouns such as 'dog'; new proper names such as 'Freddie' and new mass nouns such as 'water'; by adding new sentences some of which may be false: 'This is Freddie', 'Freddie is gone', 'Freddie is sick', 'The word "dog" is a proper name'; and by establishing appropriate rules of interpretation. These rules will state, for instance, that 'Freddie' is interpreted as a particular dog, that 'dog' applies to dogs, and that 'Freddie is sick' may be correctly asserted in situations in which the dog in question is sick and not otherwise. This developing language is a mixed one; some symbols are primitive in L, whereas others are learned and belong to the mother tongue of the child.

Since we are not concerned with the learning of sentences in general, we do not specify further the syntax of the language.

The aim of our representation is to specify intentional abilities of the cognitive system, and this we achieve as follows: the root of the tree represents the cognitive system at the moment that learning starts. At the root we place the unlearned logical resources of the system. The intentional ability of the system to refer to a member of a kind is typically represented by a proper name sorted by a count noun, e.g., 'Freddie' sorted by 'dog'. We will write '(Freddie:dog)'. The intentional ability to judge a statement to be true or false is represented by a sentence. In particular, the ability to handle questions of sameness of members of a kind is represented by sentences of the form '(a:A) = (b:A)'. Further abilities will be represented later.

Some terms that we have used may be unfamiliar to some readers, and so we will explain them briefly. By a many-sorted language, we understand a language that has different sorts such as 'water', 'dog' and 'man'. These are interpreted as the kinds WATER, DOG and MAN respectively. For reasons explained in the preceding article we do not believe that all these sorts can be reduced to a single-sort THING, in the manner of classical logic. All the terms in the language are sorted, in the sense that their appliation is dependent on appropriate common nouns. Thus 'black', as applied in conjunction with 'human skin', has a different interpretation from black as applied in conjunction with 'ink'. For a related observation see Medin and Schoben (1988). The child acquires a vocabulary of proper names ('John', 'Freddie'), count nouns ('person', 'man', 'passenger') mass nouns ('water', 'milk') and predicables ('meet', 'black', 'run', 'in the garden'). These can be combined with primitive symbols such as individual variables x, y, z, etc. and variables ranging over kinds, X, Y, Z, etc., and quantifiers such as 'there is' and 'for all'. In English, the nearest equivalents would be expressions like 'there is an x in Y' and 'Every x in X'. In L we will express the sort by means of a colon followed by a symbol for a kind. This will give us examples like : (x:person), read 'x in the kind PERSON'; (John:person), read 'John in the kind PERSON'; $\exists(x:X)$, read 'There is an individual x in the kind X'; 'Meet ((John:person), (Freddie:dog))' read 'The person John meets the dog Freddie'. Such expressions may appear cumbersome, but we will see that that is the price of clarity. In the meantime, notice that since 'stupid' as applied to the person Gussie means something rather different from 'stupid' as applied to the goose Gussie, our notation provides for this by distinguishing 'stupid (Gussie:person)' from 'stupid(Gussie:goose)'. In La Palme Reyes, Macnamara and Reyes (this volume), provision is made for generalized predicables, but initial learning must be of predicables that are individually typed.

Since word-learners must assign the words they learn to a grammatical category, they must have means to specify the symbols of L as 'entities'. To see the necessity for this, consider the two statements 'Freddie is sick' and 'Freddie is a proper name'. From the truth of both it would follow that a proper name is sick, which is absurd. What has gone wrong is that the second statement is not about a dog, but about the name of a dog, about a linguistic entity. To separate the two sorts of statement and thus block the absurd consequence, we use inverted commas to refer to the symbol. Thus, the second sentence may be stated as 'The word "Freddie" is a proper name', or simply '"Freddie" is a proper name'. Learners also need expressions for the grammatical categories of proper name, count noun and mass noun. We chose 'PN', 'CN' and 'MN' to perform those functions. Children need to form sentences (not necessarily in the mother tongue), some describing the non-linguistic world and some describing entities in the linguistic one. It is convenient to place resources describing the non-linguistic world in a language L and those describing linguistic entities in a metalanguage ML, in which there are resources to describe the (object) language L. Thus the count noun 'dog' we place in L, but the linguistic expression 'CN' we place in ML.

Bear in mind what we said about our representations. For instance, if we claim that the sentence 'The word "Freddie" is a proper name' has been added at a given state of knowledge, we do not mean that the child should be able, at that point, to assert the English phrase 'The word "Freddie" is a proper name'. What our representation is meant to imply, however, is that he must have logical resources to allow him to recognize 'Freddie' as a word (in particular as something distinct from a sneeze or a sigh) and, furthermore, that he recognizes that this word refers to a particular dog and hence that the word 'Freddie' is not of the same type as 'dog', a word which applies to all dogs.

2. Fundamental Psychological Thesis

2.1. *Aristotelean Thesis: We Can Learn to Assign Individuals to (for Us) New Kinds and Also Learn Names for the Kinds*

Plato, believing that all knowledge of kinds is innate, downplayed the role of perception. With Aristotle we hold that through our perceptual systems we can learn to assign individuals to at least some kinds that are new to us. For example, we assume that Julius Caesar had no concept of a telephone and that he did not know a name for the kind; and that today children can learn that certain objects are telephones and learn to apply the word 'telephone' to them. We imagine that in this thesis we have the support of most psychologists and philosophers. We imagine further that all psychologists and philosophers would be interested in a theory that made rational provision for such learning.

Plato was of a different opinion and he is not without contemporary followers, notably Jerry Fodor (1975). What impressed Plato was the paradox of learning with which we opened the article. Contemporary Platonists feel the paradox has never been resolved and, despairing of a solution along Aristotelean lines, opt for the innateness of the concept of dog. It is no surprise that Fodor has proposed an unlearned language of thought. We hold that he is right to have done so, though we also feel that the unlearned expressive powers he posited are too extensive. In simpler terms, we feel that the human mind is capable of learning how to categorize in various domains, of setting up count nouns and mass nouns to denote kinds and, in favourable circumstances, of learning their definitions. More concretely, this means that, while Fodor would be inclined to take our 'dog' in L as an unlearned primitive, we argue that it is a learned one. We accept fully the burden of giving a psychologically reasonable account of how it might be learned. Ultimately, what is at issue here is a satisfactory conceptualization of induction, the process of generalizing from particular experience. That would take us too far from our central concerns; but for an account of induction in keeping with the logic of kinds see Macnamara (1991). We will confine ourselves to more narrowly psychological aspects of the learning.

We realize that children cannot meet members of all the kinds for which they learn names. Frequently they learn names for kinds on the basis of pictures or descriptions of members of the kind. This applies, as Goodman has pointed out, even when the kinds, being legendary, have no members in our world. Still, who has not seen a picture of a unicorn?

We will not go into the cognitive processes that lead scientists, on the basis of perceptual observations, to posit the existence of kinds that are theoretical constructs and whose members are inaccessible to the senses even with the aid of scientific instruments.

3. Some Psychological Consequences of the Logical Theses and the Aristotelean Thesis

3.1. Psychological Theorem: There Are Psychologically Privileged Kinds

Plato's paradox of learning, together with the Aristotelean thesis, implies the presence in learners of biases to recognize certain kinds and to attach new words to those kinds. We begin with what we believe to be the most fundamental among these biases.

The world does not present itself to children as an amorphous mass or a fog, because perception divides it into perceptual individuals. That is, perception yields individuals, the figures of perceptual theory. Perceptual individuals appear to have a certain identity over movement and change of shape. Recognition of an individual as familiar is also a perceptual suggestion of identity. Perceptual individuals are situated; they are figures against a ground. And perception also suggests kinds for perceived individuals. Dogs have a sufficiently distinctive appearance that we can readily distinguish them from such similar creatures as cats and sheep. But this means that the perceptual system is already typing perceptual figures—as doglike, catlike, sheeplike and so on. Perhaps at the early stages of development, some such general kind as PERCEPTUAL OBJECT corresponding to perceptual figures is all-important. Susan Carey has strongly suggested to us the need for such a kind. While we believe she is right, we have not to date worked out the place of such a kind in the theory of kinds, and so we will use the notion in a purely common-sense manner, leaving it to a later date to work out its place in the theory. Notice, however, that because perceptual objects are being attached to perceptual figures there is no temptation to take 'perceptual object' as a universal sort.

We take PERCEPTUAL OBJECT to be the interpretation of perceptual figure. Psychologists often visualize infants as confronted with a stock of individuals which they then have to sort into kinds: buckets, bicycles, people and so on. The individuals, prior to such sorting, are, then, perceptual objects. What we require is a natural tendency to take a count noun as a name for a unique kind, a kind to which belongs as a whole the perceptual object to which the word is applied. One of the most interesting results of studies in cognition is the discovery of a set of jus such kind'"basic-level' kinds. We are not sure who discovered it. We owe our introduction to the notion to the works of Eleanor Rosch (e.g., 1977). We do not feel that we can define the notion. It seems more promising to describe it in such a way that, with the aid of examples, readers can catch on, if they do not already know the notion.

First, it is the highest level in a hierarchy of kinds – e.g., MALE POODLE, POODLE, DOG, QUADRUPED, ANIMAL – at which perceptual similarity among members is still salient. In the hierarchy given, this level is DOG. The salience of perceptual similarities at this level is revealed in several psychological tests. DOG is the highest level at which a single image comfortably represents the kind. For example, people understand an instruction to draw or imagine a dog; they are puzzled when asked to draw or imagine a quadruped, wondering if they should draw a horse or an alligator, since both are quadrupeds. The contrast in appearance between poodles and collies, for example, does not give rise to the same puzzlement. The test applies in reverse, too. When shown a picture of a prototypical dog, people tend to judge it to be a picture of a dog rather than of a quadruped or of a poodle. The effect can be seen in certain reaction times. When people are asked if a picture represents a dog, their reaction times are quicker than when asked if it represents a quadruped or a poodle. Apparently the basic level is the highest in the hierarchy where people have a standard stock of motor responses for dealing with the kind. People can think of all sorts of ways to treat a dog; they think of far fewer ways to treat a quadruped. The names for basic-level kinds tend to be shorter than those for other kinds in the hierarchy, and they tend to be used more frequently. These and other psychological results are reported in Rosch, Mervis, Gray, Johnson and Boyes-Braem (1976) and in Rosch, Simpson and Miller (1976).

Putting together the evidence, we conclude that the basic level is the highest in a hierarchy of kinds at which a kind is marked in perception. It is because of its status in perception, not cognition, that the basic level is psychologically privileged. Precisely because it is not privileged at the cognitive level, we are able to see that from a logical point of view, basic-level kinds are just one level among many. This way of looking at things puts us in opposition to several writers in the area, e.g., Posner and Keele (1968), Rosch, Simpson and Miller (1976) and more recently Lakoff (1988). For all that, our position seems quite natural, and what is more, it takes into account Osherson and Smith's (1981) trenchant criticism of the conceptual reading of basic-level kinds.

The mass noun 'gold', taken as naming an individual in the kind METAL, names an abstract individual, which therefore gives rise to no perceptual gestalt, not to mention a basic-level one. Gold, however, has a distinctive appearance, which is easy to visualize. We cannot say the same of the more general 'metal'. It follows that the notion of basic-level perceptual types can be extended to mass nouns in their interpretation as portions of some basic-level stuff.

A special attraction of basic-level theory is the feature that each perceived object belongs to at most one basic-level atomic kind (e.g., a ring) and at most one basic-level mass kind (e.g., gold). The 'at most' is to allow room for strange visual presentations. We do not know whether the visual system achieves a basic-level typing of all gestalts immediately or whether time is required. From the point of view of learning common nouns, basic-level kinds are exactly what is required, namely unique, psychologically privileged kinds. We should add that we are aware that some authors feel that the basic-level kind may change with experience. For example, FISH is a basic-level kind for most of us. For those who fish cod, perhaps, COD may become among fish what DOG is among mammals for us. But if this is so, even then there is still among cod fishers only one basic-level kind for the visual presentation of a cod, namely COD; not FISH as it is for us.

The reader may wonder that we have not mentioned Quine's proposal for psychological biasing. Quine (1960, p. 83) proposes that children are endowed with a "prelinguistic quality space" which in Quine (1969, p. 123) he claims to be "innate." The trouble with this is that it does not recognize the fundamental logical distinction between kinds (denoted by count and mass nouns) and qualities (denoted by verbs and adjectives). Quine of course speaks of objects. He called his best-known book 'Word and Object'. In Quine (1969, p. 10) he characterizes Mamma, for the child, as a "cohesive spatiotemporal convexity" and an "integrated spatiotemporal thing." Now Mamma is not just a tissue of qualities; she is not just an amalgam of pink and grey and soft and slow-moving and noise-emitting. She is an individual in the kind PERSON who has all those qualities at least some of the time. Quine makes no provision in his theory for individuals in kinds. So, despite appearances, he makes no provision for objects. That is why we could not make use of his quality space.

So far we have established only the psychological plausibility of basic-level kinds. Later, we must go on to look at several other matters, including the role that such kinds play in the learning of count and mass nouns.

3.2. The Learning Theorem

We now derive a theorem from the fundamental postulate, a theorem so fundamental that it deserves a name for itself, the Learning Theorem. We may add that its relevance to psychology extends far beyond the learning of words. We prepare the way by introducing a pair of terms.

There is a basic distinction to be drawn in psychology between the 'intentional' and the 'non-intentional'. Under both fall skills, states and events. We introduce the distinction by a few examples. A person can be in a physiological state of arousal or hunger; can have the physiological skill to tie shoelaces, type, ride a bicycle, dance; can have the perceptual skill of recognizing Greek letters; can exercise these skills by actually tying shoelaces, typing, cycling, dancing or recognizing Greek letters. On the other hand, consider such intentional states as knowing that Napolean died on St.Helena and wondering about the exact number of symphonies that Mozart wrote; such intentional skills as the ability to prove theorems in mathematics; and such intentional events as judging sentences to be true. In these examples, the intuitive difference between the intentional and the non intentional is clear enough, but how can we give a principled distinction between them?

Physiological states, skills and events can all be explained, insofar as they can be explained, in the language of physiology and physiological psychology. No doubt some are enormously complex and cannot at present be explained in any language. Yet those that can be explained, can be explained in physiological theory, and we are confident that explanations for many others will also be given in the same theory. This does not preclude a role for the intentional in the establishing of physiological states and skills, especially at the initial stages. Imagine, for example, a dancing master telling students how they should hold their partners and place their feet. If successful, however, the instruction results in habits that permit smooth and automatic performance: automatic in the sense that initial conscious effort guided by verbal instruction has been replaced by unconsciously operating motor skills. The instruction is conducive to, but not constitutive of, the resulting physiological states and skills.

The intentional, on the other hand, essentially involves strings of interpreted symbols as constitutive of its states, skills and events; strings that are interpreted as expressing truth-conditions, or, more generaly, satisfaction-conditions. Thus, for instance, a man who is in the intentional state of knowing that Napolean died on St. Helena needs symbols that refer to Napoleon and St. Helena. Furthermore, he must be able to combine these symbols to generate the string 'Napoleon died on

St. Helena' (or an equivalent one in some language), and be able to assign the truth-value true to the sentence in question.

From our definition of the intentional, it follows that the learning of words belongs to this category. The child who has learned a proper name for a particular dog must have a symbol to refer to the dog as well as the ability to combine this symbol with others to generate interpreted sentences.

Noam Chomsky (1986) has quite correctly pointed out that the picture is not as tidy as we have just presented it. For one thing, we have not been fair to perceptual processes. We propose to demonstrate the autonomy of the theory of perception from that of cognition elsewhere. Here we will briefly indicate how the proof of the autonomy will go. The crucial point is that one can fix a percept, say, of a dog, and appropriately apply the concepts dog, poodle, pet, quadruped, mammal, animal; one can fix a concept, say, animal, and apply it appropriately in connection with such perceptual figures as are afforded by dogs, birds, worms, fish, spiders and lobsters. That is, one can fix the percept and vary the concept; fix the concept and vary the percept. This effectively distinguishes the theory of perception from that of cognition--which is not, we might add, the same as ruling out top-down effects in perception.

The purpose of this digression is to highlight the distinction between the intentional or cognitive on the one hand, and the perceptual or physiological on the other. The essential difference is that all and only cognitive states and events involve the interpretation of sentences. They may involve much more, but not less. We are now in a position to state the following.

Learning Theorem: There is no purely non-intentional (physiological and/or perceptual) explanation for the acquisition of intentional skills or the existence of intentional states or events.

Proof: Intentional states, skills and events involve strings of interpreted symbols. These strings include some symbols that refer to kinds or predicates of kinds. It follows that all intentional states, skills and events involve kinds; they involve reference to kinds. But kinds, even those like DOG whose members are physical objects, are abstract. They do not interact causally with their own members or with the members of any kinds, including minds. In particular, they play no part in events under purely physiological or perceptual description. Hence the core of an intentional state, skill or event eludes physiological or perceptual explanation. This is the learning theorem.

A consequence of our theorem is that the exercise of a skill under purely physiological description cannot explain the emergence of an intentional state. In the present context, this implies that practice in pronouncing a word, even in circumstances that are constrained by a teacher to be appropriate in one way or another, does not yield a grasp of its logic or of its syntax.

Some readers may be surprised to find an impossibility statement raised to such prominence. Let us recall the fundamental role played in physics and mathematics by such statements. The second law of thermodynamics, for instance, can be stated as the impossibility of constructing a perpetuum mobile of the second kind. In Euclidean geometry it is impossible, with just compass and straight edge, to trisect an angle.

Apart from our proof of the learning theorem, several arguments have been proposed in recent times against the possibility of reducing intentional explanations to physiological ones. See especially Churchland (1984), Cummins (1983 and 1989), Davidson (1980), Stich (1983) and Putnam (1988). Though the purposes of those who argue against such reduction are varied and even incompatible among themselves, their writings can be seen as arguments for a radical division between the physiological and the intentional, and hence as arguments for the learning theorem. There are also writers seeking to reduce the notion of reference to notions of non-intentional or, as they are sometimes called, 'natural' causes--Dretske (1981 and 1988), Fodor (1987) and Millikan (1984). The inadequacies of these attempts are abundantly demonstrated by Cummins (1989). We would merely add that the basic reason for all the inadequacies lies in the theory of reference and in the central role of abstract entites in that theory, as the proof of the learning theorem shows.

We should add that our position does not commit us to dualism, any more than a similar position commits Fodor (1975) or Davidson (1980) to dualism. The reason is that dualism does not illuminate the ability to refer to abstract entities. It follows that such reference does not require dualism.

3.3.1. Unlearned Logical Resources and the Language of Thought

We now employ the learning theorem in conjunction with a linguistic postulate to demonstrate that there are unlearned logical resources. The linguistic postulate (which bears an affinity to thesis 1.3 of La Palme Reyes, Macnamara and Reyes, this volume) is that there is a dialectical relation between sentences and the words of which they are composed:

just as words in their order determine sentences, sentences determine the grammatical category and reference of each constituent word. For example, 'hand' can occur as a noun or as a verb ('Give me your *hand*' vs. '*Hand* me your cup'). In the first of these examples it applies to a body part; in the context, 'Give me a *hand* to find my glasses' it means assistance. It follows that a word is determined in grammatical category and reference only by a sentence. Presented with a word in isolation, learners have no ostensible reason to assign it any grammatical category or any semantic role. Indeed there is no reason for them to take it as a word at all. If, however, they take their teacher as applying the word to some object(s) or property(ies), then they stand a chance of assigning it a semantic role and hence, as we will see, a grammatical category. Success, however, depends not only on the expressive intent of the teacher but on learners' comprehension of that intent. That in turn depends on learners' formulating the teacher's expressive intent in a sentence of their own.

We are now in a position to state and prove a psychologically important corollary:

Corollary: There are unlearned logical resources.

Proof: Consider the first event of intentional learning in a person's life. What is learned in that event is either (i) non-linguistic in the sense of being some fact about the non-linguistic world, or it is linguistic; and if it is linguistic it is either (ii) a sentence or (iii) a constituent of a sentence. We consider the three cases separately. (i) If what is learned is non-linguistic, nevertheless the event, being intentional, makes essential use of an interpreted string of symbols. These, ex hypothesi, cannot have been acquired in an earlier event of intentional learning. By the learning theorem they cannot have been acquired solely through the exercise of non-intentional skills. Hence they are unlearned logical resources. (ii) What is learned is the grammatical structure or interpretation of a sentence. By the dialectical relation between sentences and their constituents, the grammatical structure of the sentence and its interpretation depend on the grammatical structure and interpretation of its constituents. If the learners did not already know the possible grammatical categories and possible interpretations of the constituents, they could not grasp the grammatical structure and interpretation of the sentence. Ex hypothesi the learning of the sentence is the first event of intentional learning. It follows that the learners already possessed its constituents as unlearned logical resources. (iii) If what is learned in that event is a constituent of a sentence, then the remaining words of that sentence are, by the same argument, unlearned logical resources. Notice that by the linguistic postulate there must be words other than the learned constituent to form the sentence that specifies the meaning and grammatical role of the learned constituent. Thus in all cases there have to be unlearned logical resources.

3.3.2. Criteria for Unlearned Status

While the corollary tells us that there must be unlearned logical resources, it does not tell us how to decide which ones they are. To solve that problem, we propose two conditions that such resources must satisfy. Jointly they supply us with useful heuristics. The first is that the unlearned logical resource should be a (semantic – see Carey 1982) primitive in our conceptual system. The second is that its interpretation should lack a characteristic appearance or gestalt in our extended sense of this word. We offer a few remarks in support and explanation of our conditions.

It is of course a matter of delicate choice what to count as primitive in any conceptual system. As guidelines one might propose that the resource is a linguistic universal available to everybody, regardless of education, and that children manifest command of the resource very early and without explicit instruction. Martin Braine (this volume) makes a similar suggestion.

The second condition for unlearned status, namely the lack of characteristic appearance, needs to be applied jointly with the first. We take 'dog' to be a primitive of our conceptual system; we certainly do not know how to define the word. But even if it is primitive, there is no need to consider that it is unlearned because, as we will show, it can be learned on the basis of characteristic appearance.

Where might these unlearned logical resources reside? The natural answer is in the language of thought (see Fodor 1975), with the provision that the language of thought be seen as an interpreted language and not just on a par with the computer's machine language. Computers, of course, do not interpret any of their languages in the sense we have been exploring. Indeed much of our paper constitutes an argument, perhaps more deeply motivated than any offered by Fodor, for the necessity of positing a language of thought. Moreover we simply identify the languages we have called L and ML with the language of thought. We take all the sentences in quotation marks involved in the learning of proper names, count nouns and mass nouns (to be presented below) as sentences of the language of thought. We see ourselves as specifying some of the unlearned constituents of that language. We might note in passing that Fodor's proposal has much in common with Aristotle's idea of an inner sense common to the external senses such as vision and audition: a common sense or language into which the outputs of the external senses are compiled (to use a modern idiom). It has much in common with St. Augustine's language of the heart (*De Trinitate*) a language that cannot be uttered by the mouth. The counterpart in St. Thomas Aquinas is the *verbum mentale* (mental expression). Even so bleak a philosopher as the nominalist William of Ockham retained the idea of a language of thought (*Summa logicae II*). We mention this to show that Fodor's proposal makes contact with a deep-rooted philosophical tradition.

3.4. Intentional operations

We have spoken in the preceding section about unlearned logical resources at the word level. We turn now to the other end of the dialectical relation and consider unlearned resources of a more global character. Symbols and sentences, even those of the language of thought, are inert. The learner must assemble the symbols in quotation marks in the various representations we give in section 4, impose a grammatical structure on them, and interpret them. The doctrine that there is an unlearned language of thought implies that there are unlearned linguistic skills available to the mind, skills to construct, to parse and to interpret sentences. Macnamara (1986, pp. 35 ff.) calls all these skills 'interpreters'. It seems convenient to make a division of labour and call the purely linguistic skills (sentence construction and parsing) 'parsers' while reserving 'interpreters' for the skill of interpreting. It is tempting to take both parsers and interpreters as procedure-like devices, that is, as devices that perform some *operation* when certain conditions are satisfied. We should point out, however, that the interpretation of a symbol is something that the procedures in a computer cannot perform.

So far, our representation involves sentences that the learner generates and interprets. Knowing what a sentence means, however, does not normally lead to any action. We all know what the following sentence means:

(3.1) The world will end next year

but unless persons who understand it judge that it is true, we do not expect them to perform any action that presupposes its truth, such as giving away their earthly possessions and engaging in a life of intense prayer. Likewise, unless the learner of the name 'Freddie' believes the sentence in which he learns it, we cannot expect him to perform any actions that presuppose its truth, such as calling the bearer 'Freddie' or feeding Freddie when requested to 'feed Freddie'.

How might we take account of this? It is not enough to add the words 'X judges that' to (3.1), since the sentence:

(3.2) X judges that the world will end next year

is another sentence that X might understand without necessarily judging it to be true. (Recall Lewis Carroll's story, "What the Tortoise Said to Achilles.") For this reason we employ 'judge that' not as part of the representation but as indicating that an event takes place in which a person performs the intentional act of judging a sentence to be true. The ability to judge goes beyond the parsers and interpreters of which we have just spoken.

A further fundamental intentional skill is the ability to assign kinds to individuals which have been accessed in perception.

4. Representation of Learning

4.1. Logical Aspect: Proper Names

Our representations (below) may seem unduly formal to some readers, but many considerations, some already apparent, some given in this section, seem to us to argue for their plausibility. Let us return to the example of the 15-month-old child whose parent has brought home a new puppy. The child is fascinated by the puppy and somehow picks up from the father that the name of the puppy is 'Freddie'. We represent the learning as occurring at a node in the child's expanding tree of knowledge. Let us see what is involved in the acquisition of this knowledge.

The child sees the puppy and hears the word 'Freddie'. His task is to discover that 'Freddie' refers to the puppy. At the point of learning, of course, he cannot use the word 'Freddie' on its own to refer to the puppy because that is precisely what he must learn. His intentional ability to refer to the puppy at this stage will be represented by a symbol of L. Because it is the simplest (see Macnamara 1986, p. 57), let us assume that the required symbol is the demonstrative 'this' (or rather its counterpart in L). Therefore it seems natural, as a first try, to represent his state of knowledge by a node in the tree such that:

(4.1) The sentence 'This is Freddie' belongs to the fragment of L associated with the node.

The demonstrative 'this', however, is vague. Something must steer the child from taking it as representing part of the carpet as well as the dog or as representing just the left front paw or the visible exterior. The child must end up using 'this' to designate the entire dog including the invisible interior but excluding the collar he may be wearing. In short, the interpretation of 'this' in the situation should be a member of some kind that individuates the dog and traces its identity in the appropriate manner. DOG and ANIMAL are suitable candidates. Not every CN that could be applied to the physical entity will do the job: we have seen that BUNCH OF MOLECULES will not. For reasons to be spelled out later, we assume that the basic-level kind DOG is the appropriate one to interpret (at the situation) the above demonstrative.

There is another difficulty with our representation as stated. 'This' may belong either to the language L or to English. A similar ambiguity appears in formal systems of logic, say in the formal system of arithmetic. To solve it, we distinguish between the numerals '0', '1', '2', '3'... which are symbols of the language of arithmetic and '0', '1', '2', '3',... which are the (ordinary) symbols for natural numbers of the English language. Thus the sequence of symbols 2+ 3=5 is a sentence of the language of arithmetic which is true since 2+3=5, i.e., since the operation of addition applied to the couple (2,3) gives the number 5. Notice that we have allowed ourselves an abuse of notation: we have used '+' for both the symbol of the language of arithmetic and English. Similarly for '='. We hope that this does not create confusion.

We will use a similar distinction and indicate that a word belongs in L by placing it in italics, e.g., '*this*'. Recall that the language of our representation is mixed, containing expressions such as 'Freddie' (which belongs to English) and '*this*' (which belongs to L). Recall, too, that we type a term by placing a colon followed by a common noun: e.g., (*this*:-dog) and (Freddie:dog), which are read '*this* in the kind DOG' and 'Freddie in the kind DOG' respectively. We accordingly represent the child's state of knowledge at the node representing the acquisition of 'Freddie' as:

(4.2) (i) PN ("Freddie":*word*)' is a sentence of the fragment of ML associated with the node;
(ii) The sentence '(Freddie:*dog*) = (*this*:*dog*)' belongs to the fragment of L associated with the node.

Associated with (4.2) are the rules for interpreting the sentences in quotes in (4.2)(i) and (4.2)(ii). These rules are not part of the representation of the child's knowledge; they are rather our representation of how the child must interpret the sentences containing his knowledge. The rules of interpretation, then, are expressed neither in L nor in ML but in ordinary English. Our general claim is that the child forms sentences expressing the content of the sentences in quotes, that he interprets them in conformity with the rules of interpretation, and that he judges the interpreted sentences to be true or false.

We chose to represent the kind that sorts 'Freddie' as WORD and to make PN be a predicate of that kind. An alternative would be to type 'Freddie' by the kind PROPER NAME. Our choice is guided by the desire to make representations harmonize with psychological findings and in particular with the theory of basic-level types. Now it seems likely to us that with growing familiarity, words become perceptually familiar as words; each familiar word is presented perceptually as a token of a certain type, which is a member of the kind WORD. Phonology does not distinguish among grammatical categories of words, but it takes word boundaries seriously (although it remains problematic what to treat as a word – see Sciullo and Williams 1987). Following Jackendoff (1987, chap. 14) we believe that phonology, not syntax, describes the perceptual presentation of words. This leads us to treat WORD as a basic-level perceptual type, and therefore to employ it in the representation of word learning.

We remark that the sorted demonstrative as well as the equality symbol '=', the italicized symbol PN and the underlined count nouns are examples of primitive symbols in L.

Since we make extensive use of quotation marks, a word about them is in order. As used in Tarski (1956, p. 156), their effect is to form a name for a sentence or, more generally, for an arbitrary linguistic expression of a language. Starting from that expression, we append quotation marks, left and right, to form a new expression (of the metalanguage) which is the so-called quotation-mark name of the expression. Notice the following peculiarity of this name formation: part of the name is the object denoted by the name. This is not the case with names for non-linguistic objects: a dog is not a part of its name and no matter how you analyze the word 'Freddie', you will not find the dog as one of its parts. Partly for this reason, names for expressions are tricky and confusions between use and mention are hard to avoid.

But is all this enough? If the child is to use the word 'Freddie' correctly, he needs to realize that 'Freddie' is a word that designates a unique member in a particular kind, namely Freddie in the kind DOG, and that it does so regardless of the situations in which the word is used. In particular, he needs to realize that 'Freddie' does not refer to the kind DOG or to just any individual in that kind. The child has clearly not learned the use of the proper name 'Freddie' if he calls every dog that he meets in the street 'Freddie'. The use of a proper name typed by a kind K cannot in general involve a reference to K. For example, if (Freddie:*dog*) involved reference to DOG, reference to (dog:*basic kind*) would require reference to BASIC KIND, which in turn would require reference to a higher-level kind, and so on ad infinitum. We propose that while proper names need to be typed by a common noun, apart from special circumstances there is no need to interpret the common noun.

In keeping with thesis 2a of La Palme Reyes, Macnamara and Reyes (this volume), a proper name can be described as a word that rigidly designates an individual in a kind. This means that a proper name's interpretation does not vary systematically with occasion of use. For the purposes of this paper, which focuses on learning in small children, we make the simplifying assumption that each name bearer has a distinct name. We thus represent the child in our scenario as taking 'Freddie' as designating just one dog, and doing so no matter who uses the name or when.

We can now state the psychological rules for assigning a word to the category proper name.

Rule for Classifying a Word as a PN: Assign a word to the syntactic category PN if it is read as a rigid designator of an individual in a basic-level kind.

With that we can give the rules for interpreting the sentences in quotation marks.

> (4.2)' (i) Assign the truth value *true* to 'PN ("Freddie":*word*)' if at U 'Freddie' is taken as rigidly referring to the perceptual entity to which it is applied.
>
> (ii) The sentence '(Freddie:*dog*)=(*this:dog*)' is true at the situation U if and only if the term '(*this:dog*)' is interpretable at U and 'Freddie' is a name of the dog which it is assigned as interpretation.
>
> (iii) The term '(*this:dog*)' is interpretable at U if at U there is a unique dog at the focus of attention.

Before we go on, let us be clear about what (4.2) and (4.2)' are supposed to represent. The child must recognize that 'Freddie' is a proper name, that 'Freddie' refers to a dog and not to a cat, say, and that he must be able to determine which dog is picked out by the proper name 'Freddie'. We represent these intentional abilities by (ii). He must be able to *use* the proper name in question in L, not only mention it. Notice that the fixing of the reference of 'Freddie' depends on a situation, namely the situation in which the dog in question appears and, moreover, is the only dog designated by the demonstrative '(*this:dog*)'. Nevertheless, if the child is successful in learning the name, he will use it independently of situations, because the rule of interpretation for (i) states that the name refers rigidly. In sum, we are representing the intentional ability of the child to go from perception to conceptualization. In conceptualization, the learner must specify a kind (the interpretation of '*dog*') and also a particular member of this kind denoted by '(*this:dog*)'. Similarly, the child must perceive a token of the word 'Freddie' for which in conceptualization he must specify a kind. We have suggested that the kind is WORD.

Once again, let us emphasize that our representation is not meant to imply that the child has the English words 'word' or 'proper name' to express (4.2). What we do claim is that (4.2) captures an essential element of his competence; that it specifies how he interprets 'Freddie' and classifies the word syntactically.

From a logical point of view and also from a psychological one, mistakes are possible on the child's part. Particularly at an early age, the child might mistake the proper name 'Freddie' for, say, the count noun 'dog'. Member and kind are in dialectical relation. The child is never confronted with an individual that he recognizes as such without his recognizing that it belongs to a kind that specifies what to count as an individual. So he needs to decide somehow whether to assign the new word to the individual dog or to the kind DOG. We will see that children make hardly any mistakes in doing so, but that is another matter. The decision is of fundamental importance in the learning of grammar. From the purely logical and syntactic standpoints, the feat of making the correct decisions seems well-nigh impossible.

In this section, we have followed our linguistic postulate and supplied a sentence to specify the grammatical category and interpretation of the word to be learned. Recall that we defined the logic of an expression precisely as the contribution of the expression to the truth conditions of sentences in which it occurs. This gives means to test the child's understanding of 'Freddie' through his ability to understand simple sentences in which the word 'Freddie' appears.

A word about the language L. While certain of its expressions such as 'This' are primitives of L, others are English words ('Freddie'). As a consequence, some of the sentences are linguistically mixed. In particular, the sentence in quotes in (4.2) is mixed. There is nothing to be disturbed about in this. Any sentence such as:

(4.3) The German word *'Gabel'* means the same as the English word 'fork'

that gives the meaning of an expression of one language in another language must be mixed. It cannot be that *'Gabel'* in (4.3) is a loan word in English, since the sentence claims it is German.

We might also observe that our account presupposes that the bearer of the name is present at the situations in which the proper name is learned, as indicated by the demonstrative '(*this:dog*)' in (4.2) and (4.2)'. If the name bearer is absent, some substitute for the indexical must be found. The obvious candidate is a definite description to fix the reference of the proper name – see Kripke (1972). This substitute presupposes a much greater command of language (for instance, the learner must understand the meaning of 'person') and would yield a representation that may be exemplified by:

(4.4) (i) 'PN("Aristotle":word)' is in the fragment of ML;
       (ii) The sentence 'Aristotle:*person*) = the only (x:person) such
       that (x:person) was a student of (Plato:*person*) and teacher of
       (Alexander the Great:*person*)' is in the fragment of L.

We do not spell out the associated rules of interpretation.

If the bearer of the proper name is fictitious, a demonstrative is out of the question. There is a complication in that the rule of interpretation of the definite description used to fix the reference must be so interpreted that the bearer of the new proper name is placed in a fictitious kind. Thus, though 'Sherlock Holmes', on the face of things, is assigned a member of the kind PERSON, the word 'person' must be interpreted into the counterpart of PERSON in the world of Conan Doyle's fiction. The reason is that Sherlock Holmes is not a real person, nor does he fall within the scope of the quantifier in such an expression as 'every person'. Leaving details to the reader, we might represent the learning of the name 'Holmes' by means of:

(4.5) (i) 'PN("Sherlock Holmes":*word*)' is in the fragment of ML;
       (ii) The sentence '(Sherlock Holmes:person) = the (x:person)
       such that (x:person) is the main detective in the Conan Doyle's
       stories' is in the fragment of L.

We do not spell out the associated rules of interpretation of the sentences in quotes.

The reader may remember that Macnamara (1986) was unable to give an account of the learning of a name for a fictional character because of the lack of a semantics of fictional expressions. This lack has now been supplied by M. Reyes (this volume).

4.2. Logical Aspect: Count Nouns

Let us return now to the 15-month-old child who hears his parents say 'dog' applied to Freddie and then to Rover, the dog next door. Let us suppose that the child catches on and can subsequently apply 'dog' as accurately as his parents. Gradually, too, he begins to combine the word with others to form skeletal sentences such as 'Dog allgone', 'Dog sick' in what his parents consider appropriate situations. As we mentioned at the beginning, there are several problems for the child to solve. The most obvious is to discover that 'dog' does not refer either to Freddie or to Rover, but rather to the kind to which they both belong. One trouble is that his parents cannot point directly to the kind DOG when teaching the word 'dog', but only to one of its members. At this juncture, the child cannot employ the word 'dog' to refer to anything, since that is part of what he is about to learn. Though parents often successfully teach a count noun by uttering it in the presence of one of the members of the kind it denotes, these utterances are best understood as expressing what normally adults would express by 'This is a dog' or 'Freddie is a dog'. Of course, the latter is appropriate if the child has already learned the proper name 'Freddie' for the dog in question. To have such names, however, is something of an exception because the members of many kinds lack proper names: TREE, CROW, PENCIL, etc. Since the use of the indexical 'this' is quite generally effective we will continue to employ it. There is, however, a distinction between its role in the two cases. In the learning of a proper name 'this' picks out the bearer, admittedly with the support of an appropriate count noun. In the learning of a count noun 'this' picks out in the first instance a member of a kind and only indirectly the appropriate kind itself. More concretely, without the living dog, there would be nothing to draw the child's attention to the kind through the use of the demonstratives. With this in mind, it seems natural to represent the state of a child's knowledge at a node by:

> (4.6) (i) 'CN("dog":*word*)' is in the fragment of ML associated with the node;
> (ii) The sentence '(*dog:basic kind*) = (*this:basic kind*)' belongs to the fragment of L associated with the node;
> (iii) The sentence '(dog:*basic kind*) = (dog:*basic kind*)' belongs to the fragment of L associated with the node.

The associated rules of interpretation will be spelled out shortly.

The first thing to comment on here is the expression CN occurring in the sentence of L in (i). Those of us who are grown up can usually tell a count noun in English from other words, but we might be hard pressed if asked to state how we do it. We are expecting a young child to be able to use the counterpart of the English syntactical name with comprehension. We must try to make its meaning explicit.

A count noun is a word that typically denotes a kind. At the core of a kind is a set. It follows that the extension of a count noun is conceptualized as a set, that is, as a collection of discrete elements. Some linguists have described the extension of a count noun as atomic, and some psychologists have observed that their extensions typically have perceptually recognizable boundaries. These strike us as important observations in the context of language learning, because they indicate clues that may help children to discriminate count nouns from mass nouns. For example, the juxtaposition of two dogs does not thereby yield a single dog, whereas two bodies of water can be combined to yield a larger body. The psychological salience of these facts has to do with the psychological accessibility of the boundaries of dogs even when dogs are placed side by side, and the inaccessibility of the boundaries of bodies of water when poured into a single container. (Recall that we are discussing only the basic-level kinds.)

These considerations suggest that for the theory of learning, we need a rule for assigning words to the category of count noun.

Rule for Classifying a Word as a CN: Assign a word to the syntactic category CN if it is taken as applied to perceptual entities that in combination do not yield another entity of the same kind.

The rule is semantic, non-circular and non-vacuous. It is not circular in the way that the old schoolmaster's definition of *noun* is: 'the name of a person, place or thing'. We are obliged to include under the word the walk that John took before dinner and the talks that John gave last week. In short, 'thing' is just a word for anything that can be denoted by a noun. Not much help! Some linguists try to define noun as 'the head of a nounphrase', which may lead to an axiomatic definition, but because of its circularity, it is of no assistance to a learner. Linguists also define count nouns as the class of nouns that take the plural morpheme and such quantifiers as 'many', 'one' and 'two'. But how might anyone learn the distinctive semantics of the plural morpheme and of such quantifiers as 'a', 'another', 'many', 'one', 'two'... without appreciating that they were being combined with count nouns that applied to countable discrete entities? In other words, our claim is that from the point of view of the learner in normal circumstances, a rule like the above is essential.

Our rule has the advantage of supplying a useful heuristic for deciding whether there are count nouns in languages other than English. Our rule is language neutral. The rule also supplies us with an approach to the problem of how a child, unaided, discovers that a word like 'dog' is a count noun.

We can now state the rule of interpretation for the sentence in quotes in (4.6)(i).

(4.6)' (i) Assign the truth value true to 'CN ("dog":word)' if 'dog' at U is taken as satisfying the rule for assigning words to the category CN.

A thoughtful critic has pointed out that there are count nouns such as 'surface', whose extension has a V-lattice structure. We are inclined to take them as basically mass nouns that are in common usage, combined with an implicit count noun to make them amenable to quantification, e.g., 'expanse of surface'. This seems to be correct because if 'surface' were not sometimes a mass noun, that expression would be uninterpretable. Notice that when we have to do with a genuine count noun such as 'dog' in similar construction we have to add the article: 'part of a dog', 'leg of a dog'. When we omit the article as in 'leg of lamb', 'lamb' is clearly a mass noun.

It may still not be clear how the child in our scenario learns that the English word 'dog' should be interpreted as the kind DOG. What is to prevent him guessing just that the English common noun 'dog' and the common noun of L '*dog*' denote kinds that have one member in common, namely the dog in the scenario. What tells him that the two kinds are the same? What guides him is the unique perceptual type for each perceptual figure, in fact the basic-level perceptual type.

To state the rule of interpretation of the sentences in quotes in (4.6)(ii) and (4.6)(iii), we must elaborate on the expression '(*this:basic kind*)'. When a live dog appears in the situation U, the demonstrative must refer to the basic-level kind to which the dog belongs. This suggests the following rule of interpretation.

(4.6)' (ii) a) The sentence '(dog:*basic kind*) = (*this:basic kind*)' is true at the situation U if and only if the demonstrative '(*this:basic kind*)' is interpretable at U and 'dog' is a name for the unique basic-level kind of the perceptible individual attended to.

We need of course a clause for the interpretability of the demonstrative. Tentatively, we formulate it as follows:

(4.6)' (ii) b) The demonstrative '(*this:basic level*)' is interpretable at U if at U attention is on the basic kind instantiated by an individual receiving perceptual attention.

(4.6)' (iii) The sentence '(dog:*basic kind*) = (*dog:basic kind*)' is true at U if and only if '(dog: *basic kind*)' and '(*dog:basic kind*)' are interpreted into the same kind.

The formulation of the rule for interpreting the demonstrative deliberately leaves room for situations in which no member of the kind whose name is to be learned is present.

To return to the little child. We assume that DOG is the unique basic-level kind to which the demonstrated dog belongs. Rule (4.6)(ii) shows that he needs to attend to the kind to which the demonstrated dog belongs, as well as to the dog himself. In other words, the new information is the name of that kind and not of the demonstrated individual; that individual acts as a pointer to the relevant kind – see Figure 4.1.

INDEXICAL   LIVE DOG   KIND

Figure 4.1 Schematic representation of how an indexical (hand) pointing to a particular dog can designate the kind to which the dog belongs.

Parents frequently point to pictures in books and say 'squirrel', 'fox' and so on. As a result, children learn these words for basic-level kinds. Children never seem to make the mistake of taking such words as names for pictures of animals, but as names for the animals they picture. There seems to be a difficulty: the picture of a squirrel does not fix the reference of the word 'squirrel' in the way a live squirrel does. At best the picture supplies a visual stereotype for the kind in question, which may apply to more than one basic-level kind. (Think of the Tasmanian Devil which shares with the dog a common visual stereotype.) Nevertheless, if the child masters the word 'squirrel', he must be able to apply it to exactly one basic-level kind. On this basis, we represent the learning of 'squirrel' through pictures in the same way as we did the learning of 'dog' when a live dog is present. The indexical used in connection with 'squirrel' picks out a picture that puts the learner in mind of the right basic-level kind.

(4.7) (i) 'CN("squirrel":*word*)' is in the fragment of ML associated with the node;
(ii) The sentence '(squirrel:*basic kind*) = (*this:basic kind*)' is in the fragment of L associated with the node.

The picture in the scenario serves the function of suggesting a kind. Which kind that is, is determined by the English word 'squirrel'. This merely recognizes the psychological fact that children have the general intention of joining the linguistic community of their parents. This means, among other things, adopting the decision to interpret words as parents do – rather than inventing a new, idiosyncractic language. It is this general intention that guarantees that our words behave well semantically even when we have mistaken concepts about their references. This observation applies throughout our account of word learning, but it seems particularly appropriate to draw attention to it here, when a CN has to be learned although no member of the relevant kind is perceptually presented. Of course, perceptual access to the members of the kind by some members of the speech community ensures that the kind is uniquely determined.

If, however, the kind is a fictional one like UNICORN, it cannot be uniquely determined by perceptual data, even pictures of unicorns. The distinction in this matter between real-world kinds and ficitonal ones is made by M. Reyes (this volume).

4.3. Logical Aspects: Mass Nouns

We illustrate the learning of a basic-level mass noun by a little girl who learns the word 'water' for a certain liquid she is offered to drink, for the liquid in her bath, for that in the puddles, rivers and seas she comes across. Since she encounters only portions of water and since her parents can point only to portions of water, when teaching her, we take it that the first meaning she learns for 'water' is that of the set of portions of water rather than 'water' as a name for an individual in the category STUFF.

For simplicity, let us suppose that the girl is taught the word as applying to the liquid in a tumbler in front of her. Let us suppose, too, that her mother points to the tumbler and says things like 'This is your water; drink your water'. We represent the child's knowledge at the point when she catches on as:

(4.8) (i) 'MN ("water":*word*)' is in the fragment of ML associated with the node;
(ii) The sentence '(*water:basic stuff*) = (*this:basic stuff*)' belongs to the fragment of L associated with the node;
(iii) The sentence '(water:*basic stuff*) = (*water:basic stuff*)' belongs to the fragment of L associated with a node.

Once again we assume that the little girl is familiar with the kind WATER before she learns its name. What she has to learn is that 'water' in English and *'water'* name the same stuff.

What does the predicable 'MN' mean? It picks out an extension that forms a V-lattice. This means that 'water' in the sense we are investigating denotes a kind consisting of portions of water: any set of portions of water together form a new portion, the supremum of the set, the portion that comprises all the portions in the set and nothing more. Likewise, there is an infimum of the set: the largest portion that is contained in each portion in the set. If the portions in the set are disjoint, the infimum will be the empty portion of water denoted by 'No water' or in child language as 'All gone water'. To match the corresponding rule for count nouns we now give:

Rule for Classifying a Word as MN: Assign a word to the syntactic category MN if the samples to which it is applied are taken as constituting in combination a larger sample.

It is no part of our claim that every language has the grammatical category of mass nouns. Japanese does not appear to. Our claim is rather that the grammatical category mass noun will be invoked in Japanese children's minds when learning the word for water (*mizu*), but the rest of the syntax must lead them to ignore it. Macnamara, Reyes and Reyes (this volume) note, however, that Japanese children must hold on to the semantic category of mass nouns. Because in order to apply the quantifier *san* (three) to *mizu* (water), they must add in some such partitive as *bai no* (part of). They do not use such partitives when combining *san* (three) with *inu* (dog).

The rules for interpreting the sentences in quotes in (4.8) are:

(4.8)' (i) Assign the value *true* to 'MN("water":word)' at U if at U the word 'water' is taken as satisfying the rule for assigning words to the category MN.

(ii) The sentence '(*water:basic stuff*) = (*this:basic stuff*)' is true at U if and only if a portion of water w receives perceptual attention at U and '(*this:basic stuff*)' designates the unique basic-level kind to which w belongs.

(iii) The sentence '(water:*basic stuff*) = (*water:basic stuff*)' is true at U if and only if both expressions are interpreted into the same kind.

4.4. Unlearned Logical Resources

In section 3 we proved that there are unlearned logical resources, and we laid down two criteria that decide if a logical resource is unlearned: the resource is a primitive, and it is not associated with a distinctive perceptual characteristic(s). To help decide if a resource is primitive we suggested two criteria: the resource is lexically expressed in all or almost all languages; the resource is available to children, as evidenced by their actions and words, when they are very young. We did not, however, single out any logical resources for unlearned status.

If we apply our criteria to the sentences that represent the learner's knowledge at the point of learning a proper name, we find as *primitive:*

(i) equality, '='
(ii) membership, ':'
(iii) predication 'PN("-":*word*)'
(iv) use/mention, quotation marks
(v) '*word*'
(vi) '*dog*'
(vii) indexical, '(*this:basic* K)'
(viii) PN

Every language possesses lexicalized means for expressing identity and membership in a kind, and for predicating; and clearly infants grapple with those relations long before they speak. For example, they show their appreciation of identity by refusing to go to anyone except their own mothers. They reveal their grasp of membership in kinds by treating cookies differently from plates. They reveal their grasp of predication, for example, by the way they treat some objects as their own. Admittedly, dogs' behaviour is superficially not very different from that of infants in these matters and one does not attribute to dogs the logical powers that we here attribute to infants. But as Quine (1960) has taught us with his gavagai example, children's intentional states are inevitably a matter for a reasonable but non-demonstrative assessment. Admittedly, we anthropomorphize when assessing infants' intentional states but not (usually) when assessing those of dogs. After all, an infant is an *anthropos*, whereas a dog is not.

All languages possess means for distinguishing use from mention. Mention, for instance, can be marked by such metalinguistic expressions as 'word' and 'name' or their counterparts. When children begin to speak, they are confronted by lightening switches from use to mention and back again. A child introduced to its uncle with the words 'This is your Uncle Norman' (use) may suddenly be asked to say 'Uncle Norman' (mention), and in the next breath to shake hands with Uncle Norman (use). Even small children never seem to be confused by the switch, which suggests that they have an easy command of logical resources that play the same logical role as the addition and removal of quotes. We therefore treat quotes as a psychological primitive.

Right from the beginning of language learning, children need to treat words differently from other sounds, because words have special status in revealing the intentional states of speakers, and relate in special ways to the non-linguistic world. This leads us to assign primitive status to 'word'. We do the same for 'dog', which is clearly undefined in our conceptual lives, seeing that no one at all knows how to define it. We see it as the counterpart in the language of thought of the perceptual type associated with dogs.

There is also the indexical 'this'. We take it to be an indexical that functions in conjunction with perceptual attention. It designates the perceptual figure that perception has carved out at the moment of its use. The perceptual figures to which it is applied are not assigned a common kind by the perceptual system. It follows that in itself 'this' is untyped, though as our representations of learning indicate, the first step in the interpretation of the perceptual experience will usually be to assign a kind to the object giving rise to the perceptual figure to which 'this' is applied. The universal applicability of 'this' to perceptual figures and to individuals in perceptible kinds bears out the claim that in the first instance the indexical is untyped. It would, for example, be a serious mistake to read the indexical in the learning of a proper name as typed by, say, VISUAL GESTALT, because the claim made in (4.2) is that the sort of *this* is 'dog'. But DOG does not include any visual gestalts as members. Demonstratives, as Perry (1979) and Putnam (1975) have shown, play an essential and ineliminable role in cognition. 'This' cannot be defined, and all natural languages have indexicals. It follows that we should take 'this' as a psychological primitive. There is finally the predicable PN. We do not define it. We imagine that children are guided in their learning of proper names by a psychological procedure that invokes PN when they construe their parents' words in a certain manner – in fact as applying a word as a rigid designator to an individual in a kind. Notice, however, that this procedure (if we do not miscall it) is different from the procedures of computer science, in that both its input and its output is intentional.

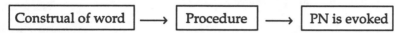

The main attraction to call this operation a procedure, in addition to fact that it produces an effect when certain conditions are satisfied, is that it seems to do its work automatically and unconsciously.

The second criterion for unlearned status (*no perceptually distinctive characteristic*) yields the following list.

(i) equality, '='
(ii) membership, ':'
(iii) predication, 'PN("-":word)'
(iv) use/mention, quotation marks
(v) '*word*'
(vi) . . .
(vii) indexical, '(*this:basic* K)'
(viii) PN

The equality of an individual with itself, though signalled by such perceptual phenomena as recognition, is really not perceivable at all, being a relation, in particular a relation between an individual and itself. Membership in a kind, though perceptually cued, is a relation to an abstract object and therefore not perceptual. Predication signals membership in a subkind; in our case the membership of a word in the subkind PROPER NAME. The distinction between use and mention is signalled perceptually in written langauge by the presence or absence of quotes or by italics; in spoken language it is not signalled at all. Since words can assume any physical form that is licensed by the phonology/phonetics of the language, words are not associated with a distinctive perceptual characteristic. Obviously the references of 'this' do not share a common perceptual characteristic. Neither do proper names. They are not, for instance, the only monosyllables in the language, neither are they reliably pronounced in a distinctive tone of voice.

Together, since they must be jointly applied, the two criteria for un-learned status yield:

(i) equality, '='
(ii) membership, ':'
(iii) predication, 'PN("-":word)'
(iv) use/mention, quotation marks
(v) 'word'
(vi) ...
(vii) indexical, '(this:basic K)'
(viii) PN

If we follow a similar pattern of reasoning in relation to the representations of knowledge associated with the learning of count nouns and mass nouns, we find four other unlearned logical resources.

(ix) 'basic kind'
(x) 'basic stuff'
(xi) CN
(xii) MN

We have decided to take (ix) and (x) as primitive partly because we do not believe they can be defined. Furthermore, many of a small child's questions (What is this?) are about the basic-level kind to which some object belongs or the basic-level type of stuff it is. Kinds and (abstract) stuff having no appearance have no perceptual characteristic. Hence our classification.

By extending the examination to the learning of words in the two other grammatical categories we consider, we conclude that CN and MN must be treated on a par with PN. Braine (this volume) is sceptical about the unlearned status of expressions for syntactic categories. While we appreciate his concerns, we feel that our suggestion of semantically conditioned procedures to invoke the syntactic-category labels goes a long way towards meeting his requirement that the assigning of words to such categories be semantically based. At the same time our suggestion recognizes the absence (so far) of semantic definitions for those categories. We admit, however, that the issue is far from settled.

5. Conclusion

Since we have proposed a number of unlearned logical resources, we feel obliged to counter an objection that has frequently been made to us.

Many people respond to our arguments by claiming that if a logical resource cannot be learned by an individual in the course of development, it could not have been acquired by the human race in the course of evolution. This is to misconceive the nature of our argument and of the learning theorem. We claim that existence of the unlearned resources cannot be explained either by intentional learning or solely through the exercise of sub-intentional skills. There is nothing to prevent non-intentional biological processes from engendering the genetic abilities to which we appeal – a position cogently argued for at length by Pinker and Bloom (in preparation). In any event we are writing a psychological essay. Our task is to explain the learning of words in certain grammatical categories by an individual, not to explain the origin of the capacity to do so in the human race.

Acknowledgments

The work here presented was done with the aid of National Science and Engineering Research Council grants to the authors. The paper was read to numerous audiences at home and abroad and benefited from their reactions. As always we are grateful for the support, encouragement and suggestions of Marie Reyes and Bill Lawvere.

References

Carey, S. (1982). Semantic development: The state of the art. In E. Wanner and L. Greitman (eds.), *Language Acquisition: The State of the Art*. Cambridge, MA.: MIT Press, p. 347-89.

Chomsky, N. (1986). Some observations on language and language learning: Reply to Macnamara, Arbib, and Moore and Furrow. *New Ideas in Psychology* 4: 363-77

Churchland, P.M. (1984). *Matter and Consciousness*. Bradford/MIT Press

Cummins, R. (1983). *The Nature of Psychological Explanation*. Bradford/MIT Press

— (1989). *Meaning and Mental Representation*. Bradford/MIT Press

Dalen, D. van (1983). *Logic and Structure*, 2nd ed. Berlin: Springer

Davidson, D. (1980). *Essays on Actions and Events*. Oxford:Clarendon

Dretske, F.I. (1981). *Knowledge and the Flow of Information*. Bradford/MIT Press

— (1988). *Explaining Behavior*. Bradford/MIT Press

Fodor, J.A. (1975). *Language of Thought*, New York: Crowell

— (1983). *The Modularity of Mind*. Bradford/MIT Press

— (1987). *Psychosemantics*. Bradford/MIT Press

Jackendoff, R. (1987). *Consciousness and the Computational Mind*. Bradford/MIT Press

Kripke, S. (1972). *Naming and Necessity*, 2nd ed., 1982. Oxford: Basil Blackwell

Lakoff, G. (1988). Cognitive semantics. In Eco U., M. Santambrogio and P. Violi (Eds.), *Meaning and Mental Representation*. Indiana University Press, p. 119-54

Macnamara, J. (1986). *A Border Dispute: The Place of Logic in Psychology*. Bradford/MIT Press

— (1991). Understanding induction. *Journal for the Philosophy of Science* 42: 21-48

Medin, D.L., and E.J. Shoben (1988). Context and structure in conceptual combination. *Cognitive Psychology* 20: 158-90

Millikan, R. (1984). *Language, Thought and Other Biological Categories*. Bradford/MIT Press

Osherson, D.N. and E.E. Smith (1981). On the adequacy of prototype theory as a theory of concepts. *Cognition* 9: 35-58

Perry, J. (1979). The problem of the essential indexical. *Nous* 13: 3-21

Pinker, S. and P. Bloom (trans.). Natural language and natural selection *Behavioral and Braine Sciences*

Posner, M.I., and S.W. Keele (1968). On the genesis of abstract ideas. *Journal of Experimental Psychology* 77: 353-63

Putnam, H. (1988). *Representation and Reality*. Bradford/MIT Press

Quine, W.V. (1960). *Word and Object*. New York: Wiley

— (1969). *Ontological Relativity and Other Essays*. New York: Columbia University Press

Rosch, E.H. (1977). Human categorization. In N. Warren (ed.), *Advances in Cross-cultural Psychology*. London: Academic

Rosch, E., C.B. Mervis , W.D. Gray, D.M. Johnson, and P. Boyes-Braem (1976). Basic objects in natural categories. *Cognitive Psychology* 8: 382-439

Rosch, E., C. Simpson, and R.S. Miller (1976). Structural basis of typicality effect. *Journal of Experimental Psychology: Human Perception and Performance* 3: 491-502

Russell, B. (1948). *Human knowledge: Its Scope and Limits*. London: Allen and Unwin

Sciullo, A.M. Di and E. Williams (1987). *On the Definition of a Word*. MIT Press

Stich, S.P. (1983). *From Folk Psychology to Cognitive Science*. Bradford/MIT Press

Tarski, A. (1956). The concept of truth in formalized languages. In A. Tarski, *Logic, Semantics and Metamathematics*. Oxford: Oxford University Press

8

Prolegomena to a Theory of Kinds

Alberto Peruzzi

1. Introduction

The discussion on meaning and reference has had a central place in contemporary philosophy of language. The problems that have emerged are not solvable by means of Procrustean definitions of meaning and reference, nor is the full range of their variety revealed by ad hoc case studies. A unifying and precise theory has to be developed and its empirical adequacy shown by its ability to handle a significant range of semantic phenomena. Yet, all attempts to achieve this goal have failed so far, because their target was language in its final stage, from the twofold point of view of both ontogenesis (adult's language) and cultural adaptation. Standard computational models of language understanding have embodied this very premise, being thus vitiated from the start by ignoring the dynamic interactions that lead to the emergence of high-level symbolic configurations. More recently, however, there is a growing realization that the search for such a unifying theory can be successful only if meaning and reference are investigated within the dynamics of cognitive development, which is a highly composite process. Correspondingly, various artificial intelligence projects now seek to design models of the formation and the stabilization of semantic capabilities (cf. analogical simulations of "naive," qualitative physics).

Until recently, logicians, linguists and psychologists have either gone their separate ways, or with scant intrinsic motivation they have borrowed the methodology of others. A proliferation of studies in cognitive science, using computational models, has undoubtedly modified the situation, in the sense that the essential questions have been precisely identified and part of their clarification consists just in showing that (i) prime aspects of semantic competence escape simulation by present digital models; (ii) widely shared logical tools are unsuited to representing the real structures of language and mind that are manifest in the common-sense world; (iii) linguistic theories devised within either cognitivism or analytic philosophy are inadequate in explanatory power or rigour. The need is for a subtler and more rigorous framework. A substantial *theoretical* contribution has come from two specific sources: the categorical treatment of syntax and semantics for formal (and programming) languages, and the psycholinguistic results on a privileged lexical level, corresponding to count nouns whose reference admits of prototypical presentation. How do these two factors interact? And how do we transfer the categorical point of view from the domain of mathematical logic and computer science to natural language? The crux of the matter lies in linking the categorical analysis of logic not to the description of the semantic steady state, but rather to the conditions that render possible the development of intentional abilities in the child language learner. (The same suggestion may be applied to AI systems, leading to the implementation of self-structuring architectures in a variable macro-physical environment.) A central point of such development consists in the perceptual/cognitive constitution of basic-level kinds (BLKs), to which a particular class of nouns refers. This line of research entails substantial methodological changes affecting: (i') adoption of a non-functionalistic philosophy by computer scientists; (ii') the adoption of a new logical set-up by analytic philosophers, and (iii') the revision of the so-called New Look in cognitive psychology and its fictionalistic aspects in dealing with linguistic primitives. These changes are needed in order to handle questions of formalization and empirical adequacy, which here concern meaning and reference.

The present paper aims at clarifying the foundations of such an approach, taking as the prime reference point the contribution provided by John Macnamara, Gonzalo Reyes and Marie Reyes's two papers that appear in this volume: "Reference, Kinds and Predicates" and "Foundational Issues in the Learning of Proper Names, Count Nouns and Mass Nouns." In this way, various aspects of the dialectical phenomenology I have worked out so far in Peruzzi (1987a, 1987b, 1988, 1989a, 1989b, 1990 and 1991a) will transpire to be pointing in the same direction as Macnamara, Reyes and Reyes. At the same time relevant differences will emerge, affecting the way logic and psycholinguistics can interact in a constructive way.

I shall confine myself to philosophical aspects, avoiding technicalities, even though some points involve familiarity with category theory and others require formal explicitation.

2. Ways of Reference in Language Learning

Referring is a characteristic activity of humans, and verbal language is the standard medium in which such activity is sedimented and rationally organized. The classical distinction between categorematic and syncategorematic expressions manifests the awareness that not every word has a meaning potential independent from other words. Some of them act as referential hooks, others as combinatorial 'strings', in representing things and facts. The function of referring is verbally exercised in two ways: an expression refers to an individual object as such, or to a kind as instantiated by an individual object – to be part of a substance may be thought of as a particular form of instantiation. Both types of reference occur in the early phases of language learning, and may be expressed diversely in different languages. In many languages the two functions are performed respectively by proper names (PNs) and common nouns, subdivided into count nouns (CNs) and mass nouns (MNs). (In the following I shall not go into the interpretation of MNs. Though corresponding to an idealized model, the adjunction displayed in Macnamara, Reyes and Reyes §2.5 gives the sense of the theoretical power and the elegance inherent in the categorical perspective on semantics of natural language.)

Both names and nouns are co-ordinated to experience through spatio-temporal localizers that ultimately reduce to the demonstrative 'this'. Therefore parallel information provided by such input systems as vision, hearing and touch is essential to reference from the beginning of cognitive development. Only after that twofold co-ordination is established, can its outputs be combined with the outputs of the predicative function, consisting in the symbolic representation of static qualities (by means of adjectives) and dynamic qualities (by means of verbs). Since every quality is relational, there is no intrinsically unary predicate – except as a systematically elliptic use.

Thus three fundamental questions arise. (1) How is it possible for a two-year-old child to learn the meaning of a PN and that of a CN? Otherwise stated, how can the bearer of a PN and the kind of which it is an instance be identified? (2) How is it possible for the child to distinguish, so early and with so few errors, between the referential functions of PNs and CNs? Take, for example, the difference in meaning between 'Freddie' and 'This dog'. (3) How do we formally represent the principles searched for under (1) and the different semantic structures under (2)?

Some qualifications! Kinds are identified on the grounds of phenomenological features: chiefly shape rather than inner chemical structure. If dogs were radio-controlled robots, nothing would change in the learning of kinds nor in the explanation of the child's competence in understanding and applying 'dog'. Similarly, the attempt to ensure constancy of reference for PNs and CNs by appealing to some causal or metaphysical theory (of the substance/accident sort) simply misses the point. On the other hand, purely relational theories of the sort envisaged by European structuralists would require of children either an implausible inductive effort or a complete misunderstanding of the words learned, since the role of any word must differ from child's to adult's idiolect. Moreover, the question of the kind assigned by children to a CN is not merely taxonomic; we must consider only features empirically accessible to them although they have to have some innate (chronogenetically emerging) biases for them – in view of 'poverty of stimulus' arguments. The battery of logical resources we ascribe to children should be restricted to those necessary to make possible and thus to explain (not simply to represent) their referential ability. Hence the only logic of kinds that could be called 'natural' is the logic followed by the child. Since it is arduous to ascribe logical competence, in the usual sense, to two-year-old children, no more than attributing to them exactly one 'logic', formalization has to shift to a deeper level of logic, that of universal constructions, for which the tools of category theory were designed. Once again, more concrete means more abstract.

There is a vast literature proving the key role of sorting by means of CNs in the reference of PNs and demonstratives. 'This is Freddie' presupposes the identification of Freddie, as, e.g., a dog: just as 'Look at this' presupposes an answer to the question 'What is this?'. Natural language can thus be thought of as generally typed, without for the moment specifying the ground types and the type constructors needed to generate new types. In addition, it is a higher-order language because there is quantification over kinds. Nevertheless, not every expression is strictly typed: adjectives and verbs are applied to different sorts with different nuances of meaning (cf. big book/big door, open the book/ open the door) in such a way that the typing affects logical inference (thieves are persons, but good thieves are not good persons).

Not even in mathematics is a single-sorted language adequate (think of the notion of vector space). True, quantifiers can be relativized, provided one can appeal to an omnicomprehensive kind: in mathematics this may be provided by the universe of sets, although since the rise of category theory, and in particular of topos theory, set theory is no longer a mandatory choice in foundations. However, strict typing of any term, embodied in the notion of topos, does not account for the flexibility of verbs in natural language. And even if by means of suitable 'comparison' functors strict typing is compatible with metaphor (cf. open the door, open the discussion), metaphor is not the unique source of flexibility.

The ability to recognize and type symbols is only a particular instance of a more general ability previously manifested by the child in perceiving. For this reason, metalinguistic ascent may be useful to focus on many logical problems, but cannot be laden with any intrinsic philosophical privilege.

With this proviso, one can still conjecture that there is a bijection between assignment of reference and assignment of grammatical category assimilating (0) and (1).

IS A(N)	INDIVIDUAL	KIND
(0) Dog	(Freddie:	animal)
(1) **PN**	('Freddie':	**word**)

which are involved in the acquisition of a PN for a dog; and also that the child's state of knowledge in the ostensive identification can be represented by:

(2) (Freddie: dog) = (**This**: dog)

(where primitive notions are in boldface).

Thus, the possibility of referring to uniquely identified linguistic or extralinguistic entities depends essentially an underlying kind (expressed by a CN). In its generality this dependence is thesis 1.3 of, Macnamara, Reyes and Reyes (this volume). Moreover, if a is identified *qua* member of a kind, then a can be a member of only one kind, codifying the *way of tracing* the identity of a. This applies to the case study concerning a person a who is counted as two passengers on different flights. In categorical terms one can easily define the relation between a *qua* X (PASSENGER) and a *qua* Y (PERSON) by means of an underlying map u: X →Y, which is not monic.

Now, does the underlying kind of a persist through any change of a in time? The answer is positive for most usual situations concerning such PNs as 'Nixon' and such CNs as 'person' which are associated with different stages (boy, adult). Yet, a semantic need can be transformed into a necessary truth no more than a metaphysical dichotomy (of the substance/accident type) can be transformed into a cognitive *a priori:* what is assumed to be constant or variable depends on the 'frame'. However, any 'frame' is ultimately the result of lifting, by metaphorization and cognitive combinations, properties of the base space of perceptual/macro-physical structures: so, there is no relativism in the dependence above, since such variability is neither autonomously principled nor arbitrary. Formally, any parametric term-morphism f: A →B in a category **C** becomes constant in the slice category **C/A**, and vice versa. Empirically, take a caterpillar which becomes a butterfly after the chrysalis stage. Imagine a child being told 'This is Freddie' of a caterpillar, and then 'This butterfly is Freddie'. One could reply: the CN 'living being' still persists. Apart from doubts about the adequacy of such a reply if referring to the child's actual learning, consider the case of a tardigrade in a dehydrated phase: does it behave like a living being? In the light of these and other similar cases, the only remaining condition is the continuity of spatio-temporal location of a with respect to some co-ordinate system K. On one hand, Kant had already realized that space-time location could not be assimilated to sorting. On the other, there are CNs (such as 'walk') with discontinuous reference, but they simply remind us that the ways of tracing identity for CNs and PNs are different (configuration prevails over position for CNs, and conversely for PNs).

This shift from absolute constancy of underlying kinds to positional continuity sums up the route that led from the Aristotelian dichotomy of substance and accident to the state-space of any dynamic system. Here, however, such space enters à la Leibniz as a net of relations among bodies, not as another substance. In particular, one cannot infer Leibniz's commitment to bare particulars from the assimilation (attributed to him) of CNs to adjectives and verbs; for the identity of any individual is positionally (beyond that attributively) determined. In monads this occurs in a self-interacting way, since each of them represents the way others represent it, even if Leibniz did not perfectly grasp the consequences of such mediated self-reference.

Summing up, in order for any demonstrative or PN to have precise reference, a (unique) CN is required, but this CN is not to be absolutely constant. Local constancy is all that is needed.

If this sortal presupposition is taken as paving the way for a 'description theory' of PNs, the mental character of the meaning of such descriptions, in addition to their non-uniqueness, leads directly to some version of linguisticized idealism. However, this would be possible only by admitting (A) a domain of bare particulars and, over it, (B) a tide of fluctuating sorts; whereas we have no cognitive access to (A), and there are cognitive constraints on (B) which prevent both Quine's arguments for the indeterminacy of translation, and Putnam's (appealing to the Löwenheim-Skolem Theorem) for the non-categoricity of reference of any CN. (A phenomenological criticism of the symbiosis between analytic philosophy and idealism is to be found in Peruzzi 1991b).

The most direct defence of a realist view of reference passes through the avowal that PNs refer rigidly. In effect, the provision laid down in Macnamara, Reyes and Reyes (this volume) for interpreting (0)-(2)

make essential appeal to such rigidity, which balances sortalization of PNs. Thus, with such simple sentences as (0)-(2), two types of basic ingredients in the interaction between semantics and cognition can be seen in action, i.e., the internal (I) and the external (E): (I) syntactic competence, recognitional capacity, and intentional ability (of the child), and (E) situational parameters and givenness of a stable, "thing-like" reality. How is this interaction successfully realized in language learning? And is the hypothesis that PNs are uniformly rigid designators really indispensable to the realistic option? To answer such questions, it is timely that the distinction between CNs and PNs be examined in psychogenesis. More specifically, how can the child understand so early that 'Freddie' does not refer to the kind DOG (i.e., to a generic individual in the kind)?

The matter might be simplified by assuming a distinct name for each relevant (animate) individual; but this would be neither necessary nor clarifying. First, it might suggest that the child takes as CNs those words that are used for different phenomena, and as PNs, words used for only one phenomenon. The point is rather that children are able to re-identify Freddie under many different presentations, and they are able to recognize a kind even if they have experience of very few specimens. Both aspects are present when a child is introduced to only one set of alphabetic letters made out of plastic stamps, and is then successively shown letters in different styles.

Nor is the child led to distinguish kinds and individuals by the presence of the article: cf. 'This is a/the dog' to 'This is a/the Freddie'. For there are languages (such as Latin) without articles, and current use of language in which the definite article precedes a PN (such as the Tuscan usage of Italian) – I will return to the indefinite article later. This remark can be generalized by saying that the child's rapid elimination of any 'confusion' between CN and PN does not depend on purely syntactic markers. There remains the possibility of prosodic traits, as of intonation and stress, tied to sensitivity for different forms of sound-curves. Yet, deaf-mute children succeed in reaching a remarkable linguistic capacity, and distinguish This-dog from This-Freddie no less quickly. The same is true of blind children. Therefore, it is not a matter of cognitive components whose activation depends on specific features of the perceptual channel employed.

Children seem to possess an innate disposition to interpret as a CN any expression associated to an indexical. Then the problem becomes how to distinguish PNs as mere labels. Whichever answer is given, a necessary condition for such a distinction consists in a fine capacity for differentially re-identifying forms, and thus in suitable quotients, i.e., in a twofold tolerance to variations called for in the use of CNs and PNs. We easily identify the same face even if it is altered by emotional or other effects, and we distinguish very similar faces as well. Consider two extreme situations, (S1) and (S2). (S1) Suppose our child has the experience of only one dog, and his verbal interactions are limited to computerized information on labelling objects in his environment. Can he understand that 'dog' is a CN instead of a PN? One might think that the unique clue available to a two-year-old child to separate PN and CN is the multiplicity of members of the same kind simultaneously accessible to him, all denoted by the same word, and this is what makes the word a CN, in view of the above location/configuration balance. (S2) Conversely, suppose many dogs are accessible to the child, but all are named 'Freddie'. With syntactic and prosodic information excluded, what would lead him to assign 'Freddie' to the category of PNs? And more, what would prevent him from using the plural and saying for, example, 'Here are three Freddies'? My answer is – nothing. For this reason, too, there is a low probability that many individuals of the same kind receive in a given environment (house, family) the same PN. Note that most PNs in Western languages are fossils of definite descriptions (by means of CNs) that played the role of locally rigid designators. There might be a community where each person is believed to be inhabited by demons of different kinds, each bearing a different PN, so that a single person is named with the PN of the demon acting in him at the relevant moment. Within such a community the child would be able to refer successfully to other humans by perceptual localization, but could not succeed by means of PNs. (In the presence of systematic correlation between PN and personal behaviour, the child would be justified in interpreting such PNs as CNs.) Moreover, if in a far future only identical unisex brothers should remain, with no behavioural difference apparent to the child, he could distinguish among them only when they were simultaneously present: rigidity of PNs would then be neither necessary nor sufficient to fix reference.

Fixing reference would still be possible in learning a language without PNs, but there would be no language at all without CNs. Correspondingly, a world where most of the kinds encountered were singletons would not be a world where children could exist, survive and develop language. On the other hand, if the variety of kinds and situations in the child's environment were far less rich than it actually is though still containing many members of each kind, the conditions for the development of a language like ours would no longer exist. So, constraints on language structure and naturalistic constraints are strictly related; understanding the details of this fine-tuning should be a prime topic of research in semantics for several years. Here, computer-aided simulation of self-modifying learning systems plays the role of testing hypotheses on the child's linguistic growth, compensating for the impossibility of systematic experimentation in psycholinguistics. As is well known, the difficulty lies in the lack of plasticity of present microworlds for expert systems.

I remarked previously that bearers of PNs and CNs are cognitively constituted as quotients over different manifolds of data. In the case of a PN, two data are recognized as equivalent if their positional features can be traced back to the same baptisimal token; in the case of a CN, they are equivalent *qua* members of the same type as *this*. In both cases there is an abstraction process, as well as a path to an indexically anchored pattern-object. As members of the same kind change through time, so cells of the same living being, bearer of a PN, change: in both cases identification is not extensional. Hesperus = Phosphorus *qua* presentations of Venus, and Freddie = Spot *qua* presentations of DOG: the two quotients are parallel, not in virtue of what is usually considered the logical structure of language, but in virtue of extralinguistic facts concerning the qualitative macro-structure of space and perception. Of that structure, logic is only a projection. The preservation of the CN 'dog' from Freddie to Spot but not of the PN is analogous to the preservation of the form of a parabola under translation, or under change of co-ordinate systems; the local coding of its points changes. It is a matter of different symmetry groups and homomorphisms – see Peruzzi (1987a) for a similar approach to rigid/non-rigid descriptions. Yet, it would be hazardous to postulate strict correlation of each group with a grammatical category. Differences among local, global and distributed semantic pointers, simultaneously present in human languages, are not necessarily mirrored in uniform grammatical differences. Expressions of distinct categories may perform the same referential function, and expressions of the same category may perform different functions. Undoubtedly, there is a typical and systematic division of semantic labour, but it remains a local division. The ways language successfully conveys information about what is fixed and what is not depend on extralinguistic factors that are activated in parallel to discourse. Lastly, the representation of such factors requires larger linguistic units, of which PNs and CNs are components, and by which they are affected, as we shall see in §4 below.

3. Bare Particulars, Modalities and ∈

The hypothesis that any term is typed may be expressed by saying that there are no bare particulars (a consequence of thesis 1.3 in Macnamara, Reyes and Reyes, this volume), which is in keeping with our lack of epistemic access to a universal kind.

The denial of bare particulars means that both quantification and identify are typed. The child's ability to handle questions of sameness has sense if applied to members of the same kind. Thus $a = b$ can only mean that, for a given kind X, $a{:}X = b{:}X$. As a higher-order language is assumed, the same holds for kinds X,Y, etc. In order to stop this infinite regress, one might postulate that there is a kind of kinds.

Yet the abandonment of absolute identity for members of kinds (so that Leibnizian, untyped, indiscernibility does not follow) is independent from the restoration of absolute identity of kinds. For all practical purposes, we manage local versions of indiscernibility, sufficient for the intended contexts of use. (As before, this is far from suggesting a relativistic view of identity. To this aim one should add the claim that there is no place for identity laws and for ordering, on a cognitively meaningful scale, different criteria of identity: an additional claim that is ungrounded from both the logical (see Macnamara and Reyes, this volume, §3) and the cognitive point of view (see §5 below). Decisions as to whether two kinds are congruent or not always involve finitely many layers of kinds, without presupposing a kind of kinds as a completed entity. Thus, a different extension of lambda-calculus can be suggested than that obtained through polymorphism, for there is not just identity between terms of the same type, which has to be given once and for all; any kind of kinds is an open entity, never entirely graspable. Localized identity is also used for kinds. So the dialectical model of referential variation for definite descriptions presented in Peruzzi (1989a) can be lifted from the first order to a higher order. Here, too, the totality of entities with their properties to be considered is specified by a 'figure' theory T together with the models of a related 'background' theory T^* – it is neither given in advance nor in a globally uniform way, but rather in a locally principled manner.

The point is that both the identity of individuals and that of kinds are traced in ways that are not just logically different: individuals are identified on the grounds of both an underlying kind and a spatio-temporal path; kinds on the grounds of configuration parameters. The semantic stability of CNs presents the same problem one meets any time one tries to describe the formation of a translocal order (structure) in a non-isolated system, as in the growth of a crystal, convection in a liquid, coherence of a laser beam, or regulation in embryogenesis. So I am not preluding an eliminative reduction of the concept of kind.

Now, any naturalistic view of language must show how idealistic consequences are avoided. But neither appeal to the rigidity of PNs nor admission of BLKs (§5) suffices to block the Kantian way opened by the 'no bare particulars' hypothesis. Only a phenomenological analysis of the notion of kind can succeed in making clear its constitution in terms of perceptual schemes. Since kinds are potentially infinite in number and the child's development takes place in a finite time, the formation of such schemes must resort to finitary resources, which can be identified in a finite set of finitely assembled topological *Urgestalts* (primitive gestalts), of either differential or algebraic character, codifying patterns of shapes and actions, shared by mind and nature, and rooting mind in nature. Each Urgestalt comes with an associated, seemingly noncomputational flexibility, i.e., a specific tolerance for variations within critical thresholds.

Without such phenomenological analysis, there would be no intrinsic reason (other than subjective biases) to separate natural kinds from arbitrary quotients of data. Absence of a naturally constrained architecture of kinds would bring us back to Poincaré's conventionalism, exported from geometry to the whole of semantics. Indeed, this result would be favoured if kinds were thought of as sets. Forgetful of the deep link between symbol and gestalt, proponents of this strategy paved the way to structuralism, cultural relativism, inscrutability of reference, and more recently, to the superficially contrasting theses of functionalists and holists.

What is primitive in the identification of kinds is a family of correlations between perceptual gestalts and differential/algebraic invariants, accessible through each sensory module and stabilized by gluing modular outputs. (In effect, children are endowed with an innate capacity to select modular information suitable for such gluing, as is manifested in early experiences of correlation, e.g., in synchronizing visual and auditory stimuli.) Unless we admit this primitive resource, the capacity to individuate members of a kind and to differentiate between them has to be considered as completely independent from the observed hierarchical structure of kinds. Consequently, the divorce embodied in analytic philosophy between logic, cognition and the physical world would be confirmed – *quod non erat demonstrandum*. If, on the other hand, the formation of kinds of concrete entities is constrained to conditions of perceptual grasping, and that of kinds of abstract entities (such as mathematical objects) to conditions of *transposed* conceptualization out of the perceptual domain by means of abstracting *(separating)* strategies, what remains of the cognitive meaning of a kind of kinds? This kind possesses neither perceptual support nor identifying conditions (separating it from what?). A kind of kinds is then just a purely formal 'foundational' requirement of closure. But we should be suspicious of it, if we are faithful to Bill Lawvere's idea of 'foundations' hoping to transfer it from mathematics to cognition.

Certainly, a kind of kinds could be kept under control by distinguishing 'small' and 'large' kinds: although this is a set-theoretic trick, out of keeping with an approach that aims to overcome the defects of set-theoretic semantics. A further delicate point is the following: individuals that are members of kinds may change; but small kinds belonging to other (large) kinds may also change, yet in the theory under review they are assumed to be modally constant. If we say that what may change is never a kind, we would restore an untenable dualist ontology of particulars and species, in contrast with the dependence of the identity of individuals on kinds (and vice versa). One might respond that what changes are only predicates, the rest being fixed (rigidity of PNs and CNs). If, however, any predicate can be turned into a kind, a much more complicated argument is needed, especially in order to preserve the dialectical relation between individuals and kinds (cf. Macnamara, and Reyes, this volume, §4.2). In contrast, my approach suggests that rigidity is just an idealization of stability. In that approach, assimilating the reference of PNs and CNs as invariants for different groups of transformations (modulo catastrophic regions) shows itself as the simplest way out of the above aporiai.

So, even if the existence of a kind of kinds is not paradoxical in itself, one should prove that in cognition there is sufficient empirical evidence for rejecting a type theory such as that introduced by Per Martin-Löf and proved to be inconsistent with such existence by Jean-Yves Girard. Extending the theory of constructions by the axiom 'Kind:Kind' serves certain purposes, yielding uniform recovery of any term qua morphism, but is not in the constructive spirit of predicative theories – see Pavlovic (1990) for a comparative categorical analysis of such type theories. In the absence of adequate empirical evidence, the above proposal of local identity and quantification over kinds appears to be a better project to pursue. It is more in agreement with the working of natural language, and also in better syntony with the shift from possible worlds to situations, advocated by many, although with remarkable differences – see Peruzzi (1987b). Situations are fundamental for the interpretation of modal discourse.

On the other hand, if CNs as well as PNs are rigid designators, predicables are the only candidates (apart from sentences) for handling modal variation (theses 1.4 and 1.5 of Macnamara, and Reyes, this volume). In this way Quine's skepticism on quantified modal logic would not apply. So, for any CN such as 'boy', '∀x:BOY. □ boy(x)' is acceptable, but '∀x: □ BOY. boy(x)' is not. Working out this intuition in a formal setting, Reyes has shown how to handle modalities in the framework of *topos* theory while imposing strong conditions on the theory of reference – see Reyes (1989). These conditions embody commitment to higher-order, intuitionistic logic (valid and complete for interpretation in toposes), to global and strict typing, and to the exponentiability of kinds. While exponentials are needed to render noun forms of verbs (actions as objects) and adjectives (quality abstracts as objects), other hypotheses on connectives and typing seem excessive, unless the range of contexts in language and cognition to be represented by such tools is suitably restricted. For example, to enrich Ω with a co-Heyting algebraic structure requires the given *topos* to be classical. This agrees with my emphasis on group actions, yet loses the semantic matching with intuitionism. Otherwise, the topos notion has to be renounced, which weakens Reyes's treatment of modalities. Hereupon other complications emerge. In particular, the incomplete and partial character of situations is sufficient to falsify the Law of the Excluded Middle, but not for constructive reasons. Moreover, there are many concrete situations for which monotonicity, embodied in intuitionistic logic, does not hold. Most of ordinary reasoning is by default, and hence non-monotonic in principle; the child cannot be modelled on an ideal knowing subject. Other obstacles for global and strict typing were considered before. As to modalities, the problem of essentialist *(de re)* predication would still be in need of clarification. Ghilardi and Meloni's (1988) categorical treatment of substitution in modal formulae shows that the distinction between *de re* and *de dicto* can be dealt with by means of presheaf semantics, through the simultaneous consideration of many accessibility maps between any two possible worlds (and the same applies to situations). Up to now, however, such treatment is confined to first-order language. On the other hand, Reyes's approach clarifies how the possible pervades the real, and this is relevant for more than philosophical discussion: think of the role of virtual particles and Feynman's path integrals in physics. The categorical framework imposes objective constraints on the use of modalities, which definitely takes us away from a convex notion of the actual. Wittgenstein claims in the *Tractatus* that logic does not deal with the world, but with the possible. By the situational character of modal notions and the intertwining of possible and real, such a dualism is now untenable.

Yet, counterfactuals remain in need of categorical analysis, and it is problematic to preserve the rigidity of all CNs and PNs in the context of such counterfactual identification as 'If cats were violins, you would be a perfect violinist'; or in the presence of such dual shifts of reference as in 'If Florence were Montréal, it would be colder' → 'If Montréal were Florence, it would be warmer'. Furthermore, modal constancy of underlying kinds raises problems not only in fairy tales (where a prince can become a frog), but even in reality. While humans do not usually change their sex, there are transsexuals. The Aristotelian distinction of substance and accidents may be valuable, for it grasps a local distribution of semantic roles intrinsic to human understanding rather than an absolute one. Thus, existence of a unique underlying kind for any given individual is not precluded. Simply stated, uniqueness is localized. Neither are we committed to resurrecting analytic truths nor do we have to resort to holism – and what is more, we cannot. Kind-ladenness of reference is holistically inconsistent with any form of modal constancy of kinds, for it is characteristic of holism that there is no fixed demarcation line between meaning and belief. Instead, localization is consistent with modal constancy. The function of rigid designation is not canonically performed by certain expressions; since reference is a local matter, permutation of semantic roles can always be accomplished within any finite set of sentences (for evidence supporting this claim see Moneglia 1987 and Peruzzi 1988, chap. 2). So even if we assume that the bearer of a PN like 'Sherlock Holmes' does not belong to the kind PERSON, but to the counterpart of PERSON in Conan Doyle's fictional world, the same strategy cannot be generalized without sacrificing the understanding of Holmes's stories. Locally distributed reference for each sentence or text avoids this difficulty. (In Peruzzi 1991b §3, a principle of invariance is introduced for the referential potential of any sentence concerning fictional entities and any claim of sceptical theses.)

The same holds true for shape Urgestalts on which object recognition is grounded. For instance, the diversity among the three kinds of curves so fundamental in perception (see Figure 1.), can be locally neutralized when referring to parts of a moving body (e.g., an arm of someone running), for factors of global invariance then become prime, whereas their

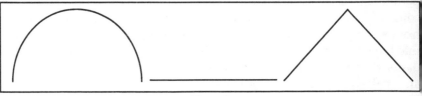

Figure 1.

diversity remains essential for the use of such CNs as 'hill', 'plain', and 'mountain'. Moreover, what is locally necessary depends on the interference between actions on objects and pre-established patterns of actions: a split glass is still a glass if the fracture is parallel to the base, but not if it is perpendicular. This points to a more central place for verbs than present type-theoretical models of language afford them.

After typing and modalities, the third topic to be addressed is the set-theoretic reading of the relationship between individuals a and kinds K.

To begin, the modal constancy of CNs might be explained by saying that while CNs do refer to sets, they are constant sets. Now if 'dog' were to denote a constant set, the use of 'dog' would differ from one day to the next, since new dogs would have been born and others would have died. Otherwise, one would have to think of the set of dogs as extending over time, through the more recent history of our planet (for simplicity's sake, to avoid evolutionary stages of present dogs and to ignore possible dogs on unknown planets), as the real reference of 'dog'. If access to this set were necessary, the child could never master the use of 'dog'. Hence, if kinds are sets, they are undoubtedly variable sets. It follows that, if CNs are to be semantically rigid, their reference cannot be to constant sets.

In a like manner, even the paradox of the ship of Theseus (all the pieces of which were changed one by one through time) can be solved not by seeking which are the "right" parts nor by modifying the power-set axiom. Note that if all the pieces were simultaneously changed, one would speak of the *second* ship of Theseus, more or less perfectly reconstructed as the first one: neither set-theoretic nor mereological relations can account for this fact in a convincing way. The body of any living being is a ship of Theseus, because cells are continuously renewed without affecting identity or disturbing identification, so that one can stick to larger units as the proper constituents: substitution of functionally equivalent parts is constrained, however, as transplant rejections testify.

Furthermore, if the direct reference of 'dog' were a variable set, the child would have to keep in mind a vast number of situational parameters to correctly map dogs in situation i to dogs in situation j, since change of situation is rarely an instance of domain extension. The memory space needed would be highly uneconomical, and the calculations involved would have to process such a vast amount of information that much more would be needed than that in which humans acquire the ability to refer correctly to dogs.

In sum, if the relationship of an individual a (such as Freddie) to a kind K (such as DOG) is membership, the link of logical analysis with language learning is lost. For cognition, what matters is not the totality of members of a kind but its representing instances. Thus, instead of a ∈ K, we are justified in thinking of a purely categorical morphism $p:a →$ K, such as that proposed in Peruzzi (1991 c), which relates to Ellerman's (1988) interpretation of predication as 'participation' in a universal. While Ellerman traces this reading of 'IS A(N)' back to Plato, the cognitive adequacy demanded on the formal setting leads to interpreting p in terms of matching a scheme in just the Kantian sense revived by F. Bartlett. In this way, the basic cognitive role of prototypes to be discussed in §5 acquires a direct logical counterpart. Since a mapping different from inclusion is needed to handle cases of the passenger/person type, we coherently proceed by representing the basic logical relation 'IS A(N)' as a map, and preserving the use of ∈ for a 'steady state' relation between finished cognitive products. Thus the way is paved for a better understanding of the role played by the 'preconceptual' in mediating identification of individuals and fixation of kinds. In effect, such mediation would be highly deprived of its structure if interpreted as ∈.

4. Dialectics

In light of what has been said so far, it becomes evident that just as kinds individuate members (viz., representing instances) through typing, T, members trace the identity of kinds through I. The mutual dependence is iconically expressed by:

$$\text{MEMBERS} \underset{T}{\overset{I}{\rightleftharpoons}} \text{KINDS}$$

Intuitively, this dialectical loop can be assumed to mean that the member/kind relationship is not of the brick/house but of the brick/arch type, and that confirms our rejecting the formalization of it as ∈.

We are not faced with a trivially vicious circle, because there is a root of the relationship at the level of prototypical individuals who properly represent the kind and therefore are universals in the sense of category theory, the representation being brought about through the activation of gestaltic resources. These control the variational procedures that underly the stabilization of prototypes, while such constrained variations guide the matching between a prototype and any given token. Furthermore, it is not simply a matter of introducing another (though peculiar) holistic view, such as that already exemplified by European structuralists and Quine's followers. For holism does not receive support through the phenomena highlighted by Gestalt psychologists, and the supposition of 'central' processes for belief fixation is in sharp contrast with the rich evidence by now accumulated in the study of both natural and artificial vision. Actually, I introduced the dual notions of local holism and local extensionality to overcome the shortcomings of global semantic holism, while at the same time preserving its valid appeal to the non-atomicity of belief – see Peruzzi (1992). For present purposes, two firm points can be found in the mutual gestaltic determination of part and whole: (1) there are well-determined principles of perception (and, in a broader sense, of figural insight) that specify when the whole prevails on the parts, and vice versa, independent of cognition – see Kanizsa (1991); (2) there are conditions of stability, for the dialectics of part and whole, that can be legitimately extended to the individual/kind case.

Since holists consider theories of meaning grounded on perceptual wholes as reductionistic, points (1) and (2) are constraints that they tend to diminish, because of the emphasis on the unregimentable manifold of ways a part receives meaning by insertion in a dominating whole. If, on the contrary, we resort to (1) as a starting point for semantics, point (2) should be equally stressed, because the growth of cognitive competence is also the result of restructuring and stabilizing referential processes, not simply of an intrinsically cumulative hierarchy of stages. This remark, clearly in the Piagetian spirit, is intended to call attention to the need for ingredients complementary to the representation of cognitive development as a path on the tree of states of knowledge, as suggested by Kripke semantics for intuitionistic logic. Consequently, formalization must also take account of such stabilizing processes, and this is particularly relevant from the logical point of view, since they are active in the dialectics by which the child's understanding of any new sentence takes place.

In fact, there is a specific linguistic manifestation of the above double-arrow dialectics in both syntax and semantics, namely, the relationship between the grammatical structure of any sentence φ and the grammatical categories of φ-constituents, as well the relationship between the interpretation of φ and that of φ-constituents. E.g., 'walk' can be both a CN and a verb, and the sentence selects which role, just as it collapses the meaning potential of an ambiguous CN such as 'state' (democratic/liquid).

The above dependence of terms on sentence (text) structure is not a prerogative of natural language due to its "imperfection." In logic the role of an individual variable x in the formula φ depends on its "environment": if it is in the range of an existential quantifier, the substitution of some term t for x in φ has to take account of other terms used in the derivation of φ.

In the light of all this, we can wonder about the possibility of integrating the context principle with the principle of compositionality, which, since Frege, remain in contrast to such an extent that some have been led to employ the contrast to measure the distance of formalized (compositional) languages from natural (contextual) ones.

On the theoretical side, much technical work is necessary to mathematize this integration. In order not to disturb the discursive tone of this paper, suffice it to say that the fundamental categorical notion required to model the dialectics of word meaning and sentence meaning is that of adjoint functor – see Peruzzi (1991c) for the definition of adjoints and a discussion of their use in logic.

On the empirical side, the question is how the child's understanding of sentences such as 'Freddie is a dog' matches such integration, when either 'Freddie' or 'dog' is a new word in the child's vocabulary. No purely linguistic fact (the above twofold dialectical relations included) is a sufficient answer, unless stable interpenetration of perception and thought with language is already achieved. In the case of the given sentence, the interference may be negligible, though non-static in view of the symmetry group interpretation of PNs and CNs. Greater extralinguistic abilities are required to grasp the meaning of compound sentences containing verbs.

Thus, the semantic role of action and sensorimotor mechanisms, previously organized into language-independent operational schemes, must be acknowledged as essential. These schemas are preconditions of the meaning of logical operations, too. With all the defects one can find in Piaget's theory of cognitive development (and particularly of logic), he grasped this point very well, balancing the priority of schemas with the admission that, without language, the sequence of successively activated schemas could be neither integrated nor controlled: the sentence provides the needed objectified structure. Unfortunately, he did not realize (see Piaget 1974) that the categorical notions of limit and adjoint allow the rendering of the correlation of action schemas and logical operations, in terms of universality.

Lastly, the need of adding type (2) constraints to those of type (1) shows that the threefold correspondence among individual/kind dialectics, gestalt patterns and categorical universals, is still insufficient as a model of language learning. If any universal is the trace of an adjunction, through which dialectical relations are manifested, we have indeed a particularly selective constraint on the emergence of complex structures out of simpler ones. In this way a gap is also filled, persisting in Piaget's reference to categories, since his sequence of (unduly global) stages is only backwardly controlled by forgetful functors, the notion of adjoint to deal with the forward part being absent. Nevertheless, we still lack a mathematical description of how such a constraint amalgamates with the local/global dialectics and the morphogenetic dynamics that provide certain gestalt patterns and not others.

Two considerations are timely and helpful. First, the ways in which a cognitive system interacts with external systems have to be taken into account, and this also applies to semantic explanation: the local/global pair cannot be separated from the internal/external pair, as is apparent in metalinguistic and indirect discourse – a case study showing the necessity of a simultaneous treatment of both pairs is given in Peruzzi (1991 a) to solve the so-called Gettier paradox. Second, the collection of cognitively relevant kinds is rooted in a basic level, where they are individuated through a minimum principle. Any minimum principle is global in character, and the construction of completions, of logical, algebraic or topological nature, is associated with uniformly defined minima. This furnishes a first link between adjoints and stability. Nonetheless, categorical description is still lacking for phenomena of instability and for the 'arrows' along which they propagate or are inhibited. For this reason, it is necessary to achieve integration of conceptual resources abstracted from situations met in algebraic topology with conceptual resources from differential topology, mainly with the notion of attractor. The motivation of such need is concrete: from early steps in language learning, explanation of progress in semantic competence demands such integration, and only with this integration can the meaning of any word be achieved, stabilized and mastered. This has direct consequences for the debate about the source of intentionality, which had in Searle's Chinese Room one of its main points of reference. It also has concrete consequences for the design of new system architectures in AI, once both cognitivistic and connectionistic ingredients are present, at different but interacting levels.

5. Basic-Level Kinds

Eleanor Rosch's contribution to psycholinguistics (see Rosch et al., 1976) can hardly be overrated: her individuation of a cognitively primary level of CNs has been widely tested, and turns out to be in closer agreement with experimental data than other alternative hypotheses. The resulting prototype theory has progressively become more articulated and more precise through numerous experimental investigations. Still, its impact on the philosophy of language has been very limited until now. Macnamara and Reyes deserve merit for having extracted from the individuation of that basic level relevant consequences for semantic theory, establishing a bridge with logic. Their main step consists in pointing out that, in order for learning of CNs to occur, every perceived figure is led back to a unique psychologically privileged kind, according to a natural tendency to map CNs to kinds. Such privileged kinds are identified with BLKs. (For brevity, we could say that these kinds are those admitting a prototype that corresponds to a maximum for perceptual similarity and a minimum of information on shape.) E.g., the kind DOG is, in this sense, privileged with respect to TERRIER (subordinate kind) and QUADRUPED (superordinate kind).

In Macnamara and Reyes (this volume) CN is semantically defined as an expression which stands for a kind, thus for either (A) atomic (such as DOG), or (B) non-atomic (such as SLICE), or lastly (C) collective kinds (such as BUNCH). The cognitive priority of atomic CNs lies in two facts: first, they do not presuppose other CNs, differently from reference to (B) and (C); and second, they are apt to sustain quantification in a direct way, different from nouns that are non-atomic, collective, or mass – the latter require combination with non-atomic CNs. Now, if we agree on the relevance of the definition given (both to avoid the usual circularity in introducing 'CN' by appealing to the notion of thing, and to explain how the child discovers that certain words are CNs), prototypical CNs should not be identified simply as those referring to kinds whose members are atomic. For MAMMAL is atomic but clearly lacks any prototype. So, whatever the conditions for atomicity involved in grasping that a demonstrated dog is an atomic individual, they bring us back to perceptual structures as essential for analysis of the notion of kind: all the more so if uniqueness of the kind underlying experience of any perceived individual has to support logical consequences. Suppose the child is shown a spherical object in motion; then the same ostensive act can be accompanied by 'ball', 'toy', 'rubber', 'round', 'throw', i.e., by many expressions of the same as well as of different grammatical kinds. How can the child eliminate the ambiguity? Briefly, the ultimate reason lies in optics and manipulation, and requires the embedding of the given presentation into a sequence of others, preceding or following. (So, the dialectics of §4 is active here too; there is no "instant rationality", as there is no instant perception in natural systems,... unless we are in a psychologist's laboratory.) This is also the way we actually proceed in eliminating ambiguity in the classical duck/rabbit and old woman's/young woman's face. Even if the bias for uniqueness of kind is innate, its satisfaction is the result of perceptual strategies that privilege atomic prototypical CNs. On the grounds of the uniqueness hypothesis, a clause for interpreting demonstratives, as in §2, point 2 above, is worked out in Macnamara and Reyes (this volume, §4.2): 'this kind' is interpretable at situation U iff there is an individual a in a unique basic-level kind K appearing at U s.t. 'this: K = a: K' holds at U.

The widely tested existence of such a basic level excludes arbitrariness in primary sorting of indexicals, and therefore rules out Quinean arguments of the Gavagai type. This closes a philosophical era based on the dogma that phenomenological data may support any parsing: as though experienced space were as conceptually amorphous as the spatial continuum is for metrics. Gestalt psychologists have shown that experienced space is not like that. On the other hand, the gravitational tensor acting on the Earth's surface makes local space not amorphous at all. Temperature and chemical bonds forge the objects that human beings are designed to recognize. The fact that only certain quotients are admissible corresponds to the fact that objects are not simply sets and that subobjects have to conform to structural constraints.

It is perfectly legitimate to leave the notion of kind unanalyzed and take it as a primitive. Yet, such a step is consistent both with platonist and with idealist stances (neither of these is excluded by the Learning Theorem in (Macnamara and Reyes, this volume), unless the naturalistic roots of emergence of kinds are adequately stressed; and a purely negative argument, aimed at criticizing as excessive the unlearned resources of Fodor's language of thought, is likewise insufficient: one has to explain why not every 'logically possible' kind is cognitively accessible. So, one is led to think that the general notion of kind is nothing more than an abstract projection of the notion of figural prototype. Lacking this, no notion would be accessible. Nor could logical abstraction be exercised, other than on empty symbols. Once perceptual kinds (of objects and actions) are stabilized, punctuating the base space with holes of referential potential (semantic attractors), cognition is activated by forgetting, metaphorizing or enriching (by imaginative recombination) the phenomenological material that thus emerges. Both basic objects and actions involve algebraic and topological features (familiar to mathematicians because of G-spaces), whose cognitive lifting finally provides us with 'manipulation of symbols'. If so, a deep revision of the status of logic is before us: it takes advantage of categorical tools, but in turn constrains their spectrum. More specifically, once one admits priority of certain kinds, prototypically rooted in structures of perception, the topological nature of basic semantic concepts and relations must become transparent through formalization. My hypothesis is that any form of predication and logical operation, and therefore the meaning of any sentence, ultimately results from algebraic transposition of concrete topological situations. This is related to the importance of verbs in the growth of semantic competence. True, CNs enter the child's vocabulary first, and verbs much later; yet, what verbs express is already a prime ingredient of kind fixation. For instance, if the spoon on the table were irremovable, it could be covered by the kind HANDLE. There are object Urgestalts implicated in kind prototypes, as there are action Urgestalts implicated in dialectical stabilization of kinds. The main examples of such verb-generators are the two pairs OPEN/CLOSE and TRANSFER/KEEP.

Granted the objective nature of BLKs, what is the position of the resulting theory of meaning for CNs with respect to popular alternative theories? The intensional view, so variously developed (as exemplified in approaches ranging from Frege to Carnap, from Montague to Katz), is grounded in principles of application and identity for members of kinds, i.e., it traces the meaning of any CN back to a set of satisfaction conditions, specifying properties by which members of the kind are individuated. A similar view appeals to 'concepts', as embodied in states of knowledge related to what should count as a kind. These states can assume the form of beliefs or of networks of 'descriptions' in a computer program.

Both views may be refined by introducing fuzzy notions and weakening the strictly procedural outlook through pragmatic parameters. In spite of this, both views encounter severe objections, as the well-known arguments by Kripke and Putnam made clear: if meanings have to be objective, they cannot be in the head, and if reference is rigid, it cannot depend on variable descriptions and subjective beliefs. Macnamara and Reyes's approach lends to such arguments, but its peculiarity consists in objecting to intensional/conceptual views of CNs' reference that they violate the mutual determination of individuals and kinds, and thus presuppose bare particulars.

One cannot say, however, that the distinctive semantic function of CNs lies in reference to kinds and that reference is inherently intentional, without providing justification of the way intentionality (which, after all, concerns subjective structures) and objective reference to kinds are fine-tuned. Admission of CNs as not mere symbols but interpreted symbols simply raises the question again of which constraints are imposed by such fine-tuning. Otherwise, we would be back to the name-object theory, the inadequacy of which motivated the structuralistic turn in linguistics (cf. Saussure's *Cours de linguistique générale*) as much as the whole intensionalist tradition (cf. Carnap's *Meaning and Necessity*). In addition, there are at least three elements to take into account: (a) Putnam (1988) has successively shown that the indexical character of rigid designation does not necessarily lead to what he names "metaphysical realism"; (b) Searle's (1983) criticisms of the reference of PNs and CNs being completely independent of subjects; (c) Dummett's (1988) attempt at a systematic conception of meaning (as Fregean *Sinn*) sensitive to the public nature of language prevents any assimilation of the grasping of meaning with either program implementation or idiolectical expansion of the 'web of belief'. Together, these three lines of thought reveal that the situation is more complex than the above considerations on CNs' referential rigidity show. Peruzzi (1991b) was written precisely to handle such complexity, showing how, from a phenomenological perspective, cognition and objectivity of reference can be dialectically unified in, and only in, a naturalistic view of language. Of such perspective, however, pattern recognition anchored to prototypical specimens is an integral part.

Any prototype is given by a pair <pattern, rule>. For example, a dog's prototype consists of a pattern of a typical dog d^*, grasped through an imprinting experience, plus a rule of similarity with d^*, corresponding to a tolerance relation. So, prototype theory avoids bare particulars. But resorting to prototypes has been criticized by noting that different imprinting experiences should lead to different prototypes, and therefore the meaning of 'dog' would change sensibly from child to child, whereas it should be constant and objective. If objectivity of reference cannot be fixed by conceptualization, it is argued, *a fortiori* it cannot be fixed by prototypes either. Actually, this conclusion does not follow. The pattern is not a pure concept, it is linked to a physical body, indexically selected, and so the rule is not a purely subjective matter. The situation is (paradigmaticaly) analogous to the co-ordinative definition of 'meter' as a unit of length, since (i) descriptions enter the definition, after which use forgets them, and keeps just the given object as canonical reference; (ii) 'meter' is used by default: the iron stick is one meter long, unless it becomes sufficiently heated. If 'meter' is absolutely rigid, no change in physics would affect its reference (against relativity theory); if it is holistically determined, any change in any part of knowledge would affect it (contrary to experimental practice). The difference lies in the fact that natural kinds are there, and their properties do not wait for definition in order to exist. And furthermore, innate biases and cognitive architecture are no less natural. Hence, a really dialectical view has to embody constrained flexibility of the similarity rule with respect to the given pattern; passing from epistemology to cognition, additional explanation is needed for the fine-tuning of CNs to BLKs.

Now, what is the source of the psychological privilege of BLKs? Gestalt theory identifies it in the perceptual saliency of such kinds, governed by a set of principles making possible the formation and the stabilization of prototypes. This could give rise to a perception-based theory of meaning. Still, the autonomy of cognition from perception is neatly reaffirmed in Macnamara and Reyes (this volume): the lack of cognitive privilege of BLKs is mirrored in logic, where all kinds are on equal footing, In fact, could logic really turn out to be autonomous from perceptual structures? One can doubt it, for (i) logical competence is achieved by what Piaget named *"abstraction réfléchissante,"* exercised on action patterns; (ii) the logic of a category of abstract kinds is sensitive to their constructive constitution (compare the logical effect of a monoid or a group action on sets). Moreover, the claim that the tree of cognitive stages has a root in perceptually characterized kinds can have relevance in semantics only if the way reference of basic CNs is determined affects the structure of either the nodes or the branches of the tree; if both structures were completely independent of the root, this would behave as if it were deprived of any structure at least for the concerns of cognition. Thus it could be treated, from the logical point of view, as occupied by bare particulars. So, if perceptual parsing of data were irrelevant for cognitive-logical architecture, the door would be re-opened to just another version of language-dressed relativism; and alternatively, if it were prescribed only by intrinsic biases of mind, there would be no obstacle to just another linguistic version of Kantian idealism. In the first case, anything goes; in the second anything is prescribed. In either case we would have an end result alien to the whole project of a logic of kinds, conceived as a part of natural philosophy. There would be no room for scientific explanation of what makes possible our basic semantic resources. So how can we avoid this dilemma?

In this connection, Macnamara and Reyes (this volume) advance two Psychological Theses: PT(1) "We can learn to assign individuals to (for us) new kinds and also learn names for the kinds"; and PT(2) "There are psychologically privileged kinds."

Apart from the fact that the discussion of PT(1) and PT(2) has already been part of previous arguments, the crucial thesis here could be a third one, i.e., PT(3) There is preconceptual access to individuals. For PT(1) and PT(2) cannot avoid the philosophical dualism we are addressing. And what is exploited to justify the learning in PT(1) and the privilege in PT(2) if not perception? The trouble is that the dialectical relation between members and kinds, in conjunction with the identification of kinds through their members, could easily engender circularity. Moreover, in a higher-order perspective, preconceptual access is at the root of the learning of *both* PNs and CNs. Since this root necessarily appeals to structures of input systems, the received view on the separability of cognition from perception is no longer tenable.

The Scylla of relativism and the Charybdis of idealism can be avoided, not by accepting rigid designation as given and breaking the flux of meaning from perception and action to cognition (making this into a sort of formal mincing machine), but rather by (and only by) focussing on the *constitution* of atomic BLKs by means of Urgestalts, which codify the topological structure of the base macro-world, and then are lifted from the base to 'abstract' fibres.

There are two immediate objections to this stance. If the privilege accorded to certain kinds for reasons of saliency should affect kinds' logical/cognitive homogeneity, then (1) alternative hierarchies of kinds would be impossible, and distance from experience, necessary to abstract thought, would be reduced to zero; and (2) alternative input systems, of either natural or artificial intelligence, would support different logics. About (1), the answer resides in the phenomenological notion of *local epoché* elaborated in Peruzzi (1988 and 1991b). About (2), we also make use of different logics in relation to different universes of discourse. Choice of logic is not an arbitrary matter: both the structure of objects and the patterns of perceptual (kinesthetic, etc.) interaction with objects contribute to establishing features of logic (and also language). Perceptual structure determines neither a unique global cognitive hierarchy nor a unique global set of operations to be formalized. This plurality of branching cognitive paths is possible because of the variety of ways of experiencing and interacting with a changing environment: it is a by-product of complexity and the possibility it offers in separating one access module from another. Logical homogeneity of 'Dogs are moving bodies', 'Mammals are vertebrate', and 'Sentences are sets of words' is reached by a *divide et impera* resource, not by a sharp demarcation line between perception and cognition. Whether or not, beyond perception and indexical reference there is just syntax, depends on how syntax is possible. Cognition consists of direct or metaphoric transposition of schemata activated at the perceptual level. This is manifest in the fact that there are no verbs that have a non-perceptual meaning, and the etymology of all 'abstract' expressions is even more revealing (understand, con-cept, de-monstration, there-fore, etc.) Symbols, too, are perceived entities, stocked in memory and ready to be managed according to combinatorial schemata. Even the understanding of syntax as recursive manipulation of symbols keeps track of the meaning lifted from configurations of objects and their actual (or imagined) *manipulation*. It stems essentially from originally meaningful *praxis*.

Likewise, the gap between thought and language concerns the fact that the human mind has parallel access to many separable sources of information, whose linearly parsed representation cannot take place without some selective reorganization. In a sense, one can say that semantics, as traditionally conceived, does not exist (i.e., as a ruled correlation of uninterpreted symbols with bare, non-structured objects).

What exists is real interaction, schematized in patterns on whose symbolization syntax operates. Reference is a particular type of action, respecting pre-established invariants. We see here that the categorical primacy of morphisms (functors) on objects (categories) has coherent application to the real bases of language and cognition.

All this affects the acquisition of kinds. The difficulties met by attempts at reconstructing the notion of kind by means of empirically grounded recursive procedures have revived innatist and platonist views. In accordance with PT(l), Macnamara and Reyes observe correctly that *some* kinds are learned through perception, which preselects admissible individuals and kinds. Nevertheless, they maintain conceptualization as autonomous from such preselection. My suggestion differs.

Some topological Urgestalts forming the schemata of any perceived kind are innate. For example, the disposition to focus on and interpret face features is of a differential nature and is activated within the first months of life. (The primary emotional role of lip configurations, as schematized in Figure 1 above, has to be stressed – reflect the first curve through the horizontal axis.) Experience does nothing more than select determinate stable configurations by means of innate space of basic forms ('micro-kinds') that are not shown separately in the experience of kinds ('macro-kinds'). Therefore, the problem of explaining the cut between perception and cognition is not raised. Conceptualization is just sedimented perceptual (static or dynamic) schematization, the trace left on the level of symbolic units from amalgamated input systems. What is more, such perspective gives a better account of how induction is possible. While the problem does not even exist for the semantical innatist, for the Aristotelian empiricist it is unsolvable (*mutatis mutandis*, Chomskyan arguments apply). Much less is it solvable if the empiricist admits the influence of globally holistic ingredients, the presence of which would largely slow the development of semantic competence on the child's part. The only reply the empiricist could ultimately offer is that the child is lucky: the world is not too complicated in his neighbourhood, and does not change too quickly. The mind develops miraculously in an extraneous world. The hypothesis of Urgestalts and their algebraic-topological structure imposes, on the contrary, severe constraints on the range of what can be a BLK. In turn, such constraints are built into the furniture of the world: light, chemical bonds, gravity, temperature, as they mould the conditions on the earth's surface, and living beings, too.

The standard argument for autonomy is that perception and cognition may vary independently from each other. This is certainly true if we take the totality of concepts on one side and the totality of percepts on the other: an ostensively presented dog may be conceptualized as a quadruped, tail moving, etc., while its conceptualization may remain constant through change of position, perspective, light, etc. In effect, we can confine attention to atomic BLKs, which are the only ones present in the child's initial vocabulary. Starting with these kinds, all others derived from them are located as super- or subordinate, neither in a necessarily algorithmic nor completely free fashion. Perceptual modalities provide themselves the needed *bricolage* for conceptual recombination. It is not difficult to produce examples of two concepts associated with one and the same percept. Indeed, what is considered here as one percept is not really such. Although perception is object-driven, any notion of object emerges out of amalgamating topological (differential, projective) Urgestalts, to each of which one 'pre-concept' corresponds, and conversely. Thus bijection occurs, but only at this level. The child's first words codify already an upper level, starting from which separability applies. Yet this should not obscure the fact that any ingredient of cognition is just the transposition of spatial structuration.

Stability of BLKs with respect to varying perceptual conditions is governed by gestalt invariance. Perception is intrinsically oriented to quotients of presentations: on its own, it takes into account the change in the figure/background relation. When the subject sees a single rotating ball, there is no stabilizing concept in addition to perceptual features constituting a closed, connected body having a surface of constant curvature, moving in three-dimensional space. Such constitution is objective as grounded in the optimal exploitation of optical information present in light, and on the dynamics of physical bodies. There is no tacit conceptual intervention, *à la* Helmholtz, in the ability to interpret variation in light gradient on different points of the ball surface relative to the background. For blind children, touch can play a similar function by affording access to features of surfaces like texture, edges, etc. Spatial abilities are not necessarily mediated by touch, nor by any specific input system, and this is the mark of the depth and universality of the 'intuition of space'. Continuous variation in curvature's constancy suggests that new entries be stocked into (discrete) lexical memory – 'deflated', 'oval'. Conceptual and perceptual variations are strictly linked. The conceptual landscape appears to be punctuated by holes of semantic potential, corresponding to object gestalts, expressed by basic CNs, with a weighted tolerance for variations (which permits the composition of CNs with adjectives); the same holds for verbs, which express action gestalts. There are instability regions in both cases. Significantly, they are not lexicalized. Consider the transition illustrated in the picture by T. Poston and I.N. Stewart (Fig. 2, below).

Here, two shape attractors corresponding to the two CNs, 'woman' and 'face', compete. The indeterminacy region is due neither to conceptual deficiency with respect to perfect perceptual focalization nor to the converse. Since all other, non-basic kinds are obtained by syntactic (combinatorial) actions, and such actions are the symbolic trace of basic action gestalts, there cannot be any cut between perception and cognition without depriving sentences of meaning.

Certainly, were our perceptual systems largely different from what they are, we would have other BLKs prototypes. Still, the correspondence of Urgestalts to objective physical properties of the world would remain untouched, since it is located on a deeper level. We could arrive at the kind DOG in an elaborated way – as do fleas, which have another access to it different from our seeing the whole moving body. In fact, we have no basic-level concept of the Milky Way. What we see are bright dots, named 'stars'. However, the Milky Way is represented as an ellipsoid, and even if it were not, its identification could still be figured as a cluster of stars, distinct from other astronomical configurations in the background of the sky. That the range of humanly accessible kinds is covered by perceptual gestalts helps to explain how language learning is possible, for at the level of features individuating BLKs, the correlation of perceptual and cognitive units collapses to identity, i.e., Gestalt = concept, as exemplified by notions such as straight, separated, moving.

Initially, the child has no lexical representation of his access to the features involved at the basic level: adjectives and verbs enter his vocabulary later than CNs. This is not by chance: the child's first problem is to name identified objects as units of action, not to be aware of those aspects corresponding to his own process of forming the concept of kind.

In this way we realize the necessity to give up the Kantian paradigm, according to which there exist two independent sources for structuring experience: forms of intuition and categories. On the basic level, perception is neither preconceptual nor postconceptual. Kinds are formal and prototype-anchored. For Kant, schemata enter the scene only in order to

Figure 2.

apply categories to experience. Instead, schemata turn out to be the result of stable amalgamation of topological Urgestalts, but come first, embody the inseparability of perception and cognition, and point in the opposite direction to contemporary philosophy of science, with its talk of "inscrutability of reference," "theory-ladenness," etc. So D. Marr's cylindric analysis of two-and-one-half- dimensional representation of objects (see Marr, 1982) and Rosch's prototypes are dialectically linked within a unifying framework.

6. Whence Psycho-Logic Starts

A fundamental postulate of Macnamara, Reyes and Reyes (this volume) is Thesis 1.2. Since reference is a form of access, we can infer that there is no access to individuals except by means of kinds. Given that reference to kinds is not physiological but rather abstract and intentional, Macnamara and Reyes (this volume) obtain what they name the Learning Theorem: "There is no purely physiological explanation for the acquisition of intentional skills or the existence of intentional states and events." Hence, in spite of the rigid character of designation by means of PNs and CNs, causal theories of reference are excluded. Actually, in the formulation adopted in the present volume, the theorem is strengthened by replacing 'physiological' with 'physiological and/or perceptual'.

The crux of the matter is the distinction between intentional and physiological. The former concerns states, skills and events involving strings of interpreted symbols to which satisfaction conditions apply (e.g., for establishing truth); the latter is confined to uninterpreted causal interactions. Reference is intentional by definition, and therefore, no purely physiological explanation (as that admissible for phrase parsing in syntax) is sufficient. Intentionality presupposes physiology but is not reducible to it. The symptom that something is not so smooth in this two-layer view has already leaked out through preconceptual ingredients in the formation of BLKs. How, in fact, does intentionality emerge from the preconceptual? If it is a completely autonomous supervenient property, such a question is deprived of most of its scientific import: it is only the description of intentional structures as end-products that matters. At the same time, all known objections to functionalistic dualism (modelled on the software/hardware paradigm) apply. On the contrary, in view of §5 above, a different approach is available based on the emergence of reference to kinds out of perceptual structures, in exactly the same way that complexity and stability of a purely physical structure graft onto local properties of its constituents under specific conditions, and onto their particular dynamics: for this same reason, I spoke of 'attractors' in §5. Thus, though semantics is not reducible to any sort of syntax (even that of the 'language of thought', to which I will come in a moment), nor to any traditional physicalism, such a super-structure does not support sharp dualism. In the presence of the link established between percept and concept on the level of Urgestalts, the Learning Theorem remains valid: one just needs to read the adverb 'purely' in its formulation as meaning 'low-level'. The naturalistic step taken, we are not confined to a one-level system organization. In physics, too, many phenomena of long-range coherence cannot be "reduced" to properties of single elements: this authorizes us to speak of theories of critical points, order out of chaos, fractals, etc., and not to speak of two (or more) physical ontologies. Similarly, we are not entitled to break into two absolutely separate layers the complex architecture of such an integrated system as the human brain/mind. (Sharp distinctions of level remain just a methodological artifice that reproduces in metalanguage the discretization of continuum yielded by means of CNs in the object language.) Otherwise one should consistently take an anti-naturalistic step, such as that proposed by Putnam (1988), which the arguments of Peruzzi (1991b) were meant to criticize.

Indeed, we have seen that built-in sortalization does not impose idealism on reference, but the Learning Theorem, as formulated, prevents a stronger conclusion: that the view codified in the theses above is inconsistent with idealism. And the reason is that, without the links to perceptual structures and bodily actions I argued for, the way is open either (i) for holistic objections to the autonomous identifiability of *any* kind as potential reference of nouns, thus affecting (given thesis 1.3) the determinacy of indexicals and PNs; or (ii) for the traditional dualism syntax of thought/physical action. Both aporetic alternatives are avoided by taking cognition as fibred over action-perception: this accounts for the possibility of fixing the percept and varying the concept, and vice versa, whereas drawing an ontological gap in between opens the door to the Chinese Room.

Attractor-based emergence, driven by object and action schemata, is on the other hand perfectly consistent with the grounding role of perception in prototypical constitution of BLKs, as well as with the anchorage of perceptual structures to physico-geometrical features common to mind and nature. The resulting 'braid' naturalism is just an amplified projection of the subject/object and part/whole dialectics, manifested on the symbolic level through the self-stabilizing link between word and sentence; and such a link is formalized in the adjunction relating compositional and contextual ingredients of meaning. Nevertheless, the success of this procedure is not warranted by purely recursive re-sources, and the conditions that make possible the mutual coherent fix-ing of word and sentence meaning possess many aspects still to be experimentally investigated and suitably mathematized.

Now, Macnamara and Reyes derive a direct corollary from the Learn-ing Theorem: There exist unlearned logical resources, to be placed with-in the stock of 'primitives', as universals of the human mind. Which are these resources? From what has been said so far, a provisional list should start with **(I) membership, (II) typed equality,** and **(III) men-tion,** i.e., reference to symbols, which embodies, of course, the notion of word, as the basic unit into which to decompose the linguistic manifes-tation of judgements, given by the semiotic ability. About (I), we have seen that it could better be interpreted as a canonical participation map-ping p, according to which, on the basic level, an individual is recog-nized as matching a pattern, while on other sub- or superordinate levels such recognition is replaced by combinatorial tools – so that one can write a $\in$ K, for any a and K of either natural or symbolic nature. Thus it is preferable to reserve $\in$ for a strictly related, yet distinct universal, i.e., the output of the process of collecting.

Although the directly linguistic nature of these (and the following) logical resources might be questioned, (I)–(III) need language to be suit-ably managed. Above all, they can operate only together with **(IV)** the notion of **kind,** linguistically expressed by means of CNs and acting as target of p. Furthermore, language learning presupposes **(V)** the index-ical skill, represented by any expression of any language having the function of the demonstrative **'this'.** (Instead of taking 'this' as not strictly typed, one could say it is parametrically typed by 'present visual gestalt', thus simply appealing to another occurrence of 'this' embed-ded in 'present'.)

The next entry on the list is **(VI)** the resource corresponding to label-ling individuals, identified by (IV) and (V) combined, in order to refer to something in the absence of the fulfilling perceptual experience; so we need the notion of uniquely **localized entity,** expressed by PNs. In its turn, the standard logical behaviour of PNs (and CNs) points to the display of **(VII)** the complementarity of **variables** and **constants** on any given referential occasion.

Passing then from word to sentence structure, §§4 and 5 lead to posit three additional resources: **(VIII) substitution** of one part by another of the same kind in a given whole; **(IX)** the capacity to activate and objec-tify dialectical relations in the form of **adjunctions,** by means of which connectives and quantifiers can be introduced; and finally, **(X)** compe-tence in **stabilization** as applied both to potential bearers of either PNs or CNs, and to the dialectics under (IX), which therefore turn out to be sensitive to local context.

The list (I)-(X) does not pretend to be exhaustive of 'logical' universals. Its purpose consists primarily in identifying the resources necessary to deal with the main aspects of language learning discussed in the present paper. In view of the essential role of topological aspects in the child's experience, other universals, related to schemata of spatial interaction and procedural uniformization, should be added. All of these primitives have then to be organized in suitable principles whose axiomatic presentation is purely categorical[1]. Note, the list above is slightly different from that in Macnamara and Reyes; yet, this difference does not, in itself, cause particular divergence in the general methodological perspective.

The question is where do such unlearned logical resources reside? Jerry Fodor's answer was: "in the language of thought," characterized in Macnamara and Reyes by its being inherently interpreted, unlike a computer's machine language. Unlearned logical resources are simply the way language of thought is basically articulated, behaving as an inner sense, independent of external senses, whose end-products are all translatable into it.

Now, even though the proper meaning of 'logic' has been somewhat dilated in order to cover all of (I)-(X), the reasons justifying such dilation do not appear to apply to 'language'. The only real language we master (to express and communicate thought) is verbal language. The new-born's early abilities in translating modular information (e.g., oral sensations into visual expectations) are better related to the geometrical meaning of 'translation' (and more generally, of 'morphism'), rather than to its linguistic counterpart. However, verbal language does not exhaust thought – see Peruzzi (1990). Moreover, as argued in Peruzzi (1988), the Self can be conceived as a sheaf of modular co-ordinated units, in such a way as to present it as the amalgamated parallel synthesis of information provided by the manifold of perception and action units. Thus we can apply Ockham's razor to such additional 'sense'. Thought can be separated from each of those units, not from them all. To use a metaphor: a blackboard, where various kinds of information is co-ordinated and unified, is not necessarily in need of being represented as a language. Moreover, verbal language does not occupy a central position with respect to all other mental modules. Of course it is a fundamental tool of the human mind, providing linearization of information acquired by parallel activated channels, yet there is evidence that thought is not linear.

What is more, if the language of thought is not in itself interpreted, it requires an interpreter. The well-known homunculus objection would be ready for application: unless interpretation is built into (or massively distributed through) perceptual structure, confirming once again that the classical dichotomy of two sharply distinct sources of knowledge is untenable, as much as the Kantian dualism between logic (as the source of the standard for reasoning) and psychology (as the description of the actual processes of reasoning) is untenable. Most of contemporary philosophy of language stems from that dualism, reinforced by Frege, and inherited by the analytic tradition. Brentano, and Husserl even more, laid the groundwork for acknowledging that the mind has access to built-in standards of correctness not only in relation to logic, but also for the whole range of products of human creativity – see Peruzzi (1989b). To paraphrase Einstein's famous dictum: logic tells psychology how to move, psychology tells logic how to bend. The constraint is mutual. The challenge of naturalizing epistemology consists just in understanding the details of the dialectical constraint. Chomsky paved the way, focussing on syntactic structures as manifestation of a biological endowment. His 'organon' was recursion theory. The extension of such an approach to semantics met insurmountable difficulties. Semantic learning does not appear to be simply procedural, being open to interference patterns among different types of information which merge in verbal language. Categorical models devised for both functional programming and higher-order type theory preserve the contribution of the computational/functionalistic approach within a wider and finer spectrum of possibilities. At the same time, the categorical turn raises stricter demands on semantics. In particular, the categorical presentation of logic allows the grasping of deep connections between cognitive development and semantic structure, which have remained unnoticed until now; and this fact is relevant to overcome the presumed ontological gap between logic and psychology.

Acknowledgments

This work was done with partial suport of a "40 percent" grant from Ministero dell'Università e della Ricerca Scientifica e Tecnologica (MURST), Italy. I wish to thank Robert Dreicer and John Macnamara for their help in improving the presentation of my ideas.

Note

1   As its title suggests, this paper was intended to prepare, not to develop, a theory of kinds. For this reason I skip here the burden of completing the list and

stating the axioms – which would really mean providing a phenomenological foundation of mathematics.

References

Dummett, M. (1988). The origins of analytic philosophy. *Lingua e Stile* 23: 3-49, 171-210

Ellerman, D. (1988). Category theory and concrete universals. *Erkenntnis* 28: 409-29

Ghilardi, S., and G.C. Meloni (forthcoming). Topology, relative topology, presheaves, relative presheaves and quantified modal logic. In C. Cellucci (ed.), *Proceedings of the Società Italiana di Logica e Filosofia della Scienza (SILFS) Congress 89*. Bologna: CLUEB

Kanizsa, G. (1991). *Vedere e Pensare*. Bologna: Il Mulino

Marr, D. (1982) *Vision*. San Francisco: Freeman

Moneglia, M. (1987). Senso e campi di variazioni: un'esplorazione sul significato di alcuni verbi causativi Italiani. *Studi di Grammatica Italiana* 13: 271-349

Pavlovic, D. (1990). *Predicates and fibrations*. Unpublished Ph.D. thesis, Utrecht: Riijksuniversiteit

Peruzzi, A. (1987a). La teoria delle descrizioni: Questo paradigma della filosofia. *Epistemologia* 10: 205-26

— (1987b). Il soggetto della logica. *Teoria* 7: 45-76

— (1988). *Noema: Mente e logica attraverso Husserl*. Milano: F. Angeli

— (1989a). The theory of descriptions revisited. *Notre Dame Journal of Formal Logic* 30: 91-104

— (1989b). Towards a real phenomenology of logic. *Husserl Studies* 6: 1-24

— (1990). Some remarks on the linguistic turn. *Teoria* 10: 117-30

— (1991a). Meaning and truth: The ILEG [Internal-Local-External-Global] Project. In T. Tscherdanzeva et al. (eds.), *Functional Semantics*. Moscow: Soviet Academy of Sciences, 53-59

— (1991b). From Kant to natural epistemology. Unpublished paper, Department of Philosophy, University of Florence

— (1991c). Categories and logic. In G. Usberti (ed.), *Problemi fondazionali nella teoria del significato*. Florence: Olschki, 137-211

— (1992). Note del seminario su semantica e cognizione. Unpublished paper, Department of Philosophy, University of Florence

Piaget, J. (1974). Structures et catégories. *Logique et analyse* 65-66: 223-40

Poston, T., and I. Stewart (1978). *Catastrophe Theory and Its Applications*. London: Pitman

Putnam, H. (1988). *Representation and Reality*. Cambridge, MA: Bradford/MIT Press

Reyes, G. (1989). A topos-theoretic approach to reference and modality. *Notre Dame Journal of Formal Logic* 32: 359-91

Rosch,E., C.B. Mervis, W.D. Gray, D.M. Johnson and P. Boyes-Braem (1976). Basic objects in natural categories, *Cognitive Psychology* 8: 382-439

Searle, J. (1983). *Intentionality: An Essay in the Philosophy of Mind.* Cambridge: Cambridge University Press

9

How Children Learn Common Nouns and Proper Names: A Review of the Experimental Evidence

D. Geoffrey Hall

Between about 18 months and six years of age, children learn new words at an average rate of several per *day* (Carey 1978; Dromi 1987). Strikingly, children readily accomplish this learning through ostensive definition. For example, young children are very good at *correctly* interpreting novel words when adults use them (e.g., "This is a dog") while simply pointing to unfamiliar solid objects (e.g., a dog). This is not a trivial ability. It implies that children are able to construe the ostensive act as one of referring (see Macnamara 1986; Baldwin 1991), and that they know how to segment the sound stream accurately to select the appropriate piece ('dog') under definition (see Gleitman and Wanner 1982). But what is perhaps most impressive, it implies that children are able to select the appropriate reference for the word, namely the kind, DOG.

Fixing a word's reference following a simple ostensive definition is an impressive ability because an ostensively defined word logically could be assigned to any of a huge number of possible referents. To be successful at learning words from ostension, children must be able to determine a word's *general* reference (e.g., whether it refers to a kind of individual, a kind of stuff, a property, an action, or an individual), and they must be able to select the correct *specific* reference within the general category (e.g., *which* kind of individual). For example, when children hear a word applied ostensively to an unfamiliar solid object (e.g., a dog), they must have the ability to determine that the word refers to a kind of individual (e.g., DOG) rather than to a kind of stuff (e.g., FUR), a property (e.g., spotted), an action (e.g., panting), or an individual (e.g., Fido). And they must also have the ability to select a *unique* kind (e.g., DOG) as the reference of the word, among the many kinds to which the word logically could refer (e.g., ANIMAL, POODLE, TAIL, PAW, PUPPY).

In this chapter, I will argue that children's ability to fix words' reference following ostensive definitions reflects implicit assumptions children hold about the reference of words used under certain conditions (e.g., to pick out unfamiliar solid objects; to pick out portions of unfamiliar non-solid substances; to pick out certain familiar solid objects). I will also suggest that these assumptions arise from children's implicit knowledge of definitions of the grammatical categories of count noun, mass noun and proper name. Recent analyses suggest that these three categories of word have semantic definitions, that is, definitions that allude to what the words are understood to refer to (see Macnamara and Reyes, this volume; Bloom 1992a; McPherson 1991; Soja, Carey and Spelke 1991). Because of these links between reference and grammatical category, I will argue also that the assumptions in question play an important role in children's discovery of the formal syntactic properties of words in these three categories (cf. Pinker 1984; Grimshaw 1981; Macnamara 1982). In other words, the proposed assumptions are relevant both to reference and to grammar.

In what follows, I will first present semantic definitions of three categories of word: common noun (count noun, mass noun) and proper name. For each category, I will describe an implicit assumption that children may initially make that would lead them not only to assign certain words in the input to that category but also to fix the words' reference. I will then review experimental findings from children learning common nouns and proper names, with an eye to examining whether these data support the existence of the proposed word-learning assumptions.

Defining the Categories and Deriving the Learning Assumptions

I first briefly summarize certain aspects of the semantics of common nouns and proper names, presented in depth in LaPalme Reyes, Macnamara and Reyes (this volume).

Common Nouns

There is a class of common nouns that on their own denote kinds; for example, 'dog', 'animal', 'water', 'liquid'. These common nouns may be called first-level nouns. I will distinguish them from second-level common nouns that acquire reference only in association with first-level ones; for example, 'group', 'crowd', 'portion', or 'gallon'. In this chapter, I will be concerned primarily with the learning of first-level nouns, and so the definitions I will provide will apply only to them.

(a) Count Nouns (CNs)

CNs are common nouns which on their own denote kinds whose members are atomic (e.g., DOG); for these kinds, CNs supply principles of identity, individuation and application. To supply a principle of individuation is to specify what counts as one member of a kind; for example, a whole dog, with interior as well as exterior parts, but excluding his collar. To supply a principle of identity is to specify which members are the same individual and which are different. For example, a dog and his mother are different dogs, whereas a puppy and a certain grown animal may be the same dog. Gupta (1980) has shown the non-triviality of this principle: a single person may be counted as several passengers. To supply a principle of application is to specify a set of conditions that distinctive of members of the kind. For example, there are certain conditions for being a dog, and these conditions differ from those for being a cat. All open class words provide a principle of application. CNs supply such a principle on their own (so do mass nouns), whereas verbs and adjectives supply them only in association with nouns. In other words, verbs and adjectives are typed by nouns.

To describe the extension of a CN as atomic is to say that (a) an arbitrary division of a member does not yield two or more members of the kind; and (b) the combining of two or more members of the kind does not yield a new member. It is this feature of the kinds denoted by CNs that explains their quantificational properties – for example, their taking plurals and their combining with such quantifiers as 'a(n)', 'many', 'several', and 'two', all of which quantify discretely, over atomic individuals.

The definition of CN suggests that children may make the following assumption in order to locate and fix the reference of words from this category. *If a word is used to pick out (what is taken to be) an unfamiliar atomic individual (with identity), then interpret it as naming the kind to which that individual belongs, and as supplying the three principles for the kind; in other words, interpret it as a CN.* But because children appear to fix a word's *specific* reference from an ostensive definition, the assumption must be more specific: Interpret the word as referring to a *unique* kind and as a *unique* CN. In other words, there must be certain *constraints* on what can qualify as an atomic individual in the extension of a word applied to an unfamiliar referent. I will call the individuals that satisfy these constraints *basic-level* individuals (after Rosch, Mervis, Gray, Johnson and Boyes-Braem 1976).

b. Mass Mouns (MNs)

MNs, like CNs, denote kinds and supply principles of individuation, identity and application for their extension. But the extension of a MN is not atomic; instead, it has a sup-lattice structure. This means that any two portions of the extension together form a third portion. For example, WATER includes the water in several glasses of water, and in combination these glasses of water form a larger portion of water. The claim about sup-lattice structure leaves open the question of whether there are minimal portions, that is, whether there are portions whose subdivisions are no longer in the extension of the kind. The definition of MNs offers insight into why they take certain quantifiers and not others. MNs take quantifiers like 'much' and 'a lot' and 'little' (in one of its senses), but not 'many', 'several' or 'two'. That is, MNs combine only with quantifiers that quantify over portions, not atomic individuals.

The definition of MN suggests that in order to locate and fix the reference of words from this category, children may make the following assumption. *If a word is used to pick out (what is taken to be) a portion of an unfamiliar stuff (with identity), then interpret it as naming the kind to which that portion of stuff belongs; in other words, interpret it as a MN.* But again, because children appear to fix a word's *specific* reference from an ostensive definition, the assumption must be more specific: children must interpret the word as referring to a *unique* kind of stuff and as a *unique* MN. Again, this claim implies that there must be certain *constraints* on what can qualify as a portion of stuff in the extension of a word applied to an unfamiliar referent. Extending a term introduced above, I will call the portions of stuff that satisfy these constraints portions of *basic-level* stuff.

Proper Names (PNs)

PNs are expressions that refer rigidly to atomic individuals in kinds, individuals that are not themselves kinds. To say that a PN refers rigidly means two things: (a) it picks out the individual at all times and in all situations, including counterfactual ones, in which the individual figures. PNs share this property with pronouns (e.g., 'he', 'she') and definite descriptions (e.g., 'The Queen of England'); and (b) it refers to the individual independent of the situation in which it is used. This is an idealization, because who is meant by 'Ralph' may depend on who happens to be speaking and to whom. Nevertheless, the reference of PNs does not vary systematically with situation of use, as does that of such pronouns as 'I' and 'you' and that of such definite descriptions as 'The Queen of England'.

There is always a CN implicitly involved in the interpretation of a PN – to handle individuation and identity. If you are introduced to an individual named 'Ralph', the CN 'person' is required to specify the kind that provides a suitable means of atomic individuation and traces the identity of the bearer. Many CNs may come into play in connection with Ralph, some having to do with just part of him (e.g., 'nose', 'face'), some with his entire person (e.g., 'student', 'man'), but they do not individuate the bearer or trace his identity suitably. To be dramatic, suppose you are introduced with the words, "This passenger is Ralph." The problem is that 'Ralph' does not name a passenger, because you are quite likely to ask "Where do you come from, Ralph?" – although Ralph is not a passenger at home. 'Passenger' does not cover the right range of situations. Therefore, 'passenger' cannot be the CN that supports the interpretation of the PN 'Ralph'. Indeed, it seems very difficult to have a PN pick out an individual in the kind, PASSENGER.

The definition of PN suggests that children may locate and fix the reference of words from this category by making the following assumption. *If a word is used to pick out an individual in a basic-level kind, and if the word is read as a rigid designator of that individual, then interpret it as referring to that individual, that is, as a PN* (Macnamara and Reyes this volume). Among other things, basic-level kinds seem to individuate the bearer and trace his or her identity in a way suitable to support the interpretation of a PN.

Experimental Evidence

I will now review experimental evidence involving children between 18 months and about six years of age, in an attempt to make the case that early word learning is guided by the implicit assumptions described earlier: (1) a word applied to (what children take to be) an unfamiliar atomic individual with identity will refer to a basic-level kind of individual, and the word will be a basic-level CN; (2) a word applied to (what children take to be) a portion of unfamiliar stuff with identity will refer to a basic-level kind of stuff, and that word will be a basic-level MN; and (3) a word applied to an atomic individual in a basic-level kind of individual and read as a rigid designator of that individual will refer to that individual, and that word will be a PN. The focus of the review will be on the period beginning at about a year and a half, because this is the point at which most (English-speaking) children begin in earnest to acquire new words (i.e., they experience a vocabulary "explosion") It is not clear that word learning in the period prior to this point (i.e., in the period from roughly one year to 18 months) is qualitatively the same (see, e.g., Dromi 1987).

Most of the evidence comes from studies of comprehension, where the interest lies in determining children's interpretation of the reference of novel words (e.g., in determining to which referents in an array of objects children will extend a novel word). A smaller portion of the evidence comes from studies of production, where the interest lies in determining children's grammatical category assignment of novel words (e.g., in determining whether children will pluralize the word, or use it in conjunction with certain quantifiers). Without both types of evidence, it is difficult to know for certain that, in interpreting any single new word, children exploit the word-learning assumptions under investigation. For example, there are certain English words that are not CNs, but that have (what we seem to take as) atomic individuals in their extensions (say, certain superordinate-level MNs such as 'furniture'). In investigating the learning of such a word from comprehension data alone, it would be easy to conclude mistakenly that children had interpreted the word as a CN (see Bloom 1992a for discussion). However, the assumptions under investigation in this paper are meant to account for the learning of words for basic-level kinds, not superordinate-level kinds. Furthermore, although many of the individual studies do report only one type of evidence, I believe that the *body* of evidence is consistent with the claim that children are guided by the assumptions under consideration.

In addition to the assumptions described earlier, I will appeal to one other assumption that children appear to make in interpreting novel words, namely, that words contrast in meaning (see Clark 1983, 1987). By making this further assumption, children avoid interpreting two words as having the same meaning. Together with the assumptions described earlier, the contrast assumption implies, among other things, that learners should tend *not* to interpret a word applied to an object for which they already know the basic-level count noun (i.e., a familiar object) as being synonymous with the basic-level count noun. An assumption of lexical contrast, then, motivates children to move beyond the preferred basic-level kind interpretation of a novel word. Several of the studies described below compare the interpretation of words for unfamiliar and familiar objects. The rationale behind such comparisons is to elucidate properties of the basic-level kind which, recall, I have defined as the interpretation of a word applied to (what is taken to be) an unfamiliar, but not a familiar, referent.

I will use certain words in specialized ways. As mentioned above, my use of the words 'familiar' and 'unfamiliar' is specialized, meaning, respectively, 'for which the basic-level noun is known' and 'for which the basic-level noun is not known'. In addition, throughout the chapter, I speak of children being taught words for "(solid) objects" or "(non-solid) substances." By 'object', I mean 'object that offers a typeable perceptual Gestalt', almost always a discrete physical object (or a drawing of one). For example, I mean something like a spoon, a dog or a chair. I do not mean to suggest an appeal to bare particulars, that is, to members of a universal atomic kind, such as OBJECT (see Macnamara and Reyes this volume). In contrast, my use of 'substance' is meant to imply 'perceptually typeable substance', where the typing is of the substance (for texture, malleability, colour, among other properties). For example, I mean something like water, milk or sand.

Count Nouns and Mass Nouns

I will focus first on the *general* hypothesis that children initially think that a word applied to an unfamiliar referent (construed as either an atomic individual or a portion of stuff) refers to a kind, and that the word is a common noun (a CN or a MN, respectively). I will save for the next section the discussion of the psychologically privileged kind, that is, the basic-level kind.

CNs

My goal in this section is to provide evidence that children initially think that any word applied to (what they take to be) an unfamiliar atomic individual refers to a kind of atomic individual, that is, is a CN. By 'initially', I mean during the period from about 18 months (perhaps earlier) until the point at which children master the referential correlates of words from more than one grammatical category (perhaps later). Actually, the period likely extends beyond the point of simple 'mastery' of these referential correlates. As will be seen, there is some evidence that children as young as two years old understand the referential correlates of words from several syntactic categories (e.g., CNs, MNs, PNs and adjectives); but other evidence suggests that children as old as four years fail to recognize these correlates - and construe *any* word applied to an object as referring to a kind of object (as a CN)- if the object is unfamiliar.

The evidence will almost all deal with how children interpret words applied to solid objects (or drawings of objects). As a result, the evidence is also consistent with the hypothesis that the assumption in question involves the notion of a *solid object*, rather than the more abstract notion of an *atomic individual*. However, there is evidence that, independently of word learning, young children treat solid objects as atomic individuals (see Shipley and Shepperson 1990), and some of the evidence reviewed below (e.g., Bloom 1992a) will suggest that preschoolers as young as three years appreciate a link between CNs and atomic individuals that are *not* solid objects (i.e., noises). These facts, plus the fact that the notion of atomic individual - not object - figures in the definition of CN, give some weight to the hypothesis that the assumption guiding learning should be framed in terms of atomic individuals and not merely solid objects (see also Bloom 1992a, 1992b).

There is evidence that preschoolers between two and five years old have learned that CNs applied to objects refer to kinds of object (e.g., Markman and Hutchinson 1984; Waxman and Kosowski 1990; Waxman and Hall forthcoming; Baldwin 1989; Waxman and Gelman 1986; Waxman 1990; Landau, Smith and Jones 1988; Jones, Smith and Landau 1991), and that not all words applied to objects refer to kinds of object (Brown 1957; Katz et al. 1974; Gelman and Taylor 1984; Landau and Stecker 1990; Taylor and Gelman 1988; Waxman and Kosowski 1990). Where does this knowledge come from? As noted earlier, children cannot be born knowing where English CNs appear in the input. But if children make the implicit assumption that CNs (words that refer to kinds of atomic individual) will be the words used to pick out (what children take as) unfamiliar atomic individuals, then children should *initially* expect that *any* word applied to an unfamiliar object will refer to a kind of object (will be a CN). The evidence in support of this hypothesis comes from two types of study: one involves comparing children's interpretations of words (including some that are not CNs) for unfamiliar and familiar objects; the other focusses exclusively on children's interpretation of words for unfamiliar objects.

First, consider those studies that have compared the learning of words for unfamiliar and familiar objects. In one experiment, Hall, Waxman and Hurwitz (forthcoming) tested two groups of four-year-olds. One group heard an unfamiliar target object (e.g., a metal garlic press) labelled with an adjective (e.g., "This is a zav one"). Children took part in a forced-choice task, where they were asked to select "another zav one." They tended to select another object of the same object kind but differing in substance kind (a plastic garlic press) rather than an object of the same substance kind but differing in object kind (a metal apple corer). In the other group, all the objects were familiar (a metal cup, a plastic cup, and a metal spoon), and children were reliably more likely to select the object matching in substance kind but differing in object kind. One interpretation of these findings is that four-year-olds have a greater tendency to interpret an adjective applied to an object as referring to a kind of object if the object is unfamiliar than if it is familiar. It is worth noting that the familiarity effect was not obtained with two-year-olds in the same task; regardless of object familiarity, two-year-olds showed a tendency *not* to select the substance kind match, and there was no significant difference between unfamiliar and familiar groups.

Markman and Wachtel (1988; experiments 4 to 6) have demonstrated a similar phenomenon. In one study, they taught three-year-old children a word modelled as a MN (or an adjective) for a target object (e.g., "This is pewter"). Children then had to say whether a new object of the same object kind but differing in kind of substance was also "pewter". If the target object was unfamiliar (pewter tongs), children tended to agree that the new object (wooden tongs) was 'pewter'. If the target object was familiar (a pewter cup), then children tended to deny that the new object (a ceramic cup) was 'pewter'.

More recently, Hall (1991) has shown the same effect in two-year-olds' learning of PNs. In Hall's experiments, children learned a word for an individual stuffed toy of an animate kind. The word was modelled as a PN (e.g., "This is Zav"). If the toy was unfamiliar (e.g., a creature), children extended the PN to a second object of the same object kind. They tended not to do this if the toy was familiar (e.g., a dog); instead, they restricted the word only to the named object, showing sensitivity to the PN syntax. Hall (1991) also found that children's spontaneous comments differed between unfamiliar and familiar conditions. If the toy was unfamiliar, children tended to treat the word syntactically as a CN, often pluralizing it, or combining it with the indefinite article or discrete quantifiers; they tended not to do this if the toy was familiar. This is perhaps the clearest evidence that children will misconstrue a word that is not a CN as a CN if it is applied to an unfamiliar object.

Instead of *comparing* children's interpretation of words for unfamiliar and familiar objects within a study, other researchers have simply examined young children's interpretation of words applied to unfamiliar objects. For example, Smith, Jones and Landau (1992) taught young three-year-olds a word for an unfamiliar geometric object. In their first two experiments, children who learned either a CN or an adjective tended to extend it to other objects of the same object kind (i.e., objects sharing the same shape). Only in one experiment (experiment 3) did they find that their subjects distinguished the words' reference, interpreting a CN as picking out objects of the same object kind, but interpreting an adjective as picking out objects sharing a salient property. However, in order to obtain this result, the authors had to make the property *extremely* salient (i.e., they placed the object in a darkened toy "cave" and shone a light on it so that the object sparkled and glowed). Smith et al.'s difficulty in showing that three-year-old children distinguish the reference of CNs and adjectives likely stemmed at least in part from the fact that the referent objects were all unfamiliar.

In a pair of papers, Soja (1992; Soja, Carey and Spelke 1991) showed two-year-olds an unfamiliar object (e.g., a copper plumber's T) and then asked them to choose between another object of the same object kind but differing in substance kind (a plastic T) or pieces of the same kind of substance (pieces of copper). Regardless of whether children heard the target labelled with a CN ("This is a blicket"), a MN ("This is some blicket"), or an unspecified noun ("This is my blicket"), they showed a strong tendency to select the object of the same object kind, rather than pieces of the same substance kind.

Dickinson (1988) has replicated Soja's findings (Soja et al. 1991; Soja 1992) with three-, four- and five-year-olds. He taught an MN ("This is some treg") and an unspecified noun ("Here is my treg") for different unfamiliar objects. Using the same design as Soja et al. (1991), he showed that children tended to select an object of the same object kind (rather than pieces of the same substance kind) after learning either type of noun, although the tendency was slightly weaker when the word was introduced as a MN than when it was introduced in an unspecified noun frame. In another experiment, Dickinson (1988) taught three-, four-, and five-year-olds a CN ("This is a treg"), a MN ("This is made of treg"), and an unspecified noun ("This is my treg") for different unfamiliar objects. In all cases, children tended to extend the word to another object of the same object kind rather than to pieces of the same substance kind, although the tendency again was weakest for the MN, especially among the oldest children. This last finding suggests some growth between three and five years in sensitivity to the meaning of the locution 'made of' as signalling reference to a kind of substance (i.e., the MN status of the word).

Gordon (1985; experiment 2) made a related discovery, although only among children above four years of age. He taught children between three and six years of age an unspecified noun (e.g., "This is the garn") for an unfamiliar object. Gordon then showed children several other objects of the same object kind and said, "Over there we have more...-what?" Gordon inferred that children who pluralized the word (i.e., said "garns") had encoded it as a CN; he concluded that those who said "garn" had interpreted the word as a MN. Gordon found that the older children (between four-and-a-half and six) readily pluralized the unspecified noun, indicating that they had encoded it as a CN, even though it had not been modelled explicitly as such. However, the younger children in his sample tended not to pluralize the word, suggesting that they did not construe the word as referring to a kind of object. This finding is somewhat surprising in light of the previous findings, because it suggests that young children *cannot* use knowledge of a referent's status as a solid object to infer that a word used to pick it out is a CN. However, Bloom (1992a) has argued that Gordon's reading of the data may be overly pessimistic about young children's ability to draw inferences about a word from its use to pick out an object; moreover, Gordon's production task may not have been well suited (e.g., may have been too difficult) for his youngest subjects (see Bloom 1992a).

Using a comprehension task, McPherson (1991) has recently found evidence that two-year-old children tend to interpret a word applied to unfamiliar objects as referring to a kind of object. She taught children a word modelled either as a CN (e.g., "These are voks") or as a MN (e.g., "This is voks") for a group of unfamiliar objects (pom-pom creatures) of two sizes, large and small. After learning the word, children were asked to provide a puppet with "a little vok" (if they had learned a CN) or "a little voks" (if they had learned a MN). Because 'a little' is ambiguous, the puppet could have been asking for a small individual pom-pom creature or a small portion of pom-pom creatures of either size. She conducted a post-test to eliminate from the analyses any children who failed to show an understanding of both senses of 'a little'. McPherson found that whether children heard a CN or a MN, they tended to give the puppet one small pom-pom creature. This finding suggests that children had interpreted the word applied to unfamiliar objects in either case as referring to a kind of object (i.e., as if it were a CN).

It is important to note that the evidence does not show that children *always* construe any word applied to an unfamiliar object as referring to a kind of object. For example, Gordon (1985; experiment 1) taught preschoolers (three- to five-year-olds) either a novel MN or a novel CN for an unfamiliar object. Referring to the object, he said either "So here we have a garn" (a CN) or "So here we have some garn" (a MN). He then asked children to produce the new word to describe a new group of objects of the same object kind. Referring to the group, he said "Over there we have more...what?" Gordon found that on most, but not all, of the trials, children interpreted the word in a manner consistent with its grammatical category (i.e., they pluralized only the CN), rather than being swayed always to interpret the word as a CN. Several concerns have been raised with Gordon's interpretation of these data (Bloom 1992a), but even if Gordon is correct that three- to five-year-olds are reliant on a word's syntactic category in interpreting its reference (rather than on the referent's status as an object) when the word is applied to an unfamiliar object, the finding does not imply that initially, children are reliant on syntax to the same degree. Gordon himself acknowledges that his subjects were old enough to have learned to rely on the syntactic cues, and his findings do not rule out the possibility that, earlier on, children relied more on the status of the referent as an unfamiliar object.

It is also worth noting the role of object familiarity in even very young children's tendency to interpret a word applied to an object as referring to *something other* than a kind of object. Unlike the preceding studies, Prasada (forthcoming) taught two-and-a-half- to three-and-a-half-year-olds a MN for a familiar object. The novel MNs he employed were familiar English MNs. For example, children heard an object (e.g., a ball) labelled as follows: "This ball is made of sponge; this is a sponge ball." Children then chose among another object of the same object kind but differing in substance kind (a wooden ball), an object of a different object kind but sharing substance kind (a sponge doll), and an object that matched in neither way (a wooden doll). Prasada found that children did *not* tend to select the object of the same object kind when asked to give "the thing that is made of sponge." On the majority of the trials, children tended to select the same substance kind match, apparently interpreting the word as referring to the kind of substance of which the object was made. One likely reason for Prasada's success at teaching words referring to substance kind for solid objects appears to be the familiarity of the referent object.

In summary, the preceding data suggest that word learners do *initially* assume that a word applied to an unfamiliar object will refer to a kind of object (be a CN). Later in the preschool years (the precise age varying with the task), this assumption appears to be countered by a tendency to rely more on previously mastered syntactic cues to word meaning (e.g., the presence or absence of the indefinite article) than on the status of the referent as an unfamiliar object. Moreover, even at a young age (e.g., as young as two and a half years), the assumption may be overruled if children already know a CN for the (basic-level) kind.

MNs

In this section, I turn to an examination of the experimental evidence supporting the *general* hypothesis that children initially assume that a word applied to (what they construe as) a portion of unfamiliar stuff will refer to a kind of stuff (the word will be a MN). As with the evidence about CNs, this evidence almost always deals with how children interpret words applied to one specific type of portion, namely, a portion of non-solid substance. As a result, the evidence is also consistent with the hypothesis that the assumption in question involves the notion of a portion of *non-solid substance*, rather than the more abstract notion of a portion of *stuff* of a certain sort. However, it seems reasonable to assume that young children treat portions of non-solid substances (e.g., milk, sugar) as portions of stuff (and not as atomic individuals), and evidence reviewed below (e.g., Bloom 1992a) suggests that preschoolers as young as three years of age appreciate a link between MNs and portions of stuff that are *not* non-solid substances (i.e., blasts of noise). These facts, along with the fact that the notion of portion of *stuff* - not *non-solid substance* - figures in the definition of MN, give weight to the hypothesis that the assumption guiding the learning of MNs is framed in terms of portions of stuff and not merely portions of non-solid substance (see Bloom 1992a, 1992b).

There is less evidence about children's interpretation of words applied to portions of substance than there is about their interpretation of words applied to objects. And to my knowledge, there have been no direct comparisons of the interpretation of words for unfamiliar and familiar substances. However, there have been several studies that have examined the interpretation of a word (a noun of some type) applied to a portion of unfamiliar substance. The results of those studies are consistent with the hypothesis that children initially interpret any word (at least, any noun) applied to a portion of unfamiliar substance as referring to a kind of substance.

For example, Soja et al. (1991; Soja 1992) taught two-year-old children a word for a portion of an unfamiliar substance (e.g., a pile of freeze-dried coffee). Children then had to choose between another same-shaped single portion of a different substance kind (a similar pile of rice-shaped pasta) and several smaller portions of the same substance kind as the target (three small piles of freeze-dried coffee). Children who heard a MN (e.g., "This is some stad") applied to the target tended to select several small piles of the same substance kind as the target. So did children who learned the word with unspecified noun syntax (e.g., "This is my stad"). Even children under two and a half years who heard a CN (e.g., "This is a stad") applied to the target did so. These findings suggest that children (below about 30 months) do show a tendency to interpret *any* word (or at least any noun) applied to a portion of an unfamiliar substance as a MN. However, children over two-and-a-half who learned a CN were more likely to select the single portion of the different substance kind (though about half still selected the three portions of the same substance kind). Because children of about 30 months of age are beginning to master the referential distinction between CNs and MNs, the older children in the Soja studies likely were interpreting the CN applied to a portion of unfamiliar substance as referring to the kind of *portion* itself, such as "pile"; in other words, they were likely interpreting the CN appropriately as referring to a kind of atomic individual.

Dickinson (1988) conducted a study with a design similar to that of Soja et al. (1991; Soja 1992), but with three-, four- and five-year-olds as subjects. He replicated the Soja findings when an unspecified noun (e.g., "This is my stad") was applied to a portion of an unfamiliar substance kind (e.g., a pile of powder or gel). Children extended the word to several piles of the same kind of substance rather than to another same-shaped single pile made of a different kind of substance.

In another study, Gordon (1985; experiment 2) showed that older preschoolers (four-and-a-half- to six-year-olds) encoded an unspecified noun (e.g., "This is the garn") as a MN when it was applied to a portion of an unfamiliar substance. The task was the elicitation task described earlier, in which children learned the word for a single portion of the substance, and then were asked to use the word to describe several other portions of the substance. Because children failed to pluralize the word in doing so, Gordon inferred that they had interpreted it as a MN. Surprisingly, Gordon found less consistent performance among the younger children in his sample (i.e., the three- to four-and-a-half-year-olds); this finding suggests that young children are less likely than older children to rely on a referent's status as a portion of substance in order to infer that a word used to pick it out is a MN. However, as noted earlier, Bloom (1992a) has made a cogent critique both of Gordon's interpretation of his findings in this experiment, as well as of the experimental task itself (i.e., that it may not have been a sensitive test of young children's interpretation).

Employing a simpler task than Gordon (1985), McPherson (1991) has recently shown that two-year-olds can exploit a referent's status as a portion of substance to infer that a word used to pick it out refers to a kind of substance. She taught children a word modelled either as a CN (e.g., "These are voks") or as a MN (e.g., "This is voks") for a portion of an unfamiliar kind of substance (a pile of tapioca pearls), consisting of grains of two sizes, large and small. After learning the word, children were asked, for example, to provide a puppet with "a little vok" (CN) or "a little voks" (MN). Because 'a little' is ambiguous, the puppet could have been asking for a small individual pearl of tapioca or a small portion of tapioca pearls of either size. McPherson carried out a post-test to eliminate from the analysis any child who failed to show an appreciation of both senses of 'a little'. She found that regardless of the status of the word as a CN or a MN, children tended to give the puppet a small portion of pearls (including pearls of both sizes). This finding suggests that children had interpreted the word modelled either as a CN or a MN applied to a portion of an unfamiliar substance as referring to a kind of substance (i.e., as if it were a MN).

Again, it is important to note that the evidence does not suggest that children *always* interpret any word applied to a portion of an unfamiliar substance as referring to a kind of substance. Gordon (1985; experiment 1) taught a group of three- to five-year-old children either a MN or a CN for a target test tube which was filled with an unfamiliar kind of substance. He asked children to produce the new word to describe other test tubes filled with the same kind of substance. He first said, pointing to the target, either "So here we have a garn" (a CN) or "So here we have some garn" (a MN). Then, pointing to the other test tubes, he said: "Over there we have more...what?" Gordon found that on most, but not all trials, children interpreted the word according to its syntactic context (i.e., they pluralized only the CN), rather than being swayed always to interpret the word as a MN (in accord with the fact that it picked out a portion of substance). But as Gordon himself acknowledged, this finding is not incompatible with the claim that children *initially* are more swayed by the referent's status as a portion of substance than by the word's status as a CN or a MN (as McPherson 1991 has shown with two-year-olds). Moreover, as in Soja (1992), children who learned the CN for the substance in Gordon's experiment could have construed the referent as an atomic individual (e.g., a test tube), and interpreted the CN as a CN such as 'test tube' or 'test-tube-full'.

In sum, the evidence reviewed in this section suggests that initially children *do* interpret a word (or at least a noun) - whether a MN, an unspecified noun, or a CN - applied to a portion of an unfamiliar kind of substance as referring to a kind of substance, that is, as a MN. Children also do come to rely on syntactic cues to reference (e.g., after two-and-a-half years of age), and this reliance eventually leads them to interpret words (other than MNs) applied to portions of unfamiliar substance appropriately. For example, it leads them to interpret a CN applied to a portion of an unfamiliar kind of substance as referring to a kind of atomic individual, where the individual is the portion itself (e.g., a pile, a puddle, a lump).

Ambiguous Referents: CN or MN?

Children appear initially to interpret a word applied to an unfamiliar solid object as a CN, that is, as referring to a kind of object (a type of atomic individual). They appear also initially to interpret a word applied to a portion of an unfamiliar non-solid substance as a MN, that is, as referring to a kind of substance (a type of stuff). The stimuli in the studies reviewed up to this point were mostly solid objects (or drawings of objects) or portions of non-solid substances - stimuli that are highly likely to be construed, respectively, as atomic individuals or portions of stuff, *independent of word learning* (e.g., Shipley and Shepperson 1990). However, many common referents can be construed *either* as atomic individuals (solid objects) *or* as a portion of stuff (non-solid substance). Certain foodstuffs such as rice, beans and peas are good examples. The nouns used to pick out these referents differ across languages in their status as count or mass. When a referent can be construed as composed *either* of atomic individuals *or* of a portion of stuff, children may have difficulty exploiting the assumptions that normally guide their locating and fixing the reference of MNs and CNs. In such cases, children may need to appeal to *previously acquired* knowledge of the referential distinction between CNs and MNs in order to discover how their particular language treats the ambiguous referent. As a result, initially (i.e., before they have mastered the referential distinction between CNs and MNs) children may err in their interpretation of words applied to such ambiguous referents. The evidence I now review suggests that children as young as three years of age can use their understanding of the grammatical distinction between CNs and MNs to constrain their interpretation of words applied to ambiguous referents.

For example, Gordon (1985; experiment 2) showed four-year-olds an ambiguous referent (i.e., beans). Children heard either a CN for one bean (e.g., "This is a garn") or a MN for more than one bean (e.g., "This is some garn"). Children then took part in an elicitation task, in which the experimenter pointed to other beans (CN condition) or other portions of beans (MN condition) and said, "Over there, we have more what?" If the word was introduced syntactically as a CN, children revealed a CN interpretation (i.e., they tended to pluralize it); if the word was introduced syntactically as a MN, children revealed a MN interpretation (i.e., they tended not to pluralize it).

More recently, Bloom (1992a) showed that three-year-old children will construe a word applied to an ambiguous referent largely in accordance with the word's syntactic frame (as a CN or a MN). Unlike Gordon (1985), Bloom used a comprehension task. Bloom presented children with both an unfamiliar ambiguous material referent (e.g., a plate of lentils) and an aural referent (e.g., a string of bells). First, children heard either a CN or a MN applied to the plate of lentils (e.g., "These are gavs" or "This is gav"). Children then were asked "Please give me a gav" or "Please give me gav." Second, children heard either a CN or a MN applied to the string of bells at approximately two-second intervals (e.g., "These are moops" or "This is moop"). Children then received a stick to hit a bell and were asked, "Please make a moop" or "Please make moop." Children showed that they could draw on an understanding of the meaning of the words' syntactic frames to disambiguate these ambiguous referents. Those who heard a CN were likely to give an individual bean and to make a single sound. Children who heard a MN were likely to give more than one bean and to make more than one sound. It is important to note that findings like Bloom's motivate the claim that the assumptions guiding word learning should be framed as involving notions like *atomic individual* and *portion of stuff*, rather than *solid object* or *portion of non-solid substance*, because sounds are neither solid objects nor portions of non-solid substance, but they can be understood as either atomic individuals (e.g., a noise) or as portions of stuff (e.g., some noise).

Gordon's and Bloom's findings indicate that when the referent of a word is perceptually ambiguous, and can be construed either as an atomic individual or as a portion of stuff, children as young as three years of age can use knowledge of the referential correlates of CNs and MNs to disambiguate their construal of the referent.

Constraints on CNs and MNs

The evidence reviewed up to this point suggests that children initially make the following assumptions when interpreting new words. (1) A word applied to (what is taken as) an unfamiliar atomic individual is a CN and refers to a kind of atomic individual; and (2) a word applied to (what is taken as) a portion of an unfamiliar stuff is a MN and refers to a kind of stuff. But *which* CNs and MNs? *Which* kinds of individual or stuff? Recall the arguments that children's success at learning words' *precise* reference following simple ostensive definitions involving unfamiliar referents suggests that there must be a *unique* kind into which such words are interpreted. A word applied to an unfamiliar referent must be taken as referring to a kind of a *unique* atomic individual or a portion of a kind of a *unique* stuff. Using a term introduced by Rosch et al. (1976), I call this unique atomic individual the *basic-level* individual, and I will extend the notion by referring also to the unique stuff as the *basic-level* stuff. This section deals with the properties of these basic-level individuals or stuffs.

Basic-level CNs

First, consider the interpretation of a CN applied to an unfamiliar object (an atomic individual). The individuals in basic-level object kinds appear to have the following properties.

(a) Intermediate Level of Shape Similarity. A first property of basic-level individuals is that they share a common intermediate level of shape similarity. The individuals in only some kinds share this level of similarity; for example, dogs do, but poodles or animals do not. There is as yet no independent definition of the degree of shape similarity associated with basic-level individuals, but it appears to be the minimum that still allows the individuals in the kind to be identified on the basis of a common shape (e.g., DOG in the hierarchy POODLE, DOG, ANIMAL). Fodor (1983), Gleitman (1990), and Macnamara (1986) all discuss the issue of explaining this property of individuals in the basic-level object kind.

Despite there being as yet no precise definition of 'same shape' associated with basic-level individuals, there is evidence that children expect that a CN applied ostensively to a set of unfamiliar objects will refer to a kind whose members share a common general shape. Horton and Markman (1980) taught four- to seven-year-old children a novel CN (e.g., "This is a danker") for each of five drawings of objects from an unfamiliar kind. They then asked children to identify kind members in a set of drawings that included old and new individuals in the kind along with non-kind member distractors. The children were more successful at this task if 'danker' referred to a kind such as SALAMANDER (in which the members share a common general shape) than if it referred to a kind such as UNGULATE (in which the members, animals like giraffes and cows, do not share a common general shape). The results suggest that children expect a CN applied to unfamiliar objects will apply to individuals sharing a common general shape and not to individuals that do not share such a common shape (see also Mervis and Crisafi 1982; Markman, Horton and McClanahan 1980).

However, it is important to note that the degree of perceptual similarity associated with basic-level individuals is only intermediate, not the highest degree of similarity imaginable. For example, Taylor and Gelman (1988; see also Taylor and Gelman 1989; Hall and Waxman forthcoming) showed that if a novel CN was applied to an unfamiliar object, then two-year-old children would extend the word to *all* individuals in the basic-level kind, even when these individuals came from two perceptually-distinct subordinate-level kinds (cf. poodles and chihuahuas among dogs). If the CN was applied to a familiar object, two-year-olds showed evidence of interpreting the word as picking out only subordinate-level individuals. In other words, although individuals such as poodles share a greater degree of perceptual similarity than dogs, if dogs are unfamiliar to children, then children interpret a novel CN applied to a poodle as if it meant DOG, not POODLE. These results provide evidence that the degree of perceptual overlap associated with basic-level individuals is in some (admittedly unclear) sense intermediate, not so high as to cover only individuals sharing subordinate-level kind membership with the labelled object.

(b) *Whole Objects*. Consider now a second property of basic-level individuals. They tend to be discrete, *whole* objects, rather than parts of objects. Thus, a dog is a basic-level individual, but a paw or a tail is not.

Recent experimental findings suggest a strong inclination to take a CN applied to an unfamiliar object as referring to a kind for the object as a whole. In Markman and Wachtel (1988; experiment 2), children saw a drawing of either an unfamiliar object (a lung) with a salient part (a trachea), or a familiar object (a hammer) with a salient part (a claw). Children then were taught the CN for the part (e.g., "This is a trachea" or "This is a claw"); in other words, the word was applied directly to the part. Children were then shown two drawings, one of the object with the part encircled and another of the object with the whole object encircled. Children were asked to choose "another trachea" or "another claw." If the object was familiar, children tended to pick the drawing with the indicated part encircled; for example, they appeared to interpret 'claw' as referring to the claw on the hammer. However, if the object was unfamiliar, children tended to pick the drawing with the whole object encircled; for example, they were more likely to interpret 'trachea' as referring to the whole lung. Shipley and Spelke (1988) and Mervis and Long (1987; cited in Mervis 1987) have also demonstrated this phenomenon.

(c) *Extensive Range of Existence*. A third property of basic-level individuals derives from the fact that all CNs provide a principle of identity - that is, CNs enable the tracing of identity of individuals in the kind across situations (e.g., times and places). Like all CNs, basic-level CNs trace individuals' identity across a certain set of situations. For example, 'person' traces the identity of individual persons across the range of personhood, and 'dog' traces the identity of individual dogs across the range of doghood. Notice that the range of situations associated with individuals traced under a basic-level CN (e.g., 'person', 'dog') is greater than the range associated with individuals traced under many English situation-restricted CNs (e.g., 'passenger', 'puppy'), although basic-level and situation-restricted individuals may coincide in certain situations (such as when a person is riding in a vehicle, or when a dog is young). Thus a third property of basic-level individuals is that their identity is traced across an extensive range of existence, rather than in restricted situations.

Recent evidence suggests that preschoolers also assume that the identity of individuals in the basic-level kind is traced across an extensive range of situations. In one experiment, Hall and Waxman (forthcoming; see also Hall 1992a) taught three-year-old children a CN (e.g., "This is a murvil") for either an unfamiliar (a creature) or a familiar (a duck) object depicted in a specific context, for example, riding in the back of a car. This is a context for which adults know a situation-restricted CN, namely, 'passenger', but children of this age do not know this word (Hall forthcoming). Children were asked to select other toys to which they believed the CN also applied. They made their selections from among a set of toys sharing an intermediate level of shape similarity, depicted both inside and outside the context of the target object (i.e., some were riding in the back of cars, some were not). Regardless of object familiarity, children tended to ignore contextual restrictions in making their choices. In other words, they interpreted the word as picking out individuals like persons, not passengers.

There was an even more striking finding. Another group of children also learned a CN for either an unfamiliar or a familiar object in the same context (riding in the back of a car), but they were given explicit information that called for a situation-restricted interpretation of the CN. They thus heard, "This is a murvil because it is riding in a car." Now, children who learned the CN for the familiar object tended to restrict their selections to objects within the same context as the target. However, children who learned the CN for an unfamiliar object were less likely to do so; they were more likely to ignore contextual restrictions in making their choices. The finding that children overlooked the information if the referent was *unfamiliar* is further evidence that the identity of basic-level individuals is traced across a range of situations, and that this range is more extensive than that associated with certain situation-restricted individuals.

In summary, there is evidence that the individuals in basic-level object kinds have three properties: they share a common intermediate level of shape similarity; they are whole objects and not proper parts of objects; and their identity is traced across an extensive range of situations and not tied to specific, highly restricted situations.

Basic-level MNs

The same logic that motivated the need to posit a basic-level CN (kind of atomic individual) motivates the need to posit a basic-level MN (kind of stuff). For example, how are learners to know, upon seeing a portion of water for the first time, and hearing a word applied to it, that the word should mean WATER and not, for example, LIQUID? How do they know that a word applied to a pile of salt should mean SALT and not POWDER? As with atomic individuals picked out by a CN applied to an unfamiliar referent, there must also be certain constraints on the properties of the portions of stuffs picked out by a MN applied to an unfamiliar referent. To my knowledge, a systematic study of these properties has not yet been undertaken. But like solid objects, portions of non-solid substances have many perceptible properties (e.g., texture, malleability, colour, though no fixed shape). Thus, it seems reasonable to guess that some of these properties may figure more prominently than others in children's interpretation of a novel MN applied to an unfamiliar non-solid substance. If this is the case, then these properties would characterize the basic-level kind of substance (stuff of a certain sort).

Input to learning CNs and MNs

Before leaving the question of the learning of common nouns, I want to draw attention briefly to an important body of evidence that seeks to establish that the input caretakers provide when teaching new words is consistent with the assumptions that children seem to adhere to in interpreting new words. After all, if the words caretakers tended to provide in ostensive definitions involving unfamiliar objects and non-solid substances were *not* consistent with children's assumptions, then word learning would be much more error-ridden. In addition to leading children to fix the correct reference, the words children hear in ostensive definitions must enable them to learn the syntactic properties associated with all words from the relevant grammatical categories.

The results from this body of evidence reveal a remarkable correspondence between caretakers' word-teaching strategies and children's word-learning assumptions. For example, when caretakers label objects for children using ostensive definitions, they tend strongly to offer CNs. For example, Ninio (1980) found that the vast majority of caretakers' ostensive definitions involving objects included CNs (see also Shipley, Kuhn and Madden 1983; Callanan 1985; Hall forthcoming). Moreover, caretakers also appear to respect the more precise constraints on interpretation, favouring basic-level CNs in ostensive definitions involving objects. For example, they prefer basic-level CNs to CNs at a higher level of abstraction (Ninio 1980; Callanan 1985; Shipley, Kuhn and Madden 1983), to CNs applying only to parts of objects (Shipley, Kuhn and Madden 1983; Ninio 1980), and to CNs that trace identity only in highly restricted situations (Hall forthcoming).

Less is known about parents' use of ostension in teaching words for portions of non-solid substances (or other stuffs). One might predict that caretakers would provide MNs, and, more specifically, basic-level MNs (e.g., "water" for a portion of water, rather than "liquid"), but more data on this question are needed.

Proper Names

In addition to learning common nouns - CNs and MNs, words that refer to kinds - children also learn proper names (PNs), words that refer rigidly to individuals that are not kinds. I now will review evidence in support of the hypothesis that children assume that a word refers to a unique individual (is a PN) if they hear the word used under certain conditions, as suggested by the definition of PN provided earlier.

What are these conditions? First, the word should be applied to (what has been taken by children to be) an atomic individual. Second, the word should be applied to an individual in a familiar kind (i.e., one for which the basic-level CN is already known). Finally, the word should be applied to a single basic-level individual, not to a multiplicity of such individuals. I break down the review of the research on the learning of PNs to address these three conditions.

Application to an Individual

Children as young as two years old understand that a word applied to an individual *may* be interpreted as a PN, referring to a unique individual. The striking finding is that children of this age expect that the individuals in only *certain* kinds merit PNs. For example, Katz et al. (1974) showed that girls who heard a PN (e.g., "This is Zav") applied to a surrogate of an animate object (a doll) interpreted the word as picking out only that doll. Girls who heard a PN applied to an artifact (a wooden block) interpreted the word as applying to either of two blocks, clearly avoiding a unique individual interpretation. These results were replicated by Gelman and Taylor (1984), who showed that if the individual was an unfamiliar animal, children tended to interpret a PN for it as referring only to that animal. If the individual was an unfamiliar block-like toy, children interpreted the PN either as picking out both the target and another block-like toy, or else (bizarrely) as picking out an unfamiliar stuffed animal also present in the array of toys (completely ignoring the fact that the word had originally been applied to a block-like toy). Gelman and Taylor's study thus provided further evidence that two-year-olds clearly differentiated between dolls or animals and blocks or block-like toys as plausible candidates for receiving a proper name.

Recently Hall (1992b) has extended these findings in two ways in a series of experiments with three- and four-year-olds. First, he examined a wider range of object kinds in an attempt to pinpoint the criterion preschoolers use to decide whether an individual merits a PN. In a first experiment, he found that children interpreted a word modelled as a PN (e.g., "This is Zavy") as picking out a unique individual if the individual was a member of a familiar kind of pet (a dog, a cat, a bird or a rabbit), but *not* if it was a member of a familiar simple artifact kind (a shoe, a balloon, a hat, a cup). In two subsequent studies, he found that other children showed a tendency *not* to interpret the same PN applied to a familiar vehicle (a car, a plane, a boat, a train) as referring to a unique individual. He also found that children *did* show a tendency to interpret a PN applied to a familiar insect (a spider, a caterpillar, a snail, a bee) as referring to a unique individual, but *only* if the insect was introduced as being possessed by (i.e., as the pet of) the experimenter. Together, these findings point out the role of (1) the specific kind of object and (2) the social importance of the particular individual (i.e., its being a pet) in three- and four-year-olds' tendency to interpret a word as referring to a unique individual (i.e., as a PN).

A second way in which Hall (1992b) extended previous findings was by showing that, when children failed to interpret a word as a PN for an individual, they were able to construe the word as having a sensible alternative reference, namely, a salient property. Hall reasoned that the sentence frame used to teach PNs (i.e., "This is Zavy") is also consistent with an adjective or a MN interpretation (e.g., "This is red" or "This is lead" rather than "This is Fred"); and so he designed test arrays that permitted children to interpret the word as referring either to a unique individual or to an unfamiliar salient property of the individual (e.g., to the fluorescent multi-coloured cross-hatches on some of the individuals, including the named individual). The results revealed that when this (and a few other) changes were made to the test stimuli and procedure of Gelman and Taylor (1984), children who failed to make a PN interpretation showed a clear tendency to interpret the word as an adjective, referring to the salient property.

Application to a Familiar Individual

Young children also seem to be more likely to interpret a word modelled as a PN for an individual as referring to a unique individual if a basic-level CN is already known, than if it is not known. That is, once children have a suitable means to specify the individual and trace its identity (i.e., they have knowledge of a basic-level CN), they show a greater likelihood of interpreting a novel word modelled as a PN as referring to a unique individual.

Previous work had suggested that two-year-olds were willing to ascribe a PN to a stuffed animate object, regardless of its familiarity (Katz et al. 1974; Gelman and Taylor 1984). However, Hall (1991) compared unfamiliar and familiar toy animals within a single study. In one experiment, he taught two-year-old children a PN (e.g., "This is Zav") for either an unfamiliar (a creature) or a familiar (a cat) target stuffed animal. Three other stuffed toys then were brought out so that, in addition to the target animal, there were the following: another animal from the target kind, an unfamiliar distractor, and a familiar distractor. Children were asked to carry out a series of actions in response to commands that included the new PN (e.g., "Can you put Zav in the box?").

Children performed differently in the two conditions. Children who learned the PN for a familiar object restricted their selections to the named object to a greater extent than did children who learned the same PN for the unfamiliar object. Those children who learned the PN for an unfamiliar object frequently extended the word to the other member of the same animal kind, treating the word as if it were a CN. Furthermore, children's spontaneous comments during the task provided additional evidence that those in the unfamiliar, but not the familiar, condition tended to interpret the word as a CN. For example, children spontaneously pluralized the word or prefaced it with the indefinite article, assigning it syntactic privileges reserved for CNs. Children did not make such comments if the animal was familiar. This finding suggests that two-year-old children are indeed more likely to interpret a PN applied to an individual as referring to a unique individual (as a PN) if a basic-level CN is already known than if it is not known.

In a second experiment, Hall (1991) used the same procedure as in the first experiment, but the target object in both unfamiliar (a new monster) and familiar (a dog) conditions was introduced with a CN that was *not* a basic-level CN; all children were told that the animal was "a pet." Hall reasoned as follows. If knowing *any* CN for an individual (e.g., 'pet') helps children to learn a PN for that individual, then mention of this CN should lead children in the unfamiliar condition to interpret the word as a PN, referring to a unique individual. However, the results of experiment 2 were very similar to those of experiment 1, suggesting that the CN that children need to know to enable them to learn a PN for an object is specifically a basic-level CN (such as 'dog' or 'cat').

Application to a Unique Individual

Finally, there is preliminary evidence (Hall in preparation) that children are more likely to interpret a word as a PN (as referring to a unique individual) if it is used to pick out one individual than if it is applied to two. This finding may seem more obvious than it is. In the real world, many people may share the *same* PN (e.g., imagine the huge number of people who share a given proper name, such as John Smith). Furthermore, young children *accept* that the same PN can apply to more than one individual (Macnamara 1982). However, acceptance of the fact that a PN can refer to many individuals does not imply that, in a particular usage, it refers to many individuals. Although they may hold no prohibition against using a PN for more than one individual, young children may find the multiplication of bearers a semantically-marked event; given a salient alternative (e.g., the object has a salient property), children may opt out of a PN interpretation and make, for example, an adjective interpretation (as in Hall 1992b).

Using stimuli and a procedure similar to Hall (1992b), Hall (in preparation) is examining whether children are more likely to make a PN interpretation of a word modelled as a PN (e.g., "This is Zavy") if the word is applied to one rather than two individuals. Preliminary results suggest that four-year-olds make a PN interpretation if one object receives the PN; they tend to select only the named object. However, if two objects receive the label, children are more likely to seek an alternative interpretation, such as a salient property; for example, they often extend the word to the two named objects and also to an object sharing a salient property with the targets (e.g., multi-coloured fluorescent cross-hatches), seeming to *avoid* a PN interpretation.

Hall (in preparation) also plans to run control conditions. In these conditions, children will hear an unambiguous PN or an unambiguous adjective for either one or two objects; in other words, the sentence frames will suggest unambiguously a PN or an adjective interpretation. The prediction is that, given unambiguous syntactic cues, children should be happy to make either a PN or an adjective interpretation, regardless of whether the word is used to label either one or two objects. The control conditions thus will attempt to show that, among other things, children have no *general* prohibition against accepting a PN as applying to two individuals, simply that they find this a semantically marked event.

In summary, experimental data concerning young children's interpretations of words modelled as PNs provides (in places, preliminary) support for the hypothesis that children assume that PNs are words that are applied to unique individuals in (certain) kinds for which the basic-level CN is known. The specific reference of a PN is simply a particular basic-level individual.

Summary

This chapter has been about the learning of common nouns and proper names. Its starting point was the puzzle posed by children's success at learning words from simple ostensive definitions, which do not specify words' reference. Semantic definitions of the categories CN, MN, and PN provided by Macnamara and Reyes (this volume; see also Bloom 1992b; McPherson 1991; Soja et al. 1991) motivated hypotheses about how, following simple ostensive definitions, children fix words' specific reference and how they learn words' formal syntactic privileges. One hypothesis was that children look out for words applied to (what they take to be) unfamiliar atomic individuals with identity or (what they take to be) unfamiliar portions of stuff with identity; children interpret these words as referring to a unique kind of atomic individual or a unique kind of stuff having certain special properties - that is, as basic-level CNs or basic-level MNs, respectively. The important role caretakers appear to play in providing basic-level CNs (and, by hypothesis, basic-level MNs) in ostensive definitions also was noted. The last claim was that children look out for words applied to unique individuals in certain familiar kinds (i.e., for which the basic-level CN is known); these they interpret as referring to the unique individual, that is, as PNs. A review of experimental data from children learning words between about 18 months and six years of age provided evidence consistent with these hypotheses, suggesting that early word learning may indeed be guided by children's implicit knowledge of semantic definitions of the grammatical categories, CN, MN, and PN.

References

Baldwin, D. (1989). Priorities in children's expectations about object label reference: Form over color. *Child Development* 60: 1291-1306

— (1991). Infants' contribution to the achievement of joint reference. *Child Development* 62: 875-90

Bloom, P. (1992a). Semantic Competence and the Bootstrapping Problem. Unpublished manuscript, University of Arizona, Tucson, AZ

— (1992b). A Theory of Constraints on Word Meaning. Unpublished manuscript, University of Arizona, Tucson, AZ

Brown, R. (1957). Linguistic determinism and the part of speech. *Journal of Abnormal and Social Psychology* 55: 1-5

Callanan, M. (1985). How parents label objects for young children: The role of input in the acquisition of category hierarchies. *Child Development* 56: 508-23

Carey, S. (1978). The child as word learner. In M. Halle, J. Bresnan, and G. Miller (eds.), *Linguistic Theory and Psychological Reality*, pp. 264-93. Cambridge, MA: MIT Press

Clark, E. (1983). Meanings and concepts. In J. Flavell and E. Markman (eds.), *Handbook of Child Psychology*, Vol. 3, *Cognitive Development*, pp. 787-840. New York: Wiley

— (1987). The principle of contrast: a constraint on language acquisition. In B. MacWhinney (ed.), *Mechanisms of Language Acquisition*, pp. 1-33. Hillsdale, NJ: Erlbaum

Dickinson, D. (1988). Learning names for materials: Factors constraining and limiting hypotheses about word meaning. *Cognitive Development* 3: 15-35

Dromi, E. (1987). *Early Lexical Development*. Cambridge: Cambridge University Press

Fodor, J. (1983). *The Modularity of Mind*. Cambridge, MA: MIT Press

Gelman, S., and M. Taylor (1984). How 2-year-old children interpret proper and count names for unfamiliar objects. *Child Development* 55: 1535-40

Gleitman, L. (1990). The structural sources of verb meaning. *Language Acquisition* 1: 3-55

—, and E. Wanner (1982). Language acquisition: The state of the state of the art. In E. Wanner and L. Gleitman (eds.), *Language Acquisition: The State of the Art*. Cambridge: Cambridge University Press

Gordon, P. (1985). Evaluating the semantic categories hypothesis: The case of the count-mass distinction. *Cognition* 20: 209-42

Grimshaw, J. (1981). Form, function, and the language acquisition device. In C. L. Baker and J. McCarthy (eds.), *The Logical Problem of Language Acquisition*, pp. 183-210. Cambridge, MA: MIT Press

Gupta, A. (1980). *The Logic of Count Nouns*. New Haven, CT: Yale Press

Hall, D.G. (1991). Acquiring proper names for familiar and unfamiliar animate objects: Two-year-olds' word-learning biases. *Child Development* 62: 1142-54

— (1992a). Persons and Passengers: Individuals and Basic-level Kinds. Unpublished manuscript, Medical Research Council, Cognitive Development Unit, London.

— (1992b). Learning Proper Names: The Role of the Kind of the Referent. Unpublished manuscript, Medical Research Council, Cognitive Development Unit, London.

—, and S. R. Waxman (forthcoming 1). Assumptions about word meaning: Individuation and basic-level count nouns. *Child Development*

—, S. R. Waxman and W. Hurwitz (forthcoming 2). How 2- and 4-year-old children learn count nouns and adjectives. *Child Development*

— (in preparation 1). How caretakers teach basic-level and situation-restricted count nouns.

— (in preparation 2). Learning Proper Names: The Role of the Number of Referents. Medical Research Council, Cognitive Development Unit, London

Horton, M., and E. Markman (1980). Developmental differences in the acquisition of basic and superordinate categories. *Child Development* 51: 708-19

Jones, S., L. Smith and B. Landau (1991). Object properties and knowledge in early lexical learning. *Child Development* 62: 499-516

Katz, N., E. Baker and J. Macnamara (1974). What's in a name? A study of how children learn common and proper nouns. *Child Development* 45: 469-73

Landau, B., L. Smith and S. Jones (1988). The importance of shape in early lexical learning. *Cognitive Development* 3: 299-321

— and D. Stecker (1990). Objects and places: Geometric and syntactic representation in early lexical learning. *Cognitive Development* 5: 287-312

La Palme Reyes, M., Macnamara, J., and Reyes, G. (1993). Reference, kinds and predicates. This volume

Macnamara, J. (1982). *Names for Things.* Cambridge, MA: MIT Press

— (1986). *A Border Dispute.* Cambridge, MA: MIT Press

— and G. Reyes (1992). Foundational issues in the learning of proper names, count nouns and mass nouns. This volume

McPherson, L. (1991). A little goes a long way: Evidence for a perceptual basis of learning the noun categories COUNT and MASS. *Journal of Child Language* 18: 315-38

Markman, E., and J. Hutchinson (1984). Children's sensitivity to constraints on word meaning: Taxonomic vs. thematic relations. *Cognitive Psychology* 16: 1- 27

—, and G. Wachtel (1988). Children's use of mutual exclusivity to constrain the meanings of words. Cognitive Psychology 20: 121-57

—, M. Horton and A. McClanahan (1980). Classes and collections: Principles of organization in the learning of hierarchical relations. *Cognition* 8: 227-41

Mervis, C. (1987). Child-basic object categories and early lexical development. In U. Neisser (Ed.), *Concepts and Conceptual Development: Ecological and Iintellectual Factors in Categorization* (pp. 201-33). Cambridge: Cambridge University Press

—, and M. Crisafi (1982). Order of acquisition of subordinate, basic, and superordinate level categories. *Child Development* 53: 258-66

Ninio, A. (1980). Ostensive definition in vocabulary acquisition. *Journal of Child Language* 7: 565-73

Pinker, S. (1984). *Language Learnability and Language Development*. Cambridge, MA: MIT Press

Prasada, S. (forthcoming). Young children's linguistic and non-linguistic knowledge of solid substances. *Cognitive Development*

Rosch, E., C. Mervis, W. Gray, D. Johnson and P. Boyes-Braem (1976). Basic objects in natural categories. *Cognitive Psychology* 3: 382-439

Shipley, E., I. Kuhn and E. Madden (1983). Mothers' use of superordinate category terms. *Journal of Child Language* 10: 571-88

—, and B. Shepperson (1990). Countable entities: Developmental changes. *Cognition* 34: 109-36

—, and E. Spelke (1988). Ostensive Definitions. Unpublished manuscript, University of Pennsylvania, Philadelphia, PA

Smith, L., S. Jones and B. Landau (1992). Count nouns, adjectives, and perceptual properties in children's novel word interpretations. *Developmental Psychology* 28: 273-86

Soja, N. (1992). Inferences about the meanings of nouns: The relationship between perception and syntax. *Cognitive Development* 7: 29-45

—, S. Carey and E. Spelke (1991). Ontological categories guide young children's inductions about word meaning: Object terms and substance terms. *Cognition* 38: 179-211

Taylor, M., and S. Gelman (1988). Adjectives and nouns: Children's strategies for learning new words. *Child Development* 59: 411-19

— (1989). Incorporating new words into the lexicon: Preliminary evidence for language hierarchies in 2-year-old children. *Child Development* 60: 625-36

Waxman, S. (1990). Linguistic biases and the establishment of conceptual hierarchies. *Cognitive Development* 5: 123-50

— and R. Gelman (1986). Preschoolers' use of superordinate relations in classification and language. *Cognitive Development* 1: 139-56

— and D. G. Hall (forthcoming). The development of a linkage between count nouns and object categories: Evidence from 15- and 21-month-old infants. *Child Development*.

— and T. Kosowski (1990). Nouns mark category relations: Toddlers' and preschoolers' word-learning biases. *Child Development* 61: 1461-73

10

Mental Logic and How to Discover It

Martin D. S. Braine

Before considering empirical ways of discovering what is in the mental logic, it seems a necessary preliminary, in order to avoid seeming to beg the question, that I discuss reasons why it is plausible to expect there to be a mental logic, and what sort of mental logic those reasons should lead one to expect. So I begin with these sorts of preliminaries, and they will, I hope, situate the concept of a mental logic in a theoretical framework within which it makes sense.

In the second section of the paper I briefly defend the notion that there must be a mental logic against two currents of today's cognitive psychological scene which have both been generally hostile to the idea of a mental logic – one a claim (that all reasoning is based on mental models), and the other a highly visible line of work (connectionism). Then, in the third section I turn to the main question in the paper. How could one determine empirically what the mental logic consists of and what does the available evidence have to say about it?

Preliminaries

I begin by making three points about mental logic.

(1) Why should a mental logic exist? Why should it have evolved? One answer is that it is needed to serve pragmatic goals. That is, I propose that the human species evolved a mental logic for purely practical purposes, to make inferences about things and events of immediate concern. Let me illustrate this interdigitation of logic and pragmatics in the service of practical goals.

Table 1 shows two little stories that are among some that my lab has considered using in experiments on practical reasoning in text comprehension. Consider the first test question on the first story – did John get a free beer? Evidently, the answer is "No," but why? Knowledge of restaurant menus tells you that the *or* in *free beer or coffee* should be taken to imply 'not both' – you get only one free, and if you want the other you have to pay for it. Later, the story says that John chose coffee. Given the premisses 'Not both free beer and free coffee' and 'Free coffee', 'Not

241

free beer' follows by logical inference. Thus the answer to the question is given by a pragmatic inference feeding a strictly logical one. Question (b) we can ignore, since that is included merely to force subjects to consider the "Can't tell" response option. To Question (c) the answer is evidently "No": presumably, based on pragmatic knowledge that food and beverage items are not free in restaurants unless explicitly offered as such by menu or waiter, the reader constructs a conditional 'If not minute steak then no free red wine'; since we are told that John chose soup and salad, which pragmatically entails that he did not choose minute steak, we conclude by logical inference *(modus ponens)* that he did not get a free glass of red wine. Again, the answer comes from an interdigitation of logical inference and pragmatic knowledge.

Table 1

Integrating Logic and Pragmatics: Sample Texts and Comprehension Questions

---

1. John went in for lunch. The menu showed a soup'n salad special, with free beer or coffee.Also, with the minute steak you got a free glass of red wine. John chose the soup'n salad special with coffee, along with something else to drink...

    (a) John got a free beer? (Yes, No, Can't tell)
    (b) John had chicken soup? (Yes, No, Can't tell)
    (c) John got a free glass of red wine? (Yes, No, Can't tell)

2. Alice had spent Saturday afternoon shopping and was feeling a bit peckish. She went into the Rali coffee shop for a coffee and a light snack. The counter was full. She sat down and ordered. Later, feeling rejuvenated, she...

    (a) Alice sat down at a table? (Yes, No, Can't tell)
    (b)Alice ordered tea? (Yes, No, Can't tell)
    (c) Alice ordered a Danish pastry? (Yes, No, Can't tell)

The second story provides another illustration of the same theme. In response to (a), Alice did sit down at a table; we know that because we know that coffee shops offer only two places to sit down – counter and tables; since the counter was full it is a logical inference that she sat down at a table ('Counter or table', 'not counter', ∴ 'table'). In response to (b), we can infer that she did not have tea, because we know that people essentially never order *both* tea and coffee ('Not both tea and coffee', 'coffee', ∴ 'not tea'). In both cases there is a smooth combination of logical and pragmatic inferences. (Question [c] we can ignore, since its only purpose is to alert subjects to the 'Can't tell' response option.)

I and colleagues have argued that one reason that mental logic evolved was to serve the practical goal of integrating information coming in at different times, or from different sources, drawing inferences that go beyond the information as given (Braine 1990; Braine and O'Brien 1991). For instance, one learns *P or Q* from one source and *not Q* from another; an intelligent being needs some mental mechanism that will integrate these pieces of information by inferring *P*; the mental logic satisfies the need. The mental logic is also involved in the comprehension of discourse and text. Some recent work (Lea, O'Brien, Fisch, Noveck and Braine 1990) suggests that it provides a set of inferences that are routinely made to integrate information from different propositions of a text. The routine role of the mental logic in comprehension has been independently argued by Sperber and Wilson (1986), who propose a psychological and pragmatic framework within which it operates in comprehension. Because it serves practical goals, the mental logic is deeply embedded within a pragmatically motivated architecture, and inferences are regularly drawn from information that includes knowledge retrieved from long-term memory, beliefs, opinions, guesses and various kinds of implicatures. Logical inferences reside comfortably in a line of reasoning with analogical, causal, pragmatic and probabilistic ones (Braine and O'Brien 1991).

(2) The second point to be made about a mental logic is that among people who have considered the idea of it (e.g., Braine 1978, 1990; Braine and O'Brien 1991; Braine, Reiser, and Rumain 1984; Johnson-Laird 1975; O'Brien 1981; Osherson 1975; Rips 1983; Sperber and Wilson 1986), there is a consensus that the mental logic must consist of a set of inference schemas together with some sort of basic program for applying them, i.e., some sort of natural deduction system. My thinking is that the basic program would operate routinely in practical reasoning and discourse comprehension, and be the first stage of processing in reasoning of a more formal sort.

(3) The concept of a mental logic is intimately connected to the concept of a language of thought. There are two reasons for this. First, to represent inference schemas, some system of representation is needed: The reasoner translates from natural-language statements into this representational system, and then reasons in this 'language of thought'. (We cannot assume that the reasoner reasons in the natural language because there are far too many ways of expressing the same proposition in a natural language – for the same inference we would need as many different inference schemas as there are ways of expressing the component propositions in the native language.) The second and ultimately more important reason is that some sort of innate format for

representing knowledge would seem to be a precondition for memory, at least for declarative memory: for a child to be able to record knowledge about the world in memory, there must be some format available for representing that knowledge – if there is no format for recording something, there is no way to record it. Now, to be adequate to the task of recording information in memory, the format would need some logical structure. For example, it would need some kind of predicate-argument structure in order to distinguish properties from the entities remembered to have the properties, and relations from the objects noticed to be related. Presumably, too, it would have to be able to represent conjunction, negation and disjunction, because memory will sometimes need to record that two properties are present, or that an expected property is absent, or that two things are alternatives. One can think of other logical structures that would be needed also, e.g., quantifying and referring devices. These arguments are some of those that Fodor (1975) presented for an innate language of thought, and are similar to some of Macnamara's (1986). Since the format is innate, the essential parts of the representational system for inferences would be universal, and so there is every reason to expect that an inference form that is easy in one language will be available and easy in another language. The inevitability of the existence of an innate information format with some logical structure provides an important additional reason, over and above the one given earlier, for expecting there to be a mental logic. Because of the fundamental nature of this mental logic, I have elsewhere referred to it as 'natural' logic (Braine 1990; Braine et al. 1984).[1]

In speaking of a 'language of thought', I do not intend commitment to all Fodor's ideas on the subject – in particular, not to his claim that the content predicates of the language of thought are innate. For an answer to Fodor's arguments for the innateness of most content predicates, and for a promising solution to the difficulties of a compositional approach to lexical meaning, see Jackendoff (1989, 1990). Actually, Fodor has very little to say about the syntax of the language of thought, although it is its syntax that defines it as a system of representation, and in which its logical properties are embodied. For my purposes, we can usefully distinguish 'syntax of thought' from 'language of thought'.

Indeed, one can contrast two 'language of thought' concepts. One is Fodor's, in which essentially everything is innate. In the other, the language of thought would be partially innate and partially acquired. The syntax would be innate; this is the innate format for representing knowledge referred to above, and the mental logic would be implicit in it; we may refer to this as the 'syntax of thought'. The content predicates would be the acquired part. Thus, the partially acquired language of thought would comprise the innate syntax with the acquired content predicates. This language of thought would be language-specific in part, and would correspond to the level of semantic representation in studies of semantic structure like those of Jackendoff (1983, 1990). One additional complexity has to be noted, however: content predicates can have complex internal structure; and the possible formats for constructing complex predicates would be universal and innate, and are best regarded as part of the syntax of thought. (An example of complex-predicate syntax is given later.) The 'language of thought' concept presumed in this paper is not Fodor's, but this second one, in which the language of thought is partially acquired.

Defence

I now defend the notion of a mental logic and language of thought against two viewpoints that have been generally hostile to it.

Mental Models

Johnson-Laird and his colleagues have repeatedly claimed that all reasoning is based on constructing and manipulating mental models in working memory, and that there is no need for a mental logic (e.g., Johnson-Laird 1983, 1986; Johnson-Laird and Byrne 1991; Johnson-Laird, Byrne and Tabossi 1990). This is not the place for a critique of the details of Johnson-Laird's theory, so I confine myself to a few general points of principle on the concept that *all* reasoning employs mental models. First, I should make clear that I have little doubt that much reasoning does use mental models; my quarrel is with the general claim and its corollary denial of a mental logic.[2]

Unfortunately, the mental models theory does not provide a definition of 'mental model'. Images are clearly included, but much else is included, too, although no enumeration is given. However, one important difference between mental models and propositions is specified: unlike propositions, models cannot contain variables, i.e., they are always concerned with specific instances. This fact immediately raises questions about whether mental models could account for *all* reasoning. Mathematical statements and mathematical reasoning seem to provide the most obvious counter-examples. Consider, for instance, a statement like 'If the sum of the digits of a number is a multiple of three, then the number is divisible by three'. How could one represent such a statement without a variable, something that represents 'any number'? Obviously, a representation that only exhibits some specific numbers would be inadequate. In addition, a proof of the statement would inevitably mention a variable ('any number'); how could one understand the proof and judge its validity if one cannot represent 'any number'? Admittedly, it is known that models often play a significant role in mathematical invention, as well as in understanding and constructing proofs, especially diagrams in geometry. However, not all proofs involve models, and even in geometry, there is much more to a proof than the diagram: principles, like the transitivity of equality, may be used, and there is invariably a generalization step, from the triangle, circle or other figure instantiated in the diagram, to any triangle, any circle, etc. – a step that involves a variable (i.e., 'any triangle', 'any circle', etc.).

A similar point applies even in a domain where the mental model theory has been worked out in some detail – Aristotelian syllogisms. The theory has gone through several versions (Johnson-Laird and Steedman 1978; Johnson-Laird and Bara 1984; Johnson-Laird and Byrne 1991). The core of the problem can be seen best in the penultimate version of the theory (Johnson-Laird and Bara 1984). Consider the following syllogism premisses, which are about the people in a certain crowded hall:

> All of the engineers are photographers.
> All of the photographers are cooks.

According to Johnson-Laird and Bara, subjects construct the following model ('e', 'p', and 'c' represent particular engineers, photographers and cooks, respectively, who are imagined to be present; parentheses enclose individuals who may or may not be present; '=' means 'is a'):

1.
$$
\begin{aligned}
e &= p = c \\
e &= p = c \\
(p) &= c \\
&\quad (c)
\end{aligned}
$$

This model suggests a tentative conclusion 'All of the engineers are cooks'. All versions of the theory say that after forming a tentative conclusion, subjects may try to falsify that conclusion by looking for other models consistent with the premisses in which the tentative conclusion does not hold. (Moreover, the better reasoners among the subjects are precisely the ones who try to falsify tentative conclusions.) However, most people shown this model – no doubt including readers of this article – know that there is no point in looking at other models (e.g., a model in which there are seven 'e's in the left-hand column), because they can see that other models consistent with the premisses are bound to yield the same conclusion as the one shown with two 'e's: no matter how many engineers, photographers, and cooks there are, the engineers are bound to be photographers by the first premiss, and cooks by the second premiss – however, *that* is a logical argument that goes beyond the model. Johnson-Laird and Bara's model does not account for this intuition, that is, it does not account for people's perception of the necessity of the conclusion without checking other models.

Perhaps mindful of this defect, in the most recent version of the theory, Johnson-Laird and Byrne (1991) propose a different sort of model for the form 'All A are B'. 'All of the engineers are photographers' would be represented by:

2.   [e]   p
                           [e]   p
                            ...

As before, each line represents an individual (e.g., each of the first two lines represents an engineer who is a photographer) and the ellipsis indicates that the model can have other lines that represent individuals in addition to those explicitly represented. The square brackets are an "exhaustivity tag," i.e., they indicate that any lines (individuals) substituted for the ellipsis must have '[~e]' in the left-hand column. Thus, if we wished, we could "flesh out" the model by adding a couple of individuals in place of the ellipsis:

                            [e]   p
                            [e]   p
                           [~e]   p
                           [~e]   ~p

'~p' is a proposition-like tag representing negation. The meaning of '[ ]' appears to be given by a tacit inference rule (which contains variables):

y is an unrepresented entry in a column that contains '[x]'

$$y = [\sim x]$$

There must also be the rule:

$$[\sim\sim x] \equiv [x]$$

Thus, there is obvious mental logic implicit in the new theory.

Having constructed model 2 with two engineers, let us consider whether we can know that it would be pointless to consider other models with a different number of engineers (e.g., seven). It seems that we again cannot know. First, the rules for '[ ]' simply forbid adding additional 'e's to the model. Since the number of 'e's chosen for the initial model is arbitrary, we are free to construct a new model with seven 'e's, and they will of course all turn out to be photographers and cooks. The theory, however, provides no way of knowing this prior to actually constructing the new model. So we have still not accounted for the perception of the necessity of the conclusion without checking other models. In sum, even within the mental-models theory, one would have to have the logic of *all* in order to know that one has looked at all the necessary models for these premisses.

Connectionism

From much recent literature, both that advocating and that criticizing connectionist models, it is easy to get the impression that connectionism and the notion of a syntax of thought are incompatible (e.g., Fodor and Pylyshyn 1988; Rumelhart and McClelland 1986; Smolensky 1988). However, it is far from clear that there is any inherent incompatibility between these notions. As against Fodor and Pylyshyn, it seems to me a serious tactical error for supporters of the notion of a language of thought to appear to favour classic serial models over parallel ones: it seems indisputable that massive parallelism is pretty characteristic of the brain; that being so, there is evidently a way of realizing a language of thought in a parallel mechanism. We should find out how it is done, and not put our money on serial mechanisms.

At the moment there are too many open questions and unresolved serious issues that prevent assessment of whether and how a language of thought and a mental logic might be implemented in a connectionist architecture. On the one hand, semantic networks are a classical way of realizing predicate-argument structure, and it appears that these can readily be implemented in a connectionist system; moreover, spreading activation seems to have a more natural implementation in a connectionist system than a serial one. On the other hand, such models (e.g., Shastri 1990) are localist; and while they provide a sketch of how a parallel system might realize a language of thought, there is the crucial problem that no algorithm is available for learning what the units represent in such localist systems. The available algorithms pertain to distributed representations, but there are formidable problems (Fodor and

Pylyshyn 1988; Fodor and McLaughlin 1990) in handling linguistic structure (e.g., constituent structure) with distributed representations, although it is an active area of current connectionist research (e.g., van Gelder, 1990). Moreover, the learning algorithms for distributed representations face the profound problem of catastrophic interference (McCloskey and Cohen 1989; Ratcliff 1990) – new learning is much more destructive of prior learning in connectionist nets than in people. It seems that the interference of new learning with old learning is catastrophic precisely because of the distributed nature of the representations: that is what makes the problem a profound one, and until there is a solution to it, the ultimate usefulness of this class of model for human learning is bound to be in serious question.

Discovering the Mental Logic and the Syntax/Language of Thought

To return to the main issue, the nature of the mental logic and the syntax of thought, I can see three empirical routes which could contribute information about them. The first route is through reasoning, and it focusses most directly on the basic inference forms of the mental logic. The second is through universals of language, and the third is through what is semantically and syntactically most primitive in language acquisition. Both of the latter two focus on the nature of the representational system more directly than on inference. I shall discuss each in turn (and all unfortunately, rather briefly).

The Approach through Reasoning

Traditionally, most work on logical reasoning has focussed on reasoning error, as if it were error rather than correct reasoning that required study and explanation. The notion of a mental logic involves a reversal of focus – towards identifying the forms of inference that people make easily and correctly. The approach through the study of reasoning has developed a general methodology, although the empirical work has focussed almost exclusively on the mental propositional logic. Methodologically, the concept of a mental logic prescribes that the basic inference schemas of the logic should have certain properties. Empirical work can then proceed to identify the inferences that have these properties. A natural logic based on inference schemas entails that there is a set of logically valid schemas, each of which has the following properties:

(1) Each schema is psychologically valid: subjects use it essentially

errorlessly on maximally simple problems that could be solved using it.

(2) Each schema is psychologically elementary: the inference it defines is made in a single step, not as the end product of a chain of inferences. (See Braine et al. 1984 for illustration of methods of obtaining evidence relevant to elementariness.)

(3) Each schema is psychologically primitive – available early to children.

(4) Each schema is universal: it has Properties (1) to (3) in all cultures and languages.

In addition, the set of schemas as a whole should have properties that warrant its being called a 'logic' (e.g., an interesting relation to some standard system). Finally, there should be a simple routine for applying the schemas that is an integral part of ordinary text and discourse comprehension, and the first step in reasoning.

Let us consider whether there is evidence for each of these properties. The evidence is most ample for propositional logic, which I consider first, though incomplete even for that. For propositional logic, there is a set of schemas for which Property 1 has been demonstrated and for which Property 2 is arguable on the basis of a mixture of experimental evidence and commonsensical argument (Braine et al. 1984). With respect to Property 3, there is a substantial amount of evidence, but with lacunae; and Property 4 has not been directly investigated. I return to Properties 3 and 4 shortly. Also, I think it will be clear to anyone who inspects it that the set of schemas as a whole (e.g., Braine 1990, Table 1) warrants being called a 'logic'. Finally, for evidence and argument that subjects have a simple routine for applying the schemas, used both in reasoning problems and in text comprehension, see Braine et al. (1984), Fisch (1991) and Lea et al. (1990).

I will say a little more about Properties 3 and 4. English *or* and *if*, and their translation equivalents in the approximately half-dozen other languages investigated, appear fairly early in development, typically during the third year; *and* and negation appear even earlier (e.g., Bates 1974; Bloom, Lahey, Hood, Lifter and Fiess 1980; Bowerman 1986; Kuczaj and Daly 1979; Lust and Mervis 1980; Pea 1980). When they appear, they are almost always used in a semantically appropriate way, suggesting that children have an early grasp of their meaning. What is the nature of the meaning grasped? There are two potential ways in which the meaning of a connective might be specified. One is by the inferences that it sanctions; the other is by truth-conditions. There are several reasons for thinking that the meaning is more likely to be given by inferences than by truth-conditions. First, there is little evidence for the use of truth conditions in studies of deductive reasoning (e.g., Osherson 1975; Braine and Rumain 1983), but plenty of evidence for inference schemas (e.g., Braine and Rumain 1983; Braine et al. 1984; Fisch 1991; Lea et al. 1990; Osherson 1974, 1975b, 1976; Rips 1983). Second, there is an intuitively clearer relation of connective meaning to inference. Thus, there are intuitively tight correspondences between the meanings of particular connectives and particular inference schemas; these are such that, if someone were not able to make the inferences, one would be inclined to say that they did not understand the connective. For instance, consider *if* and *modus ponens*.[3] If someone did not understand that the consequent of an *if-then* statement has to be true if the *if*-clause is fulfilled, one would judge that they did not understand *if*. *Or* is similarly related to certain inference schemas, the most obvious being the schema: *p or q; not-p* / ∴*q*. Here again, one would be much inclined to say that someone did not understand *or* if they did not understand that, when there are only two alternatives and one of them is found not to hold, then the other must hold. The relation of meaning to truth-conditions is more opaque. For *if,* people notoriously do not make truth judgments that conform to the standard truth table of the conditional; moreover, those judgments that they do make easily are just the ones that are easy to make by short chains of inference (Braine and O'Brien 1991).[4] In the case of *or,* children show competence at making standard inferences before they are able to make sensible truth judgments (Braine and Rumain 1981). Finally, there is direct evidence for spontaneous conditional inference in the conversations of preschool children (Scholnick and Wing 1991).

On Property 4, I know of no specific survey of languages, but the well-known languages of Europe and Asia appear to have connectives that are at least approximately equivalent to *and, or* and *if.* Negation can be presumed to be universal, even if only because work on universals (e.g., Comrie 1989) would have found room for comment if someone had found a language without it (which is hard to imagine). Comrie (1986) discusses the typology of conditionals across languages; he presumes that all languages have them but finds variation in the formal devices used to signal conditionality. As noted earlier, the connectives translating *or* and *if* appear early in the development of children in the languages investigated just as they do in English, and conjunction and negation also appear early. In sum, although much investigation remains to be done, the existence of similar early-developing connectives in unrelated languages, taken with the great frequency of such connectives across languages, is certainly consistent with the notion of a universal mental propositional logic, and may be hard to explain otherwise.

In addition to mental propositional logic, there must be other mental logics, e.g., predicate and modal logics. I have been working on a hypothesis for a tentative mental predicate logic. However, progress is more difficult here, because to state inference schemas for a predicate logic requires a complex representational system, whereas stating schemas for a propositional logic makes few demands on a representational system. For a propositional logic all one needs are connectives and variables for propositions, whereas a mental predicate logic requires one to make difficult assumptions about the internal structure of propositions in the syntax of the language of thought. I will not discuss hunches about the representational system here, but will point out that there is evidence that important aspects of the mental predicate logic are developmentally very primitive.

First, there are reasons for thinking that the concept 'all' is available early to children. For instance, it is one of the very few logical notions that Piaget (Inhelder and Piaget 1964) accepts as available pre-operationally; also, reasoning of the form 'All A are F, x is an A, so x is an F' can be elicited easily in five-year-olds (Harris 1975; Smith 1979); in addition, a variety of well-known errors apparently having to do with intersection or inclusion of classes have been shown to have to do with comprehension processes that involve guessing based on plausibility combined with poor mastery of relatively subtle aspects of English structure (e.g., Bucci 1978; O'Brien, Braine, Connell, Noveck, Fisch, and Fun 1989; see Braine and Rumain 1983, pp.300-302 for a review).

Second, grammatical devices that are the natural language analogs of existential instantiation are available quite early in children. I have in mind the use of pronouns and definite NPs that have indefinite NPs as their antecedents ('I saw a man yesterday. HE/THE MAN...'). Such pronouns and definite NPs are in effect discourse names for existentially instantiated objects, and they are present in the speech of most three-year-olds (e.g., Maratsos 1974).

In addition to defining a canonical set of primitive inferences, the approach through reasoning can provide an important constraint on hypotheses about the representational system: it must be able to represent inference schemas perspicuously, as well as the train of thought that people go through in solving the deductive problems that they are able to solve.

The Approach through Language Universals

By any theory, the syntax of the language of thought must constrain the syntax of natural languages, and would be expected often to be directly reflected in the syntax of natural languages. Working backwards, universals of syntax are excellent candidates for being properties of the syntax of the language of thought. In reading recent work on language universals (e.g., Comrie 1989) and on linguistic work oriented towards language-of-thought issues and semantic structure (e.g., Jackendoff 1983, 1987, 1990; Pinker 1989; Rappaport and Levin 1988), tentative conclusions about a number of features of the syntax of the language of thought came to mind. No originality for the observations is claimed, and the following list largely echoes Jackendoff; it is intended as purely suggestive, and is far from exhausting what work on language universals has to tell us about the syntax of the language of thought.

(1) There is a categorization of entities by ontological category, e.g., Material entities, Locations, Times, Actions, Events, Propositions. Moreover, there appear to be subcategories of these, e.g., Material entities divide into Objects (individuated) and Substances; Locations comprise Places, Paths, etc.

(2) The language of thought has a predicate-argument structure. In addition, there are functions that build reference to arguments compositionally – the functions map one ontological kind of argument into another, e.g., locative prepositions like *in* and *on* map object arguments (e.g., *the chest, the bed*) into place arguments (e.g., *in the chest, on the bed*, as in *Put the shirt in the chest/on the bed*). There are also functions that build predicates out of predicates, often adding or subtracting an argument, e.g., 'make + NP + VP' = MAKE–VP (NP), with NP as the non-Agent argument of the complex predicate MAKE-VP. Much the same functions appear over and over again in different languages, without actually being universal.

(3) Predicates easily tend to become arguments. For instance, in 'Somebody erased the master tape – Well, George didn't do it', *it* refers to the action of erasing the master tape; thus, this action is predicate of the first proposition, but argument in the second. Similarly, in 'George is in jail – the police put him there', *there* refers to a place (in jail) that is an argument of *put;* the place is predicate in the first proposition and argument in the second. It seems that there must be an abstraction operator that, given an action- or place-predicate, automatically conceives of an entity that is the action or place and that can serve as an argument referred to by a subsequent referring expression.

(4) There are some primitive relational predicates that repeatedly occur in the meanings of words (though they do not exhaust their meanings) and that are drawn upon to mark (i.e., distinguish) arguments.
Examples are CAUSE, ACT, GO, TO, and these seem to provide the
basis of 'thematic' categories (Jackendoff 1987) – for instance, the NP
argument of CAUSE is an Agent, and having an Agent subject is part of
the semantic representation of all causative verbs.

(5) Two identifiable and different devices – (a) relative clauses and (b)
embedded (genitive) arguments – are used to delineate arguments or
argument sets. Thus, (a) there is an analog of relative clauses ('The Xs
such that...'); (b) the predicates used to identify arguments may themselves have arguments (e.g., 'The mayor OF NEW YORK' as in *The may-
or of New York lives in Gracie Mansion)* – thus, 'mayor' is a predicate with
two arguments, a person and a city; because the person argument remains undefined if the city is unknown, when *mayor* is used to identify
an argument of some other predicate (e.g., the argument of the predicate 'lives in Gracie Mansion'), the city is embedded as part of the argument NP, its function signaled by the genitive marker *of.*

As I said above, the list is intended to be merely suggestive. However, I
believe that much progress could be made fairly quickly towards forming a well-developed hypothesis about the syntax of the language of
thought. I am impressed that the linguistic literature contains a great
deal of relevant work and theorizing that has been done with various
goals, but which could be harnessed to the task of formulating such a
hypothesis.

The Approach through Language Acquisition

Fodor (1975), following the computer metaphor, argues that in learning
their native language, children learn a compiler between the language of
thought and their language. As noted earlier, the notion of a 'language of thought' adopted here is not quite as nativist as Fodor's. However, a claim essentially similar to his is still appropriate – that children
learn a mapping between the syntax of the language of thought and the
grammar of their language. If this claim is correct, it would follow that
there is a third empirical route into the syntax of thought – by examining what is developmentally most primitive in grammar. In this
scheme, the child's syntactic primitives are the primitives of the syntax
of the language of thought. These would include the predicate/argu-
ment distinction, connectives and ontological categories, along, no
doubt, with many other notions, too. It is worth noting, incidentally,
that although ontological categories played no role in the earlier discus-

sion of reasoning, they are strongly implicated in analyses of semantic structure (e.g., Jackendoff 1990), as noted in the preceding section, and there is evidence for their primitiveness in recent work with young children (e.g., Keil 1989; McPherson, 1991; Soja, Carey, and Spelke 1991; Spelke 1990; however, most of the work has focussed on the object/substance distinction).

There is, of course, a very strong counter-claim to this neo-Fodorian conception in the literature: Chomsky has vigorously argued for innate natural-language syntactic primitives – primitives like NP, VP, N, V, A, P, Subject of, etc., of a universal natural language grammar. However, it is not possible to account for language acquisition with just Chomsky's primitives, because, as various people have noted, beginning with Fodor (1966), in order for such primitives to be useful to a child, the child must have a means of recognizing instances of them in the input. We are thus led to the 'bootstrapping' proposal (Grimshaw 1981; Pinker 1984), that the child has innate semantic flags for each of the innate Chomskyan categories: on their first encounter with language, children assign words for objects to the noun class, object arguments to NP, words for actions to Verb, agents to Subject, etc., and their initial rules are based on this assignment. In sum, the Chomskyan theory has to assume two kinds of primitives – the natural language syntactic categories and a parallel set of semantic categories that are quite similar to the neo-Fodorian syntax-of-thought categories.

From the perspective that I have been taking, the positing of these natural language syntactic primitives seems curiously gratuitous – why would nature have bothered to give us two such similar sets of primitives? Of course, in adult languages (and indeed quite early in development) the syntax-of-thought categories and the natural language syntactic categories do not match perfectly (e.g., nouns often do not represent concrete objects nor verbs actions), and the mismatch has to be explained. Nevertheless, the semantic (syntax-of-thought) categories could be the child's starting point for the natural-language syntactic categories, as Macnamara (1972) suggested. The mismatch need not mean that two independent sets of syntactic categories are present innately; it could emerge as a consequence of the mapping (learning) process. Parsimony demands that this possibility be thoroughly investigated before it is assumed that an innate set of natural-language syntactic categories exist in addition to the categories of the syntax of thought. What is at issue, therefore, is whether a learning theory can be constructed that accounts for the emergence of the natural-language syntactic categories, given just the syntax-of-thought categories as primitives.

I have shown elsewhere (Braine, 1992) that such a learning theory can be obtained by a rather straightforward modification of Pinker's 'boot-strapping' theory (Pinker 1984, chap. 3), which is the best specified current theory of the acquisition of phrase structure. Pinker's theory posits both types of primitives. However, it can be reformulated, without loss of precision or scope, with only syntax-of-thought categories as primitives. The reformulated theory posits a tendency on the child's part to categorize words and phrases according to their category in the syntax of thought. Because of this tendency, the initial word and phrase categories of the natural language correspond to categories of the syntax of thought. Then, over time, the learning procedures already formulated in Pinker's theory adjust the extensions of these initial natural-language categories so that they come to match those of the standard adult grammatical categories of the language the child is learning.

A simple example may serve to illustrate how the reformulated theory works. We suppose, with Pinker, that in the absence of applicable grammatical rules the child uses semantic and pragmatic information from the context to construct a parse-tree for an input sentence, and then derives rules from the tree. Assume that a child has no grammatical rules of English yet but knows the words *man* and *jump*; the child sees a man jump and hears the sentence *The man jumped*. Understanding and parsing the sentence involves assimilating the scene into the innate information format, i.e., coding its elements by ontological category and predicate/argument status, and labelling the words and phrases accordingly. Thus, because the child knows that a man is an object and jump an action, and that the *man* is argument to predicate *jump*, the child can construct the tree of Fig. 1, and then read off the rules shown. The expressions 'construct the tree' and 'read off the rules' are partly metaphoric. By 'construct the tree', what is meant is that the child perceives the sentence as having two parts, an Object-Argument Phrase *the man* and an Action-Predicate Phrase *jumped*, and also perceives the first component as having two parts, *the* and an Object-word *man*. 'Reading off the rules' means that the child registers that a sentence can consist of an Object-Argument Phrase followed by an Action-Predicate Phrase (the order being part of the regularity registered), and that an Object-Argument Phrase can consist of *the* and an Object-word (again, in that order). We may assume that rule registration is initially weak but solidifies as similar sentences and scenes are encountered.

Now let us move forward in time, past a number of such sentences and scenes, to the point at which the rules of Fig. 1 are solidly learned. Our child now hears the sentence *The wind stopped*. Assume, again with Pinker (and also with Schlesinger [e.g., Schlesinger 1982],[5] that where

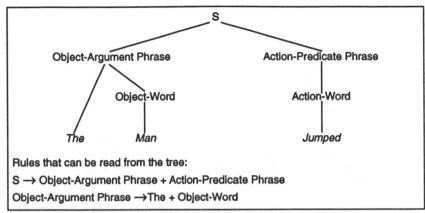

Figure 1. Parse-tree for 'The man jumped', which a child might construct given the sentence, the scene, knowledge of the words 'man' and 'jump', and innate syntax-of-thought categories.

there are known rules that are applicable, the child always uses them first when trying to understand a novel sentence. Applying the rules involves using phrase position and function words like *the* to construct the tree. After constructing the tree, the child puts the category information of the tree into the lexical entries for the words (Pinker 1984). According to these assumptions, the child constructs the tree of Fig. 2. Annotating the lexical entries entails that *wind* becomes marked in the lexicon as an Object-word, and *stop* as an Action-word. Note that this means that the category Object-word, which initially contained just *man* and other names of objects, has now come to include a word that does not designate an object, namely *wind*; likewise, the non-Action-word *stop* has come to be included in the category Action-word, which previously contained only words for actions like *jump*. Similarly, Object-Argument-Phrase has come to include phrases like *the wind*. As this kind of learning procedure operates over time, assimilating many input sentences, the extension of the category Object-word converges on the extension of Noun; similarly, the extension of Action-word converges on that of Verb, and the extension of Object-Argument-Phrase on that of NP. Thus, de facto, the child comes to have Nouns, Verbs, and NPs – what one calls the categories is of no importance. In short, given a learning procedure of this sort, word-and phrase-categories that begin as reflexes of categories of the syntax of thought grow into the syntactic categories of the language being learned. The lack of a good one-to-one match in the adult language between the syntax-of-thought categories and the natural-language syntactic categories is a consequence of the nature of the learning process.

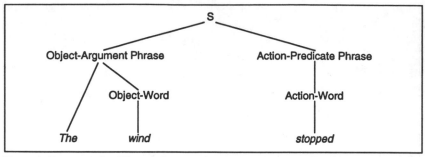

Figure 2. Parse-tree for 'The wind stopped', which a child might construct after having learned the rules of Figure 1.

In sum, there is a third method of investigating the syntax of thought empirically – by discovering what is developmentally most primitive in grammar. The effort to improve and perfect the learning theory referred to above will necessarily force the construction of precise hypotheses about the semantic structures (i.e., the categories and form of the syntax of thought) that provide the point of departure for learning. Given that the same learning theory should be applicable to any language, there is no reason to doubt that there are enough empirical constraints that particular hypotheses can be confirmed or invalidated.

Summary and Conclusions

I began by arguing that an intelligent species would need a mental logic to integrate information arriving from different sources or at different times, and that there is indeed evidence for a stock of elementary logical inference forms that people use for such practical purposes. A consensus exists that the core of such a mental logic would be a set of easy inferences defined by schemas. These would be represented in a system of semantic representation akin to Fodor's 'language of thought': I argued, like Fodor, that there must be an innate proposition-like format – a syntax of thought – to provide a basis for semantic representation and for a child's initial encoding of knowledge in memory. Such a format would necessarily embody a good deal of logical structure, and the inference schemas of the mental logic would use it.

Mental models alone, precisely because they lack variables, could not perform the representational and inferential functions served by this syntax of thought and mental logic. Nor is there reason to think connectionism incompatible with them.

The paper discussed three complementary ways in which the mental logic and the syntax of thought can be investigated empirically –

through reasoning, through linguistic universals and by discovering what is semantically and syntactically primitive in language acquisition. The reasoning route searches for types of logical inferences that are closely tied to the meanings of natural-language logical particles, inferences that are made easily and develop early, and that conserve these properties across languages. There is strong suggestive evidence for such a set of propositional inferences that would indeed form a mental propositional logic. Facts like the apparent primitiveness of quantifying and instantiating devices in language provide reason to believe that the mental logic extends well beyond a propositional logic, but the available evidence is too fragmentary to define its specific nature.

The other two empirical routes focus on the structure of the representational system rather than on inference. I enumerated some probable features of the syntax of the language of thought to exemplify what can be culled from linguistic work on links between semantic and syntactic representation in languages. The approach through language acquisition depends on the idea that children learn a mapping between the syntax of the language of thought and the grammar of their language. I show how this idea is viable in that it can, in principle, account for acquisition without requiring innate natural-language syntactic primitives. Thus, since the child begins with just the syntax of thought, it is potentially reconstructible from study of the beginnings of grammar.

In sum, there are means to investigate empirically the specific nature of a mental logic and that of the basic syntax of semantic representation; and there is enough evidence to indicate that the investigative enterprise will be productive.

Acknowledgments

The work for this paper was supported by grants from NSF (BNS-8409252) and NICHD (HD20807, Project 2). David O'Brien has been an important colleague in the work on reasoning.

Notes

1 Thus it is, of course, to be distinguished from logic learned in logic courses, or from logic textbooks or from other sources.

2 It has been argued (e.g., Rips 1986) that there is much mental logic implicit in Johnson-Laird's theory, so it should not be advanced as a claim about 'reasoning without logic' (e.g., Johnson-Laird 1986). I think Rips is right – and I cite an example of tacit logic later – but, since the model is different from the kind of model based on inference schemata for which I (and Rips) have argued, I let this point go by.

3 *Modus ponens* is the inference form: *If p then q; p / ∴.q.*

4 For example, the judgment that an *if*-statement *(if A then B)* is false, given that the antecedent is true and the consequent false, is easy to make because applying *modus ponens* (from *if A then B* and *A*, one deduces *B*) leads immediately to a contradiction *(B and not-B).*

5 For discussion of truth conditions defined in terms of possible worlds, see Braine and O'Brien (1991).

6 As noted in Braine (1992), where the account is developed in detail, there is much formal similarity between Pinker's "bootstrapping" theory and Schlesinger's "semantic assimilation" theory.

References

Bates, E. (1974). The acquisition of conditionals by Italian children. *Proceedings of the 10th Regional Meeting of the Chicago Linguistic Society.* Chicago: Chicago Linguistic Society

Bloom, L., M. Lahey, L. Hood, K. Lifter and K. Fiess (1980). Complex sentences: Acquisition of syntactic connectives and the semantic relations they encode. *Journal of Child Language* 7: 235-61

Bowerman, M. (1986). First steps in acquiring conditionals. In E. Traugott, A. ter Meulen, J.S. Reilly and C.A. Ferguson (eds.) *On Conditionals.* Cambridge: Cambridge University Press

Braine, M.D.S. (1978). On the relation between the natural logic of reasoning and standard logic. *Psychological Review* 85: 1-21

— (1990). The 'natural logic' approach to reasoning. In W.F. Overton (ed.), *Reasoning, Necessity, and Logic: Developmental Perspectives.* Hillsdale, NJ: Erlbaum

— (1992). What sort of innate structure is needed to 'bootstrap' into syntax? *Cognition* 45: 77-100

— and D.P. O'Brien (1991). A theory of *if*: A lexical entry, reasoning program, and pragmatic principles. *Psychological Review* 98: 182-203

—, B.J.Reiser and B. Rumain (1984). Some empirical justification for a theory of natural propositional logic. In G.H. Bower (ed.), *The Psychology of Learning and Motivation: Advances in Research and Theory.* New York: Academic Press

— and B. Rumain (1981). Development of comprehension of *or*: Evidence for a sequence of competencies. *Journal of Experimental Child Psychology* 31: 46-70

— and B. Rumain (1983). Logical reasoning. In J.H. Flavell and E.M. Markman (eds.) *Handbook of Child Psychology,* Vol. 3, *Cognitive Development.* New York: Wiley

Bucci, W. (1978). The interpretation of universal affirmative propositions: A developmental study. *Cognition* 6: 55-77

Comrie, B. (1986). Conditionals: A typology. In E. Traugott, A. ter Meulen, J.S. Reilly and C.A. Ferguson (eds.), *On Conditionals*. Cambridge: Cambridge University Press

— (1989). *Linguistic Universals and Linguistic Typology: Syntax and Morphology*. Chicago: University of Chicago Press

Fisch, S. (1991). Mental Logic in Children's Reasoning and Text Comprehension. Unpublished Ph.D. dissertation, New York: New York University Press

Fodor, J.A. (1966). How to learn to talk: some simple ways. In F. Smith and G.A. Miller (eds.), *The Genesis of Language*. Cambridge, MA: MIT Press

— (1975). *The Language of Thought*. Cambridge, MA: Harvard University Press

— and B.P. McLaughlin (1990). Connectionism and the problem of systematicity: Why Smolensky's solution won't work. *Cognition* 35: 183-204

— and Z.W. Pylyshyn (1988). Connectionism and cognitive architecture: A critical analysis. *Cognition* 28: 3-71

Grimshaw, J. (1981). Form, function, and the language-acquisition device. In C.L. Baker and J.J. McCarthy (eds.), *The Logical Problem of Language Acquisition*. Cambridge, MA: MIT Press

Harris, P. (1975). Inferences and semantic development. *Journal of Child Language* 2: 143-52

Inhelder, B., and J. Piaget (1964). *The Early Growth of Logic in the Child*. London: Routledge and Kegan Paul

Jackendoff, R. (1983). *Semantics and Cognition*. Cambridge, MA: MIT Press

— (1987). The status of thematic relations in linguistic theory. *Linguistic Inquiry* 18: 369-411

— (1989). What is a concept, that a person may grasp it? *Mind and Language* 4: 68-102

— (1990). *Semantic Structures*. Cambridge, MA: MIT Press

Johnson-Laird, P.N. (1975). Models of deduction. In R.J. Falmagne (ed.) *Reasoning: Representation and Process in Children and Adults*. Hillsdale, NJ: Erlbaum

— (1983). *Mental Models*. Cambridge, UK: Cambridge University Press

— (1986). Reasoning without logic. In T. Myers, K. Brown and B. McGonigle (eds.), *Reasoning and Discourse Processes*. London: Academic Press

— and B. Bara (1984). Syllogistic inference. *Cognition* 16: 1-61

— and R.M.J. Byrne (1991) *Deduction*. Hove, UK: Lawrence Erlbaum Associates

— R.M.J. Byrne and P. Tabossi (1989). Reasoning by model: The case of multiple quantification. *Psychological Review* 96: 658-73

— and M. Steedman (1978) The psychology of syllogisms. *Cognitive Psychology* 10: 64-99

Keil, F.C. (1989). *Concepts, Kinds, andCognitive Development*. Cambridge, MA: MIT Press

Kuczaj, S.A., and M.J. Daly (1979). The development of hypothetical reference in the speech of young children. *Journal of Child Language* 6: 563-79

Lea, R.B., D.P. O'Brien, S.M. Fisch, I.A. Noveck, and M.D.S. Braine (1990). Predicting propositional logic inferences in text comprehension. *Journal of Memory and Language* 29: 361-87

Lust, B., and C.A. Mervis (1980). Development of coordination in the natural speech of young children. *Journal of Child Language* 7: 279-304

Macnamara, J. (1972). The cognitive basis of language learning in infants. *Psychological Review* 79: 1-13

— (1982). *Names for Things: A study of Child Language*. Cambridge, MA: MIT Press

— (1986). *A Border Dispute: The Place of Logic in Psychology*. Cambridge, MA: MIT Press

Maratsos, M.P. (1974). Preschool children's use of definite and indefinite articles. *Child Development* 45: 446-55

McCloskey, M., and N. Cohen (1989). Catastrophic interference in connectionist networks: The sequential learning problem. In G.H. Bower (ed.), *The Psychology of Learning and Motivation: Advances in Research and Theory*. San Diego, CA: Academic Press

McPherson, L.M.P. (1991) *A little* goes a long way: Evidence for a perceptual basis of learning for the noun categories COUNT and MASS. *Journal of Child Language* 18: 315-53

O'Brien, D.P. (1981). The Development of Propositional Reasoning from the Perspective of a System of Inference Rules. Unpublished Ph.D. dissertation, Philadelphia, PA: Temple University

—, M.D.S. Braine, J. Connell, I. Noveck, S. Fisch and E. Fun (1989). Reasoning about conditional sentences: Development of understanding of cues to quantification. *Journal of Experimental Child Psychology* 48: 90-113

Osherson, D.N. (1974). *Logical Inference: Underlying Operations*. Vol. 2 of *Logical Abilities in Children*. Hillsdale, NJ: Erlbaum

— (1975). Models of logical thinking. In R.J. Falmagne (ed.), *Reasoning: Representation and Process in Children and Adults*. Hillsdale, NJ: Erlbaum

— (1975). *Reasoning in Adolescence: Deductive Inference*. Vol. 3 of *Logical Abilities in Children*. Hillsdale, NJ: Erlbaum

— (1975). *Reasoning and Concepts*. Vol. 4 of *Logical Abilities in Children*. Hillsdale, NJ: Erlbaum

Pea, R.D. (1980). Development of negation in early child language. In D.R. Olson (ed.), *The Social Foundation of Language and Thought: Essays in Honor of Jerome Bruner*. New York: W.W. Norton

Pinker, S. (1984). *Language Learnability and Language Development*. Cambridge, MA: Harvard University Press.

— (1989). *Learnability and Cognition: The Acquisition of Argument Structure*. Cambridge, MA: MIT Press

Rappaport, M., and B. Levin (1988). What to do with theta-roles. In W. Wilkins (ed.), *Syntax and Semantics, 21, Thematic Relations*. New York: Academic Press

Ratcliff, R. (1990). Connectionist models of recognition memory: Constraints imposed by learning and forgetting functions. *Psychological Review* 97: 285-308

Rips, L.J. (1983). Cognitive processes in propositional reasoning. *Psychological Review* 90: 38-71

— (1986). Mental muddles. In M. Brand and R.M. Harnish (eds.), *Problems in the Representation of Knowledge and Belief*. Tucson, AZ: University of Arizona Press

Rumelhart, D.E., and J.L. McClelland (1986). PDP models and general issues in cognitive science. In D.E. Rumelhart, and J.L. McClelland (eds.), *Parallel Distributed Processing: Explorations in the Microstructure of Cognition*. Vol. 1, *Foundations*. Cambridge, MA: MIT Press

Schlesinger, I.M. (1982). *Steps to Language: Toward a Theory of Language Acquisition*. Hillsdale, NJ: Erlbaum

Scholnick, E.S., and C.S. Wing (1991). Speaking deductively: Preschoolers' use of *if* in conversations and in conditional inference. *Developmental Psychology* 27: 249-58

Shastri, L. (1990). Connectionism and the computational effectiveness of reasoning. *Theoretical Linguistics* 16: 65-87

Smith, C.L. (1979). Children's understanding of natural language hierarchies. *Journal of Experimental Child Psychology* 27: 437-58

Smolensky, P. (1988). On the proper treatment of connectionism. *Behavioral and Brain Sciences* 11: 1-23

Soja, N.N., S. Carey and E.S. Spelke (1991). Ontological categories guide young children's inductions of word meaning: Object terms and substance terms. *Cognition* 38: 179-211

Spelke, E.S. (1990). Principles of object perception. *Cognitive Science* 14: 29-56

Sperber, D., and D. Wilson (1986). *Relevance: Communication and Cognition*. Cambridge, MA: Harvard University Press

van Gelder, T. (1990). Compositionality: A connectionist variation on a classical theme. *Cognitive Science* 14: 355-84

11

The Semantics of Syntactic Categories: A Cross-Linguistic Perspective

Emmon Bach

And so we might go on examining the various parts of speech and showing how they not merely grade into each other but are to an astonishing degree actually convertible into each other. The upshot of such an examination would be to feel convinced that the "part of speech" reflects not so much our intuitive analysis of reality as our ability to compose that reality into a variety of formal patterns. A part of speech outside of the limitations of syntactic form is but a will o' the wisp. For this reason no logical scheme of the parts of speech – their number, nature, and necessary confines – is of the slightest interest to the linguist. Each language has its own scheme. Everything depends on the formal demarcation which it recognizes.

Yet we must not be too destructive. It is well to remember that speech consists of a series of propositions. There must be something to talk about and something must be said about this subject of discourse once it is selected. This distinction is of such fundamental importance that the vast majority of languages have emphasized it by creating some kind of formal barrier between the two terms of the proposition. The subject of discourse is a noun. As the most common subject of discourse is either a person or a thing, the noun clusters about concrete concepts of that order. As the thing predicated of a subject is generally an activity in the widest sense of the word, a passage from one moment of existence to another, the form which has been set aside for the business of predicating, in other words, the verb, clusters about concepts of activity. No language wholly fails to distinguish noun and verb, though in particular cases the nature of the distinction may be an elusive one. It is different with the other parts of speech. Not one of them is imperatively required for the life of language.

– Edward Sapir

0. Plan

A grammar shows how to make expressions of a language by combining expressions into expressions. The classes of expressions to which a grammar refers are the syntactic categories of the language (under description by that grammar). A semantic description of the language gives us the interpretations of the expressions of the language. The question before us here is this: what kinds of meanings go with what kinds of expressions? That is a very big question. I will confine myself to a couple of specific instances of the question. But first I need to say a little bit by way of background about categories of grammars and categories of meanings.

0.1. Background: Categories of Grammar

There are two ways in which we can classify linguistic expressions. One way is on the basis of "size" and independence: phrases, words, parts of words, bound and free morphemes, and so on. Call that the *vertical* dimension. The other – which we might call *horizontal* – has to do with distinctions like those of the traditional parts of speech: nouns, verbs, adjectives, and so on. The bases of this second kind of classification are a mixed bag, but are certainly partly semantic: "a noun is a name of person, place, or thing," and so on.

The sources for my discussion of syntactic categories here are three: the "parts of speech" of the traditional Western European grammarians; the features and categories of some contemporary syntactic theories that follow the so-called X-bar tradition; and the classes of categorial grammar.

One important question about categories is: to what extent do different languages show differences in their categorial systems?

I will generally follow the convention of Montague (1973) and use 'categories' for the syntax and 'types' for the semantic classifications. Also: mostly I will use 'syntactic' in a broad sense and understand it to include both phrasal and morphological – that is, word-internal – phenomena.

0.2. Semantic Interpretation

I will assume here without discussion an interpretation in the tradition of model-theoretic semantics. We can call the set of possible objects, sets, functions, and so on, that are to serve as the universe of denotations for the expressions of a language a *model structure*. So a first stab at answering the basic question under scrutiny is to ask whether the categories of the grammar correspond systematically to the kinds of things in our model structures. The most definite and detailed answer to that question that I know of is given in standard theories of interpreted categorial grammars, and I will take that set-up as a convenient and concrete starting point.

1. Some Systems of Syntactic Categories

1.1. A Categorial System

The syntactic categories of a categorial grammar are specified by giving a set of primitive or basic categories and a recursive definition of an infinite set of derived or functor categories. The functor categories encode an i-place operation, i argument categories, and a resultant category. Syntactically, the expressions belonging to a set indexed by a functor category f – hereafter, simply "in a category f " – combine with the appropriate number of expressions in the argument categories in the manner specified by the operation to form an expression in the resultant category. If we limit our operations to the two two-place operations of concatenation of the functor to the left or to the right (symbolized by the conventional slashes 'leaning toward' the argument expression / and \), then we will have a bidirectional 'binary' categorial grammar. Take t and e as primitive categories (as in Montague 1973, for Ajdukiewicz's s and n), then we will have categories for functors like these:

1. t/e, e\t, t/t,…, (e\t)/e,…

So suppose we have a grammar with these expressions:

2. e: John, Mary
    e\t: walks, runs
    (e\t)/e: loves, sees,

Then we can build (or analyse) expressions like these:

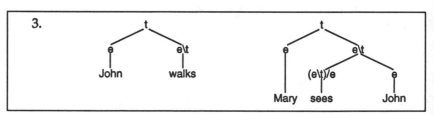

3.

Here is a simple model-structure for the extensional interpretation of a categorial language/grammar:

4. model-structure:
    truth-values {0/, 1}
    A: set of individuals
    F: hierarchy of functions built out of those elements

If we take that together with some apparatus for doing quantification (say, a set of assignments of values to variables), we have all that we need for a standard interpretation of a categorial version of the predicate calculus with the following match between categories of the language and types of the interpretation:

Syntax:	Semantics:
t formulas	truth values
e individual terms	individuals
(variable, constants)	
$a \backslash b, b/a$	functions from a type things to b type things

If the language includes categories for the connectives and negation, then the interpretation will include truth-functions of the familiar sort. The interpretations of the one-place predicates can equivalently be thought of as sets, transitive verbs as functions from individuals to sets, and so on. To get to the full system of an intensional interpretation such as that of Montague's fragment in PTQ (i.e., Montague, 1973) all we need to add is a set of possible worlds and a set of times. (See Oehrle et al. 1988, for a collection of recent papers in categorial grammar, and Bach 1988, for an exposition of the general framework I assume here. This exposition in terms of Montague's version of a possible world semantics is motivated primarily for purposes of concreteness and illustration. I endorse the general thrust of model-theoretic semantics but consider it to be the job of the linguistic semanticist to discover the most adequate model structure for dealing with natural language[s]. For a general and relatively nontechnical introduction to model-theoretic methods and some recent directions and problems, see Bach 1989.)

One of the hallmarks of categorial grammars (and related frameworks) is that the relationship between syntactic categories and semantic types is completely determined by the general theory (indeed, Ajdukiewicz, 1935, called his categories *semantic categories*). Notice, however, that the kind of semantic property that is specified in this functional relationship is completely structural. Nothing whatsoever is required as to the inner content of the semantic types. This fact suggests a useful distinction for us to follow here: on the one hand, we can ask what the various classes of syntactic items do in the economy of building up denotations for complex expressions and, on the other, we can ask about the kinds of things that are included in the denotations of the items. Call these two aspects *external* and *internal* semantics. Of course, there is some connection between these two aspects of meaning: in

English, *hat* and *love* are one- and two-place predicates, respectively, and it is not surprising that it is not the other way around. But we must not jump too fast. Many languages distinguish certain kinds of necessarily possessed items like noses and heads, and hats might be among them in some culture, while for loving we have Montague's examples (Montague 1969, 1974, p. 161, n.8):

5. To love is to exult.
6. To love is to exalt.

The main argument I will try to develop is that there is a very firm semantic link between aspects of the external or structural semantics of expressions and the syntactic categories of natural languages. It is primarily in the internal semantics of the syntactic categories that we see considerable crosslinguistic variation and looseness. But even here there are certain prototypical elements of content that go with the major syntactic classes. (Henceforth, I will follow the notational conventions of Montague's PTQ in one more respect by using angled-bracket 'argument first' notation for semantic types, with no presumptions about order. So the semantic type – ignoring intensions – corresponding to the categories t/e and $e \backslash t$ will be $<e,t>$.)

1.2. X-Bar Categories

Let us now consider systems of categories that fall into what Chomsky refers to as "some variety of X-Bar theory" (Chomsky 1982,: p.5). Such systems appear at first blush to differ radically from that of the categorial system that we have just looked at. The system is based on a number of features with binary values (Verbal, Nominal, and so on) and a single-feature (Bar) with more values (three or four). Labels like $V^{\emptyset}$ ('V zero'), N'' ('N double-bar') are then taken to be just abbreviations for some combination of feature-specifications (+V, -N, $\emptyset$-Bar; -V, +N, 2-Bar for the examples just given). The two types of features appear to correspond in part to the 'horizontal' and 'vertical' dimensions mentioned earlier: for example, the value $\emptyset$ ('zero') is generally reserved for what we usually think of as words, while higher Bar values go with phrases.

At first glance, it might seem that the distinction between words and phrases corresponds to the distinction in Montague grammar between the sets of "basic expression" (B_a) and the sets of expressions derived by the rules (P_a) (cf. PTQ, i.e., Montague 1973), but this is not correct. The first syntactic rule (S1) in PTQ is not a rule at all in the technical sense of Montague's general theory, but simply a statement that the sets of basic expressions are subsets of the sets of non-basic expressions. It would be possible to exploit the distinction in some way to capture a difference like that assumed between expressions of X^0 and higher bar-level X's, but as it stands the distinction is not of this sort. Compare the discussion in di Sciullo and Williams (1987) of the difference between lexical items or "listemes" and words (of various kinds).

It is easy to see that the relationship between syntactic categories and semantic types cannot be a function in an X-Bar system. Consider the category of verbs, encoded as V, which stands for the feature specifications [+V, -N]. Among the items that would presumably be included in the set of Verbs we find intransitives like *walk*, transitives like *see*, ditransitives like *give*, items like *put* that require two arguments (nominal object and directional adverbial), and so on. Clearly, no reasonable semantics could consider these items to represent the same semantic types. These examples show that the syntactic categories of an X-Bar system are not strictly comparable to the categories of a categorial grammar. Rather, the things that are most like the categorial classes are items associated with a combination of syntactic features and subcategorizations. Hence, we must not make too much of the fact that categorial systems project an infinite set of categories and the X-Bar systems a "very finite" set. Without some limit on the subcategorizations of an X-Bar system, there could be an infinite number of possible classes associated with combinations of syntactic features and subcategorizations.

There are two ideas about the relationship between syntax and semantics that have been enunciated by works in the tradition of X-Bar syntax. First, the Crosscategorially Uniform Semantic Interpretation Hypothesis (CUSIH) was proposed by Jackendoff (1977, see Williams 1981): it says that the interpretation of items at a given bar-level will be fixed and independent of the particular category that the item belongs to. So, for example, all lexical items will have interpretations of the same type, since they are all of the bar-level 0. I believe that this idea is best understood (within the present context) as claiming that the semantic operations associated with a particular construction at a given level will be the same across 'horizontal' categories. For example, nominal and verbal counterparts will be interpreted as functions taking their complements as arguments, optional elements at level 1 will be interpreted as restrictive modifiers, and so on. We will return to this question below in the context of comparing the denotations of verbs and nouns. (In Montague grammar and extensions thereof, these two examples are both instances of the single semantic operation of functional application.)

Second, within the framework of Relational Grammar it was proposed that there is a uniform mapping from semantic properties of lexical items to the relational structures associated with them in the initial stratum. This Uniform Alignment Hypothesis (Perlmutter and Postal 1984; Rosen 1984) was adapted to the X-Bar framework by Baker (1988) and stated in terms of Thematic Roles as the Uniformity of Theta Assignment Hypothesis (UTAH): every lexical item with a given cluster of thematic role assignments will appear in D-Structures of a determined type. This hypothesis seems to be a revival of some form of the hypotheses about the relationship of semantics and syntax associated with the program of Generative Semantics. Unfortunately, it is difficult to test these claims without some explicit semantic theory, so far lacking in both frameworks.

1.3. Traditional Parts of Speech

The parts of speech that are distinguished in the lore of our school grammars and popular works on language are inherited from the Greek and Latin grammarians (Steinthal 1890-91). In the heyday of structuralism in America there was a reaction to this terminology, based as it was on particular Indo-European languages, so that in this period many linguists refrained altogether from the use of such words as Noun, Verb, Adjective. A second influence on terminology of that era was a strong scepticism about semantics. Since part of the traditional characterization of the parts of speech was clearly semantic ("a noun is the name of a person, place, or thing"), it was felt that the technical terminology of linguistic should be free of this semantic taint. Hence, the use of such colourless terms as 'Class I' words, and the like (see the works of C.C. Fries on English grammar, for example).
It is interesting that the transformational-generative tradition inherited both the scepticism of the American structuralists about semantics and an entirely traditional set of categories. Moreover, suspicions about a Western European or Latinate bias in the categories seem to have been completely lost, to the point where syntactic descriptions of the most widely different languages are often couched in the traditional terminology without any comment or question.

1.4. Grammatical Relations

There is a completely different set of concepts that we inherit from traditional terminology: subjects, objects (direct and indirect), and so on. Although I am following a more or less standard line here in assuming that these categories are derived and relational in character, it should be noted that these grammatical relations or functions play important and differing roles in various current theories. In some theories (Relational Grammar and Arc-Pair Grammar) the counterparts to these terms are primitives. The quotation from Sapir at the head of this essay shows that there is an important connection between these notions and some of the traditional terms ('nouns' and subjects, 'verbs' and predicates). (I will mention another set of terms, the so-called thematic roles or relations below in section 3 on internal semantics).

2. External Semantics

Conventionally, the three predicative classes of the Western European grammatical tradition are represented in elementary logic books and classes as corresponding to a single family of predicates of varying 'adicity' or 'arity': simple (one-place) predicates, two-place predicates (relation symbols), and so on. From a categorial perspective, in the case of one-place predicates, we would have items of type $<e,t>$, that is, functions from individuals (entities) to truth-values. On the assumption that proper names and personal pronouns are expressions of the category (and type) e we should be able to put such an expression together with a name to get a truth-bearing expression, that is, a sentence or a formula:

7. Mary walks.

Now, in a language like English, no adjective, common noun or un-tensed verb can stand in the place of *walks* here:

8. *Mary happy
    *Mary doctor
    *Mary walk

(I assume that a form like *walk* in *Mary and John walk* contains a phono-logically null suffix and is tensed, like the form *walks* in example 7 above.) Let us call an item like *walks* a 'predicative'. We can extend the term to include items that take varying numbers of arguments, such as tensed transitive verbs, and distinguish them if need be by indicating their arity or adicity (one-place, two-place, and so on). Traditionally, this predicative function has been associated with the category of verbs, but as we can see in the English example, sometimes members of the category Verb need some extra dressing or help to carry out this func-tion. In X-Bar terms this extra "stuff" is associated with the category of INFL (or some related category).

The category of names is sharply distinguished in the classical logical tradition from complex NPs like the subject in this sentence:

9. Every fish swims.

Montague (1973) showed how to preserve the syntactic/semantic integrity of the NP by treating such items as denoting generalized quantifiers, that is, families of sets (type: $<<e,t>,t>$ in an extensional version). He also assimilated singular names to the same category (and type), so the expression *Mary* in an example like (7) is interpreted as the family of sets to which the individual Mary belongs. If the set of things denoted by *walks* is a member of that family, then the sentence is true (in a world at a time). In this set-up, the category and type of determiners is fixed as functors that take common nouns to make expressions for generalized quantifiers.

We can go on to indicate the primary distinguishing marks of the other two major classes of (common) nouns and adjectives. Common nouns function primarily as sortal bases for generalized quantifier expressions and for forming complex common nouns via adjectives and relative clauses, while adjectives function primarily as operators on common nouns to make common nouns (thus I am taking the attributive use as the primary one for adjectives).

The canonical external semantics of Nouns, Verbs and Adjectives can now be illustrated in an example like the following:

10. Every	little	dog	barks.
DETERMINER	ADJECTIVE	NOUN	VERB
$<<e,t>,<<e,t>,t>>$	$<<e,t>,<e,t>>$	$<e,t>$	$<e,t>$

It is hard to imagine a natural language that did not allow the construction of expressions corresponding to these particular functions or uses of lexical items. It is easy to imagine natural languages that did not distinguish at the level of lexical classes between items that could enter directly into these positions or functions. What is necessary is some kind of grammatical machinery to allow the functions or uses of the undifferentiated lexical items to be marked in a not intolerably ambiguous way. Among unnatural languages the predicate calculus, supplemented with some such grammatical machinery as variables (perhaps of higher orders) and binders (like lambdas) is an example of such a language. Among natural languages, perhaps classical Chinese is an example. In the next section I will take up some languages that have been claimed to have only a single open class of predicatives.

2.1. Nouns and Verbs in Some Particular Languages

Languages of the Northwest coast of North America have often been cited as languages that have only a single open class of predicative expressions, especially languages of the Wakashan family (for example, Nootka or West Coast, Kwakiutl or Kwakw'ala). (Jacobsen 1979 provides a careful review of the general literature on this topic for Nootkan [the sources of which are some writings of Sapir and Swadesh] as well as a detailed examination of the question for Nootkan with special attention to Makah, with the conclusion that Makah does show a contrast between nominal and verbal items after all. See also Kinkade 1983 for a discussion of Salish, and Robins 1952 for an earlier review of the general question.)

To get an idea of what the phenomena are that have led to this conclusion, consider sentences like the following Haisla examples:

11. Dexwdusi. 'That was/is a rabbit' (-i 3 person, remote)
12. Duqwelan dexwdus. 'I saw a rabbit.'

Boas (1947) and Swadesh (1939) cite examples like the following, to show that we can interchange stems to get matched pairs with the same stem acting in a predicative and a more "nominal" or specificational role (these from Kwakw'ala; see Boas 1947, p. 280, retranscribed here):

13. N'i'kida bəgwa'nəm. 'That one said, it was the man'
14. Bəgwa'nəmida n'i'ka. 'It was the man he [i.e. who] said'

There has been a certain confusion in the literature about the question of nouns and verbs because of a failure to distinguish between (common) nouns and noun phrases or terms (compare the quotation from Sapir at the head of this essay). Traditional logic is correct in saying that common nouns and verbs (as well as predicative adjectives) are to be interpreted as referring to sets or relations (or properties, etc., depending on the particulars of your basic interpretative set-up). Terms, on the other hand, are either referring expressions denoting individuals or generalized quantifiers, as we have seen. In either case they are the kind of expressions that can go with predicatives to make sentences (truth-bearing expressions and other parallel types associated with various kinds of speech acts).

Recently, Eloise Jelinek [in preparation] has proposed an interesting new angle on the question of syntactic categories and their semantic reflexes. She argues that another language of the Northwest, the Salishan language Samish (or Straits Salish), lacks a contrast between nouns and verbs, and that as a consequence, Samish does not use noun phrase quantification (generalized quantifiers) at all. If this conclusion is correct, it would support very strongly the idea that the central characteristic of common nouns is to act as sortal bases for generalized quantifiers. Of course, this language like every other does provide the means for expressing quantification, that is, for making general statements of various kinds. In fact, the means that are exploited in Samish – higher order predicates, affixation and auxiliary elements interpreted as unselective binders (Lewis 1975, Heim 1982, Diesing 1989, Kratzer 1989)– are familiar from other languages and necessary for some kinds of sentences. Jelinek's proposals are extremely interesting both within the context of discussions like the present one about the relationships between categories and types, and because they offer an entirely new slant on questions of syntactic typology.

There is another, not unrelated claim that Jelinek makes about Samish: it is an example of a kind of language which she has elsewhere (1984) characterized as the type of a "pronominal argument language." According to this hypothesis, there is a typological difference among languages which can be seen as a difference in the mapping to semantic categories: there are simply no predicates in the sense of this essay. What appear to be predicates are in fact logically full sentences or formulas, which contain pronominal arguments (perhaps phonologically null). Such languages do not have full NP (term phrase) arguments at all. Rather, the NP's that appear in sentences are to be understood as adjuncts, appositive amplifications of the minimal content given by the pronominal argument of the verbal element in the sentence.

Here are some examples from Jelinek's work and an illustration of her conclusions about differences between the logical forms or interpretations of some sentences in English and Samish:

15. Cey ce sweyqe 'He works, the (one who is a) man'
16. Sweyqe ce cey 'He (is a) man, the (one who) works'

17. English: Salish (Jelinek):
    walk' (j)   Walk' (x) & john' (x)
    Walk' (x) & man' (x)   Walk' (x) & man' (x)
    EVERY(man') (walk')   ALL (Walk' (x), man' (x)) [see (i)]
                                       (ALL: unselective binder)

One important area to look at in figuring out the relationships and differences between nouns and verbs is that of nominalizations of verbs:

18. ...the destruction of the city by the United States...
19. The United States destroyed the city.

According to the hypothesis of Jackendoff mentioned above (CUSIH) the relationship must be the same: for both, we have a function/argument relationship. David Dowty (1989) has proposed an interesting hypothesis about the way in which function/argument relationships are expressed in nominal and verbal constructions. It has often been noted that the arguments of nouns are optional, while those of verbs are obligatory in the normal case (Grimshaw 1990 argues that this optionality is illusory). Dowty observes that there have been two principal ways for exhibiting the logical form of predicates and their arguments. One – the Ordered Argument method – is that familiar from standard logic book treatments of the predicate calculus, with the difference between *John sees Bill* and *Bill sees John* exhibited (as in these English examples) by the order of the term expressions in a formula: *See(j,b)* vs. *See(b,j)*, or the like. The other – the method of Thematic Role Assignment – is reminiscent of languages with case-marking and the kinds of structures proposed in Fillmore's Case theory (1968) and various representations of thematic roles (θ-roles). In this method, we might have something like markers such as Agent and Theme associated with the terms in the example just given. Dowty suggests that natural languages might exploit both methods, and in a language like English the first method would be associated with verbal constructions, the second with nominal constructions. Note that this would give a direct explanation for the optionality of nominal arguments, especially if expressed along the lines of a Davidsonian representational scheme like that worked out by Parsons (1990).

If Dowty's ideas about nominal and verbal constructions hold up, one could raise an interesting question about languages that appear not to have a lexical constrast between nouns and verbs. There is an old idea that some languages as a whole are primarily verbal or primarily nominal. This idea could be given a precise form in line with Dowty's hypothesis.

Examples like (18) and (19) cannot fail to bring to mind the whole question of the status of events and other similar things in the semantics of English and other languages. The relevant question here is whether there is some special affinity between verbs and events (and the like) on the one hand, and nouns and things, stuff and so on.

3. Internal Semantics

The traditional school definitions of the parts of speech make reference to what I am calling here the *internal semantics of the categories*. It is here that the scepticism of modern linguists – expressed, for example, in the first paragraph cited from Sapir at the head of this essay – has been most vocal.

In his paper on "Grammatical Categories," Whorf drew a distinction between overt categories such as those we have been discussing (nouns, verbs, etc., but also morphosyntactic categories like grammatical gender and so on) and covert categories, which lead a more hidden life. He stated that the covert categories seemed to be more important in inquiring into the psychological or metaphysical import of linguistic distinctions. In any case, the distinction provides a useful frame for discussing some aspects of the internal semantics of some syntactic categories.

3.1. Overt Categories

In the second paragraph of the quotation from Sapir's *Language*, we can see a suggestion about a semantic link between the external semantics of the classes of nouns (or noun phrases!) and verbs and their internal semantics, the typical kinds of semantic values that they have. We might understand Sapir's suggestion like this: utterances of sentences often or primarily express propositions. The canonical form of such a sentence (a statement) is that of making an assertion about something. The thing about which we make an assertion is generally some sort of a stable entity – "a person or a thing" – while what is predicated of the entity is "generally an activity in the widest sense of the term, a passage from one moment of existence to another," and the prototypical meaning of a verb is activity.

Discussions of questions like these have often been hampered by too rigid expectations or claims that are too rigid. Probably the right way to think about a claim about the semantic import of a certain syntactic category is in terms of prototypical or stereotypical connections. There are clear cases of objects that are prototypically associated with the category of common count nouns – various middle-sized objects of interest to humans – and clear cases of actions and event types that are prototypically associated with transitive verbs – actions under control of agents that affect some object. We expect these differences to be reflected, on the whole, in languages that draw a distinction in their grammars between count nouns and transitive verbs. (There is a fairly extensive literature following this line of thought; a good recent discussion may be found in Croft 1991.)

3.2. Covert Categories

To my mind, some of the most interesting parts of natural language semantics are those that appear "below" the level of the big categories like
verbs, nouns, adjectives and so on, in the various kinds of subcategories
that show up in various ways, more or less covert, more or less gram-
maticized in one language or another. I am thinking here of distinctions
like those between mass and count nouns, the distinctions between
stage-level and individual-level predicates (Carlson, 1977), and the various distinctions having to do with what are variously called verb-clas-
sifications, *Aktionsarten*, types of *eventualities* (what I barbarously refer
to occasionally as "eventology"). It seems to me that the basic conceptual matrix for these and other kinds of distinctions is quite universal,
and that working out the "logic" of such distinctions in various languages may be the place where linguistics can contribute most to the
goal of understanding cognition. By way of illustration, let me just take
one set of distinctions to stand in for many.

3.3. Unaccusativity

In a number of languages, intransitive verbs seem to come in two varieties, associated with various syntactic contrasts such as selection of
auxiliaries, differing case-marking, possibility of impersonal passives
and so on. Some examples:

Perfect Auxiliary Selection

In some Romance and Germanic languages, the (formal) perfect tenses
or aspects are construed with two different auxiliaries, one corresponding to English *have*, one to *be:*
Dutch:

20.	Zij heeft (*is) geslapen.	'She slept'
21.	Zij is (*heeft) gekomen.	'She came'

Italian:

22.	Ha (*è) dormito.	'(S/he) has slept'
23.	È (*ha) venito.	'(S/he) has come'

Subject Case Marking

In Lakhota (and some other Siouan languages) one-place predicates
(and in a more limited way, transitives as well) must be divided into

two classes according to the case form which a surface structure subject affix assumes. For first- and second-person-singular subjects, we have these contrasts:

Lakhota:
24. Machuita 'I'm cold'   Nichuita   'You're cold'
25. Wathi   'I dwell'   Yathi   'You dwell'
     (Boas and Deloria 1941, p. 23 ff., 78. Thanks to George Whirl-
     wind Soldier for help with Lakhota.)

The affixes for the first class of predicates are (almost) formally identical to the affixes for objects of transitive verbs; thus the system is reminiscent of the ergative/absolute case systems of some languages (but is actually quite different).

Passives of Intransitive Verbs

Some languages allow not only passives of transitive verbs as in English, but also passives of intransitive verbs, usually with some meaning like 'there is V-ing going on' (I have avoided the term Impersonal Passives, because this term has connotations that can be misleading). German and Dutch are examples of such languages. Again there seems to be a split: some intransitives do, others do not allow this construction:

Dutch:
26. Er werd gedanst.   'There was dancing going on'
27. *Er werd geploft.   '[There was exploding going on]'

What is intriguing about these phenomena is that there are clear semantic correlations across languages with respect to these disparate characteristics. What is puzzling is that these correlations are anything but complete and exact, so that any attempt to predict the complete membership of such classes from the semantics seems doomed to failure. The factors that seem to be involved are verbal aspect, agentivity, "activeness" of the property denoted by the verb and a link to the object relation for some typical transitive verbs, as seen in pairs like these for English:

28. Mary opened the door.
29. The door opened.

In various ways, the subjects of verbs like intransitive *open*, and others that have been called 'unaccusatives', exhibit properties that are associated with objects, and these phenomena then are quite rightly of crucial importance for theories which emphasize the importance of such grammatical relations. They are of importance, above all, for Relational Grammar, a theory in which a large part of the basic work on unaccusativity was done and which provided inspiration to work in a very wide variety of frameworks.

The study of such phenomena is of the utmost importance for coming to understand the conceptual bases of language. A promising line of thought about the semantic import of such covert categories as well as the internal semantics of the overt categories touched on above is to attribute the generalizations that we find not to the theory of language per se, but to the acquisition process. In this way we may be able to do justice both to the undoubted similarities that we find crosslinguistically as well as to the many conflicting and exceptional phenomena that exist. (A very stimulating recent discussion of such issues can be found in Dowty 1991.)

Note

Epigraph: Edward Sapir (1921), pp. 118-19.

References

Ajdukiewicz, Kazimierz. (1935). Die syntaktische Konnexität. *Studia Philosophica* 1: 1-27. English translation (1976) in Storrs McCall, (ed.), *Polish Logic: 1920-1939*. Oxford: Oxford University Press

Bach, Emmon. (1968). Nouns and noun phrases. In Emmon Bach and Robert T. Harms (eds.),*Universals in Linguistic Theory,* New York: Holt, Rinehart and Winston, 90-122

— (1988). Categorial grammars as theories of language. Richard T. Oehrle, Emmon Bach and Deirdre Wheeler (eds.), *Categorial Grammars and Natural Language Structures*. Dordrecht: Reidel, 17-34.

— (1989). *Informal Lectures on Formal Semantics*. Albany: SUNY Press

— Eloise Jelinek, Angelika Kratzer, and Barbara H. Partee, (eds.) (In preparaion.) *Quantification in Natural Languages.*

Baker, Mark. (1989). *Incorporation*. Chicago: University of Chicago Press.

Carlson, Greg N. (1977). Reference to Kinds in English. Ph. D. dissertation, Amherst: University of Massachusetts.

Chierchia, Gennaro. (1984). Topics in the Syntax and Semantics of Infinitives and gerunds. Ph. D. dissertation, Amherst: The University of Massachusetts.

280

Emmon Bach

Croft, William. (1991). *Syntactic Categories and Grammatical Relations*. Chicago and London: The University of Chicago Press.

Diesing, M. (1989). Bare plural subjects, inflection, and the mapping to LF. In E. Bach, A. Kratzer, and B. Partee, (eds.), Papers on Quantification, National Science Foundation report, Amherst: University of Massachusetts

Di Sciullo, Anna-Marie and Edwin Williams. (1987). *On the Definition of Word*. Cambridge, MA: MIT Press

Dowty, David R. (1989). On the semantic content of the notion of 'thematic role'. In Gennaro Chierchia, Barbara H. Partee, and Ray Turner (eds.), *Properties, Types, and Meanings* (Dordrecht/Boston/London: Kluwer), Volume II, pp. 69-129

— (1991). Thematic proto-roles and argument selection. *Language* 67:547-619

Fillmore, Charles J. (1968). The case for case. In Emmon Bach and Robert T. Harms (eds.), *Universals in Linguistic Theory* (New York: Holt, Rinehart, and Winston), pp. 1-88

Grimshaw, Jane. (1990). *Argument Structure*. Cambridge, MA: MIT Press

Heim, I. R. (1982). The Semantics of Definite and Indefinite Noun Phrases. Ph. D. dissertation, Amherst: University of Massachusetts.

Jackendoff, Ray S. (1977). *X'-Syntax: A Study of Phrase Structure*. Cambridge, MA: MIT Press

— (1990). *Semantic Structures*. Cambridge, MA: MIT Press.

Jacobsen, William H., Jr. (1979). Noun and verb in Nootkan. In Barbara S. Efrat, (ed.), *The Victoria Conference on Northwestern Languages* (Victoria: British Columbia Provincial Museum), pp. 83-155

Jelinek, Eloise. (1984). Empty categories, case and configurationality. *Natural Language and Linguistic Theory* 2:39-76

— (1988) Quantification without Nouns in Salish. Unpublished paper presented at the Symposium on Cross-Linguistic Quantification, Linguistic Society of America, New Orleans 1988

— (In preparation). Quantification in Straits Salish. To appear in Bach et al. *Quantification in Natural Languages*

Kinkade, Dale. (1983). Salish evidence against the universality of noun and verb. *Lingua* 60:25-40

Kratzer, A. (1989). Stage-level and individual-level predicates. In E. Bach, A.Kratzer, and B. Partee, (eds.), Papers on Quantification, National Science Foundation report, University of Massachusetts.

Langacker, Ronald W. (1987). Nouns and verbs. *Language* 63: 53-94

Lewis, D. (1975). Adverbs of quantification. In E. L. Keenan, (ed.), *Formal Semantics of Natural Language*, Cambridge: Cambridge University Press

McKeon, Richard, (ed.) (1941). *The Basic Works of Aristotle*. New York: Random House

Montague, Richard. (1969). On the nature of certain philosophical entities. *The Monist* 53: 159-94 (Paper 5 in Montague 1974, pp. 148-187)

— (1973). The proper treatment of quantification in ordinary English. Paper 8 in Montague (1974), orginally published in K.J.J. Hintikka, J.M.E. Moravcsik and P. Suppes (eds.), *Approaches to Natural Language: Proceedings of the 1970 Stanford Workshop on Grammar and Semantics*. Dordrecht: Reidel, 1973, pp. 221-42

— (1974). *Formal Philosophy*. Richmond Thomason (ed.), New Haven, CT: Yale University Press

Oehrle, Richard T., Emmon Bach, and Deirdre Wheeler, (eds.) (1988). *Categorial Grammars and Natural Language Structures*. Dordrecht: Reidel

Parsons, Terence. (1990). *Events in the Semantics of English: A Study in Subatomic Semantics*. Cambridge, MA: MIT Press

Perlmutter, David M., and Paul M. Postal. (1984). The 1-advancement exclusiveness law. In Perlmutter and Rosen (1984), pp. 81-125

— and Carol G. Rosen (eds.) (1984). *Studies in Relational Grammar 2*. Chicago: University of Chicago Press

Robins, R. H. (1952). Noun and verb in universal grammar. *Language* 28: 289-298

Rosen, Carol G. (1984). The interface between semantic roles and initial grammatical relations. In Perlmutter and Rosen (1984), pp. 38-77

Sapir, Edward. (1921). *Language: An Introduction to the Study of Speech*. New York: Harcourt, Brace (Rpt., n.d., Harvest Books)

Steinthal, H. (1890-91). *Geschichte der Sprachwissenschaft bei den Griechen und Römern mit besonderer Rücksicht auf die Logik*. Vols. I, II. Berlin: Dümmler

Whorf, Benjamin Lee. (1956a). Grammatical categories. In Whorf (1956b)

— (1956b). *Language, Thought, and Reality: Selected Writings of Benjamin Lee Whorf*. John B. Carroll (ed.). Cambridge, MA: MIT Press

Williams, Edwin S. (1981). Language acquisition, markedness, and phrase structure. In Susan L. Tavakolian (ed.), *Language Acquisition and Linguistic Theory* (Cambridge, MA: MIT Press) pp. 8-34

— (1983). Semantic vs. syntactic categories. *Linguistics and Philosophy* 6: 423-46

12

Some Issues Involving Internal and External Semantics

Francis Jeffry Pelletier

1. Introduction

Emmon Bach's paper (this volume) raises a number of interesting issues, especially the questions "What is quantification, anyway?" and "What is the range of different ways in which quantification can be manifested?" Of course such questions bring up philosophical issues of how we can know whether such-and-such construction in this or that language *really* is or is not quantification.

For example, Bach cites Jelinek (1989) as arguing that Samish (or Straits Salish) does not use noun phrase quantification at all, but rather that it uses auxiliary elements interpreted as unselective quantifiers (Lewis 1975 and Heim 1982). Thus there are no phrases like the English 'all bears', but instead such apparent quantification over all bears is dealt with by quantifying over what bears always do. According to this view, the Samish sentence is more faithfully translated 'Bears always eat fish' than as 'All bears eat fish'. Those of us sharing Quine's Indeterminacy of Translation doubts might raise our eyebrows at this claim.[1] After all, by hypothesis there is no distinction in Samish between different types of quantifiers, and so within the language there is no reason to think the auxiliary ought to be translated as the adverbial quantifier 'always' rather than the nominal quantifier 'all', is there? Well, the evidence for Jelinek's claim really is that it fits into a much broader picture of the Samish language as a whole – that Samish has no contrast between common nouns and verbs, that it is a "pronominal argument language," etc. Once again, though, it would seem that each of these claims themselves is subject to the Quinean doubts, and therefore the whole broader picture can be challenged. This is not the place to do that, however, because in any case, Bach does not take any "Whorfian flying leap" from Jelinek's claim. Rather, he quite sensibly says that any quantificational claim we can make in English can be equivalently expressed in Samish – and conversely, the difference between languages is not in their expressive power, but in the *ways* in which things are expressed, especially whether things are expressed lexically.

This internal/external semantics distinction is a crucial distinction, and many of the debates that currently rage in semantics could benefit from the realization that the participants just are not talking about the same aspect of semantics: one side asserts something of internal semantics while the other denies it of external semantics. After discussing the distinction and its usefulness, I will consider a topic which might at first seem rather remote from the distinction, but which can benefit from a clearer appreciation of the internal/external semantics distinction.

This topic concerns the issue of *semantic compositionality* – the claim that the meaning of a syntactically complex whole is a function of the meanings of its parts together with the manner in which these parts are combined. Bach (this volume) says, "there is a very firm semantic link between aspects of the external or structural semantics of expressions and the syntactic categories of natural languages." One way of taking this (but perhaps not the only way) is as a claim that external semantics obeys the principle of semantic compositionality. And if this is what Bach means, then because he is contrasting internal and external semantics here, it is also natural to think of him as denying that internal semantics obeys the compositionality principle.

Another topic which I would very much like to discuss, but for which I have no time, concerns "covert categories." About such things, Bach says:

> Some of the most interesting parts of natural language semantics are those that appear "below" the level of the big categories like verbs, nouns, adjectives and so on, in the various kinds of subcategories that show up in various ways, more or less covert, more or less grammaticized in one language or another. I am thinking here of distinctions like those between mass and count nouns.... The basic conceptual matrix for these and other kinds of distinctions is quite universal, and working out the "logic" of such distinctions in various languages may be the place where linguistics can contribute most to the goal of understanding cognition. By way of illustration, let me just take one set of distinctions to stand in for many.

The "one set of distinctions" that Bach considers is that called "unaccusativity phenomena." Perhaps on a different occasion I will consider what the study of mass and count nouns might teach us about cognition (for a start, see Pelletier 1991).

2. The Internal/External Semantics Distinction
and Its Usefulness

(A) The professional linguist/semanticist who comes from a philosophical logic background or who, some years ago, was trained in linguistics at U. Mass., Stanford-Santa Cruz, U.C.L.A., U. Texas or one of their numerous outposts, will typically identify "real semantics" with external semantics. Ask such a person what is the meaning or semantics of, say, 'tadpole' or 'swim', and we will receive an answer like this: it is a function on possible worlds/information states which, in each possible world/ information state, picks out the set of objects which are tadpoles (or: which swim) in that possible world/information state. An outsider might ask what the point of such a semantics is. Is it not circular? Uninformative? Non-instructive? Non-learnable? And furthermore does it not make such "obviously wrong" claims as: an N^0 like 'tadpole' is just as similar in meaning to a V^0 like 'swim' as it is to an N^0 like 'building'. (According to external semantics all three mean some function on possible worlds which picks out some set in each world. The set of tadpoles is "just as similar" to the set of swimmers as it is to the set of buildings.)

But if we make an internal/external semantics distinction, we can readily admit that we have here two different conceptions of semantics. And perhaps both are worth study; but it would be wrong to expect external semantics to do the job of internal semantics.

(B) The professional linguist/semanticist who comes from a philosophy of mind or a psychology background or who was trained in linguistics at U.C.-Berkeley, U.C.-San Diego, Brandeis or one of their numerous outposts, will typically identify "real semantics" with some psychological manifestation – either an individual's psychological representation or with some socially generated and publicly accepted representation. Ask such a person what the meaning of 'tadpole' is and you might get some picture or prototype or stereotype, possibly with collateral information concerning parentage, size, slimness, edibility and future development.[2] Ask about 'swim' and you will perhaps get a picture of some activity prototypically involving water, locomotion and methods of breathing. An outsider might ask what the point of such a semantics is. What do such pictures have to do with reality?" After all, a picture or prototype (or any representation, more generally) is just an item in some language – a pictorial or representation language. We still require some "hook-up" between this pictorial or representation language and the world. As Lewis put it, "we still don't know the *first* thing about semantics – viz., under what conditions is a sentence true?" (1972, p. 170).

Once again, though, it seems to me that the internal/external semantics distinction can be pressed into service. Prototypes (whether generated by an individual or by society) and representations generally are interesting and worthy of study. Such internal semantics, however, should not be confused with external semantics.

(C) When I read modern "Sapirians" (e.g., Lakoff 1987 and other cognitive grammarians), I sometimes find myself believing that languages could divide the world up in all kinds of different ways. Languages need not have the categories 'mammal' or 'fish'. They might even have a single lexical item for the items we put into the three separate categories 'women', 'fire', and 'dangerous objects'. Languages perhaps need not have the concept of 'enduring physical object' (which can be continuously referred to, despite its having undergone vast changes). They might instead have lexically instantiated notions of 'manifestations-of-rabbithood', or maybe of 'instantaneous stage of x', and (what we call) objects might be describable only by lengthy combinations of these lexically manifested concepts. Perhaps they might only have the concept of 'event' as a lexical primitive, and then (what we call) objects have to somehow be described by circumlocution as such-and-such a portion of an event. Indeed, maybe even the concept or meaning of such a basic notion as time might be different between languages. Perhaps one language views time as 'future in front of us, past behind us', while another views time as 'our being able to see all that has happened, and the unseen future coming at us from behind'.

But then I catch myself and say, like Sapir, that everyone and all cultures express *something* by language. So they all want to indicate a topic/subject and to say something about this topic/subject. "It might be done in an unusual way," I say to myself in such moments, "but any statement of theirs can always be analyzed as a topic/subject and a predicate. So, such quasi-linguistic items are universal across languages and are not bound to individual or cultural psychology."

Once again it seems to me that the external/internal semantics distinction can help here, although exactly how is less than clear.

3. Issues of Compositionality

The Principle of Semantic Compositionality is the principle that the meaning of a complex expression is a function of (and only of) its parts together with the method by which those parts are combined. As stated, the principle is vague or underspecified at a number of points, such as: "what counts as a part," "what is a meaning," "what kind of a function is allowed" and the like. In this very general form, The Principle makes no assumptions about what the parts of a complex expression are, nor does it put any restrictions on what constitutes the function of parts-and-whole. Nor does it make any assumptions about what is meaning, nor does it say how to tell whether two expressions have the same or different meanings. Such vagueness and underspecification, however, have not stopped some people from treating The Principle as obviously true, true almost by definition. Nor has it stopped some others from attacking it both on empirical grounds and on theoretico-methodological grounds.

As an empirical comment on the sociology of linguists and philosophers, let me just point out that those who support The Principle are philosophical logicians and linguists from U. Mass./ Stanford/U. C.-Santa Cruz/U. Texas/etc., whereas those who oppose The Principle are cognitive scientists and linguists from U. C.- Berkeley/U. C.- San Diego/Brandeis/etc. Generally, the supporters trace intellectual heritage through Montague; the opponents call themselves cognitive grammarians. Although there are certainly substantive differences within each of these groups on all sorts of matters (including even issues concerning compositionality), for terminological convenience I will call the two groups 'U. Mass. theorists' and 'Berkeley theorists'.

The existence of the two divergent groups described above suggests to me a "Cognitive Science Compromise": both the supporters and the opponents are right about the Principle of Semantic Compositionality–but they are talking about different notions of semantics. The U. Mass. notion of semantics (i.e., external semantics) *is* compositional. The Berkeley notion of semantics (i.e., internal semantics) is *not* compositional.

Although in general I am a great believer in cognitive science compromises in which everyone can be right, in this case I would rather propose "Pelletier's Middle Road": both U. Mass. and Berkeley theorists are *wrong* about The Principle of Semantic Compositionality. Internal semantics *is* compositional; but external semantics is *not* compositional.

We cannot really discuss here the complex issue of compositionality in any detail or with any care. So, I must just content myself with caricatures and with discussing only the "weakest" ("strongest"?) form of compositionality: that very general characterization given above. Any further restrictions on compositionality, such as "the meanings must be regular across constructions" or "the allowable functions must be systematic" and the like, are not directly under discussion. (It might be noted, however, that if the general form of compositionality is false, as I argue it is for external semantics, then it must also be incorrect to affirm any theory of general compositionality which is also regular and systematic.)

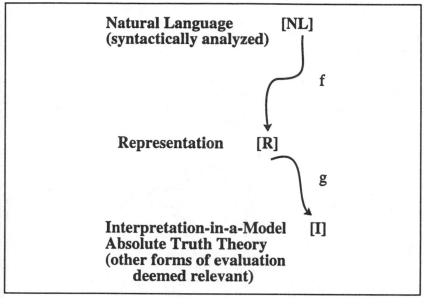

Figure 1: A picture familiar from the philosophy of language and logic, and from many linguistic theories.

Figure 1 gives a generic description of the portion of linguistic theory that I wish to examine. It is a picture familiar from philosophy of language and logic, and from many different linguistic theories. One is given a syntactically analyzed natural language, and correlates elements of it (typically sentences) with some representation. And then one further "interprets" this representation with respect to a model or "the world," or whatever is deemed relevant.

The (stereotypical) proponents of the U. Mass. theory are *Eliminativists* (see Figure 2). The 'f •g' indicates some way of combining the output of f to form an input to g. Since the (stereotyped) eliminativists believe f and g to be functions, they tend to believe that '•' designates function composition.

And the (stereotyped) proponents of the Berkeley theory are *Straight Representationalists*, where there simply is no level of interpretation beyond the level of representation. (See Figure 3.)

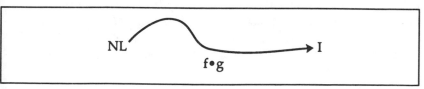

Figure 2: Eliminativism as a way to remove the level of representation.

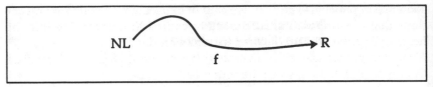

Figure 3: Straight representation as a way to remove the level of interpretation.

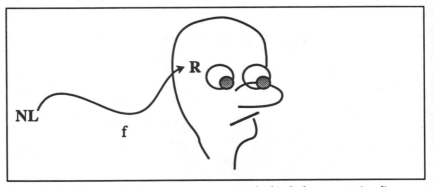

Figure 4: Straight mental representation as a particular kind of representationalism.

In fact, most Berkeleans are *Straight Mental Representationalists* (although the feature of mentalness will not enter into my further discussion). (See Figure 4.)

The reader will notice that there is no structural difference between eliminativism and straight representationalism (Figures 2 and 3). Both postulate a (syntactically analyzed) natural language and some semantic correlate.

We should note just how implausible it is to add The Principle of Semantic Compositionality to this picture. If compositionality were true, then the relation between NL and the semantics S (either I or R, depending on the theory under discussion) would be a *function*. That is, for each item from NL there would be exactly one[3] counterpart in S. In other words, there would be no ambiguity except for what could be traced to individual lexical items. What might otherwise appear to be ambiguity would be traced to differing items of NL – i.e., "It appears that there is just one item in NL which has these two meanings, but really there are two different sentences of NL here." This is the strategy taken by Montague, for instance, in explaining why it appears that sentence (1) below has two meanings: one in which Kim wants to marry some particular person who happens to be a Dane, and another in which Kim has a condition on who is marriageable – the person must be a Dane.

1.   Kim wants to marry a Dane.

Rather than say that (1) is ambiguous, Montague says that there are in fact two sentences here, distinguished by different syntactic rules being applied at different points in its derivation. (The quantifying-in rules being applied at different times. See Montague 1973, especially p. 255.)

Adoption of compositionality requires the wholesale use of this strategy. There simply can be no ambiguity at all (other than lexical ambiguity) in either eliminativism or direct representationalism, if one adds compositionality. There can never be cases of one and the same syntactic structure, using identical basic parts, but where there are two or more different meanings.[4] But is that not all rather silly? Are not each of the following sentences counter-examples to that position, and are there not a great many more examples?[5] Do not each of sentences (2a) to (2e) have exactly one syntactic analysis, and yet are they not also ambiguous?

2a. Every linguist in the room knows two languages.
2b. John wondered when Alice said she would leave.
2c. When Alice rode a bicycle, she went to school.
2d. The philosophers lifted the piano.
2e. The Canadian family used less water last year than the preceding year.

To maintain the compositionality principle, theorists have resorted to a number of devices which are all more or less unmotivated (except to maintain the principle): Montogovian "quantifying-in" rules, "traces," "gaps, "quantifier raising" rules, distributivity/collectivity features, genericity features and many more.

Eliminativism and direct representationalism, when combined with compositionality,[6] are also incompatible with any form of synonymy – lexical (e.g., 'attorney' and 'lawyer'), phrasal (e.g., 'a circle' and 'a locus of all points on a plane equidistant from a given point'), and sentential (e.g., 'Dentists usually need to hire an attorney' and 'Tooth doctors commonly require the professional services of a lawyer'). The argument for this is a reductio. Assume compositionality to be true, and consider (for example) the cited instance of sentence ambiguity. If 'Dentists usually need to hire an attorney' meant the same as 'Tooth doctors commonly require the professional services of a lawyer', then (3a) below would have to mean the same as (3b) – since they were put together by the same rules from parts that mean the same, and the principle of compositionality says that this is all that comes into play when considering the meaning of the whole.

3a. Kim believes that dentists usually need to hire an attorney.
3b. Kim believes that tooth doctors commonly require the professional services of a lawyer.

But it is quite clear that Kim might believe one of the embedded sentences without believing the other (one can make up all kinds of stories about how this might come about), and thus (3a) might be true while (3b) is false. But from this it would follow that (3a) and (3b) do *not* mean the same thing. Therefore compositionality is incompatible with sentential synonymy. This argument can be extended to phrasal and lexical synonymy. If 'a circle' means the same as 'a locus of all points on a plane equidistant from a given point', then sentences (4a) and (4b) below would mean the same, since they are formed/analyzed by the same rules from parts that mean the same (this is all that is required by the principle of compositionality to guarantee sameness of meaning):

4a. Saying a circle is a circle is the same as saying a circle is a circle.
4b. Saying a circle is a circle is the same as saying a circle is a locus of all points on a plane equidistant from a given point.

But since (4a) and (4b) mean the same (which some might already find objectionable), it follows that (5a) and (5b) must mean the same, since they are formed/analyzed by the same rules from parts that mean the same, which is all that is required by the principle of compositionality to guarantee sameness of meaning:

5a. Kim believes that saying a circle is a circle is the same as saying a circle is a circle.
5b. Kim believes that saying a circle is a circle is the same as saying a circle is a locus of all points on a plane equidistant from a given point.

We know, however, that Kim might believe one and not the other; thus one of (5a) and (5b) can be true while the other is false, and therefore (5a) and (5b) *cannot* mean the same – contradicting the principle of semantic compositionality.

Though obviously the argument can be extended to lexical synonymy, I will not do so here. Instead I ask: can it really be true that there is no synonymy of any sort in natural language? How could language ever be learned if that were true? How could we ever explain person A to person B by "re-phrasing his words"?

We have seen that neither eliminativism nor straight representation-alism can embrace semantic compositionality if they also wish to hold on to the existence of either ambiguity or synonymy. And it is quite clear that no principle so highly theoretical should be allowed to over-turn the manifest facts of language such as the existence of synonymy and ambiguity. But now note this important observation: the sort of se-mantic phenomena we are here considering concern *external semantics* exclusively. All this worry over the existence of a function from syntac-tically analyzed natural language into some semantic representation, and all the worry over ambiguity and synonymy, concerns "what the various classes of syntactic items do in the economy of building up de-notations for complex expressions," to use Bach's characterization (this volume) of external semantics. These phenomena do not at all concern themselves with "the kinds of things that are included in the denota-tions of syntactic items" (to use his characterization of internal seman-tics). From this I conclude that *external semantics does not obey the principle of semantic compositionality.* So, although there might be "a very firm link between aspects of the external or structural semantics of ex-pressions and the syntactic categories of natural languages" (as Bach characterizes the main argument of his paper), this very firm link is *not* semantic compositionality, nor is it anything which would imply se-mantic compositionality (e.g., the "rule-to-rule hypothesis").

Though my discussion of compositionality's interplay with external semantics has been brief, I will now discuss even more briefly and still less thoroughly compositionality's interplay with internal semantics. Recall that the Berkelean conception of a semantic value is a prototype or stereotype or picture (etc.), and that this may be either "individual" or "social." This is the *internal* semantic value, to use Bach's terminolo-gy. Let us consider prototype formation as a particular version of this sort of theory. Such a semantic item is either atomic or is composed of (mental? prototypical?) parts. In the latter case, the parts of the com-pound prototype and how these parts are assembled simply define the prototype. How could this sort of construction (or analysis) of a whole from its very own parts *fail* to be compositional?

Furthermore, if we were to assume that somehow the compound pro-totypes might fail to be some function of their parts and of the manner in which these parts are put together, then we will find ourselves unable to account for meaning-learning. How could we, as meaning-learners, ever come to understand complex prototype-meanings unless we did so on the basis of having already understood the simpler parts of the prototype and the ways in which these parts are put together to form the larger prototype? (Well, one way would be for us just to learn the new prototype as an unanalyzed whole. But that would be to treat the larger prototype as not really being built up from its parts – as being itself an atomic prototype. And surely not all our meanings can be atomic. Surely there are too many meanings to learn, for us to do this with all of them. Even if there is not literally an infinite number of them that must be learned, there are still too many meanings for each to be learned as atomic. In any case, introspection shows that many of our mental/social meanings *are* functionally composed from simpler parts.) In addition to requiring compositionality in order to learn the internal semantics of complex items, we require compositionality to understand the internal semantics of novel combinations of natural language. Once again, even if there is not literally an infinite number of things that need to be understood, there are still too many of these novel combinations of the simpler prototypes for us to claim that they can all be understood as atomic concepts. Although this novelty argument is commonly used to argue for compositionality of external semantics (e.g., by Davidson and his followers), its true force comes more to the fore when we consider internal rather than external semantics.

So in light of the foregoing, what would a prototype which violates compositionality look like, according to the Berkeleans? Langacker (1987) gives an example of such a prototype (and refers to it throughout as a proof of the falsity of compositionality):

> Suppose that at a particularly popular American football game, say a Superbowl, the organizers staged a half-time extravaganza which included a young woman draped in an American flag climbing a flagpole and then swinging down to the tune of some particularly patriotic music. At the end of this mesmerizing spectacle, the announcer says "Ladies and gentlemen, let's hear it for our patriotic pole-climber!!" So much in keeping with the psyche of the country is this show that *all* the football games came to have such a show at half-time, and this event (and the woman who participates) became known as 'the patriotic pole-climb(er)'.[7]

The reason that Langacker perceives this to be a violation of compositionality is that (after the custom has been established) he sees something in the (mental? social?) prototype of 'patriotic pole-climber' which is not in the (mental? social?) prototypes of the three individual terms – 'patriotic', 'pole' and 'climber' – and also not in the way these were combined (mentally? socially?).[8] How does Langacker know this? Well, he has seen the prototype of 'patriotic' (etc.) in other circumstances, and there is something in the present new circumstance which does not occur in any of the old ones. And he has seen the effect of this sort of mental combination of prototypes before (the kind used here to put together the three simpler prototypes to form the complex), and he does not see how that effect could possibly generate the present "something new" in the complex.

But when Langacker's reasoning is put like this, we see that it has no force at all against the proponent of compositionality. The compositionalist merely asserts that, in the given example, the prototypes for 'patriotic', etc., do in fact combine so as to yield precisely the sort of prototype required. (The compositionalist might remind Langacker that part of the "stuff" that goes into forming this prototype has to do with the phrase's origin in the half-time entertainment of a football game. And it may be this part which is being ignored by Langacker when he says that he finds something in the complex prototype which he cannot find in any of the parts.) Of course compositionalists have no *argument* for this position--they merely assert that it is possible, and that nothing Langacker has said has shown otherwise. The patriotic pole-climber just is not the knock-down example of non-compositionality that Langacker pretends it is.

The prototype-learning argument and the prototype-understanding argument convince me that *internal semantics does obey the principle of semantic compositionality*. And there has been no evidence offered to support the claim that complex mental or social meanings are not compositional.

4. A Concluding Remark

This concludes my brief remarks on The Principle of Semantic Compositionality that have been occasioned by Bach's discussion of the distinction between internal and external semantics. As I said at the outset, his paper raises many other topics that are also worthy of discussion (I hope to follow up on some of them at another time). Bach's paper has the features of all his earlier ones: it is chock-full of extremely interesting, informative and provocative remarks.

Notes

1 The implicit claim that all quantification can be reduced to one type might also raise eyebrows. Is there not a difference between the two types of quantifiers even in the simple example cited? Does not 'Bears always eat fish' imply that bears are always eating? But does not 'All bears eat fish' instead say that each bear has the habit/ability/propensity to eat fish? And if these two senses can be distinguished in Samish (as surely they can be), then is there not in fact a nominal-quantifier-versus-adverbial-quantifier distinction

available in Samish? So what would it mean to say that Samish "has no noun phrase quantification at all" (as Bach puts it)?

2   Pictures, prototypes and stereotypes are not the only sorts of representations such theorists might find acceptable. I use them simply as easy-to-state examples, and intend my discussion to generalize to other possible representations.

3   We assume here that the function is *total* – that each item in NL in fact does have some correlate in S. The theory could still obey the compositionality principle without this assumption; the function relating NL and S might be *partial*. In this case some members of NL would not have a meaning, but those that did have a meaning would have exactly one counterpart in S.

4   Not like 'Teaching students can provide a learning experience', which has two obviously distinct syntactic analyses. I mean instead that there cannot be cases where the identical syntactic analysis yields two different meanings.

5   For those having difficulty seeing the ambiguities: (a) is ambiguous between each linguist's knowing some two or other languages, versus all linguists knowing the same two; (b) is ambiguous between John's wondering about the time of Alice's departure, versus wondering when Alice said it; (c) is ambiguous between 'In the past, on those days that Alice rode a bicycle she rode it to school', versus 'In that period of time in the past when Alice was a bicycle-rider, during that period she also attended school'; (d) is ambiguous between each of the philosophers lifting the piano, versus their doing it all together; and (e) is ambiguous between the total water used by all Canadian families this year being less than last year, versus the water used by the average Canadian family this year being less than that used by the average Canadian family last year. (With regard to [2e], compare the sentence 'The American consumer purchased 8,000 BMWs last year', where it is clearly that the sum total of all American consumer purchases included 8,000 BMWs, with 'The American consumer purchased 1.9 video cassettes last year', where it is clear that the average American consumer purchased 1.9 video cassettes.)

6   Plus a few other obviously true assumptions. I will assume: (a) that if sentence X is true and sentence Y is false, then X and Y cannot have the same meaning; (b) that all sentences of the form 'Kim believes that S' (where 'S' is a sentence) are formed/analyzed by the same syntactic rule(s) from 'Kim', 'believes' and 'that', plus whatever went into the formation/analysis of S; (c) that for any two syntactically distinct sentences, it is possible to imagine a person who believes one of them but disbelieves the other.

7   The passage cited is a shortened paraphrase of Langacker's original.

8   Something about social practices, perhaps. Or something about the esteem in which such people are held. And perhaps something about its effect on the future history of American football.

References

Bach, Emmon (this volume). The Semantics of Syntactic Categories: A Cross-Linguistic Perspective

Heim, Irene (1982). The Semantics of Definite and Indefinite Noun Phrases. Ph.D. dissertation, Amherst, MA: University of Massachusetts

Jelinek, Eloise (1988). Quantification without Nouns in Salish. Unpublished paper presented at the Symposium on Cross-Linguistic Quantification, Linguistics Society of America, New Orleans,1988

Lakoff, George (1987). *Women, Fire, and Dangerous Objects* (Chicago: University of Chicago Press)

Langacker, Ronald (1987). *Foundations of Cognitive Grammar*, Vol. 1: *Theoretical Prerequisites* (Stanford, CA: Stanford University Press)

Lewis, David (1972). General semantics. In D. Davidson and G. Harman, *Semantics of Natural Language* (Dordrecht: Reidel)

— (1975). Adverbs of quantification. In E. Keenan, *Formal Semantics of Natural Language* (Cambridge: Cambridge University Press)

Montague, Richard (1973). The proper treatment of quantification in English. Reprinted in R. Thomason (ed.), *Formal Philosophy* (New Haven, CT: Yale University Press)

Pelletier, Francis Jeffry (1991). Mass terms. In B. Smith (ed.), *Handbook of Metaphysics and Ontology* (Munich: Philosophia Press)

13

Husserl's Notion of Intentionality

Dagfinn Føllesdal

Intentionality is the central theme of phenomenology, its *Generalthema*, Husserl tells us in *Ideas* (§ 84). All of phenomenology can be regarded as an unfolding of the idea of intentionality.

It is well known that Husserl's interest in intentionality was inspired by his teacher, Franz Brentano. However, there are many differences between Husserl's treatment of this notion and that of Brentano. In this paper I will first discuss these differences and then consider further features of Husserl's notion of intentionality that go beyond the issues considered by Brentano.

Intentionality as Directedness

In *Ideas*, Husserl retains the following basic idea of Brentano: we understand by intentionality the peculiarity of experiences to be "consciousness *of* something".[1] Husserl's formulation comes close to Brentano's oft-quoted passage from *Psychology from an Empirical Point of View*: "Every mental phenomenon is characterized by what the scholastics in the Middle Ages called the intentional (and also mental) inexistence of an object, and what we could also call, although in not entirely unambiguous terms, the reference to a content, a direction upon an object...".[2]

However, already at this starting-point there is an important difference between Brentano and Husserl. While Brentano says straightforwardly that for every act there is an object towards which it is directed, Husserl focusses on the "of"-ness of the act. There are two reasons for this difference. First, Husserl wants to get around the difficulties connected with acts that lack an object. Second, Husserl aims at throwing light on what it means for an act to be "of" or "about" something. I will begin by discussing these two differences.

Acts that Lack an Object

First, I will discuss acts that lack an object. Brentano's thesis may seem unproblematic in the examples Brentano considered: just as when we love there is somebody or something that we love, so there is something that we sense when we sense, something we think of when we think, and so on. However, what is the object of our consciousness when we hallucinate, or when we think of a centaur?

Brentano insisted that even in such cases our mental activity, our sensing or thinking, is directed towards some object. The directedness has nothing to do with the reality of the object, Brentano held. The object is contained in our mental activity, "intentionally" contained in it. And Brentano defined mental phenomena as "phenomena which contain an object intentionally."[3]

Not all of Brentano's students found this lucid or satisfactory, and the problem continued to disturb both them and Brentano. Brentano struggled with it through the rest of his life, and suggested, among other things, a translation theory, giving Leibniz credit for the idea: when we describe an act of hallucination, or of thinking of a centaur, we are only apparently referring to an object. The apparent reference to an object can be translated away in such a way that in the full, unabbreviated description of the act there is no reference to any problematic object. There are two weaknesses of Brentano's proposal. First, unlike Russell later, Brentano does not specify in detail how the translation is to be carried out. Secondly, if such a translation can be carried out in the case of hallucinations, etc., then why not carry it out everywhere, also in cases of normal perception? What then happens to the doctrine of intentionality as directedness upon an object?

One of Brentano's students, Meinong, suggested a simple way out. In his *Gegenstandstheorie*, [4] Meinong maintained that there are two kinds of objects: those that exist and those that do not exist. Hallucinations, like normal perception, are directed towards objects, but these objects do not exist. Brentano was not happy with this proposal. He objected that, like Kant, he could not make sense of existence as a property that some objects have and others lack.

Husserl's solution was, as we noted, to emphasize the 'of'. Consciousness is always consciousness *of* something. Or better, consciousness is always *as if of* an object. What matters is not whether or not there is an object, but what the features are of consciousness that makes it always be as if of an object. These three words, 'as if of', are the key to Husserl's notion of intentionality. To account for the directedness of consciousness by saying only that it is directed towards an object, and letting it remain with that, is to leave us in the dark with regard to what that directedness is. This leads us to the second reason why Husserl diverged from Brentano. Husserl wanted to throw light on just this issue: what does the directedness of consciousness consist in? He made it a theme for a new discipline. This discipline is phenomenology.

What is Directedness?

Husserl uses the label 'noema' for those features of consciousness that make it directed. I shall not discuss the notion of noema now. I did that at the American Philosophical Association Western Division meeting here in Chicago 23 years ago. Instead I will now go into aspects of Husserl's theory of intentionality that I have not earlier discussed in writing. To grasp what the directedness of consciousness consists in, to understand better the word 'of' in Brentano's *Psychology from an Empirical Point of View*, which was emphasized by Husserl, let us note that for Husserl, intentionality does not simply consist in consciousness directing itself towards objects that are already there. Intentionality for Husserl means that consciousness in a certain way "brings about" the existence of objects. Consciousness "constitutes" objects, Husserl said, borrowing a word from the German idealists, but using it in a different sense. I put the phrase 'bringing about' in quotation marks to indicate that Husserl does not mean that we create or cause the world and its objects. 'Intentionality' means merely that the various components of our consciousness are interconnected in such a way that we have an experience as of one object. To quote Husserl: "the object is 'constituted'– 'whether or not it is actual' – in certain concatenations of consciousness which in themselves bear a discernible unity in so far as they, by virtue of their essence, carry with themselves the consciousness of an identical X."[5]

Here and in many other places, Husserl's use of the reflexive form 'an object constitutes itself' reflects his view that he did not regard the object as being produced by consciousness. Husserl considered phenomenology as the first strictly scientific version of transcendental idealism, but he also held that phenomenology transcends the traditional idealism-realism distinction, and in 1934 he wrote in a letter to Abbé Baudin: "No ordinary 'realist' has ever been as realistic and concrete as I, the phenomenological 'idealist' (a word which by the way I no longer use)."[6] In the Preface to the first English edition (1931) of *Ideas*, Husserl stated:

Phenomenological idealism does not deny the factual [*wirklich*] existence of the real [*real*] world (and in the first instance nature) as if it deemed it an illusion.... Its only task and accomplishment is to clarify the sense [*Sinn*] of this world, just that sense in which we all regard it as really existing and as really valid. That the world exists...is quite indubitable. Another matter is to understand this indubitability which is the basis for life and science and clarify the basis for its claim.[7]

An Example

However, let us now look at an example to see more clearly what Husserl is after, Jastrow and Wittgenstein's duck/rabbit picture. Actually, in order to come closer to Husserl, we should modify the example and consider not a picture but a silhouette of the real animal against the sky.

When we see such a silhouette against the sky, we may see a duck or a rabbit. What reaches our eyes is the same in both cases, so the difference must be something coming from us. We structure what we see, and we can do so in different ways. The impulses that reach us from the outside are insufficient to uniquely determine which object we experience; something more gets added.

The Noema, Intentionality

This something more that gets added, this structure that makes up the directedness of consciousness, Husserl called the noema. Our consciousness structures what we experience. How it structures it depends on our previous experiences, the whole setting of our present experience and a number of other factors. If we had grown up surrounded by ducks, but had never even heard of rabbits, we would have been more likely to see a duck than a rabbit when confronted with the above silhouette; the idea of a rabbit would probably not even have occurred to us. According to Husserl, in principle our experience in a given situation can always be structured in different ways: what reaches our senses is never sufficient to uniquely determine what we experience. Only in a few rare cases, such as in the duck/rabbit example, can we go back and forth at will between different ways of structuring our experience. Usually we are not even aware of any structuring going on – objects are simply experienced by us as having a structure.

The structuring always takes place in such a way that the many different features of the object are experienced as connected with one another, as features of one and the same object. When, for example, we see a rabbit, we do not merely see a collection of coloured patches, various shades of brown spread out over our field of vision. (Incidentally, even seeing coloured patches involves intentionality: a patch is also a kind of object, but a different kind of object from a rabbit.) We see a rabbit, with a determinate shape and a determinate colour, with the ability to eat, jump, etc. It has a side that is turned toward us and one that is turned away from us. We do not see the other side from where we are, but we see something which has an other side. It is this peculiarity of our consciousness that Husserl labels *intentionality*, or directedness. That seeing is intentional, or object-directed, means just this: the near side of the object we have in front of us is regarded as a side of a thing, and the thing we see has other sides and features that are co-intended, in the sense that the thing is regarded as more than just this one side. The noema is the comprehensive system of determinations that gives unity to this manifold of features, and makes them aspects of one and the same object.

Here, as on many other points, there are striking similarities between what Husserl calls 'intentionality' and Quine 'indeterminacy'. Husserl's notion of constitution of objects corresponds to Quine's notion of reification, particularly what Quine calls 'full reification', as opposed to 'perceptual reification'. I quote Quine, from a manuscript that will be out later this year:

> I reserve 'full reification' and 'full reference' for the sophisticated stage where the identity of a body from one time to another can be queried and affirmed or conjectured or denied independently of exact resemblance. Such identification depends on our elaborate theory of space, time, and unobserved trajectories of bodies between observations. Prior recognition of a recurrent body – a ball, or Mama, or Fido – is on a par with our recognition of any qualitative recurrence: warmth, thunder, a cool breeze. So long as no sense is made of the distinction between its being the same ball and its being another like it, the reification of the ball is perceptual rather than full. A dog's recognition of a particular person is still only perceptual, insofar as it depends on smell.[8]

At this point it is important to note that the various sides, appearances or perspectives of the object are constituted together with the object. There are no sides and perspectives floating around before we start perceiving, which are then synthesized into objects when intentionality sets in. There are no objects of any kind, whether they be physical objects, sides of objects, appearances of objects or perspectives of objects, without intentionality. And intentionality does not work in steps. We do not start by constituting six sides and then synthesize these into a die; we constitute the die and the six sides of it in one step.

As we have noted, the word 'object' must be taken in a very broad sense. It comprises not only physical things, but also animals, persons, events, actions and processes, as well as sides, aspects and appearances of such entities. We should also note that when we experience a person, we do not experience a physical object, a body, and then infer that a person is there. We experience a full-fledged person; we encounter somebody who structures the world, experiences it from his or her own perspective. Our noema is a noema of a person: no inference is involved. Seeing persons is no more mysterious than seeing physical objects: no inference is involved in either case. When we see a physical object we do not see sense data or the like and then infer that there is a physical object there; our noema is the noema of a physical object. Similarly, when we see an action, what we see is a full-fledged action, not a bodily movement from which we infer that there is an action.

Filling

In the case of an act of perception, its noema can also be characterized as a very complex set of expectations or anticipations concerning what kind of experiences we will have when we move around the object and perceive it, using our various senses. We anticipate different further experiences when we see a duck and when we see a rabbit. In the first case we anticipate, for example, that we will feel feathers when we touch the object; in the latter case we expect to find fur. When we get the experiences we anticipate, the corresponding component of the noema is said to be *filled*. In all perception there will be some filling: the components of the noema that correspond to what presently "meets the eye" are filled – similarly for the other senses.

Such anticipation and filling distinguish perception from other modes of consciousness, for example, imagination or remembering. If we merely imagine things, our noema can be of anything whatsoever, an elephant or a locomotive standing here beside me. In perception, however, my sensory experiences are involved; the noema has to fit in with my sensory experiences. This eliminates a number of noemata which I could have had if I were just imagining. In my present situation I cannot have a noema corresponding to the perception of an elephant. This does not reduce the number of perceptual noemata I can have just now to one, for example, of you sitting there in front of me.

It is a central point in Husserl's phenomenology that I can have a variety of different perceptual noemata that are compatible with the present impingements upon my sensory surfaces. In the duck/rabbit case this was obvious, we could go back and forth at will between having the noema of a duck and having the noema of a rabbit. In most cases, however, we are not aware of this possibility. Only when something untoward happens, when I encounter "recalcitrant" experience that does not fit in with the anticipations in my noema, that I start seeing a different object from the one I thought I saw earlier. My noema "explodes," to use Husserl's phrase, and I come to have a noema quite different from the previous one, with new anticipations. This is always possible, says Husserl. Perception always involves anticipations that go beyond what presently "meets the eye," and there is always a risk that we may go wrong, regardless of how confident and certain we might feel. Misperception is always possible.

The World and the Past

We constitute not only the different properties of things, but also the re-lation of the thing to other objects. If, for example, I see a tree, the tree is conceived of as something which is in front of me, as perhaps situated among other trees, as seen by other people than myself, etc. It is also conceived of as something which has a history: it was there before I saw it, it will remain after I have left. Perhaps it will eventually be cut and transported to some other place. However, like all material things, it does not simply disappear from the world.

In this way, my consciousness of the tree is also a consciousness of the world in the space and time in which the tree is located. My conscious-ness constitutes the tree, but at the same time it constitutes the world in which the tree and I are living. If my further experience makes me give up the belief that I have a tree ahead of me because, for example, I do not find a tree-like far side or because some of my other expectations prove false, this affects not only my conception of what there is, but also my conception of what has been and what will be. Thus in this case, not just the present but also the past and the future are reconstituted by me. To illustrate how changes in my present perception lead me to reconsti-tute not just the present, but also the past, Husserl uses an example of a ball which I initially take to be red all over and spherical. As it turns, I discover that it is green on the other side and has a dent:

> the sense of the perception is not only changed in the momentary new stretch
> of perception; the noematic modification streams back in the form of a retro-
> active cancellation in the retentional sphere and modifies the production of
> sense stemming from earlier phases of the perception. The earlier appercep-
> tion, which was attuned to the harmonious development of the "red and uni-
> formly round," is implicitly "reinterpreted" to "green on one side and
> dented."[9]

Values, Practical Function

So far I have mentioned only the factual properties of things. However, things also have *value* properties, and these properties are constituted in a corresponding manner, Husserl says. The world within which we live is experienced as a world in which certain things and actions have a positive value, others a negative. Our norms and values, too, are sub-ject to change. Changes in our views on matters of fact are often accom-panied by changes in our evaluations.

Husserl emphasizes that our perspectives and anticipations are *not* predominantly factual. We are not living a purely theoretical life. According to Husserl, we encounter the world around us primarily "in the attitude of the natural pursuit of life," as "living functioning subjects involved in the circle of other functioning subjects."[10] Husserl says this in a manuscript from 1917, but he has similar ideas about the practical both earlier and later. Thus in the *Ideas* (1913) he says: "this world is there for me not only as a world of mere things, but also with the same immediacy as a world of values, a world of goods, a practical world."[11]

Just as Husserl never held that we first perceive sense-data, or perspectives or appearances, which are then synthesized into physical objects, or that we first perceive bodies and bodily movements then infer that there are persons and actions, so it would be a grave misunderstanding of Husserl to attribute to him the view that we first perceive objects that have merely physical properties, and then assign to them a value or a practical function. Things are directly experienced by us as having the features – functional and evaluational as well as factual – that are of concern for us in our natural pursuit of life.

Horizon

When we are experiencing an object, our consciousness is focussed on this object, the rest of the world and its various objects being there in the background as things we "believe in" but not the current focus of our attention. The same holds for most of the innumerable features of the object itself. All these further features of the object, together with the world in which it is set, make up what Husserl calls the *horizon* of that experience. The various features of the object, which are co-intended, or also-meant, but not at the focus of our attention, Husserl calls the *inner horizon*, while the realm of other objects and the world to which they all belong, he calls the *outer horizon:*

> Thus every experience of a particular thing has its *internal horizon*, and by "horizon" is meant here the *induction* which belongs essentially to every experience and is inseparable from it, being in the experience itself. The term "induction" is useful because it suggests [*vordeutet*] (itself an "induction") induction in the ordinary sense of a mode of inference and also because it implies that the latter, for its elucidation to be completely intelligible, must refer back to the original, basic anticipation....
>
> However, this aiming-beyond [*Hinausmeinen*] is not only the anticipation of determinations which, insofar as they pertain to this object of experience, are now expected; in another respect it is also an aiming-beyond the thing itself... to other objects of which we are aware at the same time, although at first they are merely in the background. This means that everything given in experience has not only an internal horizon but also an infinite, open, *external horizon of*

objects cogiven.... These are objects toward which I am not now actually turned but toward which I can turn at any time. ...all real things which at any given time are anticipated together or cogiven only in the background as an external horizon are known as real objects (or properties, relations, etc.) *from* the world, are known as existing within the one spatiotemporal horizon.[12]

Let us take a simple example of an item belonging to this outer horizon. If I had asked you, as you were entering this room, what your expectations were, you might mention something about friends you expected to meet, a lecture you expected to hear, and so on. It is highly unlikely that you would mention that you expected there to be a floor in the room. Yet, because I saw you confidently stepping in, I have every reason to believe that you expected that there would be a floor here. You did not think about it, your attention was directed to other things, but you had a disposition that you acted on. Also, if I had asked you whether you expected there to be a floor in the room, you might have wondered why I asked such a trivial question, but you would probably have answered yes.

Expectations and beliefs are dispositional notions. We count as beliefs not only thoughts that we are actively entertaining, but also those that we rarely think about, for example, that 2+2=4. We do have a problem when we try to delimit exactly what beliefs we have. The method of questioning is not reliable. On the one side, it gives too much: remember how in the *Menon* a skilled questioner uncovers that the slave boy has the most unexpected geometrical beliefs. Plato took this as evidence for his theory of *anamnesis*. On the other, it yields too little. As Freud and others have taught us, we often sincerely deny that we have beliefs that seem all too apparently to underlie our actions.

The most reliable criterion, one which we often fall back on, is to assume that people have those beliefs that best explain their actions, including their verbal activities. However, then a further problem is that the states we appeal to in order to explain people's actions are not exclusively cognitive states. Also various physical states are needed, and skills of various kinds that are often hard to classify as mental. Thus while our arithmetical skills are presumably mental, our skills in swimming or walking can hardly be classified as mental. Then we have tricky intermediate cases, such as one's keeping a standard distance to partners in a conversation, where the standard may vary from culture to culture. Is keeping this distance a matter of a tacit belief that it is the proper distance? Or is it a matter of a bodily skill which is gradually acquired as one grows up in this culture? And what about the way we sign our name?[13] Obviously, cognitive activities are involved in the process that brought us to sign it the way we do – we had to learn the alphabet, we had to learn our name, and so on. But also, in our semi-automatic way of signing it, bodily skills are involved to a great extent. Various personality traits play a role, as do certain general traits of our culture.

Opinions concerning examples such as these may vary. One of our problems is that we have no clear-cut way to settle such issues, lacking a precise definition of what is to count as mental, what as physical. However, there is obviously an interplay here, both in the process that leads to the skill and in the skill itself, and any satisfactory theory of intentionality must heed such an interplay. The noema may still be defined as a structure, but the anticipations that are related through this structure are not merely the anticipations involved in seeing, hearing and the like, but also the anticipations involved in kinesthesis and bodily movement, where when something "goes wrong" we are aware of it. We are familiar with this experience of "going wrong" from cases of misperception: we cannot always tell exactly what went wrong, but we are aware that something went wrong.

As I have mentioned, Husserl states already in *Ideas* that we encounter the world "not only as a world of mere things, but also with the same immediacy as a world of values, a world of goods, a practical world."[14] In later manuscripts, particularly from 1917 on, he focussed more and more on the role of the practical and the body in our constitution of the world. We discussed earlier one side of this, namely that we experience objects as having practical or functional properties, and not just factual ones. Husserl is very clear and explicit that they have. I am now concerned with a different and more difficult issue, namely in what way the various features of the world – be they factual, valuational and practical – are reflected in the noema. Here Husserl is less explicit and more tentative.

In an earlier paper,[15] I tried to show that Husserl would consider our anticipations as not merely beliefs – about factual properties, value properties and functional features – but also as bodily settings, which are involved in kinesthesis and also play an important role in perception and in the movements of our body. In numerous passages, some of which I quoted in that paper, Husserl talks about practical anticipations and the role of kinesthesis in perception and bodily activity.

Intersubjectivity

Husserl emphasizes, early and late, that the world we intend and thereby constitute, is not our own private world, but an intersubjective world common to and accessible to all of us. Thus in the *Ideas* he writes:

"I continually find at hand as something confronting me a spatiotemporal reality [*Wirklichkeit*] to which I belong like all other human beings
who are to be found in it and who are related to it as I am."[16] Husserl
stresses the shared, intersubjective nature of the world particularly in §
29 of *Ideas*, which he entitles "The 'Other' Ego-subjects and the Intersubjective Natural Surrounding World." There he says: "I take their surrounding world and mine Objectively as one and the same world of
which we are conscious, only in different ways [*Weise*].... For all that,
we come to an understanding with our fellow human beings and together with them posit an Objective spatiotemporal reality...."[17]

In the later works one finds similar ideas, particularly in the many
texts that have been collected by Iso Kern in the three volumes of the
Husserliana devoted to intersubjectivity, but also in many other works,
for example, in the *Crisis:* "Thus in general the world exists not only for
isolated men but for the community of men; and this is due to the fact
that even what is straightforwardly perceptual is communal.[18] Husserl
discusses in great detail empathy and the many other varieties of intersubjective adaptation that enable us to intend a common, intersubjective world. For these discussions I refer you to the three volumes on
intersubjectivity that I just mentioned.[19]

Existence

The above passages express one further and final feature of Husserl's
notion of intentionality which I have not yet mentioned. It is rarely discussed, in spite of its importance: intentionality does not just involve directedness upon an object, but also a "positing" of the object, to use
Husserl's term – an experience of the object as real and present, as remembered, or as merely imagined, etc. I repeat the pertinent parts of the
above passages: "I continually find at hand as something confronting
me a spatiotemporal reality..."; "we come to an understanding with
our fellow human beings and together with them posit an Objective
spatiotemporal reality...."

The same idea of the reality of the world is repeated with almost the
same words when Husserl discusses the life-world in the *Crisis*, for example in § 37, where he says:

> "the lifeworld, for us who wakingly live in it, is always there, existing in ad-
> vance for us, the 'ground' of all praxis, whether theoretical or extratheoretical.
> The world is pregiven to us, the waking, always somehow practically inter-
> ested subjects, not occasionally but always and necessarily as the universal
> field of all actual and possible praxis, as horizon. To live is always to live-in-
> certainty-of-the-world."[20]

Husserl discusses this *thetic* character of intentionality, and, correspondingly, of the noema, in many of his books and manuscripts. He was particularly concerned with what gives reality-character to the world. Like William James, whom he read already when he made the transition to phenomenology in the mid-1890s, he stressed the importance of the body (and the inflictions upon our body) for our sense of reality. As James put it: "Sensible vividness or pungency is then the vital factor in reality..."[21] Husserl could also have subscribed to James's observation that: "The fons et origo of all reality, whether from the absolute or the practical point of view, is thus subjective, is ourselves."[22]

I will let this passage from James end my paper, since it gets a double meaning in Husserl, and so well expresses the core of Husserl's view on the reality of the world. The subjective, ourselves, is the fons et origo of all reality in two senses, a transcendental and an empirical: we constitute the world as real through our intentionality, and the reality-character we give it is derived from our being not merely transcendental subjects, but empirical subjects with a body immersed in a physical world.

Notes

1 Edmund Husserl, *Ideas*, 188.20, Husserl's emphasis.

2 Franz Bretano, *Psychology from an Empirical Point of View*, Vol. I, Bk. 2, chap. I (Leipzig: Duncker und Humblot, 1874), p. 85, reprinted in *Philosophische Bibliothek* (Hamburg: Felix Meiner, 1955, 1st ed. 1924), p. 124. Here quoted from D.B. Terrell's English translation of this chapter in Roderick M. Chisholm, (ed.), *Realism and the Background of Phenomenology* (Glencoe, IL: Free Press, 1960), 50.

3 Franz Bretano, Editor of *Pholosophische Bibliothek*

4 Meinong, *Gegenstandstheorie*,

5 Edmund Husserl, *Ideen*, § 13S, original edition, 281, Husserliana III,1, 313.16-20. Kersten's translation, 325.

6 Letter quoted in Iso Kern, *Husserl und Kant. Eine Untersuchung über Husserls Verhältnis zu Kant und zum Neukantianismus* Phenomenologica 16. (The Hague: Martinus Nijhoff, 1964), 276, n.

7 Edmund Husserl, Preface to the Gibson's translation of Ideas (London: Allen & Unwin, 1931). Here from the German version in Husserliana V,152.32-153.5, my translation.

8 W.V. O. Quine in "Reactions," comments on papers presented at a conference on Willard Van Orman Quine's Contribution to Philosophy, San Marino, May 21-26, 1990. To be published in the Proceedings of the conference, edited by Umberto Eco and Paolo Leonardi.

Dagfinn Føllesdal

Edmund Husserl, *Erfahrung und Urteil*, § 21a, 96 = 89 of Churchill and Ameriks' English translation, (Evanston, IL: Northwestern University Press, 1973).

10 *Husserliana* IV,375.31-33. The manuscript dates from 1917, but was copied during the first half of the 1920s, and it is possible that the word 'Lebenswelt' came in then.

11 Husserl, *Ideen*, § 27, Husserliana III,1,58.13-19 = Kersten, 53. I have changed his translation slightly.

12 Husserl, *Erfahrung und Urteil*, § 8, 28-29, Churchill and Ameriks, 32-33.

13 This example came up in conversations with David Wellbery.

14 See note above.

15 Dagfinn Føllesdal, "Husserl and Heidegger on the role of actions in the constitution of the world." In E. Saarinen, R. Hilpinen, I. Niiniluoto and M. Provence Hintikka, (eds.), *Essays in Honour of Jaakko Hintikka*. (Dordrecht, Holland: Reidel, 1979), 365-378.

16 Husserl, *Ideen*, § 30, Husserliana III,1,61.15-18 = Kersten's translation, 56-57, slightly modified by me.

17 Husserl, *Ideen*, § 29, Husserliana III,1,60.16-26 = Kersten, pp. 55-56.

18 *Krisis*, § 47, Husserliana VI,166.19-22 = Carr's translation, p.163.

19 Isokern,

20 Husserl, *Krisis*, § 37, Husserliana VI,145.24-32 = Carr's translation, p.142.

21 William James, The Principles of Psychology (New York: Dover, 1950) Vol. 2, chap. XXI, 301.

22 Ibid., 296-97.

14
Referential Structure of Fictional Texts

Marie La Palme Reyes

1. Preliminaries

1.1. *Introduction*

The commonplace observation that motivated this work is that we can understand narrative fictional texts, although to do so we are forced, as in fairy tales and fables, for instance, to allow for a wide variety of possibilities that seem to contradict our system of background beliefs. But if this is so, how can we understand fictional texts? I do not confront this question directly, but remark that certain aspects of our understanding of fiction are quite systematic and, in fact, may be formulated in the systematic way that we call logic or, more precisely, logic of fictional texts. This logic will be partly "unveiled" through an analysis of reference, that is, an analysis of the relation between words and their reference. As we will see, the analysis of this relation will permit us to deal in a new way with the well-known problems of existence, possibility and identity which lie at the heart of the fictional phenomenon.

The concentration on reference to the exclusion of connotation does not imply that I deny connotation a role in the understanding of fictional texts and, more generally, of literary texts. It only means that I will limit my investigation to the realm of reference, and show that this realm is richer and more rewarding than one may have thought.

This paper is more the foundation of a program to be developed than the program itself. There are many aspects that are just hinted at. For instance, what does literature say about the world? I have established a basis that enables one to think about that question in a precise manner. "The moratorium on referential issues has by now become obsolete. Freed from the constraints of the textualist approach the theory of fiction can respond again to the world creating powers of imagination and account for the properties of fictional existence and worlds, their complexity, incompleteness, remoteness, and integration within the general economy of culture." (Pavel 1986, p. 10). Pavel's ambition is mine also, but I am content to make a beginning in this program. Even a beginning will involve us in philosophy, logic and the theory of fiction. First a look at an important predecessor.

1.2. Parsons's Theory of Fiction

Parsons (1980) is interested in the same problems that I deal with, and has carefully developed both a formal system and a semantics that share some features with mine. Here, I stress only those aspects of his theory for which I offer a different approach.

Parsons develops his views in the context of a general theory of non-existent objects. He proceeds by identifying certain objects of fiction with certain non-existent objects. The idea is to view Sherlock Holmes, for instance, as an object that has exactly those properties that are attributed to Sherlock Holmes in Conan Doyle's novels. Some objects that owe their existence entirely to the storyteller such as Sherlock Holmes and Dr. Watson, Parsons calls objects "native" to the story. Objects such as London and Gladstone, Parsons calls "immigrant." (I shall assume, for the sake of argument, that Gladstone meets Sherlock Holmes in one of Conan Doyle's novels. I could have taken, for instance, the example of Sarasate, a real Spanish violinist mentioned in Conan Doyle's "The Read-Headed League.") Notice that in Parsons's theory, a fictional object such as Sherlock Holmes that is native in one novel may be an immigrant in a novel by another author.

Parsons has identified the native objects of fiction with a set of properties. On the other hand, Parsons holds that 'Gladstone' in Conan Doyle's novels refers to the real man who was Prime Minister of England, and that 'London' refers to the real city of that name in England. In the same way Parsons would maintain that 'Sherlock Holmes' refers to the fictional object of Conan Doyle's novels in any work in which he is an immigrant object. For Parsons, then, "fictional object" does not mean "non-existent object," since real objects as well as non-existent ones occur in fiction. This theory has the surprising consequence that, in order to understand the story, we are forced to change the logic of English, as the following considerations show. Assume that in the story, Sherlock Holmes shook hands with Gladstone. The ordinary logic of English tells us that Gladstone also shook hands with Holmes. But shaking hands with a fictitious being is not a property that we can attribute to the real Gladstone. Hence we are forced to conclude that 'A shakes hands with B' may be true while 'B shakes hands with A' may be false.

Parsons develops a formal system and a corresponding semantics to handle the peculiar relations that may hold between real and non-real objects. For real objects, his system is true to the original intuitions about the logic of English. The same holds for non-real objects, as, for instance, when Sherlock Holmes meets Dr. Watson. The problem arises only when there are extensional relations such as 'meeting', 'shaking hands' or 'kissing' between real and non-real objects.

When Parsons speaks of an object having a property "in a story", he means something like an object's having a property "according to" a story. He does not take the story to be a "possible world" as discussed in possible-worlds semantics. A non-real object in a story is highly incomplete, in the sense that whether the object has or fails to have some property is not always decidable. For instance, in Conan Doyle's novels, there is no way to decide whether Holmes had a birthmark on his left leg. There would have been no way to decide whether or not he played on a Stradivarius if one of the stories, "The Adventure of the Cardboard Box," had not told us that he did. In possible-worlds semantics, on the other hand, every object is complete, since the worlds are complete by definition.

1.3. Some Criticisms of Parsons's Position

(i) Since characters such as Sherlock Holmes are identified with sets of properties such as 'is a detective', 'lives on Baker Street', 'owns a Stradivarius', etc., it is impossible to talk counterfactually about them. This leads to trouble. In the story "The Man with the Twisted Lip," the main character, Neville St. Clair, was present when the police forcefully made their way into the room in which he had been seen by his wife shortly before. Identify characters with the properties actually attributed to them in the story and it becomes logically impossible for Neville St. Clair to have the property 'not to have been in the room in question at that moment'. Yet the whole story is incomprehensible if we do not consider this possibility. It was this very possibility that eventually led Sherlock Holmes to solve the mystery of the disappearance of Neville St. Clair. This criticism has also been made by Pavel.

(ii) The properties of Sherlock Holmes change according to the situations of the story: he may be in London at his club, or on a train or in a coach, etc. Hence we need to make precise the sense in which he has those properties that are attributed to him in the novel. Parsons seems to consider only such non-changing properties of Sherlock Holmes as 'is a detective', 'lives on Baker Street', etc. Move to changeable properties and you find an inconsistent set: 'is in London', 'is away from London', 'is on a train', 'is in a coach', 'is sleeping', 'is awake', etc. Not taking situations into account, Parsons has no way to avoid the resulting confusion.

(iii) The change of the logic of relations makes a normal or natural understanding of a literary text impossible. Readers will automatically conclude that Gladstone shakes hands with Holmes when reading that Holmes shakes hands with Gladstone. Such inferences are part of our very understanding of a language, and cannot be laid aside when language is used in literary texts.

(iv) Another problem of a logical nature is the way Parsons's theory handles quantifiers and hence the way it deals with questions of generality. Suppose we read in a novel that a large group of people form a line, each holding a flag, but blue and red flags alternate along the line. Parsons does not have enough fictional objects, corresponding to distinct sets of properties, to interpret such a statement correctly, since his quantifiers range over characters only. Characters are individualized, fictional objects of the story, and since the members of a crowd are not individualized they are not characters. Although Parsons discusses crowds in his book, he never does so in the context of quantifiers, a context that creates real difficulties for his approach, as the example shows.

(v) A last criticism arises from the fact that Parsons talks about "objects" or bare individuals. La Palme Reyes, Macnamara and Reyes (this volume) show that reference to an individual has to be supported by a kind, and that the kind cannot be the universal kind THING. This rules out bare individuals.

2. The Referential Structure of Fictional Texts

The basic thesis to be developed in this paper is that fiction is not different from reality as far as reference is concerned. In my view, the expression 'Sherlock Holmes' is a proper name that refers rigidly, just as 'Richard Nixon' does. We can follow *his* exploits, *his* deductions and *his* whereabouts through countless adventures in Conan Doyle's books.

But this implies that the analysis of reference done by La Palme Reyes, Macnamara and Reyes for reality is applicable also to fictional texts, and therefore that kinds, members of kinds and predicates of kinds are needed to interpret count nouns (CNs) and mass nouns (MNs), proper names (PNs) and predicables (mainly adjectives and verbs). I will, in fact, base myself on the theory developed in La Palme Reyes, Macnamara and Reyes, especially on the thesis laid down in the early part of the paper.

2.1. Kinds and Situations in Literary Texts

A literary text may contain expressions like 'men', as in Conan Doyle's novels (1983); 'troll', as in the Moumine stories of Tove Janssen (1986); or 'Lilliputians', as in *Gulliver's Travels* (1957). All these expressions function as CNs. Furthermore, a text may contain expressions like 'Sherlock Holmes', 'Moumine', or 'Flimnap' which play the role of PNs in their respective stories, as well as expressions of the kind 'the man with the twisted lip', which are definite descriptions. The text also contains expressions such as 'meet' or 'shake hands', which function as predicables. I then postulate the existence of kinds to interpret the basic CNs, particular members of the corresponding kind to interpret PNs and predicates to interpret predicables. I further postulate that predicables are interpreted with the ordinary logic of English. For instance, we know that if the troll Moumine meets another troll Mu, then Mu meets Moumine, despite the fact that our knowledge of trolls is rather meagre. In section 2.2, I will present a more precise version of my thesis. For the moment, I will describe where the kinds that I have postulated "live."

I need to introduce the notion of *situation in a story*. Martínez Bonati (1981 and 1972, pp. 68-69) distinguishes different levels in a story, consisting, on the one hand, of what is said by the narrator and, on the other hand, of what is said by the characters. This does not exclude the possibility of the narrator being one of the characters. What is said by the narrator constitutes the basic level of narration-description. This level consists of assertive phrases (as opposed to exclamations or interrogatives) of a "concrete and particular nature expressed by the narrator". These assertive phrases form the declaratory discourse which, when interpreted, constitutes the world of the story. The declaratory discourse is transparent and should lead us directly to the world of the story. To find the narrator in a story is not always straightforward. The narrator may or may not be present in the story; the narrator may even be one of the characters. For Martínez Bonati, to understand literary phrases is to unveil the situation immanent in the phrase.

Notice that the story may present contradictions; the author may make mistakes. We then automatically try to reinstate coherence: our further understanding of the story depends on our succeeding. It is not my goal to explain how to succeed. I just take for granted that we do.

A situation in a story is the interpretation of actual and counterfactual partial descriptions of the world of the story. Some situations are actual; some counterfactual. Some of these are described in the narrative; others are deduced from what is described. For instance, in the story "A Scandal in Bohemia," Dr. Watson says to Sherlock Holmes: "You would certainly have been burned had you lived a few centuries ago." To understand, one must consider a counterfactual partial description of a world when witches were burned at the stake for seeming to be endowed with special powers. The other actual and counterfactual partial descriptions whose interpretations make up the situations in a story are those that are needed to provide the coherence of the story and determine the range of possibilities allowed by the text. Thus a science fiction story allows for a wider range of possibilities than a realistic novel which, for instance, sticks to the physical and biological possibilities of dogs as grasped at the time of the writing of the realistic novel. Nowadays, because of comparative studies of volume versus area, we know that dogs cannot measure seven meters. A story in which dogs measure seven meters would not, then, be a realistic one. Notice that these partial descriptions are often deduced from the written text of the story with the help of background beliefs. For instance, if Gladstone is mentioned in one of the stories, we complete the story with a partial description of Gladstone as Prime Minister of England that we interpret as an actual situation of the story, although the text may fail to provide such a description. These last descriptions not obtained directly from statements of the story were not considered by Martínez Bonati.

Let me emphasize again that I am not using the notion of 'possible world'. Possible worlds are complete, whereas I envisage partial descriptions only. Indeed, incompleteness is a characteristic feature of literary works, and it would be irrelevant and probably hopeless to try to complete the partial descriptions that are given by the narrative-descriptive level of the story. It seems important to point this out, since some authors, for instance Mates (1986, p. 252), question the cogency of the notion of counterfactual world, precisely because it maybe impossible to control what other changes are entailed by replacing any factual situation with a counterfactual one. My situations avoid the problem by being incomplete.

I will often contrast the expression 'real world' and 'world of the story', meaning thereby no more than that the two are disjoint, sharing no situation in common. I should also remark that I do not confine possibilities to logical ones. Just as 'our world' has its 'real' possibilities, the world of a story has its set of *relevant* possibilities defined by the story itself. In the world of the story we must be able to discuss and consider types of possibilities that would be impossible in the real world. The range of such possibilities varies from one story to the next. We do not expect supernatural elements to invade a Conan Doyle story. Our faith in the coherence of his stories is reinforced when, at the end of the "The Hound of the Baskervilles," we are given a very simple and realistic explanation for the appearance of the devilish beast. A supernatural explanation would have been very much out of place.

2.2. Language of the Literary Text and its Interpretation

There seem to be two inconsistent intuitions with respect to statements about men, for instance, in a story. On the one hand they might seem to refer to real men, since part of the interest of fiction is precisely the fact that it reveals something about the real world. Parsons seems responsive to this intuition. On the other hand, these statements in fiction about men seem to refer to characters of the novel, since Holmes would certainly include Dr. Watson and Moriarty in the range of his quantifier 'every man'. There is a corresponding problem with the reference of PNs. Assume that Sherlock Holmes refers to Gladstone and his Irish policy. Holmes seems then to refer to the real man, and hence the name 'Gladstone' in his mouth would refer to the man who was Prime Minister of England. On the other hand, if Holmes shakes hands with Gladstone in one of Conan Doyle's novels, the name 'Gladstone' seems to refer to a character of the novel. When Sherlock Holmes refers to Gladstone, he can say "the man with whom I shook hands," which is a property that the real Gladstone does not have; the real Gladstone did not shake hands with Holmes. This suggests that after all, 'Gladstone' in Holmes's mouth refers to a native character of the novel who has, however, something to do with the real Gladstone.

My hypothesis is that 'man' in the story is interpreted as a kind that is native to the story and that if Gladstone shakes hands with Sherlock Holmes, then 'Gladstone' and 'Sherlock Holmes' are interpreted as members of that kind and hence they have the same 'ontological status'. Furthermore, I postulate ordinary relations between the members of these kinds, namely, relations that follow the ordinary logic of English. Thus, if Holmes shakes hands with Gladstone, Gladstone shakes hands with Holmes.

We must enrich the language defined in La Palme Reyes, Macnamara and Reyes (this volume) with the CNs, PNs and predicables that are specific to the literary text. To distinguish the expressions (and their interpretations) native to the literary text from those that are not, I will add an asterisk (*). For instance, I will write *troll** for the sorts representing the CN 'troll'. Capital letters indicate the interpretation of sorts.

The interpretation of *man* is written as MAN in the real world, but the interpretation of the same sort in the world of the story is written as MAN*. In other words, I do not introduce a different sort to designate the men of the story. Instead, I interpret the same sort differently in the different worlds. After all, we use the same words when we tell a story! Similarly the single name 'Gladstone' will be interpreted sometimes as a member of the kind MAN and sometimes as a member of the kind MAN*.

Sherlock Holmes uses the expression 'every man' to refer to men of "his reality," i.e., to men of the story. But why not assume that we have a single set that embraces both the real men and the men of the story? The answer is that we cannot allow an individual man to belong to both worlds. We do not include Dr. Watson when we refer to 'every man', although Sherlock Holmes certainly does include him when he speaks about all men. More dramatically, if a real bomb killed every man in the Baker Street of Edwardian England, it would not touch either Dr. Watson or Holmes.

Crowds (in particular, crowds of people) are considered by Parsons as characters by themselves, and no means of individuating the members of a crowd are provided. I have already given an example in section 1.3 to show that we sometimes need to quantify over the individual members of a crowd. Parsons does not have enough fictional objects, correlated with sets of properties, to interpret these statements correctly, since his quantifiers range over characters only. I do not have this problem, since I have postulated the kind MAN* in the story. So in the example of the crowd, the quantifiers range over MAN* and we have enough men to interpret that sentence.

A pair of twins presents us with similar problems. Let us suppose that nothing in the story permits us to distinguish between the twins. Since each twin is a member of the kind PERSON*, we can individuate them. Even if the story supplies no distinguishing properties, we can still distinguish between them, talk counterfactually about them and wonder, for example, what would have happened if one of them had blue eyes and the other had brown eyes.

We know that the sentence 'Gladstone meets Bertrand Russell' is true in those situations of the real world where Gladstone meets Bertrand Russell. Similarly the sentence 'Gladstone meets Sherlock Holmes' will be true in those situations of the story where Gladstone meets Sherlock Holmes. The constant term *meet* is interpreted as a function that associates with Gladstone and Sherlock Holmes the sets of situations of the world of the story in which Gladstone meets Sherlock Holmes.

Postulating that the logic of the relations should be the same in the real world and in the world of the story implies that the logic of *meet* is the same for the two following sentences: 'Russell meets Gladstone' and 'Sherlock Holmes meets Gladstone'. If 'Russell meets Gladstone' implies that 'Gladstone meets Russell' so in the same way 'Sherlock

Holmes meets Gladstone' implies that 'Gladstone meets Sherlock Holmes'.

The connection between the real world and that of the story depends on the transference of relevant background beliefs to the world of the story. The transfer of the logic is just a particular instance of this process. In general, we transfer the minimal amount of background beliefs that enables us to understand the story and make it coherent. We impose this set of relevant background beliefs as true in the world of the story. Since we cannot compare situations across worlds, we cannot transfer a sentence that depends on a specific situation for the computation of its truth-values, unless we have introduced such a specific situation as being an actual situation of the story (as explained in section 2.1.). In general, sentences may be transferred only if they are "independent" of situations. Modally closed sentences satisfy this condition; we do not require specific situations to compute their truth-values. As an example, we may transfer the modally closed sentence that expresses our background belief that in a parliamentary democracy, the prime minister is ultimately responsible for the security of the country.

Thus, to understand the role of Gladstone in the story, we introduce situations in the story and assume those modally closed statements of our background beliefs about the real Gladstone who was Prime Minister of England.

We could say that the Gladstone of the story is a counterpart of the real Gladstone. Notice, however, that in spite of obvious similarities with Lewis's (1986) notion of counterpart, there are profound differences between these two notions. In the first place, our counterpart of Gladstone does not have all properties of the real Gladstone, but only some of them. Which ones depends on the story. In the second place, and this is the most important difference, our counterpart of Gladstone cannot occur in either the real or counterfactual situations of our world. It is Gladstone himself who appears in counterfactual situations of the real world. Similarly, it is the Gladstone of the story himself who appears in the counterfactual situations of the story. This of course is a consequence of the fact that PNs are rigid designators.

Our theories about the kind MAN* in Conan Doyle's stories, for instance, are given by the transfer of our background beliefs about man. In the case of a "realistic" story by other authors like Balzac, Zola or Mauriac, we can understand the story with our usual theories of man, since nothing in the story clashes with our theories. In the case of fairy tales or science fiction, on the other hand, we transfer only beliefs that do not contradict the story. For instance, to understand the story of the three little pigs, we postulate the kind PIG* whose members have properties obtained from our theories of pigs... and of men. We transfer only the beliefs that do not clash with the story. We do not transfer the knowledge that pigs cannot talk. In Swift's novel, the conditions for being a Yahoo or a Lilliputian come mainly from the story itself and are supplemented by our anthropomorphic vision. In Conan Doyle's novels, we bring to the understanding of the story our theories of men almost entirely. Conan Doyle wants his men to "look like" our men... and the best way to obtain this result is to say nothing about "his" men since then he can be assured that our background beliefs will not clash with his stories. In this sense, our understanding of the story does not clash with our background beliefs.

Let us now look at the following problem. In one of Tove Jansson's stories there are two trolls, Moumine and Mu, who meet. 'Meet' is interpreted as a function that associates with two trolls, say, Moumine and Mu, the set of situations of the world of the story in which Moumine meets Mu. But since trolls do not exist in our world, what kind of background beliefs can we transferred about their meeting? What does it mean that two trolls meet? 'Meet' is sorted: the meanings of two continents meeting and two dogs meeting are different. Since nothing in the story is said about the meeting of two trolls, we must transfer some background beliefs to understand this sentence. Fortunately, we know that the trolls in these stories are animals. The kind ANIMAL is a kind of our world. To understand the meeting of two trolls, we transfer to the world of the story the relevant modally closed statements, such as that the relation of animals meeting is symmetric.

My approach is in the spirit of Model Theory (see, for instance, Barwise 1977). It is to build a model for literary texts in such a way that when 'run', 'meet', etc., are interpreted, the text in conjunction with the transferred background beliefs is true. The contrast between dogs running and motors running in a story is the same as in our world. To illustrate from mathematics, consider the relation of order. A relation of order is anything that satisfies the axioms of order. It does not make sense to say that the order defined among the natural numbers is the same as the one among the reals. Of course if we restrict the order defined on the reals to the naturals we recover the order defined on the naturals.

Macnamara has pointed out the following difficulty with the notion of background beliefs and the transfer mechanism. Suppose one of the clients of Dr. Watson complains about gout and is told to drink less port. The position I have stated is that, to understand Dr. Watson's advice, we must transfer those of our background beliefs about port and gout that do not clash with the story. Since today we do not believe that port causes gout, we cannot understand this advice. It seems, therefore, that we need to bring the background beliefs of the relevant period (for instance those of Edwardian England when it was thought that port caused gout) in order to understand Dr. Watson's advice. Similar remarks apply to novels that are supposed to take place, say, in the Middle Ages, even if these novels have been written by modern authors. It is amusing to remark that this example of gout and alcohol is also discussed by Zenon, the hero of *L'Oeuvre au noir* by Marguerite Yourcenar (1968).

A final remark on the nature of the kinds (*) of the story. According to Putnam (1983), it is impossible to determine kinds uniquely, his reason being essentially that we have non-standard models for first-order theories. Putnam's position does not take into account the fact pointed out by Searle that we seem to be able to determine kinds uniquely by pointing to some of their members. Since this possibility is not available in the world of fiction, Putnam's argument seems to be correct for that realm. We cannot point to a man of the story (namely a member of the kind MAN*) and say "Hamlet" or "this man." We cannot fix interpretations of CNs uniquely, even with the aid of drawings of members of a given kind such as TROLL. If the drawings are slightly altered, the question of whether or not the drawings still represent a troll does not make sense. Trolls lack internal structure. While, then, Putnam's remark may not hold for real-world texts, it does hold for fictional ones.

2.3. Characters

In our world, Sherlock Holmes is a fictitious being, a character, a member of the abstract set of *Ur*-elements (i.e., elements which are not themselves sets) constitutive of the kind MAN* of the story.

I call a member of this abstract set a *character* in the story. Thus, the CN 'troll' is interpreted in our world as the set of all trolls, namely, the set of the kind TROLL* of the story. This notion of character differs from that which has been usually used in theories of fiction, where character is taken to mean members of the abstract set that are individualized in the story. As I emphasized at the beginning of this paper, I do not believe that the consideration of characters in this restricted sense suffices to describe the logic of fiction: we may lack individualized characters to interpret our quantifiers correctly. More importantly, we are not able to interpret counterfactual statements about Moumine, Hamlet and Sherlock Holmes in our world, since those characters do not appear in any situation of our world.

Notice that I have used English as a metalanguage to describe the relation between the formal language and its interpretation. To interpret the formal language, we required a set of situations (given by the story) and kinds of the story. Since all of this was described in the metalanguage, namely English, we are able to describe events of the story by referring to situations and members of the kinds. Thus, we can say: "In a given situation, such and such was the case," or, more precisely, "In a given situation, such and such a statement holds." Notice, however, that one cannot interpret the statement in question into the real world.

In my theory I do not define a character as an individual concept, that is, as a constant function from situations into a set of individuals. Montague (1974, p. 124) and Gupta (1980) consider each member in a kind as an individual concept. If we were to interpret 'Sherlock Holmes' as an individual concept, then Sherlock Holmes would be a constant function whose domain is the set of situations of the world of the relevant story and whose value is an individual. But there is no way to bridge the situations of the world of the story with those of the real world to obtain an individual concept of our world whose domain is the situations of our world. In Montague's theory, Sherlock Holmes could become a real man in a possible world and a character in another; we cannot distinguish between reality and fiction. All the entities are on a par: man and unicorn and troll and number. Our approach has the advantage of separating constitution from constituency (intuitively existence) in a given kind, since constituency is an added structure independent of the constitution of the kind itself. Because of this separation, we can "freeze" a given kind of the world of the story by forgetting the existence predicate. We can freeze the kind MAN* of Conan Doyle's stories and thus have Sherlock Holmes as a character in our world; but he remains a "situationless" character about whom we cannot talk counterfactually. If fictitious persons were just characters, namely, members of an abstract set, we could not make sense of the following sentence from *Six personnages en quête d'auteur* by Pirandello (1977): "Quand un personnage est né, il acquiert aussitôt une telle indépendance, même vis-à-vis de son auteur, que tout le monde peut l'imaginer dans nombres d'autres situations où son auteur n'a pas songé à le mettre" (When a character is born, he becomes so independent, even from his author, that everybody can imagine him in many situations that the author himself did not envisage).

I definitely distinguish between fiction and reality. Sherlock Holmes can never be a real man. Martínez Bonati (1981, p. 56) writes: "As such (Don Quixote) is a fiction and independently of the existence of a possible real model, we have to say with rigour that Don Quixote has not existed.... Don Quixote as a type on the other hand can exist in real models. These distinctions are obvious but anyway very often ignored."

The reason we need a new kind to talk about Sherlock Holmes in our world (after all, Sherlock Holmes is a man and we have the kind MAN in our world) is that, unlike real men, Sherlock Holmes cannot appear in any real or counterfactual situations of our world. We certainly do not include Sherlock Holmes when we refer to 'every man'. For similar reasons, if we were to find animals in our world having all the stereotypical attributes of unicorns, they would still not be unicorns. This seems to be consistent with what Kripke (1980, p. 24) says: "Further, I think that even if archaeologists or geologists were to discover tomorrow some fossils conclusively showing the existence of animals in the past satisfying everything we know about unicorns from the myth of the unicorn, that would not show that there are unicorns."

Besides the "frozen" kinds there are kinds that are abstract in any world in the sense that their members cannot appear in any situation of any world. Thus, these kinds can be interpreted in all worlds. As an example, since Holmes mentions natural numbers in "The Adventure of the Musgrave Ritual" in connection with measurements of a tree, we must postulate the kind NATURAL NUMBER* to interpret his computations. However, this kind is the same abstract kind NATURAL NUMBER that we need to interpret our own computations. Holmes's notion of natural number is exactly the same as ours. In fact, the kind NATURAL NUMBER is a kind whose members never appear or occur in any situations of any world. In this sense, their members are abstract in any world. That cannot be said about Holmes. Holmes is a man who lives in his world, and the men of that world constitute a concrete kind of that world, although an abstract kind of ours. Holmes may appear in situations of his world; a natural number never.

2.4. Metamorphosis

My theory has been designed to accommodate metamorphosis in a very straightforward way. In La Palme Reyes, Macnamara and Reyes, we explain the connections between the kinds BABY, ADULT and PERSON. We interpret every postulate of the nominal category, for instance, 'A baby is a person', as a map (that we call *underlying map*) from the kind BABY into the kind PERSON. Metamorphoses in fairy tales may be explained by considering further underlying maps. The problem with this approach is that we do not always have such maps and kinds at our disposal, and to understand literary texts, we are sometimes forced to create some artificial kinds. The kind SOUL of many religions is required to state metempsychosis, suffering in hell and resurrection. The man who lived and the reborn (man) have the same underlying souls, they are identical as members of the kind SOUL.

As an aside, let us remark that van Baaren (1962, p.107) says that in Buddhism there is no such thing as an immortal soul that, surviving death, could help to explain reincarnations. He then asks: but what is it that revives again? And he concludes that, according to our occidental categories of thought, it is impossible to answer. We need a certain continuity to explain change. Otherwise we cannot understand the question "What is it that changes?"

The film *Ladyhawke* (prod. Richard Donner and Lauren Schuler, dir. Richard Donner, 1985) offers an interesting case of metamorphoses. Two lovers were condemned by a jealous bishop never to see each other under their human form. At dawn, the lady becomes a hawk and spends the day on the hand of the knight, her lover; at dusk, the hawk becomes a lady while the knight is metamorphosed into a wolf. The hawk does not know that it has undergone metamorphosis and has some relation to a being that is in love with the knight. Similarly, the wolf does not know that it has undergone metamorphosis and that it has some relation to a being that is in love with the lady. Nevertheless, as humans, the knight knows that the hawk is his metamorphosed lady and the lady knows that the wolf is her metamorphosed knight.

To understand this story, we must then postulate a kind to handle the identity and the change. The background beliefs of our linguistic community will probably not allow us to postulate the kind SOUL, since, in this linguistic community, animals are not supposed to have a soul. In the fairy tale "Beauty and the Beast," the kind SOUL could perhaps explain the metamorphosis because the Beast has a very anthropomorphic behaviour and aspect. So we could say that the underlying soul of the Beast is the same as the underlying soul of the Prince. In *Ladyhawke* however, we must consider another kind. I suggest the kind LIVING BEING. The living being that underlies the hawk is the same as the living being that underlies the lady. In this particular example, unlike most fairy tales, the theories of hawk and wolf are taken unchanged from our background beliefs and do not exhibit any anthropomorphic features.

Acknowledgments

This paper is based on a part of the third chapter of my doctoral thesis (Reyes 1988), written at Concordia University under the supervision of a committee consisting of my thesis advisor, Professor M. Szabo, together with Professors I. Bellert and M. Hallett. I would like to express my gratitude to all of them for their generous help during my studies. I also owe a great debt of gratitude to Professors J. Macnamara and G. E. Reyes for many suggestions, helpful criticisms and their patient reading of different versions of this paper. The revision of the paper was supported by a Social Sciences and Humanities Research Council postdoctoral fellowship awarded to the author. A final word of thanks to Professor Steven Davis for his careful editing of the paper.

References

Baaren, Theodorius Peiter van (1962). *Les Religions d'Asie*. Traduit du néerlandais par M. Autressoux. Marabout Université. Zeist, NL: Gérard et C°, Verviers et W. de Haan N.V.

Barwise, J. (ed.) (1977). *Handbook of Mathematical Logic*. Studies in Logic, Vol. 90. Amsterdam: North-Holland Publishing Company

Doyle, C. (1983). *Sherlock Holmes*. Greenwich Unabridged Library Classics. New York: Chatham River Press

Gupta, A. K. (1980). *The Logic of Common Nouns*. New Haven and London: Yale University Press

Janssen, T. (1986) Papa *Moumine et la mer*. *Pappan hoch havet* [1965]. Holger Schildts Forlag. Translated from Swedish by Caroline Tabourin. Livre de poche jeunesse. Paris: Librairie Générale Française

Kripke, S. A. (1980). *Naming and Necessity*. Oxford: Basil Blackwell

La Palme Reyes M., J. Macnamara and G. E. Reyes (This volume). Reference, kinds and predicates

Lewis, D. (1986). *On the Plurality of Worlds*. Oxford: Basil Blackwell

Macnamara, J. (1986). *A Border Dispute*. Cambridge, MA: Bradford/MIT Press

Martínez Bonati, F. (1981). *Fictive Discourse and the Structure of Literature*. Translated by Philip W. Silver with the author's collaboration. Ithaca and London: Cornell University Press.

— (1972). *La Estructura de la Obra Literaria*. Barcelona: Editorial Seix Barral, S. A.

Mates, B. (1986). *The Philosophy of Leibniz*. New York and Oxford: Oxford University Press

Montague, R. (1974). The proper treatment of quantification in ordinary English. In R. H. Thomason (ed.), *Formal Philosophy: Selected Papers of Richard Montague*. New Haven and London: Yale University Press

Parsons, T. (1980). *Nonexistent Objects*. New Haven and London: Yale University Press

Pavel, T. (1986). *Fictional Worlds*. Cambridge, MA and London: Harvard University Press

Pirandello, L. (1977). *Six personnages en quête d'auteur*. Translated from Italian by Michel Arnaud. Folio 1063. Paris: Gallimard

Putnam, H. (1983). Models and reality. In H. Putnam, *Philosophical Papers, Realism and Reason*. Cambridge: Cambridge University Press

Reyes, M. [La Palme] (1988). A Semantics for Literary Texts. Unpublished Ph.D. thesis, Montreal: Concordia University.

Swift, J. (1957). *Gulliver's Travels*. New York: Pocket Books

Yourcenar, M. (1968) *L'Oeuvre au noir*. Folio 798. Paris: Gallimard

15
How Not to Draw the
de re/de dicto *Distinction*

Martin Hahn

Introduction

Philosophers since Aristotle have thought that to discover the laws of logic is to discover the laws governing thought. Until relatively recently, that has meant only that logic captures the way we reason, or the way we ought to. But when symbolic logic was born in the nineteenth century, another connection between logic and cognition arose with it. The formal sentential structures it gave us were taken to represent the real structure of thoughts, their logical form. Thoughts, on this picture, have sentence-like contents and their representational properties are like the semantical properties of a language. A formal system can be used to provide an analysis of the structure of such a "language," making its semantical properties perspicuous and formal semantics possible to construct. Formal logic, in other words, can be used to represent the *logical form* of thoughts.

There are two ways this can be done, one direct the other less so. The present paper is part of a larger project to show that the direct way is the right way. This is worth arguing for, if only because the indirect method has held the day so far. The logical form of thoughts, on the prevalent view, is going to be discovered in the course of discovering the logical form of natural language sentences. The project is to construct a formal language with explicit logical form which captures the underlying deep form of sentences of, say, English (or perhaps of particular uses of sentences of English).

The connection between this project and cognition is an old one. Both Russell and Frege noted that there was a special problem of providing an analysis of sentences which ascribed, in Russell's felicitous phrase, propositional attitudes to people: 'John believes that *scampi* are not shrimp', 'Jodi hopes that the *risotto* is not overcooked', 'Frank fears that his *soufflé* will not rise'. First, what these sentences attribute to John, Jodi and Frank seem to be cognitive states and, in the words of David Kaplan, if you are going to write the semantics of the word 'love', you are going to say some things about love. But more importantly, the embedded that-clauses in propositional attitude ascriptions provide a description of the content of the cognitive states ascribed, and so in giving the logical form of the whole sentences, one will provide the logical form of the contents of the cognitive states ascribed. This last thesis is widely held among philosophical logicians, although I believe that it is false. The relationship between the content of cognitive states and that of the that-clauses ascribing those states is much more complex.

Thus, if we are to discover the logical form of thoughts, we have to take the route of applying our formal techniques to thought-contents themselves rather than to their ascriptions.[1] Most of this paper is devoted to an argument against the prevalent indirect way of characterizing the logical form of thoughts. In the last part, I will sketch the beginnings of an answer to how, using the direct approach, one might get the results which have eluded us. The question which the indirect method cannot resolve but the direct can is how to draw a distinction between *de re* and *de dicto*, as applied to cognitive states. But first, let me explain why I think that the *de re/de dicto* distinction is more than some obscure medieval bit of terminology; why I think any theory of cognition has to be able to draw it, i.e., what problem will be solved by drawing it correctly.

Why a *de re/de dicto* Distinction?

Naturalistic accounts of the mind are, of necessity, torn between two conflicting intuitions. On the one hand, it seems clear that our mental states constitute relations with objects in the world around us. Biologically, my belief that Hoshi makes the best sushi in town is one end of a continuum whose other end is occupied by a story of how amoebas detect the presence of nutrition. All organisms, and many other things in the world, react to changes in their environment. Our cognitive states are just very sophisticated versions of the same old story. At least some cognitive states, on this account, constitute a relation between the thinker and a particular object, set of objects, or state of her environment. Such relations play an important role in explaining our behaviour: I reach for the last piece of salmon-skin roll because I believe no one else wants it, for example. The object to which my belief relates me had better be the very object sitting on the pretty Japanese tray if the explanation is to go through.

The other horn of our dilemma is the representational, intentional nature of mental states. The above rudimentary explanation of behaviour only works on the supposition that I correctly identify the salmon-skin roll in question. I would have behaved in exactly the same way if there had been a plastic replica of a salmon-skin roll on the platter, and conversely, I would not have behaved that way even with a real roll there, had I misidentified it as a plastic replica. Considerations like these, as well as ones concerning the thinker's assent to and dissent from belief-attributions, have led theorists to the conclusions that (a) all of our cognitive contents are intentional (or opaque, in Quine's oft-borrowed metaphor), and (b) that the relational sense of propositional attitudes is irrelevant to the cognitive scientist.[2] These conclusions have not often been argued for in detail, and are by no means universally accepted. Probably the best known and most thorough argument for them is to be found in Fodor's "Methodological Solipsism as a Research Strategy in Cognitive Science" (1981).

Unfortunately, the intuition that our thoughts essentially constitute relations to the world does not go away so easily. As Brentano, who articulated this mess for us so persuasively in 1870, put it: "It is paradoxical in the highest degree to say that what a man promises to marry is an *ens rationis* and that he keeps his word by marrying a real person" (1966, p. 174).

Now, commitment to the intentionality of thought does not necessarily lead us to endorsing an *ens rationis* as the object of my marital intentions, but however we account for them, if they are intentional it is not clear exactly how they constitute a *relation* between me and a particular woman. After all, it follows from their intentionality that my mental states might be the same if the woman did not exist, or if two women satisfied the mental descriptive contents equally well, or if I also had utter horror of marrying my own mother who, as Oedipus found out, may well be identical to the object of my desires. *Relations* properly so called, by contrast, hold between existent objects under whatever description or none. Brentano's problem, stripped of its commitment to intentional objects, is thus to explain how it is that our cognitive states constitute a relation between us and objects in the world even though such states are essentially intentional.[3] This, I take it, is nothing other than the traditional problem of intentionality.

It has seemed to many people that the most straightforward way out of the quandary was to distinguish between two senses of 'mental state'. So, using belief as a stand-in for all propositional attitudes, we distinguish between the relational sense of 'belief' and the intentional sense. The two kinds of belief are, mistakenly in my view, often called *de re* and *de dicto* respectively. Cognitive science only has an interest in *de dicto* (i.e., intentional, 'opaque') belief. Whatever real relations to medium-sized dry goods people have in virtue of having these beliefs, the issue is not a matter for psychologists but for someone else. Fodor writes:

> My point, then, is *of course* not that solipsism is true; it's just that truth, reference and the rest of the semantic notions aren't psychological categories. What they are is: they're modes of *Dasein*. I don't know what *Dasein* is, but I'm sure there's lots of it around, and I'm sure you and I and Cincinnati have all got it. What more do you want? (1981, p. 253)

Now, stripping away the gratuitous but funny snipes at neo-Heideggerian cognitive scientist-philosophers, I want to defend this view of Fodor's – even though he himself may not hold it any more. What I will argue is that, as far as the issue about relational and intentional beliefs goes, Fodor and others who hold this view are right. The argument usually given against them by direct reference theorists and their heirs is based on a confusion engendered by importing genuine issues about the structure of intentional cognitive states, in particular the distinction between *de re* and *de dicto* beliefs properly so called, into the account of the semantics of ascriptions of belief. And the problem arises, I shall argue, precisely because the semantics-of-natural-language tradition has the wrong view about the relationship between logic and cognition. One way of putting this is that Fodor is right about there being two senses of 'belief', but it does not follow from this that there are two kinds of beliefs rather than just two ways of attributing a single intentional state. The arguments used against views like Fodor's are based on just this confusion.

That is the negative thesis of this paper. The positive account in the last part of this paper is the first step in an account of *de re* cognitive states, intentionally construed, and a plea for formal methods to be applied directly to the contents of thoughts, in the tradition of the early Husserl. The point will be that Brentano's worry resurfaces as does the tension between the intentional and relational intuitions concerning propositional attitudes, even if we construe all cognitive states as intentional. Fodor's dichotomy, while important and correct, does not solve the problem of intentionality. The *de re/de dicto* distinction is one between two ways a thought can be about an object, i.e., of solving the problem. It is a semantical distinction between two sorts of cognitive states, reflected in the logical form of their contents.

Before launching into the argument proper, two caveats. While I wish to defend Fodor's view that the relational sense of belief is irrelevant to cognitive science, I do not want to defend methodological solipsism as a whole. That is because I am convinced by Tyler Burge's (1979, 1982,

1986) entirely different arguments that an individualist semantics of cognitive state contents is impossible.

The second caveat is that I do not wish to argue about terminology. There is good precedent for construing the *de re/de dicto* distinction as applying to reports of propositional attitudes rather than the attitudes themselves. Insofar as I think that there is an important distinction to be drawn concerning reports, I do not want to lay any special claim to the terms '*de re*' and '*de dicto*'. I have interpreted them as distinguishing kinds propositional attitudes, but have no quarrel with those who use them in the other sense. My only quarrel is with those who run the two senses together.

Ascriptions, Scope and Quantifying in

As early as Russell's "On Denoting" (1905), philosophers were aware of the possibility of permutations of quantifiers (or description-operators) and belief-operators and the apparent difference in the meaning of formulae like:

(1) $\qquad\qquad\qquad \text{Bel}_{\text{Fred}}(\exists x)Fx$

and:

(2) $\qquad\qquad\qquad (\exists x)\text{Bel}_{\text{Fred}}Fx$

Bertrand Russell writes:

> [W]hen we say 'George IV wished to know whether Scott was the author of *Waverley*', we normally mean 'George IV wished to know whether one and only one man wrote Waverley and Scott was that man'; but we *may* also mean: 'One and only one man wrote *Waverley,* and George IV wished to know whether Scott was that man'. In the *latter* 'the author of *Waverley*' has a *primary* occurrence, in the former, a *secondary.* The latter might be expressed by 'George IV wished to know concerning the man who wrote *Waverley* whether he was Scott'. This would be true, for example, if George IV had seen Scott at a distance and had asked 'Is that Scott?' (1905, p. 53)

The contrast here is between something like:

(3) $\qquad\qquad \text{WK}_{\text{GIV}}\ (\exists x)(y)[(Wy\leftrightarrow x=y)\&x=s]$

and:

(4) $\qquad\qquad (\exists x)(y)[(Wy\leftrightarrow x=y)\&\text{WK}_{\text{GIV}}\ x=s]$

Similar contrasting pairs can be constructed when definite descriptions do not get the Russellian treatment, and even with proper names. This can be done by means of eliminating them in favour of descriptions in the way Russell (1956) suggests: 'Scott' becomes 'the author of *Waverly*' or even 'the man named Scott', or changing them into predicates *à la* Quine (1960): 'Scottizes', or more simply as the pair:

(5) $Bel_{Fred}(\exists x)x=a\&Fa$

and:

(6) $(\exists x)x=a\&Bel_{Fred}Fa$

the latter being a simple rendering of the philosophese:

(7)   Of *a*, Fred believes that it is *F*.

Now, the difference between the odd- and even-numbered formulae is a syntactic one which we can describe in terms of permutation of components, of relative scopes, or of primary and secondary occurrences. But, given either the project of constructing a canonical, logically perfect language of science (Russell's, Frege's and Quine's project), or of providing the semantics of natural language, the interesting question is what *semantical* distinction the pairs mark for us.

I shall argue that Russell's story of when one might use (4) is roughly correct. But the waters are quite murky here and the issue is controversial to say the least. To say more: many theorists have been ambivalent as to the meaning of the even-numbered formulae. The best way to set out this ambivalence is to look at its origins in Quine's "Quantifiers and Propositional Attitudes" (1976).

Quine sees that the semantical interpretation of (2), (4) and (6) is problematic in formal systems which are extensional and first order, and where quantifiers are interpreted in the standard objectual manner. The familiar problem, in a nutshell, is that the contexts created by belief-operators are referentially opaque but the variable of quantification is a device of pure reference. An existential generalization is true if and only if there is an object which satisfies the relevant open sentence. It has to be the *object*, under whatever name or none in Quine's phrase. Thus all instances of the quantification which refer to the same object must be true. But that is just what the opacity of belief-contexts fails to guarantee. So quantifying into opaque contexts, or equivalently, the exportation of quantifiers out of them, seems to be without a semantic interpretation in first order, extensional logic, given an objectual reading of quantifiers.

All of this creates a problem for Quine, as well as a little burgeoning philosophical industry in propositional attitude attribution analysis, only because he is not willing to say of propositional attitudes, as he is for modal logic: "so much the worse for quantifying in" (Quine, 1963). I am not here interested in either Quine's, or anyone else's solutions to the problem.[4] My only interest is in why philosophers have found it worthwhile to solve the problem, i.e., what it is that Quine and his followers thought (2), (4) and (6) expressed that needed to be captured by their semantical interpretations. What is the meaning of exportation?

To see that this is not an easy question, note that among other things, Quine says that the difference between:

(8)   Ralph believes that $(\exists x)(x$ is a spy)

and:

(9) $(\exists x)$(Ralph believes that x is a spy)

"is vast; indeed, if Ralph is like most of us, (8) is true and (9) is false" (1976, p. 186). But later Quine tells us that "exportation should doubtless be viewed in general as implicative" (p. 190). One does not have to be a philosopher or logician of Quine's calibre to notice a tension here. It is not often that we can derive a stronger assertion from a weaker one. The two intuitions at war here are that, on the one hand, there is patently a difference between believing that someone in particular is a spy and believing that there are spies; on the other, that from

(10)   Ralph believes that Ortcutt is a spy.

Proposition (9) follows by existential generalization.

But it will be remarked, quite correctly, that the content attributed in (10) is very different from that in (8) and therefore one should not expect the two sentences to bear the same relation to (9). Granted. But Quine and some of those who followed have wanted to treat the two relations as one, characterized syntactically as exportation (of the existential quantifier out of the opaque context). Furthermore, I am about to argue that they were right in this.

What Exportation Cannot Do

Quine is genuinely ambivalent about the meaning of exportation, as the two quotations we just saw show. On the one hand, he sees it as a reporter's prerogative to let selected positions shine through as transparent and export as needed (1960, p. 199). In the later "Intensions Revisited" (1981) he argues that exportation is allowed in a contextually (pragmatically) delimited set of cases. On the other, he tells us that what is being captured is an important difference in Ralph's state of mind. In fact, the argument in "Quantifiers and Propositional Attitudes" is that we have to provide an interpretation exported versions of attitude ascriptions precisely *because* they capture an importantly different kind of belief.

Quine's terms for these two sorts of beliefs were 'relational' and 'notional', but the more common terminology has been the medieval *'de re'* and *'de dicto'*. His argument for the importance of the relational (*de re*) sense of belief is, however, curious. It concentrates on (8) and (9) and the two readings of each of the following:

(11)	I want a sloop.
(12)	Ctesias is hunting unicorns.
(13)	Ernest is hunting lions.

Of (11) he says, amusingly, that we need to distinguish between wanting a particular sloop in the harbour and wanting mere relief from slooplessness (1976, p. 185). Proposition (8), as we saw, makes Ralph like most of us, while (9) would interest the FBI. Similar remarks are made, mutatis mutandis, about (12) and (13). Other philosophers have occasionally used examples like these as particularly clear cases of the *de re/de dicto* distinction (e.g. Burge 1977, p. 340). The curious fact is, however, that such cases are triply beside the point here.

First, (11) through (13) display an ambiguity between readings on which there is and is not a specific object indicated by an indefinite noun-phrase, a phenomenon which has little to do with propositional attitudes, or even referential opacity, as is seen from its occurrence in, for example:

(14)	Fred goes to a meeting every Thursday.

Indeed, it is not even clear that the standard treatment of the +/- specific distinction as a scope ambiguity will work. The sentence:

(15)	There's a fly in my soup.

has two readings. The usual one is the complaint to the waiter announcing that the soup is not fly-free, on the other reading the speaker has a particular fly in mind and continues by naming it "Herbert" and describing its swimming technique.[5] But there seems to be no operator in (15) whose scope could be wider than that of the indefinite description.

Second, as applied to propositional attitudes, it does not line up with any recognizable version of the *de re/de dicto* distinction.[6] Consider, for example, the belief that the person who has been asking strange questions about the philosophy department, whoever he might be, (or, for that matter, the man in the brown hat) is a spy. Or consider Ctesias's hunting a specific unicorn, namely the most beautiful one in the woods. Such beliefs and desires, based as they are on general considerations, certainly do not involve one in any kind of *special* relation with a *res*.[7] If (11) describes my wanting the largest sloop in Philadelphia (whichever one it is), my desire is specific and I do not crave mere relief from slooplessness. But my desire is *de dicto* on any construal of that distinction as applying to kinds of attitudes that I know of.

Quine's own gloss on the distinction between (8) and (9) in terms of what would interest the FBI confirms, interestingly enough, the point that specific contents are not necessarily *de re* and that the former, if anything, is captured by (9). The FBI, it turns out, has an interest in many uniquely specifying descriptions of spies and does not require one to have a special relation to the *res* to be an informer. The issue of which descriptions are of interest and which not is complicated and, fortunately, beyond the scope of this paper. It is clear that they do not find it interesting that the shortest spy is a spy. But they would take some interest in the information that the head of the milk marketing board is a spy, and would certainly welcome such information from someone who did not have the faintest idea who heads the board but has noticed strange fluctuations in the price of milk, a code-like regularity in the misprints on milk cartons, etc.

And third, again as applied to propositional attitudes, the distinction between specific and non-specific indefinite noun-phrases cannot be captured by the permutation of components Quine thinks is required. It is true that "the incorrectness of rendering (12) in the fashion

(16) $(\exists x)(x$ is a unicorn. Ctesias is hunting $x)$

is conveniently attested by the non-existence of unicorns," in Quine's words (1976, p. 185). But while the zoological lacuna makes that reading impossible, it does not take away the fact that (12) displays the +/- specific ambiguity. There is a large difference in Ctesias' cognitive state when he is out to get any horse-like beast with a single aphrodisiac horn, as opposed to when he is out to hunt down the unicorn he saw the night before munching on his cabbages. Furthermore, we should note that Ernest would behave no differently while hunting a specific lion, were the fierce beast he saw near camp only an illusion. But exportation commits us to the existence of these beasts, and thus it had better not be the way we render the specific reading.

So Quine's main argument to show that quantifying in has to be given an interpretation fails. But it fails, in part, for an interesting reason. Because the existence of our objects of thought is never guaranteed, nor can we be counted on to identify these objects correctly when they present a different face to us, it is unlikely that the exported version of a propositional attitude ascription will mark a new kind of mental state, one with a different *intentional* content. I shall return to this point below.

But all this does not mean that exportation is not needed. In fact, the distinction between belief *reports* in which exportation (or at least existential generalization) was applied and ones where it was not seems to me to be important and interesting in its own right. Its import is independent of the issue of whether it corresponds to some distinction between different mental states. There is a striking difference between the two forms of report. The "exported" versions commit us (the reporters) to the existence of an object and, if along with existential generalization we export the whole denoting expression, to the referential success of said expression. Furthermore, in the unexported version we have more of a commitment to reporting the referring content in a way the thinker of whom we are speaking would find acceptable.[8]

There is as good a case for the indispensability of this distinction as there is for that of the first one. The reasons are, however, rather different. That there is a distinction between general and specific beliefs is a fact about our mental lives which is hard to deny. The demand for the exported form, on the other hand, stems from our need to link our reports of mental states with ones of other facts, as in the case of my marrying the girl next door because I think she will make a fine wife, driving the Renault because I trust that it is mine, etc. If we could not move from the fact that someone has a certain propositional attitude to his being related to some *object*, our everyday and scientific explanations of individual behaviour as well as much of the social sciences would be impossible. In other words, exportation satisfies one of the intuitions I describe above as driving some philosophers to distinguish *de re* from *de dicto*.

Exportation does, by its very nature, commit us to quantifying into propositional attitude ascriptions. So Quine's dilemma is best located here. The specific/non-specific distinction, by contrast, does not clearly demand such quantification. While every legitimate case of exportation will be a report of a propositional attitude with a specific content, exportation is never *required* in reporting specific beliefs and often is prohibited (as in the case where someone is hunting what they believe to be a particular unicorn or looking for the person fully responsible for governing Canada). We have thus located the technical problem and separated it so far from anything directly relevant to there being different *kinds of beliefs* and other propositional attitudes.

How Export Permits Are Issued

For all that, Quine's paper has given rise to much work on the distinction between *de re* and *de dicto* attitudes. To be sure some philosophers, notably John Searle in *Intentionality* (1983), have argued that the distinction is nothing other than the one I just drew between reports where the reporter is, and ones where she is not committed to the existence and correct description of the object of belief. But there have been many more who have maintained that there really are two kinds of cognitive states here; two sorts of belief-contents.

Starting with the unexported version of a report, we can distinguish – according to this tradition – between those cases where we may export, and those where we may not. It has seemed all along that, aside from the cases where a lacuna in the furniture of the world prohibits exportation, there are others where we cannot export for quite a different reason: the thinker's relation to the object is somehow too "accidental." Much work has been done on specifying what a non-accidental relation would be, ranging from Donnellan's having someone in mind (1966), through Kaplan's being *en rapport* (1971) to Hintikka's knowing who (1967). The idea is that we can export the referring phrase, and thus place it in a transparent position, in cases where the thinker *really* has something in particular in mind, some *res* to which she is in a special relation in virtue of her cognitive state.

I want to suggest that these attempts are engendered by a confusion, found in Quine, and perhaps inherited from him. The problem is another consequence of the failure to distinguish *reports* of beliefs from *beliefs*. There are two questions to be asked: "When can we export?" and "When does a person's belief put him in a special enough relation to a *res* to be a different kind of belief?" The answer to both of these is: "When the relation between the thinker and the object is not too *accidental*. Too *accidental* for what? The answers ought to be rather different in the two cases.

Exportation, as I have argued, captures a distinction between *reports*. We export the singular term or existential quantifier when we need to say something about the relationship between the thinker and some object of which he is thinking. We do this when it suits our conversational and explanatory purposes. The question: "When can we export?" is ambiguous. It can either be asking when exported belief reports are true, or it could be asking when they are appropriate. If all we want to preserve in exportation is truth-value, the answer is not all that difficult: an exported report is false if no object is picked out by the exported term, if we misdescribe the object, or if there is no mode of presentation of the object under which the thinker has the belief ascribed. If, on the other hand, the demand is for the criteria of appropriateness, the simple answer is: "When the exported version fulfils our explanatory and conversational purposes."

The distinction ought to be familiar. David Kaplan points out that while the report 'The host spilled wine all over my suit' may be quite true, strictly speaking, it is not conversationally appropriate if it could also have been made using the sentence 'I spilled wine all over my suit'. The notion of conversational (broadly speaking, since it clearly applies even in scholarly writings, sermons, etc.) inappropriateness is often used to explain why we can claim that a sentence in a given context is really true in spite of the fact that there is, intuitively, something drastically wrong with it. Unfortunately, the notion of conversational implicature, as developed in H.P. Grice's pioneering work (1989, p. 1-144), is so powerful as to be subject to abuse. It is much too easy to allow oneself to bite the bullet when one's favourite theory predicts semantical simplicity in a seemingly complex situation, hoping that any bad taste will be mopped up by the generic notion of conversational implicature. I do not think that such is the case here.

We make such exported reports whenever we want to indicate that there is a relation between the person of whom we are speaking and some object to which we, the reporters, refer. Quine's term 'relational' is thus quite appropriate. It is plausible then, that such a report ought to be true whenever there is such a relation. Now, even in the most "pseudo de re" case, as Kaplan and Burge call them, there is *some* epistemic relation between the thinker and the object. So if I think about the first child born in the twenty-first century, whether or not I dub it Newman1, to use Kaplan's famous example (1978), there is no doubt that *some* epistemic relation between myself and that person exists. Immediately, I can be mistaken *about her*, if I think that she is going to be male, for example. There is no denying that at a minimum, it is true that my mental states are related to that person by the relation of denotation (i.e., my thought picks the person out descriptively).

From this it follows that exportation always preserves the truth of the original ascription so long as the exported term succeeds in referring to an object of which the thinker is thinking, under some mode of presentation or other. The main objection to this conclusion is the alleged existence of counter-examples. Thus, it is argued that in exporting and substituting from:

(17)   John F. Kennedy believed that the president of
              the USA in 1985 would live in the White House.

to:

(18)   R. Reagan is such that JFK believed that
              he would live in the White House.

we move from truth to falsehood (as opposed to from a conversationally appropriate attribution to one that is not).

But we must be careful here not confuse (18) with the more plausibly false:

(19)   JFK believed that Ronald Reagan
              would live in the White House.

The problem, in a nutshell, is that in English *both* the exported and the unexported versions are ambiguous, or at least there is no clear distinction between them. This is attested by the fact that the *exported* version is notoriously difficult to express clearly. We resort to logicianese 'such that' formulations and various stressed 'of's and 'about's and 'concerning's, or to other ways of stressing that we mean to pick out the object of thought under whatever name or none. And, in the opaque unexported case, we do in fact allow some substitutions of co-referential terms so long as they do not mislead.

The distinction is thus a philosophical one, inspired by the fact that quantified logic on its standard interpretation makes a sharp distinction between sentences in which the quantifier reaches across an opacity-forming operator and those in which it does not. There are then two distinct questions: (a) what does such a distinction capture? (i.e., what is the difference between the meanings of the two syntactic forms?), and (b) how shall we translate English sentences? I am interested in the first question and claim that all we capture by the distinction is a difference between reporting the whole propositional attitude *qua* content,[9] and reporting a relation between the subject and the object thought about. About English, then, the question under present discussion is not: "When is a certain syntactic form appropriate?" but rather: "When is it appropriate to treat a referring expression used in making a belief attribution as occurring in a transparent position?"

It seems to me, then, that if we read (18) as an unequivocal case of a report with an exported referring expression, there is good reason to believe that it is true after all. JFK, of course, was not thinking of R. Reagan *qua* Reagan, or even *qua* anything but the president of the USA in 1985. But for all that, his thought succeeded in referring to that person and is true if and only if that person was duly elected and lived in the White House. It did constitute a relation between JFK and Reagan, no matter how slight, in virtue of that denoting relationship. To insist that such a relation is too slight to allow exportation would be a mistake because it turns out that the closeness of the speaker/object relation does not determine even the appropriateness of exportations, much less their truth-value.

What determines whether or not an exported report of a mental state is appropriate is whether or not it fits the particular conversational and explanatory purposes at hand to describe someone's mental state as a relation between the person and some other object. The "closeness" of the epistemic relation between thinker and object is often irrelevant. Now, the case against counting all exportations from true ascriptions as true (if they satisfy the other conditions listed above) rests on just such intuitions of what is acceptable. But if we took acceptability to be the criterion of truth, truth would vary from occasion to occasion with our conversational and explanatory purposes. This seems wrong, and so I take the source of our unease with (18) to be the fact that it is hard to imagine under what circumstances such an exported attribution would be appropriate.[10]

The appropriateness of exportation depends on our purposes in performing it. For example, we cannot explain or predict how I respond to the entrance of Bernard J. Ortcutt on the basis of a (true) exportation from:

(20)   Hahn believes that the man who sold U.S.
            secrets to the Russians should be killed.

where this is my only belief about him. Such an exportation would thus be inappropriate. The problem here seems to be the lack of a sufficient epistemic relation between Ortcutt and me to make that belief affect my actions in these circumstances. But what relation would suffice will vary from belief to belief and context to context.

In the following case the epistemic relation between thinker and object is no more intimate, and an exportation *is* appropriate because a conversational purpose is fulfilled by it. A friend mentions he would like to meet the person with the best academic record at the university. It takes a little research at the dean's office, but you find out who that is and, on meeting them at a party, you say: 'I have a friend who would like to meet you'.[11] There is nothing unusual here and you are correctly reporting your friend's wishes, exporting a term referring to a person to whom he has no special epistemic relation.

So how did the lack of a more intimate epistemic relation undermine exportation in the case of (20)? Only indirectly. Our stated purpose in exporting was to explain my behaviour on Ortcutt's entrance and such an explanation would only work if I *knew* that Ortcutt is the spy. However, such an indirect influence is not always there. In different circumstances or for a different purpose, the move would be appropriate. Suppose, for example, that the discussion concerns the death penalty and everyone knows (except for me) that Ortcutt is a spy. I express the belief attributed to me by (20), and immediately two friends whisper to one another: "We'd better tell Ortcutt to be careful. Hahn thinks he should be killed."

To repeat: whether or not an exportation is acceptable in given circumstances doesn't depend on anything the sentence could plausibly be taken to assert, such as the existence of a special kind of relation between thinker and object. Instead, it varies with the conversational purposes of the reporter. The variations in these are such that we would not want to base semantical values on them, and they are more plausibly relegated to pragmatics. Thus the unacceptability of exportations signifies (except in the cases specified by the truth-conditions I gave) conversational inappropriateness and not falsity.

The question of when exportation is permitted in either sense (i.e. in the sense of being truth preserving or in the sense of being conversationally appropriate) is in sharp contrast to questions of delineation of a special kind of propositional attitude. Still, it does seem that there are some propositional attitudes in which the relation between the thinker and the object thought about is somehow different, more intimate than in other cases. My belief that my mother is a woman is very different from my belief that Shakespeare's mother was a woman (since all mothers are), though I hold both with equal certainty. The first is *about* my mother for me in a very different way from the way the second is about Shakespeare's. What is the difference?

It is this difference between *de re* and *de dicto* beliefs that Kaplan would seem to be trying to capture with his notion of being *en rapport* (1971) with the referent of a singular term in a belief-content ascription. The account is presented as a criterion for the permissibility of exportation, but being *en rapport* fails as a criterion of appropriateness of exportation. It is both too strong and too weak.

The case of the friend who wishes to meet the best student at the university shows the criterion is too strong. Exportation is permitted even though no *en rapport* relation exists. The case is only a particularly blatant case of a common phenomenon. We do not require anything nearly as strong as being *en rapport* to allow exportation. In the case of (20), for example, all we need to add to my belief system to make the exported version explanatory is the conviction that the next person who walks into the room will be the dreaded spy (whoever he may be).

But the criterion is sometimes too weak as well. It is true that often we may export when the thinker is *en rapport* with the object. But not always. Failures of existence of the object are an obvious case in point. But further, we may not export, no matter how acquainted the thinker may be with the object, in situations where the point of the report is to say how the object is represented for him. Such exportation will be at best misleading. When I say: "I can't believe that my mother could reject me" in a discussion of maternal love in general, the report of this belief performed in a supermarket in the form: 'Do you see that woman over there picking through the tomatoes? Well, Hahn can't believe that she could reject him' is, at best, odd.

Another range of cases where the thinker's being *en rapport* does not *ipso facto* grant us export permits is suggested by Perry in his influential paper, "The Problem of the Essential Indexical" (1979). One presumably has a *de re* relation to oneself. Perry's case is one where a person in a supermarket is unaware that sugar is spilling from a torn bag in the cart he is pushing down the aisle. Now suppose that the person notices a trail of sugar and wonders who is making the mess. Such a person believes that he is not spilling sugar *and* is *en rapport* with himself. And yet, it would be grossly misleading (though strictly true) to say that he believes of the person making a mess that he is not spilling sugar.

A further type of case where exportation is problematic even though the beliefs seem to be *de re* can be drawn from Kripke's examples in "A Puzzle About Belief" (1979). There, Pierre has two *de re* beliefs: that London is not pretty, and that Londres is pretty – even though he *is en rapport* with the city. Awkward as this way of reporting them is, it is often preferable to the exported versions if we are trying to capture Pierre's state of mind. In many situations the exported versions of these belief reports would be inappropriate. In the course of trying to explain why Pierre saves every penny for a vacation in the country, the observation 'he believes of the city he lives in that it is pretty' is true, but counterproductive.

To recapitulate, the problem with the attempt to specify when exportation is permitted by laying down criteria for a special intimacy between thinker and object is that it is a quest for two different things. In "Quantifying In," Kaplan is trying both to give the rules for granting export permits, and to delineate two kinds of beliefs. If I am right, such a project is doomed from the start. Whether we call the two kinds of belief 'relational' and 'notional' following Quine, or we use the more current terms 'de re' and 'de dicto', the connection between having a certain kind of relation to the object of one's thought and exportation is at best complex and tenuous. The two goals of the project do not coincide and no single criterion will do both jobs.

Direct Reference and *de re* Belief

Issues of export permits are thus independent from ones concerning the taxonomy of propositional attitudes. The most popular account of the *de re/de dicto* distinction, the one associated with direct reference theory, fails to take this into account.[12] The starting point of this conception is an observation about language. While some singular expressions, notably definite descriptions, denote in virtue of specifying a set of conditions the referent uniquely satisfies, names and indexicals refer directly. The point can, but need not, be put in terms of propositions. Propositions expressed by sentences containing the latter terms are called 'singular' because they cannot be reduced to a general proposition. In addition to attributes, they contain an irreducibly singular element (perhaps the object itself) whose only function is reference.

If instead of believing that the man in the brown hat was a spy, Ralph had believed that Bernard J. Ortcutt was a spy, then he would have believed a proposition which contained (a direct reference to) Bernard J. Ortcutt, the man. He would then be related to Ortcutt *simpliciter*, not Ortcutt under a guise. No mode of presentation or meaning would play an intermediary role between what Ralph believes and Ortcutt. Moreover, Ralph would be so related in virtue of one of his beliefs, not merely because we the reporters ascribe such a relation to him. Here, then, we have a notion of a different *kind* of *belief* content. The belief is *of* Ortcutt in a way Ralph's other beliefs were not. This captures the difference between my belief that my mother is a woman and the one that Shakespeare's mother was a woman. My thought is related directly, non-descriptively, to my mother. I only refer to Shakespeare's mother by description.

Exportation from positions occupied by directly referential terms is always allowed, in fact it is in general implicative. The reason for this is that such terms are "scopeless." Their only function is to refer, and so they refer whether they are in or out of opaque contexts. The only difference there might be between:

(21)   Ralph believes that Ortcutt is a spy.

and:

(22)   Of Ortcutt, Ralph believes that he is a spy.

is that the former but not the latter attributes to Ralph the use of the name 'Ortcutt'. The latter follows from the former, on this view, and so it is not surprising that it says *less* than the unexported version.

We now have a new special relation between thinker and object in place of Kaplan's *en rapport*. Exportation is permitted in those cases where the thinker has a singular belief. It follows from the fact that someone has a singular belief about some object that there is an object to which he is related. Such a view of certain kinds of belief has far-reaching consequences. In particular, since such beliefs relate one to objects "transparently," it would seem that some relations between the mind and its objects are not intentional. Furthermore, *de re* attitudes depend for their identity on the objects they are about. Their content makes essential reference to an external object and cannot be individuated without reference to that object. In describing Ralph's state of mind by (21), reference to Ortcutt is made. And there is no other way of describing what Ralph is thinking. Being *de re* is essentially just that, of an *object*.

But if there are such essentially *de re* cognitive states, then it would seem that some states are irreducibly relational and thus not intentional in Fodor's sense. Thus Fodor's solution to the dilemma with which we started would be wrong, and methodological solipsism impossible.

Some Problems of the Direct Reference View

On the direct reference view the *de re/de dicto* distinction separates kinds of mental states. But the view is so struck by the fact that there is some connection between *de re* attitudes and transparent (i.e., exported) reports that it transfers some of the properties of the latter to the former.

So, since the object of transparent reports must exist if they are true, the objects of *de re* beliefs must also exist. Since such reports are true given any description of the object or none, *de re* beliefs must also be independent from the conception which the thinker has of the object. There is only a relation between the speaker and the object, no mode of presentation mediates between them. And, since there is no difference between the exported and unexported version of reports using directly referential terms, beliefs correctly reported by these must be the *de re* ones. This conclusion of the direct reference theory of *de re* belief leads to a whole range of familiar problems.

In a nutshell, this way of drawing the distinction between *de re* and *de dicto* beliefs fails to capture two *mental* kinds. There are several problems. How is it possible for someone's mind to be related *directly* to a referent? Singular propositions are sometimes said to have the referent itself as a constituent. But how can an object itself get "into" the mind? The way for the direct reference theorist to meet this challenge is to retreat from the position that some mental states have objects in their contents. Instead, one can see the states as being irreducibly relational. The question then is: what is it about the person *in himself* that makes him related to one object rather than another? The direct reference theorist has no explanation available to him.

The notion of a mental state is not well defined, but some criteria of individuation of such states seem quite plausible. *De re* propositional attitudes do not fare well when some of our normal criteria are applied. It would seem, for example, that there is no phenomenological difference nor any difference in the power to explain behaviour, between the desire to find Rudolf where Rudolf exists and one where he does not (so long as the thinker is not aware of the lacuna). But on the direct reference theory, the latter is not even the same *kind* of belief as (i.e., has a radically different content from) the former, since there are no *de re* beliefs without objects. It is implausible that the content of one's propositional attitudes *requires* that their object exist. In fact, it was just this view that led intentionality theorists at the turn of the century to conclude that there must be special, intentional objects.

An even more serious problem is that, in fact, there does seem to be a mode of presentation even in the case of proper names and other directly referential terms. How else does one explain cases like Pierre's? He believes of London *qua* London that it is ugly and of London *qua* Londres that it is pretty. But the direct reference theory predicts that there is no distinction between beliefs specified as being about *London* and about *Londres*. One can recall or construct many such cases, including ones where the thinker uses one name to refer to what he thinks are two different people, as in Kripke's case about Paderewski, or one name for two different people, etc. Kripke's Paderewski case shows that the issue is not simply that one ought not to allow substitution of co-referential names in opaque contexts. If the direct reference theory is correct about language, as I tend to think it is, such substitution ought to be allowed. But disallowing it does not solve the problem in trying to extend the theory to propositional attitudes. These do seem to involve modes of presentation. Pierre thinks of Paderewski the pianist differently from the way he thinks of Paderewski the statesman, even though he knows that 'Paderewski' is a proper name and so is directly referential and not an abbreviation of 'the greatest Polish statesman' or 'the pianist whom my mother adores'.

In a word, mental states, even when directly referential terms are in-volved, are intentional and, to explain how they relate to ordinary ob-jects, we need just the rich notion of content which direct reference predicts they cannot have. One can introduce, if one wishes, a not fully intentional notion of belief on which it is a relation between a thinker with a certain propositional content and an object. Such a concept of mental state might even be useful in various ways. I have no objection to reifying that which is attributed to a person by an exported belief re-port, if such a move serves some purpose. I just do not think such a con-ception squares with our notion of a mental state.

Direct reference theorists are well aware of these problems. As Scott Soames put it: "If it weren't for propositional attitudes, direct reference would probably be uncontroversial" (1989, p. 393). The responses have ranged from an orgy of bullet-biting, through more-or-less covert rein-troductions of modes of presentation to dark Wittgensteinian sayings about the impossibility of a semantical theory.[13] The problem, as I see it, is that few are willing to give up on the premise that the semantics of propositional attitude ascriptions reveal the structure of cognitive state contents.

This premise and the consequence of direct reference theory that some terms can occur only in transparent (i.e., purely referential) posi-tions lead directly to the counter-intuitive conclusion that there are non-intentional mental states. The problem is compounded by the fact that it seems, on the face of it, that the direct reference view does have some-thing to say about cognition. After all, many of the arguments for it have concentrated on the speaker's understanding of referring expres-sions.

My proposal is to deny the premise and, at the same time, to provide an alternative account of how the insights of direct reference semantics are relevant to cognition.

Toward an Intentional Notion of *de re*

The account I propose has been suggested by Tyler Burge,[14] but germs of it can be found in Donnellan's work on reference (1966).[15] It has some analogues in David Kaplan's recent work[16] and is first found, I believe, in Husserl (1962). Its strength is that it retains all of the insights of the direct reference theory while leaving *de re* beliefs intentional. Husserl proposes the notion of the determinable X in *Ideas* 131 in connection with perception. He regards every mental attitude as intentional, including perception. I will not argue for it here because others have (Miller 1984, Smith and McIntyre 1982), but Husserl had a coherent notion of perception understood intentionally, i.e., so it does not follow that if I see a cat, there is a cat there which I see, nor that I see the cat, the animal, no matter how described.[17]

Now, perceptual beliefs are prime candidates for *de re* propositional attitudes. When one sees an object before one's eyes, the intention is to refer to *that* object, whatever description it might or might not satisfy. The use of the indexicals 'this' and 'here' is also paradigmatic in perceptual beliefs. Thus Husserl's notion of determinable X stands a good chance of helping us out of the dilemma that *de re* beliefs seem to be direct while all beliefs must be intentional and thus mediated by a mode of presentation.

The content or *noematic Sinn* of a perceptual belief has two different kinds of elements for Husserl.[18] It has attributive elements. Many would call the 'concepts' today, the term Burge prefers in his work on *de re* belief. These are familiar to us because Frege thought all *Sinne* were composed of them exclusively, Russell seems to think that most discourse and thought consists in commenting on the distribution of attributes in the world, and, before direct reference came into vogue, it was generally accepted that both linguistic and mental reference was achieved by means of attribute-specification.

The determinable X is an entirely different element. It is purely indexical (directly referential in the sense that it has no conceptual content, though not in the sense that its referent must exist for it to be meaningful). Its only function is as a sort of focal point for attributes: it explains the difference between the situation where F, G and H are all attributes of one object and the situations where F applies to one and G and H to another, or where none apply to any. In itself, however, it does not determine an object. It seems at first a strange element of thought. Its only function is to refer to a particular object. It does not say anything about its referent. But unlike the direct reference theorist's 'this' or 'Charles', its identity is not tied to the identity of the object. That is, which thought

I have when I think something whose content has 'X' and 'is green' in it, is not determined by which object I happen to be looking at. I could have the very same thought if the object was, unbeknownst to me, switched for another or was only a mirage to start with. I could also have *different* thoughts with those elements in the content while looking at the *same* object on different occasions, were I unaware of the identity. Needless to say, the attributive parts of the content do not determine the identity of the X and thus of the entire content either.

All of this is merely a consequence of the fact that contents with an X in them are still fully intentional; an X is not an element which guarantees a non-intentional relation to an object. Its function is internally determined. We are faced with a dilemma. If we try to introduce an element into thought whose function is *directly* to refer to an object *and* we insist on the full intentionality of mental states, we end up with mysterious contents individuated neither by the objects nor by their elements. The X is by definition featureless.

The solution which will allow us to have both direct reference and full intentionality is in fact parallel to a solution to a similar dilemma in direct reference theory. Kripke and Donnellan want to maintain that the *only* meaning of a proper name is its referent but they also want to hold, reasonably enough, that the connection between name and referent (and the identity of the name itself) is not a magical necessary bond but can be explained by contingent facts about human linguistic behaviour (Donnellan 1970, Kripke 1980). If we hold that the *meaning* of a term is what explains the connection, the puzzle is insoluble. The insight needed is that it is something *outside* linguistic meaning, in this case chains of uses, which explains how names attach to objects. Similarly, if we insist that it is the *content* which explains how and to what an X attaches we will not be able to do it.

It is very clear in Husserl that the determinable X comes into play only when we compare whole series of perceptual beliefs. Its function is to mark which attitudes are considered as being about the same object.[19] We regard certain experiences as being about the same object as others regardless of whether there is continuity of attributes or not. Such continuity provides *evidence* that the same object is present, but is not constitutive of our treating it *as* the same object. We keep track of these identities across beliefs as we go through various experiences, trying to keep each connected string of beliefs consistent and to find the right string for each new piece of information. All of this "bookkeeping" is outside the content of any particular belief. Instead, it is a matter of its external connection to other mental states which are taken to be about the same object.

It is thus somewhat misleading to talk of *the X* since there will have to be a different one for every intentional object a person keeps track of. The *X*'s will have to be subscripted in some way, though of course which subscript an *X* has makes no difference to the content of any single belief. The situation is, as Tyler Burge suggests, similar to that of bound variables in predicate calculus. It makes no difference which variable occurs in which open sentence. Their identity and function is entirely exhausted by the linkage between them and with quantifiers. Similarly, *de re* beliefs one by one and by themselves do not yet have a determinate referent and thus content. These are determined by the whole chain of beliefs taken to be about the same object.

We thus have a distinction between *de re* and *de dicto* beliefs which keeps them both fully intentional. The latter are fully conceptual or attributive, the former purport to be about a particular object. Of course, even a *de dicto* attitude may constitute a relation to an object – as in my desire to own the largest yacht in Philadelphia. Conversely, a *de re* attitude need not constitute such a relation at all – as in Virginia's hope that Santa will be good to her this year.

But while both are intentional, and both may constitute a relation to an object, the account of how this might be is different in the two cases. In other words, the problem of intentionality we started with – namely to explain how such relations are possible given the intentionality of the mental – gets different solutions. For *de dicto* ones the solution will likely be broadly in the Frege/Russell[20] mode: the object thought about, if one exists, is the one that satisfies the set of attributive conditions specified by the content. For *de re*, the solution will likely have something to do with the perceptual/causal origins of the chain of attitudes tied with a particular *X*.

De re and *de dicto* attitudes are thus importantly different from one another, both structurally and in how they are tied to the world. But this difference cannot be captured by either semantic or syntactic criteria applied to sentences ascribing propositional attitudes, if I have argued successfully.

Acknowledgments

This paper has its roots in my Ph.D. dissertation. I am grateful for comments on various written and oral versions of this material from Tyler Burge, David Kaplan, Keith Donnellan, Derk Pereboom, Steven Davis and, of course, Philip Hanson. Their lack of responsibility for my mistakes goes without saying.

Notes

1 I will speak freely and often of the contents of mental states in ways which seem to commit me to some very strong, perhaps Platonist, version of realism concerning them. In fact, I am a metaphysical agnostic about them. I believe my points are fully compatible with instrumentalism about content. That is, even if one takes content-talk to be merely a useful and convenient way of talking about human behaviour from a Dennettian "intentional stance" (Dennett 1978, 1987), there can be representational structure to the contents we ascribe, and this structure may not be captured by the that-clauses used. After all, contents are supposed to have predictive and explanatory value in our science of human behaviour. If I can show, as I think I can, that taking contents to be the occasion-meanings of that-clauses gives us the wrong results, I have the conclusion I want without any objectionable reification of contents.

2 The term 'opaque' originally applies to linguistic contexts – it is short for 'referentially opaque', a condition of a position occupied by a name, variable, or other referring device which does not allow unrestricted substitutivity of coreferential terms or existential generalization *salva veritate* (Quine 1960, 1966, 1976). The term has been widely extended to apply to mental states (Quine 1960, Fodor 1981). Given its metaphorical character, such an extension is relatively harmless: there is the opaque (intentional) sense of 'seeing' on which when I see a dagger it does not follow that it exists, and there is the transparent (relational) sense on which it does follow. To philosophers raised on the idea of the veil of perception, such a metaphorical use of Quine's 'opacity' terminology comes naturally. I will have much more to say below about what Quine, and others, might mean by 'relational'.

3 The notion of intentionality at stake here ought to be clear. 'Intentional' means roughly 'representational' with the understanding that the familiar failures of identity or existence of the intended object are possible. 'Intentional' does not mean merely *directed* or, with emphasis standing proxy for clarity, *of* or *about*. Berkeley's account – or, for that matter, Brentano's – account of the relation between the mind and its (immediate) object makes it intentional in the second sense, but not the first. Failures of existence or identity cannot occur where the *of* relation is necessarily incorrigible.

4 The problem of the interpretation of quantifying in is, in my view, not a philosophical one but a technical one, once it becomes clear why it is that we do not want to say "so much the worse for propositional attitude ascriptions." The latter question is what I am trying to answer there. That is not to say that inquiring into what opacity is and how, formally, to deal with it is not difficult or interesting. One need only look at the subtleties of Kaplan's "Opacity" (1986).

5 I am grateful to Professor Hedberg of the Simon Fraser University Linguistics Department for pointing this example out to me. Examples like this are

discussed in some detail in Chastain's seminal "Reference and Context" (1975).

6 I am relying here, perhaps unfairly, on the reader's familiarity with "the" *de re/de dicto* distinction as it has been used in the literature. Later, I will sharpen just what "interesting standards" might be.

7 To anticipate somewhat, this is a way of making the by- now familiar point that the construction where one quantifies into the propositional attitude ascription is no guarantee that the attitude is really *de re*. I am avoiding the terminology favoured by Kaplan and Burge which labels these *'pseudo de re'*. The reason for this is that on my view a linguistic construction is not the sort of thing which is or is not *de re*, pseudo or otherwise; and the attitudes themselves seem to be *de dicto, tout court*.

8 I say *more* of a commitment because the degree of such commitment seems to be only a matter of conversational propriety even in the unexported case. So given Quine's story about Ralph who thinks Ortcutt is a spy when he spots him in a brown hat under suspicious circumstances but not when he sees him at the beach because he does not realize it is the same person, to say of Ralph that he believes that the man he has seen at the beach is a spy is no worse than misleading in some conversational contexts, false in others. On the other hand, to say that, of the man at the beach, Ralph believes that he is a spy (or some such natural language expression which is to make it clear that *we*, the reporters, take responsibility for the denoting phrase used) involves us in no commitment to reporting *how* he is thinking of Ortcutt.

9 To whatever standards of accuracy are appropriate. It is simply false, it seems to me, that what follows a 'that-' clause has to be exactly "what is in the head" (whatever that means) of the person to whom the content is attributed. It might be distorted in various ways to make it comprehensible to the audience or merely grossly simplified because that is all the accuracy required in the context. Furthermore, it can be quite different from what the person herself would say or even agree to, were she asked to report her own state of mind. The reasons for this can range from self-deception, through lack of the ability to understand one's own views, to certain kinds of (non-radical) lack of linguistic competence. Obviously, this is not the place to argue for this, but I am suggesting that the recently much discussed principle of disquotation (Kripke 1979) is simply false.

10 Hard, but not impossible. Let us suppose that it turns out that JFK had discovered structural faults in the White House and thought that, sometime in the early 1970s, the place would have to be evacuated for major re-construction which would take some 10 years. Now, someone explaining this to you might go through the list of presidents since then and say: "JFK was pretty sure all presidents until about 1972 would live in the White House, but not after. That makes Ford borderline and Carter out of the question. But now, Reagan after 1984, by the time you get to him, JFK was sure he would live there again."

11 For sticklers: "You are such that my friend Ralph strives that he meet you."

12 I am thinking, of course, of Donnellan's (1970) and Kripke's (1980) work on proper names and Kaplan's (1978) on indexicals. A more complicated issue is the place of Donnellan's work on definite descriptions (1966) in the theory of direct reference. My conjecture is that the results are of a rather different kind, but I will not argue for this here.

13 It is not always easy to tell the bullet-biting from the reintroductions of modes of presentation. This is certainly so in Kaplan (1989), Salmon (1981), Soames (1989) and others. The dark Wittgensteinian sayings can be found, with increasing frequency, in the work of Howard Wettstein.

14 The idea first appears in "Belief de re," a more full working out in "Russell's Problem and Intentional Identity." There is reason to believe Burge himself does not hold the view I am defending here.

15 Donnellan characterizes the referential use of a definite description as one where the speaker has someone in mind to refer to. This idea has never had much of an influence on philosophers interested in the semantical consequences of Donnellan's work. For them, the claim that such uses are non-attributive, i.e., do not find the referent by description, has played the central role. But let us take seriously Donnellan's suggestion that the referent is "what the speaker had in mind," and add what ought to be obvious: that we can intend to refer to things that do not exist, that we need not be able to identify the intended referent under every guise. (Consider Schliemann's state of mind before his discovery and whether it would have been any different had the site of Troy not existed.) We are not likely to come up with a direct reference view of referential uses then. That would require that such descriptions always take wide scope, i.e., that the object exist and the intended reference be under whatever description or none.

16 I have in mind his notion of a virtual word, discussed in recent seminars and lecture series. Kaplan emphasizes the importance of the speaker's (thinker's) use of a name as a single name (referring to a single object) regardless of its use in the community.

17 The idea that there is an entirely intentional sense of all sensation-words is by no means a new one. One can find it explicitly defended in Descartes's second Meditation.

18 Husserl calls the part of what he calls 'content' or 'noema' which many modern theorists think of as the content 'noematic Sinn' The other part of Husserlian content, the 'way of being given', 'gegebenheitsweise' contains an indexical reference to the thinker as well as a mental correlate of what Searle, following Austin, calls the 'illocutionary force'.

19 See Ideas (1966, pp. 337-38) for this and also Miller's illuminating discussion (1984, pp. 63-69). This does not mean that the first time I see a what I take to be a new object and refer to it mentally as an X, my thought is meaningless. The function of the X in this case is precisely that it starts a chain of thoughts

about what I take to be the same object. So even if another thought about it never occurs to me, the series is thereby started.

20 There is a complication for Russell, since he thought there were logically proper names which had some sort of a primitive relation to their referent. So for Russell, this account is right only for thoughts where these do not occur. See chap. 3 of my dissertation (Hahn 1990) for more details.

References

Almog, Joseph (1986). Naming without necessity. *Journal of Philosophy* 83: 162-85

Brentano, Franz (1973). *Psychology from an Empirical Standpoint*. L. McAlister (ed.). New York: Humanities Press

Burge, Tyler (1977). Belief de re. *Journal of Philosophy* 74: 338-62

— (1979). Individualism and the mental. In P. French, T. Uehling, H. Wettstein, (eds.), *Studies in Metaphysics*. Vol. IV, Midwest Studies in Philosophy. Minneapolis: University of Minnesota Press

— (1982). Other bodies. In A. Woodfield, (ed.), *Thought and Object*. Oxford: Oxford Universtity Press

— (1983) Russell's problem and intentional identity. In J. Tomberlin, ed., *Agent, Language and the Structure of the World*. Indianapolis: Hackett Publishing, 79-110

Chastain, Charles (1975). Reference and context. In K. Gunderson (ed.), *Language. Mind and Knowledge*. Vol. VII, Minnesota Studies in the Philosophy of Science. Minneapolis: University of Minnesota Press: 194-269

Donnellan, Keith (1966). Reference and definite descriptions. *Philosophical Review* 77: 281-304

— (1970). Proper names and identifying descriptions. *Synthese* 21 (October): 203-15

Dreyfus, Hubert (ed.) (1982). *Husserl, Intentionality and Cognitive Science*. Cambridge, MA: MIT Press

Fodor, Jerry (1981). Methodological solipsism considered as a research strategy in cognitive psychology. In his *Representations*. Cambridge, MA: MIT Press

Føllesdal, Dagfinn (1982). Husserl's notion of noema. Reprinted in Dreyfus (ed.) (1982), Husserl, Intentionality and Cognitive Science. Cambridge, MA: MIT Press, 73-80.

Frege, Gottlog (1968). The thought. In E.D. Klemke, (ed.), *Essays on Frege*. Urbana: University of Illinois Press, 507-36

— (1970). On sense and reference. In P. Geach and M. Black (eds.), *Translations from the Philosophical Works of Gottlob Frege*. Oxford: Basil Blackwell, 56-78

Grice, Paul (1989). Logic and conversation. In his *Studies in the Way of Words*. Cambridge, MA: Harvard University Press, 1-144

Hahn, Martin (1990). Intentionalty, Direct Reference and Individualism. Ph.D. dissertation. Los Angeles: UCLA

Hintikka, J. (1967). Individuals, possible worlds and epistemic logic. In *Nous* 1: 33-62

Husserl, Edmund (1962). *Ideas*. W.R.Boyce Gibson (trans.). New York: Collier Books

Kaplan, David (1971). Quantifying in. In L. Linsky (ed.): *Reference and Modality*. Oxford: Oxford University Press

— (1977). Demonstratives. In J. Almog, J. Perry and H. Wettstein (eds.), *Themes from Kaplan*. New York: Oxford University Press, 481-563

— (1978). Dthat. In Peter Cole (ed.), *Syntax and Semantics*. New York: Academic Press, 221-53

— (1986).Opacity. In Lewis Edwin Hahn and Paul Arthur Schilpp (eds.), *The Philosophy of W.V.O. Quine*. La Salle: Open Court, 229-89

Kripke, Saul (1979). A puzzle about belief. In A. Margolit, *Meaning and Use*. Dordrecht: Reidel, 239-83

— (1980). *Naming and Necessity*. Cambridge, MA: Harvard University Press

Linsky, Leonard (ed.) (1971). *Reference and Modality*. Oxford: Oxford University Press

Miller, Izchak (1984). *Husserl, Perception and Temporal Awareness*. Cambridge, MA: MIT Press

Perry, John (1979). The problem of the essential indexical. In *Nous*. 13: 3-21

Quine, W.V.O. (1960). *Word and Object*. Cambridge, MA: MIT Press

— (1963). Reference and modality. In his *From a Logical Point of View*. New York: Harper and Row, 139-51

— (1966). Three grades of modal involvement. In his *The Ways of Paradox*. Cambridge, MA: Harvard University Press: 158-76

— (1976). Quantifiers and propositional attitudes. In his *The Ways of Paradox*. Cambridge, MA: Harvard University Press: 185-96

— (1981). *Theories and Things*. Cambridge, MA: Harvard University Press

Russell, Bertrand (1905). On denoting. *Mind*. 14: 479-93. Reprinted (1956) in R.C. Marsh (ed.), *Logic and Knowledge*. London: George Allen & Unwin, 41-56

— (1956). The philosophy of logical atomism. In R.C. Marsh (ed.), *Logic and Knowledge*. London: George Allen & Unwin: 173-281

Salmon, Nathan (1986). *Frege's Puzzle*. Cambridge, MA: MIT Press

Searle, John (1983). *Intentionality*. Cambridge: Cambridge University Press

Sleigh, Robert (1967). On quantifying into epistemic contexts. In *Nous* 1: 1-31

Soames, Scott (1986). Direct reference and propositional attitudes. In Lewis Edwin Hahn and Paul Arthur Schilpp (eds.), *The Philosophy of W.V.O. Quine*. La Salle: Open Court, 392-420

Smith, David and Ronald McIntyre (1982). *Husserl and Intentionality*. Dordrecht: Reidel

Wettstein, Howard (1991). *Has Semantics Rested on a Mistake?* Palo Alto, CA: Stanford University Press

16
Cognitive Content and Semantics*
Philip P. Hanson

Do cognitive state ascriptions reveal the logical form of cognitive state contents? Not in general, says Hahn, because the interpretation of cognitive state ascriptions, which their logical form would make perspicuous, can include "direct reference" to objects in the world, whereas cognitive state contents are "essentially intentional" in a way that excludes such direct reference. But, Hahn continues, it is a mistake to suppose that, in general, the logical form of cognitive state contents *should* be (fully) revealed by cognitive state ascriptions, the received view to the contrary notwithstanding.[1] Instead, the interpretation of cognitive state ascriptions is importantly keyed to purposes and ontological commitments of ascribers: *pragmatically*, to their *appropriateness* for use in connection with the (e.g., explanatory) purposes and ontological commitments of particular ascribers in particular contexts of ascription; *semantically*, to whatever purposes or commitments the linguistic community has conventionally enshrined in the *truth conditions* it attaches to the sentences.

It is possible, of course, to be sceptical about intentionality, semantics, direct reference and all that.[2] But for those of us who would like not to be, Hahn's line sounds promising. Perplexing problems appear, however, when we move from this preliminary statement to a more detailed articulation – problems, e.g., about the nature and causal-explanatory credentials of cognitive contents, about the individuation of cognitive states, about the role of cognitive state ascriptions in psychological explanations, about the scope of semantics, and about the point of an account of the logical form of cognitive contents.

Hahn wants us to apply our formal techniques directly to thought contents themselves rather than to their ascriptions. But this seems like hard advice to follow, given our apparent lack of direct access to thought contents.[3] It is also hard to see how cognitive contents can be characterized except through the sentences of public language. So will not the logical form of thought contents *have* to be captured, if at all, by the logical forms of whatever linguistic structures we must use to describe them?

I.

Let us begin with an intuitive, pretheoretic, or "vernacular" (see above, n.2) characterization of the central notion of cognitive state content. To believe, for instance, is to believe *something*: that 2+2=4, that snow is black, that Sir John A. MacDonald was the first Prime Minister of Canada, or that Santa is an elf. Call *what* is believed the belief's content. On the received view, a belief is completely individuated by specifying the believer, the time of the belief and its content. And it is supposed to be definitive of a *de dicto* interpretation of a standard belief ascription of the form '*S* believes that *p*' that the that-clause – i.e., the 'that' followed by the declarative sentence for which '*p*' stands – expresses the "propositional" content of the ascribed belief.[4] When a belief is true (false) it is because of its true (false) content. And the 'cognitive closure' of one's set of beliefs supposedly reflects pretty much the closure of the contents of one's "atomic" beliefs under logical operations and relations like logical implication and equivalence, subject only to the incompleteness, inadequacies or inherent limitations in the believer's grasp of the contents of her beliefs, her grasp of logical relations, or her reasoning capacities. What we need, then, from a theory of the logical form of cognitive contents is their truth conditions, and on the received view we can get these simply by extracting them from the truth conditions of belief ascriptions on their *de dicto* interpretation.

But, besides being the bearer of a truth value, a cognitive content is also supposed to give a belief its specific relevance to given contexts of psychological explanation; and this combination of constraints on giving the logical form of belief contents creates problems. For instance, the content determines the "subject matter" of the belief, what it is about. A belief about some existing object thereby relates the believer to that object in a way that may be pertinent to the explanation of the believer's (e.g., object-directed) behaviour. The trouble is, by virtue of the intuitive notion of content, each belief has a content, and each therefore has a subject matter whether or not that subject matter actually exists. Beliefs whose subject matters are merely, as it were, *ens rationis*, e.g., beliefs about Santa, nevertheless have subject matters and contents in the only sense intuitively relevant to being a belief. And it seems to follow from this that nothing about the content *per se* contributes in a determining way to the believer's relation to an actually existing subject matter when there is one.

This leads directly to Brentano's Problem. For as Hahn emphasizes, appealing to particular relational – broadly speaking "referential" or "representational" – features of our cognitive states seems necessary in psychological explanations of our behaviour, if only because our behaviour is itself typically characterized as directed towards or otherwise relating us to objects, properties, and so on in our environment. Yet if, as Fodor says and Hahn approvingly quotes, "truth, reference, and the rest of the semantic notions aren't psychological categories" (p. 327), what contribution can a *purely intentional* content which excludes these make to the explanation of behaviour? Brentano's Problem à la Hahn just is the problem of explaining "how it is that our cognitive states [can] constitute a relation between us and objects in the world" (p. 326), even though they would be the same states with the same contents even if they did not, other things being equal.⁵

Hahn therefore needs a solution to Brentano's Problem, and goes on to sketch one. But before turning to it, we would do well to notice that Fodor's previously quoted remark ruling out any 'semantic notion' as a psychological category begs the question considerably. It assumes that ascribing any semantic property to a cognitive state turns it into a relational state, thereby undermining its intentionality. But this is far from obvious. Let us distinguish between truth and reference, on the one hand, and truth *conditions* and reference *conditions* on the other, where by these latter we mean *interpretive rules*, not the extralinguistic states of affairs or objects that may satisfy those rules. Interpretive rules in and of themselves are surely semantic yet non-relational. To grasp such a rule does not in and of itself seem to constitute a relation with the extralinguistic conditions that may satisfy it. In this connection it should also be noted that by the "semantic content" of a natural language sentence, Hahn appears to mean the proposition expressed by it, which is surely distinct both from the interpretive rule(s) associated with it and from the conditions in the world that may satisfy those rules.⁶ So semantic content does not appear to exhaust semantics. This means that the semantic status of cognitive contents cannot be settled simply by showing that they are not semantic contents in the technical sense of propositions expressed.

Hahn's solution to Brentano's Problem has three key elements. The first is the rather compelling point that if cognitive states *do* relate to worldly items even though they *need not*, then such relations must be contingent, and lie outside the state's cognitive content proper. It is these contingent connections, e.g., perceptual/causal connections, together with the cognitive states themselves, that we are really appealing to in psychological explanations of behaviour. But there are, he thinks, no *de re* cognitive states whose content constitutively incorporates such relations or relata. It is because so many illustrious philosophers have thought otherwise that he spends so much time defending this negative claim. Against the postulation of such "worldly" *de re* cognitive states he argues that the reasons that have been given for postulating them are bad reasons that confuse the semantic or pragmatic interpretation of natural language ascriptions of such states – which ascriptions *can* imply relations to worldly items – with the cognitive content of the states themselves.

The second element is the familiar but controversial thesis that cognitive states have or involve "modes of presentation" or "guises" of their contents, such that the same content can be believed under different modes of presentation. Thus Ralph may believe that Cicero *qua* 'Cicero' was a Roman orator, or may instead believe that Cicero *qua* 'Tully' was a Roman orator.[7] Hahn accepts a direct reference construal of proper names, in which there is no semantic difference between the ascriptions 'Ralph believes that Cicero was a Roman orator' and 'Ralph believes that Tully was a Roman orator', provided that 'Cicero' and 'Tully' are co-referential names. But at the same time he insists that there can be a difference in these two beliefs not captured by the semantics of their ascriptions, because of their different modes of presentation. Modes of presentation are needed to explain, in this instance, why Ralph recognizes a propositional content as one that he believes when it is characterized one way, but not when it is characterized another semantically equivalent way. Besides challenging the cognitive or causal-explanatory significance of directly referential construals of belief ascriptions, the postulation of guises also challenges the received view of the individuation of beliefs, something direct reference theorists are quick to point out.

The third element is a psychologically privileged sense of content – "intentional content proper" – distinguishable (when it needs to be, cf. n.1 above) from the semantic, i.e., propositional contents expressed in cognitive state ascriptions. Hahn's intentional content has the interesting though perhaps problematic feature of admitting of a kind of indeterminacy, a feature that figures in what Hahn provocatively characterizes as a "purely intentional *de re/de dicto* distinction" among beliefs. Briefly, the intentional content of a *"de dicto* belief" is a fully determinate structure of concepts or attributive conditions of the familiar Fregean sort. Whereas the intentional content of a *"de re* belief" is a not fully determinate mixed structure of Fregean attributive conditions and occurrences of Husserl's determinable X. The determinable X is not a worldly object (or *res*) nor does it determine one, though it purports to refer to one. Yet it is not an attributively conceptual item either. The determinable functions rather as a directly referential indexical to which concepts may attach when they purport to be about the same thing.[8] So

I can believe *de dicto* that the best sushi bar in Canada is in Vancouver. Or I can believe *de re* that, as it were, X is in Vancouver, where the 'X' purports to pick out an otherwise unspecified subject matter, which, though it may turn out to be a certain sushi bar (e.g., via a perceptual connection), is not determined to be so by the 'X'.

Is there supposed to be a connection between the second and third elements, i.e., between the modes of presentation thesis and the determinable X thesis? The closest Hahn comes to drawing one is when he claims that "Husserl's notion of determinable X stands a good chance of helping us out of the dilemma that *de re* beliefs seem to be direct while all beliefs must be intentional and thus mediated by a mode of presentation" (p. 344). How so? A possibility proposed later is that the determinables may best be thought of as constituents of *guises* rather than, as Hahn would have it, of contents.

II.

Hahn wants a purely intentional *de re/de dicto* distinction among beliefs. But what would that be? Taking our cue from his title, we can ask: *What is this distinction not?* Obviously it is not supposed to be any distinction that is not a distinction among beliefs, or that is not in some appropriate sense a *de re/de dicto* distinction, or that is not purely intentional. And Hahn argues convincingly that a number of would-be *de re/de dicto* distinctions among beliefs fail one or more of these conditions. A brief review will bring to light what Hahn is after. First, Hahn's distinction is not Quine's distinction between "notional" and "relational" beliefs, since the latter distinction, *contra* Quine, fails to mark any distinction among beliefs as opposed to belief ascription sentences. Second, it is not the distinction between non-specific and specific construals of beliefs. This Hahn takes to be a genuine distinction among beliefs, which Quine also confusedly invoked, he tells us, to justify his notional/relational distinction. But it is not a *de re/de dicto* distinction, because both non-specific and specific construals can be understood as *de dicto*. Thus I might believe that a yacht has been stolen, meaning non-specifically some yacht or other, any yacht, none in particular. Or I might believe that a yacht has been stolen, meaning a specific one, e.g., the largest yacht in Philadelphia, whichever one that is. Now even though my belief is specific, it need involve no relation to a real yacht.

But is that not acceptable? Hahn wants an intentional *de re/de dicto* distinction among beliefs, one which does not involve relations to worldly items essentially. Why is this not such a distinction? Hahn's thinking here seems to be that the specific object is identified descriptively, or attributively, so that no *"special* relation with a *res"* (p. 332, emphasis his), presumably not even with an *ens rationis*, need be involved.[9] So what we may glean from this is that a genuine intentional *de re/de dicto* distinction among beliefs should mark a distinction among ways of being related to objects in virtue of one's beliefs.

Third, Hahn's intentional *de re/de dicto* distinction as applied to beliefs is not the distinction between beliefs about a thing with which the believer is not *en rapport* and beliefs about a thing with which she is. While this, too, can mark a distinction among beliefs, it can be at best, Hahn thinks, a *distinction of degree* amongst intentionally *de re* beliefs, while at worst a distinction that also fails to be intentional. Thus I am *en rapport* with my mother but not with Shakespeare's. In that respect my belief that my mother is a woman differs from my belief that Shakespeare's mother was a woman. But both beliefs may relate me essentially to an *ens rationis* (lending itself to the best case), and also contingently and non-intentionally to a worldly item (lending itself to the worst case).[10] What we may glean from this is that the distinction between ways of being related to something that Hahn wants must be a distinction of kind and not merely of degree.

Fourth and finally, Hahn's distinction among beliefs is not the distinction between, on the one hand, beliefs that are about an item because their content is a Fregean proposition containing an attributive conceptual element that picks out the item, and on the other hand beliefs that are about an item because their content is a Russellian singular proposition that contains the item. Here at last is a distinction of kind between ways of being related to an object. The trouble now is that while some belief ascriptions are true when semantically interpreted in terms of Russellian singular propositions, such propositions are not properly intentional, and so no belief can have such a proposition as its cognitive content. What Hahn seems to be looking for, then, is a *distinction like this last one, but purely intentional.* And he claims to have found it, in what is, in effect, an intentional analogue of Russellian singular propositions. Instead of an ordered pair (in the simplest case) consisting of a worldly item followed by a concept, the intentional analogue is an ordered pair consisting of an occurrence of the determinable *X* followed by a concept (p. 344). Let us dub these latter "Husserlian singular propositions," though as we shall see, whether or not they really are a kind of proposition is debatable.

What is the determinable? It *looks and sounds* like just a piece of syntax, intuitively a strange sort of thing to be *in* a content as opposed to being *assigned* one. This is a sticky issue. Hahn says the following: that the determinable functions like an indexical and its only function is to refer to a particular object, to individuate an otherwise unspecified subject matter, but that it is meaningful whether or not its referent exists (p. 344); that which determinable occurs in a *de re* belief will make no difference to the belief's content, though there will have to be a distinct determinable for each distinct subject matter of *de re* beliefs;[11] that Husserlian singular propositions cannot, taken singly, serve as *determinate* contents for the reason that an occurrence of a determinable X in a particular *de re* belief does not by itself have a determinate reference (p. 346). However Hahn intimates that while a *de re* belief taken singly lacks determinate content, a *de re* belief taken together with the whole chain of beliefs involving the same determinable can have it. He hints that there might be some sort of quantification (existential?) over the whole chain yielding a determinate referent for the determinable, and thus a determinate content (p. 346).

If Husserlian singular propositions taken singly are not determinate contents, then taken singly they have no determinate truth value and cannot enter into the logical relations reserved for propositions. Yet intuitively beliefs *are* true or false taken singly, and their contents *do* enter into such relations. This indicates vividly just how far Hahn has moved away from the received view of contents and of why we need an account of their logical form. But intuitively the contents of beliefs are also essentially intentional, and given the behaviour to be explained, it seems as though this denial of truth-bearer status may be necessary if we are to have an account of cognitive content that preserves the causal-explanatory role of content while remaining intentional.

As for chains of beliefs, I see how (e.g., existential) quantification would give them a determinate semantic content, and thus truth value, but how would it yield a determinate *referent*, which is surely required for a determinate *de re* content? Presumably not in terms of some object *uniquely satisfying the associated attributive conditions*. It is hard to see how there could be any guarantee of this; but in any case it seems like just the sort of thing Hahn *wants not* to be guaranteed, given that determinables are supposed to be directly referential. One might take the beliefs to be about intentional entities uniquely satisfying the descriptive conditions. But this too is implausible, and Hahn properly resists it; my belief that X is in Vancouver is about a particular sushi bar, not an *ens rationis*. Now if among the chain of beliefs containing the determinable is a perceptual belief that causally links the determinable to the intended referent, then perhaps the referent is "determined" in this way, but since it is not thereby *purely intentionally* determined, why would this determination of referent imply a determinate *intentional de re* content for the beliefs? *Contra* Hahn, the cost of a fully intentional *de re* belief may be its lack of a fully determinate intentional *de re* content, even when taken together with the other beliefs that share its determinable.

Perhaps what Hahn has in mind is merely that the *function*, not the referent, of a determinable is determined by the whole chain of beliefs that share it and are therefore taken to be beliefs about the same thing. But while their bookkeeping aspect may be so determined, that is merely an aspect of what Hahn has already identified as their referential function, and it is very unclear how even their referential function, let alone their referent, is determined just by a determinable occurrence's internal links with other occurrences.

All this still leaves unanswered the question of what constitutes the 'meaningfulness' of the determinable. Husserlian singular propositions are *individualistic* entities, and Hahn tells us that he agrees with Tyler Burge that "an individualist semantics of cognitive state contents is impossible" (p. 328). That seems compatible with there being an individualist semantic *component* to an overall relational semantic story about cognitive contents, perhaps of the sort Fodor has proposed. But while Hahn does side with Fodor's commitment to intentionality, nowhere does he contemplate the Fodorian idea of a "narrow content," or, e.g., the Kaplanesque idea of "semantic character," to explain the claim that the determinables are meaningful even when they fail to pick out anything.[12] Yet whatever it is that contingently determines the worldly referent of a determinable when it has one, there must be *something about the determinable itself* (but not, of course, a Fregean attributive condition) which facilitates and helps to sustain that referential tie. Such a feature would seem to be semantic by virtue of its role, and so a semantics for cognitive contents needs to tell us what it is.

Hahn likens the determinables to indexicals, and indexicals are directly referential and meaningful even when they do not refer, just like Hahn says determinables are, so let us briefly consider Kaplan's semantics for indexicals as a possible model for the meaningfulness of determinables. According to Kaplan, indexicals have "semantic character," which is taken to be an interpretive, rule-like component of meaning that they have independent of a context of utterance: and which, together with such a context, determines an unique referent in that context. For instance, the semantic character of indexical 'I' is the rule that, relative to a given "context of utterance," 'I' refers to the speaker in that context: while apart from such a context 'I' does not refer at all. Semantic character is not propositional content. Rather, character plus context determines content.[13] Now, could we think of Husserlian determinables having a "cognitive semantic character" akin to this? The problem of its specification would be to characterize in some sufficiently general rule-like way (that could plausibly be taken to be grasped at least implicitly by a cognitive agent) a set of internal (psychological) and external (contingently occurring) conditions given which the occurrence of a determinable would pick out an unique and stable (i.e., not contextually relativized) referent.

I have no idea whether this is possible. But here I am just going to assume that determinables are, in fact, governed by some such interpretive rules. For I find it hard to suppose that the meaningfulness of an occurrence of a determinable can consist merely in (anything like) its syntactic links with other occurrences of the same determinable. That seems to me to be a kind of category mistake. If the point of a theory of the logical form of cognitive contents is to make their intentional semantics perspicuous, then if it postulates Husserlian determinables, it needs also to postulate the intentional basis of their referential role. And what other options are there?

III.

Turning finally to Hahn's construal of the semantics of natural language belief ascription sentences, recall his claim that, contrary to the received view, it is false that in giving the semantics of a standard belief ascription sentence – a sentence like 'John believes that scampi are not shrimp' – one thereby gives the content of the belief. But if the embedded that-clause does not express the content of the belief, then, at least on the traditional conception of belief individuation, no determinate belief is attributed by the sentence. Yet was it not the content that was supposed to be crucial to belief-desire explanations, explanations formulated using standard belief ascription sentences?

Hahn is careful to distinguish semantic from pragmatic issues in the interpretation of belief ascriptions. Very roughly, matters of truth conditions attaching to the ascription are semantic for him, while matters of the appropriateness of the ascription to the purposes of the ascriber in a context are pragmatic. I have no quarrel with this general line of demarcation. But it leaves unanswered the crucial issue of what gets built into the truth conditions.

The possibility of meaningful belief-desire explanations seems to depend in part on it being possible for people to *share* such cognitive states, i.e., have type-identical ones. I believe that the ozone layer is being depleted, and so do others. This makes it possible to explain certain shared patterns of behaviour that we may exhibit by appealing to our shared beliefs. How does the nature of belief allow for this? The received view is that beliefs are relations to propositions, and thus individuated by their propositional contents, and that sharing a belief means having beliefs with the same propositional content. But if Russellian singular propositions are admitted as possible contents, then we have the problems, first, that they are not intentional, and second, that a certain apparent *opacity* in some of our belief ascriptions remains unaccounted for. Thus Pierre may believe that *Londres* is pretty while not believing that London is, even though, given a direct reference construal of names, the respective embedded that-clauses of these ascriptions express the same Russellian singular proposition. So we might instead think of beliefs as relations not to propositions but to the internal counterparts of natural language sentences, guises.[14] But while this gives us as much opacity as a substitutivity principle could be sensitive to,[15] it makes sharing of beliefs a relatively rare phenomenon.

The move often taken in response to this, and a move Hahn has already made, is to make beliefs a kind of three place relation: to say that beliefs are related to propositions *under* guises (or "modes of presentation" or "internal representations" or "sentences of mentalese"). For Maggie to believe that London is not pretty or that scampi are not shrimp there must, on this construal, be some mode of presentation or other under which she believes a certain proposition (Russellian singular in both cases, provided that natural kind terms, like names, are directly referential). But this does not automatically help. If the requirement is that there be a *particular, specified* guise, then that again interferes with our wish to attribute shared beliefs. If on the other hand the requirement is merely that there be *some mode of presentation or other* under which the proposition is believed, then instead there is a failure of opacity: e.g., Ralph ends up believing that Tully was a Roman orator after all, since there is *some* guise under which he believes it[16]

It may be that Hahn is not bothered by this.[17] But if the apparent opacity of such ascriptions is linked to a real aspect of the belief itself – its mode of presentation – and not just some contextual explanatory purpose or ontological commitment of the ascriber, why not make the opacity semantically real by making the truth conditions more sensitive to the peculiarities of the mode of presentation? If so, there can then be a kind of link after all between the semantics of belief ascriptions and the intentionality of belief contents (see below).

But in that case what seems to be needed, if it can be had, is *just the right amount of constraint* on features of the guise, constraint that is strong enough to capture the opacity, but weak enough to permit sufficient sharing of beliefs. It would have to be a delicate balance. Suppose that we let one guiding constraint on co-referential substitutions into the embedded that-clauses of natural language ascriptions be *the preservation of cognitive function of the attributed belief.* Then, for example, if Ralph associates a different determinable with 'Tully' than he does with 'Cicero', the cognitive function of his belief that Cicero was a Roman orator will fail to be preserved under a substitution of 'Tully' for 'Cicero.'

I propose that we let modes of presentation be the primary bearers of intentionality, and let determinables be features of them. And where a determinable is involved, let the mode of presentation involve the whole chain of beliefs, and therefore include all the internal representations of concepts and singular terms attached in the believing way to the given determinable. Husserlian singular propositions on this conception turn out to be a splicing together of part of a guise and part of a Fregean proposition (see Fig. 1). So a determinable will not be a

---

Representations of:

I.   A Russellian Singular Proposition

$$< a, Fy >$$

where 'a' is the name of some particular individual, and 'Fy' expresses the concept of having some particular property.

II.   An Husserlian Singular Proposition

$$< 'X_1', Fy >$$

where "'X_1'" names a particular (internal) determinable, and 'Fy' is as above.

III. A Mode of Presentation

$$< 'X_1', 'a_i', 'Fy_i',... >$$

where "'X_1'" is as above, "'a_i'" names an internal representation of a public language name, and "'Fy_i'" names an internal representation of the concept expressed by 'Fy', and we let the mode of presentation include all the internal representations of concepts and singular terms attached to the determinable.

Figure 1.

constituent of a cognitive content after all. But its "cognitive semantic character"[18] in the sense previously posited can be. Like an Husserlian singular proposition, the resulting mixed structure will not in itself be a bearer of truth values and so not a proposition. But it will be just as intentional and, I claim, more uniformly semantic.

Guises and parts of guises, in and of themselves, seem to be merely syntactic, and as such not a kind of content nor essentially bonded to a content. But on the proposed conception they are the bearers of *intentional, cognitive* content by virtue of the interpretive, internally grasped rules that may govern them and by virtue of the concepts or attributive conditions they may express. And they can also be the bearers of *semantic, propositional* content of either the Fregean or Russellian singular variety, by virtue, this time, of the concepts they may express plus any constituent entities they may have when the contingencies of external circumstance conspire with their interpretive rules in the appropriate way. When their cognitive content and semantic content are distinct, the former will not determine the latter.

The connection I have in mind between the semantics of belief ascriptions and the intentionality of beliefs is via a "principle of substitution" that, in effect, places an important additional constraint on the "cognitive closure" of beliefs envisaged by the received view. The principle, for substitution of co-referential names and other singular terms into embedded that-clauses of standard cognitive state ascriptions on their *de dicto* (notional) reading, is that substitution is to be permitted, as a matter of semantic convention, when and only when an internal representation of the co-referential expression occurs in the mode of presentation of the believer's cognitive content. Of course a belief ascription *per se* will typically give relatively little information about what appears in the guise. So the more collateral information about the believer's state of mind, gleaned from a variety of sources including verbal behaviour, the more sure-footed and confident applications of our principle can be. Though a semantic principle, its application is practically constrained.[19]

Acknowledgment

I would like to thank Martin Hahn for his reactions to an earlier version of this commentary, and for several helpful discussions. Alas, I cannot blame him for any inadequacies that remain.

Notes

* Page references in the main body of the text are to Martin Hahn's paper in this volume.

1. Though nothing Hahn says challenges the claim that an embedded clause that lacks embedded, directly referential devices, such as the ascription 'Susan believes that preferring antique furniture is an affectation', can give the cognitive content of Susan's belief.

2. There is Quine: "Brentano's thesis of the irreducibility of intentional idioms is of a piece with the thesis of the indeterminacy of translation. One may accept the Brentano thesis either as showing the indispensability of intentional idioms and the importance of an autonomous science of intention, or as showing the uselessness of intentional idioms and the emptiness of a science of intention. My attitude, unlike Brentano's, is the second. To accept intentional usage at face value is...to postulate translation relations as somehow objectively valid though indeterminate in principle relative to the totality of speech dispositions. Such postulation promises little gain in scientific insight if there is no better ground for it than that the supposed translation relations are presupposed by the vernacular of semantics and intention." *Word and Object* (Cambridge, MA: MIT Press, 1960), p. 221.

3. Worse, if instrumentalism is the appropriate theoretical stance towards cognitive contents, and in n.2 Hahn explictly refuses to rule it out, then there is nothing to have access to, direct or otherwise!

4. Cf., e.g., S. Kripke, "A Puzzle About Belief," in A. Margalit (ed.), *Meaning and Use* (Dordrecht: Reidel, 1979) p. 242. Hahn also has a very interesting and useful discussion of the 'exported forms' of standard belief ascriptions and their relation to unexported forms. But since I agree with most of what he says in this connection, I will largely set it aside here.

5. Hahn's use here of 'constitute' may mislead, as on one reading it would make the worldly items *constituents* of the mental states, which pretty straightforwardly *contradicts* the supposition that such states are individuated by their intentional contents. But as I interpret him, he means merely to stress that in an important sense it is no accident when these states relate us in particular ways to worldly objects, it is even their *function* to do so. The question is how they can have and fulfil this function while still being essentially intentional.

6. A complication here of course is that among the propositions Hahn wants to countenance are 'Russellian singular propositions' which have worldly elements. More on these below.

7. Modes of presentation are not peculiar to names. Ralph may believe that Cicero was a Roman orator *qua* 'declaimer', or even *qua* 'Tully was a Latin declaimer'. This suggests, of course, that the relation between a guise and its cognitive content is a lot like the relation between a natural language

sentence and its semantic content. Note also that where the only differences are in the attributive expressions involved, Ralph can come to realize that these are different modes of presentation of the same content merely by reflecting on the relations between the senses of the expressions. Not so when the differences involve directly referential expressions.

8. Though unlike an ordinary proper name or demonstrative, its value is not supposed to vary from context to context.

9. Cf. p. 326. But this is surely not to deny that such relations *might* be involved. Suppose that someone tells me that the largest yacht in Philadelphia is the 'Liberty Belle'. If this is true, then my specific belief may now connect me in a special way to a real yacht via the association of the embedded description with the name. Even if the person is simply whimsically inventing a name for a would-be yacht that does not exist (there being no yachts in Philadelphia), then my specific belief may nevertheless at least seem to connect me in a special way to an *ens rationis*.

10. Of course I also believe *de dicto* that all mothers are women, from which it may appear to follow both that Shakespeare's mother was a woman and that my mother is a woman. But if we construe 'Shakespeare's mother' as a functor and thus a rigid designator given that 'Shakespeare' is, then my causal link to Shakespeare's mother via my causal links to Shakespeare (having properly acquired the term) constitute a relation to her, though not direct and vivid enough to put me *en rapport* with her. And neither this relation nor my vivid perceptual relation to my mother are implied by the *de dicto* general belief. So if these relations are taken to be part of the respective beliefs, then those beliefs are *not* implied by the *de dicto* general belief after all.

11. This has implications for the individuation of Hahn's *de re* beliefs. Presumably John's belief that X_1 is in Vancouver and his belief that X_2 is in Vancouver are distinct beliefs, since they concern distinct subject matters. But since their *contents* are allegedly not thereby distinct, they must be individuated not only by their content but also by their determinables. If I am right that determinables are best viewed as features of guises (see below), then this is just a special case of the significance of guises for the individuation of beliefs previously noted.

12. Cf. J. Fodor, *Psychosemantics* (Cambridge, MA: MIT Press, 1987); and D. Kaplan "On the Logic of Demonstratives," *Journal of Philosophical Logic* (1978): 81-98.

13. This may suggestively be compared with Fodor's slogan that 'narrow' (individualistic, intentional) content plus context determines 'wide' (relational) content. Cf. Fodor, *Psychosemantics*, chap. 2.

14. I am assuming that these are ontologically independent enough so that one can have a belief relation to a guise without thereby having a belief relation to the proposition under it.

15. A substitutivity principle cannot be sensitive to intentionally distinct interpretations that hinge on construing a *single* proper name as referentially ambiguous.

16. Note that one must distinguish this from exported versions, in which, e.g., Ralph believes of Tully that he was a Roman orator, or in which Tully is such that Ralph believes him to be a Roman orator. I agree with Hahn that these are not semantically equivalent to the unexported version. Cf. Hahn's discussion of his sentences (18) and (19).

17. In his discussion of exportation, Hahn suggests that if the truth value of the report is all that needs to be preserved when we export, then one of the conditions for such preservation is that there be some mode of presentation of the object under which the believer has the ascribed belief. And this suggests that Hahn's truth conditions for unexported ascriptions of beliefs whose embedded clauses express Russellian singular propositions would handle modes of presentation in the same way. That is, the truth conditions would require that there be a mode of presentation, but would place no further constraints on it.

18. I.e., the interpretive rule itself, not a mere statement of it.

19. I believe that this limitation afflicts other genuinely semantic phenomena in a way that has occasioned confusion about their semantic status. For a discussion of this issue in connection with another kind of example, see my "Explaining Metaphorical Interpretations," *Poetics* 9, (1980): 441-56.

NATIONAL UNIVERSITY
LIBRARY   SAN DIEGO

9199